Philosophy and Jurisprudence in the Islamic World

Philosophy in the Islamic World in Context

Edited by
Peter Adamson, Nadja Germann, Reza Hajatpour,
Ulrich Rudolph and Georges Tamer

Volume 1

Philosophy and Jurisprudence in the Islamic World

Edited by
Peter Adamson

DE GRUYTER

ISBN 978-3-11-055197-6
e-ISBN (PDF) 978-3-11-055238-6
e-ISBN (EPUB) 978-3-11-055218-8

Library of Congress Control Number: 2019939540

Bibliographic information published by the Deutsche Nationalbibliothek
The Deutsche Nationalbibliothek lists this publication in the Deutsche Nationalbibliografie; detailed bibliographic data are available on the Internet at http://dnb.dnb.de.

Cover image: © Zuheir Elia
Printing and binding: CPI books GmbH, Leck

www.degruyter.com

Table of Contents

Preface

For many authors of the Islamic world "philosophy" was synonymous with "Aristotelianism," and modern-day scholars largely follow suit. Even while admitting that other influences, both Greek (Neoplatonism) and indigenous (*kalām*), affected the development of philosophy in the Islamic world, historians of philosophy have typically concentrated on issues that are at home within the Aristotelian course of study: logic and philosophy of language, epistemology, philosophy of mind, natural philosophy, metaphysics, ethics, and political philosophy. This despite the fact that philosophers nowadays recognise subfields of their discipline that had no place in the Aristotelian curriculum.

This is sensible enough for areas where the Islamic tradition has little to say. It isn't clear that a specialist in, say, decision theory, existentialism, or philosophy of quantum mechanics—even one with historical sensibilities—is missing out on a lot by not knowing Arabic or Persian. (Although, never say never.) But for many subdisciplines that have emerged in more recent times, the Islamic world offers riches. This has not gone unnoticed when it comes to such topics as philosophy of religion. But other areas would reward increased attention, such as aesthetics, philosophy of action, and philosophy of medicine.[1] The present volume will, it is hoped, show that philosophy of law deserves a place on that list. Indeed, legal theory was an obvious choice for inclusion in the new series of which this book is a part. The series as a whole will look at various aspects of Islamic culture, investigating their intrinsic philosophical significance and also the question of how these cultural phenomena interacted with, and exerted influence upon, philosophy taken in the strict sense. Other planned volumes will, for instance, be looking at philosophy in the context of Arabic grammar and linguistics, poetry, translations, and mysticism.

Why is jurisprudence such an obvious candidate for this broader approach? First, because so many authors of the Islamic world contributed to both philosophy and jurisprudence. It is easy to reel off a list of famous names from whom we have both philosophical and juridical works: al-Ghazālī, Ibn Rushd (Averroes), and Fakhr al-Dīn al-Rāzī leap readily to mind, and the first two feature heavily in the present volume.[2] Ulrich Rudolph looks at al-Ghazālī's treatments of the sciences and the place of jurisprudence within these classifications. He

1 For the latter see Adamson and Pormann 2017. The present volume is something of a sequel, approaching law in the same spirit as this previous collection approached medicine.
2 For a philosophically rewarding study of Fakhr al-Dīn's legal thought see Opwis 2012.

https://doi.org/10.1515/9783110552386-001

argues that al-Ghazālī offers no truly explicit answer to the question of how practical philosophy relates to the study of law, but that his works opened the way for later authors to answer that question. Ibn Rushd is far more forthcoming here, as established in Ziad Bou Akl's paper, which conversely addresses the legal status of philosophy itself. Central figures of the classical period (roughly, the third–sixth centuries AH, ninth–twelfth centuries AD) who are not particularly known for their connection to jurisprudence, like al-Fārābī and Ibn Sīnā (Avicenna), were in fact well aware of developments in that field and developed their own thought with an eye to contemporary legal concerns. This is shown below in the contributions of Feriel Bouhafa and Hannah Erlwein.

As for the post-classical period, the *madrasa* educational system meant that nearly all authors who are of interest to the historian of philosophy at least enjoyed some training in jurisprudence. To take one particularly celebrated period, this would apply to Mullā Ṣadrā and other Safavid philosophers. (Ṣadrā called his own teacher Mīr Dāmād "lord (*sayyid*) of philosophers and the master of the jurists."[3]) Or, to take a more understudied period, the *dars-i niẓāmī* curriculum devised in Islamic India gave young scholars a formation in logic as they worked towards a possible career as jurists. In the nineteenth century Ṣiddīq Ḥasan Khān (d. 1400/1890) duly integrated jurisprudence into his curriculum of the sciences, which was still organised on broadly Aristotelian principles.[4]

Just as figures we usually classify as philosophers often had legal interests, so significant jurists often made philosophical contributions. The genre of works devoted to the "principles of jurisprudence" (*uṣūl al-fiqh*) is the closest thing we have in Islamic civilization to a sustained reflection on philosophy of law. Accordingly, a number of the papers collected here look either at debates within *uṣūl al-fiqh* or at the writings of significant authors in the history of this genre. Few were more significant than al-Shāfiʿī, founder of an eponymous legal tradition that became one of the four main schools of Sunnī jurisprudence. As Georges Tamer shows in his contribution, al-Shāfiʿī's poetry reflects ethical concerns, as he develops an ascetic—one might say "stoic," in a non-technical sense—worldview that is intended to shield the believer from the disappointments

3 Quoted from Rizvi 2018.

4 I here draw on a forthcoming paper by A.Q. Ahmed, "What Was Philosophy in Late Pre-Modern Muslim India?" to appear in U. Rudolph et al., *Concepts of Philosophy in Asia and the Islamic World*, vol. 2 (Leiden: Brill, 2019). It should be noted that Asad Ahmed and Robert Gleave have also edited a recent collection of papers on philosophy and law, which appeared as *Oriens* 46 (2018). It features some of the same contributors and is strongly recommended as a complement to the studies offered here.

brought by change and the passage of time. A later author who is primarily classified as a jurist, Ibn Taymiyya, is well known for having engaged with philosophy, especially with his notorious critique of logic.[5] In the present volume Jon Hoover finds that he too has something to contribute to the history of ethics in the Islamic world and can be seen as a forerunner of utilitarianism, something that has been suggested also with respect to Fakhr al-Dīn al-Rāzī.[6]

Alongside ethical questions, the most philosophically rewarding debates in the Islamic legal tradition have to do with legal reasoning. Here we are dealing with issues of relevance to logic and meta-ethics, which are extensively represented in the papers collected below. Some contributors have chosen to focus on just one figure to illuminate the connections between juridical reasoning and logic. Joep Lameer discusses the famous Ẓāhirī jurist Ibn Ḥazm, who, like his fellow Andalusian Ibn Rushd or, somewhat further east, Ibn Taymiyya and Fakhr al-Dīn, should be familiar to both historians of philosophy and historians of law. Lameer points out that the classification of actions as impermissible, permissible, and obligatory is closely parallel to the three core notions of modal logic, namely impossible, possible, and necessary. Remarkably Ibn Ḥazm has noticed this too and shows that the rules governing modal inferences in Aristotelian logic can thus be transposed to a legal context.

We have already observed that *madrasa* education required fledgling jurists to become acquainted with logic. So it is unsurprising that as we move forward in history, many authors begin to deploy logical tools—especially those they found in the massively influential Ibn Sīnā—in their analyses of legal reasoning. A second paper on al-Ghazālī, by Felicitas Opwis, gives us one example. She shows how for him logic is a crucial tool for jurists quite generally, and can be used to validate reasoning by analogy in particular. As she points out this would have been suggested to him by the fact that the Arabic word *qiyās* was used both for analogical arguments in law and syllogisms in Aristotelian logic.[7] Nora Kalbarczyk looks more broadly at how a number of *uṣūlīs* (that is, authors who write on *uṣūl al-fiqh*), engaged with Avicennan logic to evaluate an argument pattern we can call *argumentum e contrario*, "argument from the contrary." For instance, if we have a rule that tax is owed on sheep that are not free-grazing, does that mean it is *not* to be paid on sheep that *are* free-grazing?

5 See Hallaq 1993 and more generally Krawietz and Tamer 2013.
6 See Shihadeh 2006.
7 For discussion of the double meaning of *qiyās* in Ibn Rushd, see Bou Akl 2018b.

The study that ends this volume, Walter Edward Young's investigation of the legal concept of *darawān*, returns us to a central question of logical reasoning, which concerns the legitimacy of *qiyās*. Under what circumstances can one transfer a ruling from one class of things to another on the grounds that the "cause" justifying the ruling in one class also applies to the other? The debate over *darawān* concerns a specific answer to this question, which invokes "co-present" and "co-absent" properties. The idea is that, for instance, if grape-wine has the property of being intoxicating and the property of being forbidden, then anything else that has the first property (intoxicating) should have the second (being forbidden); and conversely for co-absent properties. The idea is simple, but the debate over the legitimacy of such inferences is not, especially because of the role of causation, which is held to license such transfer of properties. Here we have another point of contact between Aristotelian logic and legal reasoning, since in Aristotle too a syllogism must have a middle term that is causally explanatory if the syllogism is to be truly demonstrative.

While it is clear that the abovementioned studies touch on meta-ethics as well as logic, other contributions deal more squarely with meta-ethical questions. Amir Mohammad Emami and Mirza Mohammad Kazem Askari point out that another legal debate has a strong connection with the idea of "moral luck," that is, that one's moral blameworthiness (or, less alarmingly, praiseworthiness) may depend on factors outside one's control. It may be noticed that this paper deals almost solely with Shīʿī legal thought, the tradition also discussed by Robert Gleave. His topic is also a meta-ethical one raised in *uṣūl* texts: if we find that something is not forbidden in the sources of the law (the Qur'an, *ḥadīth*, and for these authors the authority of the Imāms), may we immediately infer that it is therefore permitted? Or rather, given that we do make such an inference, on what basis do we do so? Here there were two camps, with one holding that permission is a kind of default in the absence of prohibition, the other that there is no legal assessment at all (and *a fortiori* no prohibition). As Gleave points out, there is at least a family resemblance between this debate and the famous *kalām* problem of whether non-existent things (here, the absence of a ruling) are "real" enough to bear predicates.

Obviously the goal of this volume is not to offer a complete survey of figures or topics for which legal and philosophical concerns coincide. To the contrary, it is hoped that the reader will come away with the sense that the interrelation of law and philosophy is nearly pervasive in Islamic culture, and that a more or less indefinite amount of research could be devoted to similar topics in various chronological periods and geographical regions. While the contributions do, as we've seen, range fairly widely in terms of chronology, and touch on both Shīʿī and Sunnī legal thought—and with Ibn Ḥazm even Ẓāhirism, not just the mainstream schools—it would be easy to think of major topics that go unmentioned here. In particular, the volume does not include any study of the interplay between law and philosophy among Christian or Jewish authors in the Islamic world, even though this too would be a promising direction for enquiry. (Just consider that Maimonides was simultaneously the most important legal and philosophical mind of medieval Judaism.) Nor do the papers included here touch on contemporary developments.[8] So this is far from an exhaustive inquiry of the fascinating and far-reaching connections between philosophy and law in the Islamic world. It would perhaps be too pessimistic, to conclude with Socrates and al-Shāfiʿī (quoted by Tamer below), that "the more I know, the more I know that I know nothing." But when it comes to the complex connections between these two disciplines, it seems likely that the more we know, the more we will realise that we don't know everything.[9]

8 For a relevant contribution by one of our authors, which draws connections to some of the medieval thinkers discussed in the present volume, see Opwis 2005.

9 I would here like to record my immense gratitude to Hannah Erlwein for her extensive help getting this volume ready for press, and also making a number of insightful remarks on draft versions of the papers. I am also grateful for support from the Deutsche Forschungsgemeinschaft, sponsors of the research project "Natur in politischen Ordnungsentwürfen: Antike, Mittelalter, frühe Neuzeit," and from the Fritz Thyssen Stiftung, which provided funding for a workshop at which some of the papers included here were first presented. My thanks also to Rocio Daga, Mostafa Najafi, and Devin Stewart who participated at that event, and finally to Sophie Wagenhofer at De Gruyter and my fellow series editors for helping this book project to reach completion.

Georges Tamer

Philosophical Reflections in the Poetry of al-Shāfiʿī

1 Introduction

In Arabic, there are two words for philosophy: the old Semitic word *ḥikma* and the word transmitted from Greek *falsafa*. While the conception of philosophy designated by *falsafa* is closely connected to its classical meaning with its various theoretical and practical subdivisions, a much wider scope of philosophical cognition is encompassed by the concept of *ḥikma* which originally means "wisdom". In Arabic philosophical writings, both terms are used sometimes interchangeably.[1] However, it is the term *ḥikma* which is mostly used by Sufis and Muslim theosophists, like Ibn ʿArabī (d. 638/1240) and Suhrawardī (d. 587/1191), that has philosophy's broader sense denoting the entirety of intellectual activity in its rational and spiritual forms.[2]

It is also in this broader meaning of philosophy that poetry including wisdoms and philosophical reflections can be studied as philosophical poetry.[3] This genre is present in the literary history of the Arabs from its known origins. Pre-Islamic Arab poets were already busy reflecting upon calamities of life, death, time, and fate, articulating their philosophical reflections in verse form.[4] Most prominent among these poets is Zuhayr b. Abī Sulmā (d. c. 609) whose *muʿallaqa* includes famous verses of wisdom (Arberry 1957, 114–19).[5] In particular, those elegies in which female and male poets mourn the death of relatives lend themselves to gnomic verses addressing human powerlessness against death and the necessity to live in a virtuous fashion, a mode of behavior

I came across the topic of this article during a research stay at the Sheikh Nahyan Center for Arabic Studies & Intercultural Dialogue at the University of Balamand (Lebanon) in March 2017. I wish to thank the director of the Center and president of the university, Dr. Elie A. Salem, and his team for their hospitality and manifold support.

1 This is also the case in Avicenna's *ʿUyūn al-ḥikma* or in Averroes' *Faṣl al-maqāl fī mā bayna al-sharīʿa wa'l-ḥikma mina al-ittiṣāl* which is dedicated to the investigation of the epistemological state of philosophy from the standpoint of Islamic jurisprudence.
2 For a discussion of both concepts, see Nasr 1996.
3 On philosophical poets, see, for instance, Santayana 1910; Hodgson 1980.
4 On the topic of time in pre-Islamic Arabic poetry, see, for instance, Tamer 2008.
5 See also verses of wisdom in the *muʿallaqa* of Ṭarafa b. al-ʿAbd (Arberry 1957, 87).

https://doi.org/10.1515/9783110552386-002

capable of granting a legacy of remembrance.[6] Facing the specter of death, worldly matters appear of little value, and history resembles a sequence of recurring deadly events. This leads one to see annihilation everywhere: the present generation is doomed to perish just as earlier ones did.[7]

In reaction to the extravagant lifestyles developed under the Umayyads from the end of the second century AH (first half of the eighth-ninth century AD) onwards, a stream of religious thought emerged calling people to renounce worldly pleasures and live in a condition dominated by piety, voluntary abstinence, and social justice. One of the influential early figures in this movement was the theologian al-Ḥasan al-Baṣrī (d. 110/728) who pleaded for an ascetic way of life (*zuhd*). It is remarkable that he was also one of the earliest Muslim theologians who defended human free will (*al-qadariyya*) against those who believed in the determinism of divine predestination (*al-jabriyya*). The earliest collection of ascetic verses in Arabic (*zuhdiyyāt*) goes back to Sābiq al-Barbarī (d. 99/718 or 100/719), a contemporary of al-Baṣrī (Wagner 1987, 121). Ascetic poetry flourished, however, in the time of the Abbasids. An attitude of *tawakkul*, or unqualified trust in God, developed out of the attitude of abstinence and world renunciation. Abū l-ʿAtāhiya (d. 210/825 or 211/826) was the main representative of this new genre of poetry. Besides Islamic religious ideas, ascetic poems include classical philosophical gnomologia which were transmitted from Greek into Arabic and enjoyed wide popularity (Rosenthal 1965, 352–54; 1971; Gutas 1975). Indian and Persian wisdom literature constituted another line of transmission brought into Arabic in the early Abbasid period. The most famous work in this field is Ibn al-Muqaffaʿ's *Kalīla wa-dimna*. Ascetic poetry became in a later period part of the Sufi poetic tradition (Wagner 1987, 128–29), containing a considerable amount of philosophical and spiritual reflection.

Many a *faqīh* composed poetry. Some verses are ascribed, for instance, to Mālik b. Anas, Abū Ḥanīfa, and Aḥmad b. Ḥanbal. Some other jurists who composed poems are ʿUrwa b. Udhayna, ʿAbdallāh b. al-Mubārak, Ibn Ḥazm, and Ibn al-Qayyim al-Jawziyya. Another author of poetry was al-Shāfiʿī (d. 204/820), very well known as an influential jurist and founder of one of the four schools of *fiqh* in Islam. His poems and verses are scattered in several biographical works and literary collections. His edited *Dīwān* includes 179 alphabetically ordered pieces

6 Famous are, for instance, the elegies of the female poet al-Khansāʾ on her brother Ṣakhr.
7 On the motif of "Ubi sunt qui ante nos fuerunt?" in old Arabic poetry, compare Becker 1924. The poet ʿAdī b. Zayd from al-Ḥīra is known for such philosophical reflections (Toral-Niehoff 2013).

with a total count of 590 verses.[8] An appendix includes additional 21 pieces ascribed simultaneously to al-Shāfiʿī and other poets. Their authorship cannot be definitively determined (al-Shāfiʿī 1996, 6–7).[9]

Born in 150 AH/767 AD in Gaza or Ashkelon, Muḥammad b. Idrīs al-Shāfiʿī grew up in Mecca where he received his education. In addition to Qur'an, *ḥadīth*, *fiqh*, and grammar, he mastered poetry. The famous grammarian and critic al-Aṣmaʿī (d. 213/828 or 216/831) reports that he studied the poetry of the pre-Islamic Arab poet al-Shanfarā and corrected the poetry of the tribe Hudhayl and determined its authenticity under al-Shāfiʿī's supervision (al-Shāfiʿī 1996, 5; 1979, 24). In accordance with the habit of young scholars in the medieval period, al-Shāfiʿī traveled to several cities in the Abbasid state, including Baghdad, in order to meet established scholars and learn from them. He settled in Egypt where he became a renowned jurist. He died in 150 AH/820 AD.

The majority of the verses of the *Dīwān* contain epithets of wisdom and reflections on the best way of life that are mainly characterised by devotion to obtaining and conveying knowledge, acts that steer one away from sensual pleasures. The main virtue praised there is satisfaction (*zuhd*) which lets man renounce needs and live happily with that which he possesses. According to Iḥsān ʿAbbās, the religious nature of al-Shāfiʿī's poetry did not allow it to benefit in the literary sense from the stylistic features found in the poetry of the Hudhalites or other contemporaneous poets (al-Shāfiʿī 1996, 7). On the other hand, it seems possible that al-Shāfiʿī adopted Greek gnomologia in his verses. The famous literary critic al-Mubarrad (d. 285/898) testifies to a similar stylistic adoption in the poetry of the "philosophical poet" Abū l-ʿAtāhiya (Gutas 1975, 464–465).

A critical assessment of al-Shāfiʿī's verses reveals that his ascetic insights are intrinsically related to his views on time. For this reason, I will focus in the present study on his understanding of time, and how this understanding affects his philosophy of life in general. As his views on time share many similar character-

8 According to Ibn Khallikān and al-Dhahabī, al-Shāfiʿī composed a great amount of poetry which did not survive (al-Shāfiʿī 1996, 6).

9 ʿAbbās points out the difficulty of determining the authenticity of al-Shāfiʿī's poetry, as his verses were mixed with verses of his followers or with ascetic verses of poets like Abū l-ʿAtāhiya, Maḥmūd al-Warrāq, or even Abū Nuwās. Another edition of the *Dīwān* known to me is the one composed by Zuhdī Yakan that was subsequently edited and redacted by his son Muḥammad (Beirut: Yakan and Mneimne Publishing Houses, 1400/1979). Quoted verses in the present article are taken from ʿAbbās's edition of the *Dīwān* (that is, al-Shāfiʿī 1996). Yakan's edition is referred to by al-Shāfiʿī 1979.

istics found in works of pre- and early Islamic poetry, such similarities will be highlighted.

2 Al-Shāfiʿī's Views on Time and Life

The most important observation when looking at al-Shāfiʿī's understanding of time, as it is articulated in his poetry, is that he, like old Arab poets, conceives of time as an agent of events in the lives of individuals and communities (al-Shāfiʿī 1996, 2.1–2, 12–13):

> Let days do whatever they will; keep quiet when destiny decrees (*idhā ḥakama al-qaḍāʾu*).
>
> Don't fear the accidents of nights; the accidents of the world do not linger [forever].
>
> God's dominion (*arḍu llāhi*) is wide, but when destiny afflicts (*nazala l-qaḍā*) space becomes narrow (*ḍāqa l-faḍāʾu*).
>
> Let the days act treacherously anytime; medicine would never keep death away.

Echoing pre-Islamic Arabic poets, al-Shāfiʿī seems to adhere to a deterministic conception of life based on the conviction that time is the source of inconveniences. However, as time flows, events change with it. Nothing in the world is interminable. For al-Shāfiʿī, this observation functions in times of misery as a source of hope.

In accordance with a conception of time deemed irreversible, negative events, particularly death, are viewed as inevitable; nothing can stop them or protect man against them (al-Shāfiʿī 1996, 2.11). Even the physician who cures people from their diseases cannot avert a predetermined destiny (*maqdūru l-qaḍā*) (al-Shāfiʿī 1996, 1.1). As evil events vary, death is universal; all humans are decreed to die (al-Shāfiʿī 1996, 1.3):

> The healer and the healed, he who brings the medicine, who sells it, and who buys it: all of them perish.

In one verse, al-Shāfiʿī integrates an ancient Oriental idea which continued to persist into the Islamic period: everything which occurs has been recorded on a tablet in heaven and is, therefore, predetermined and immutable (al-Shāfiʿī 1996, 34.1):

> Concern is superfluous (*al-hammu faḍlun*); destiny vanquishes (*wa'l-qaḍā ghālibun*); what happens is that which was written on the tablet (*wa-kāʾinun mā khuṭṭa fī l-lawḥi*).

Predetermined events unfold in the due course of time within regularly recurring intervals. Thus, there remains nothing for man to do but to blame time (*wa-adhummu dahrī*), which is held to be the cause of these events.[10] However, in al-Shāfiʿī's poetry, this attitude is combined with the belief that God's command (*amr*) is higher than one's own command (al-Shāfiʿī 1996, 71.1–2). What follows, therefore, is the necessary submission of one's own will to God's will (al-Shāfiʿī 1996, 39.3–4):

> I am resigned if God wants something (*usallimu in arāda llāhu amran*) and leave what I want to that what He wants;
>
> My will has no significance (*wa-mā li-irādatī wajhun*) when God wants (*arāda llāhu*) for me what I don't want (*mā lā urīdu*).

Like other thinkers of great faith who are confronted with the classical problem of how to explain the existence of evil in the world, and, at the same time, keep believing in the omnipotence of God, al-Shāfiʿī considers unexpected misfortunes to be predetermined by God and brought forth by time. As these misfortunes cannot be avoided, the believer has no other choice but to accept them and submit him- or herself to the will of God. Submission to God's will leads to a comforting state of detachment, serenity, and satisfaction. This state is described abundantly in the *Dīwān* (al-Shāfiʿī 1996, 39.2, 54.1–4, 85.1–2, 113.1–3), as can be observed in the following verses (al-Shāfiʿī 1996, 55.1–3, 170):

> I put on the firm armor of contentment in order to protect my honour and treat it like a treasure.
>
> I don't fear the treacherous time (*al-dahra*); its aim is to hit me with death and poverty.
>
> Against death I have God and His forgiveness, against poverty, endurance and patience.
>
> Do you want to live in wealth? Then if you are in a certain state, be ready to accept a worse one.

Through a life style of self-sufficiency, bad situations like poverty, decease, and death can be dealt with in a sovereign fashion. Being ready to expect the dete-

---

10 In a *ḥadīth*, Muḥammad forbids Muslims to curse time ("*lā tasubbū l-dahr*") for causing unpleasant events, because they are actually cursing God who is the real creator of all that happens to them. Different versions of this text and an overview on related debates in early Islam can be found in Tamer 2008, 199–205. On *sabb al-dahr* as a literary topic, see Abū l-Faraj al-Iṣfahānī 1972, 2000; Rosenthal 1983.

rioration of one's conditions can be viewed as a type of wealth, since it means that one possesses more mental power than is really needed to overcome present difficulties, according to al-Shāfiʿī. Belief in God and His mercy grants one strength in such situations. However, it is not only the belief in, and self-submission to God which help one deal with events characterised by the presence of evil. Hope arises also from the observation that negative developments in life do not last forever, as mentioned above: they are caused by time and will. They shall inevitably pass like all discrete periodisations (al-Shāfiʿī 1996, 63.1–2):

> The consequences of calamities are selected (*khiyāru*); the days of evil are short, not lasting.
>
> Neither misery nor felicity remains, when night and day alternatively return (*idhā karra laylun thumma karra nahāru*).

Like pre-Islamic Arabic poets, al-Shāfiʿī (1996, 53.2) calls the perpetually recurring day and night "the everlasting new two" (*al-jadīdayni*). Time consists, furthermore, of two days: a safe and a perilous one. Life is divided into two parts: a happy and a troubled one (al-Shāfiʿī 1996, 60.1). Radical change of life circumstances belongs to the nature of time which gives and returns what it gave (al-Shāfiʿī 1996, 81.3):

> Days get back what they bestowed upon you; it is custom of the days to demand the return of the loan.

According to al-Shāfiʿī, life is unjust: many a person enjoys a pleasant situation which he or she does not deserve; and many a person is deprived of that what he or she deserves (al-Shāfiʿī 1996, 10.1–2). However, changes caused by time can undo this kind of injustice and take revenge for iniquity (al-Shāfiʿī 1996, 22.5–6):[11]

> Would an unjust person enjoy injustice (*al-ẓulma*) as a way of life (*madhhaban*) and persist arrogantly on adhering to it infamously,
> So leave him to the misfortune of the nights (*ṣarfi l-layālī*); they will collect for him what he did not expect.

As a result of this observation, al-Shāfiʿī (1996, 81.1–2) advises people to be generous to each other, as they cannot keep their possessions due to the changing effects of time. It is better that they give away that which they cannot keep. This generous attitude is, in his view, connected with deep contentment and aban-

11 Further verses 7–10.

donment. In this sense, wealth consists in the renunciation of wealth (al-Shāfiʿī 1996, 22.4). Time is unreliable (al-Shāfiʿī 1996, 58.2–3):

> You thought well of the days as were good, and did not fear the bad [things] which fate (*al-qadaru*) brings,
> The nights made peace with you; you were deluded by them; when nights are clear, grief occurs.

Al-Shāfiʿī thus concludes that people share with time the quality of treacherousness; there are no real friends in the world (al-Shāfiʿī 1996, 47.2). It is a waste of time to search for them (al-Shāfiʿī 1996, 78.3). He draws from this pessimistic view the recommendation that one should live in solitude "like a monk in his monastery" (al-Shāfiʿī 1996, 72.1), then "people are a disease, their nearness is the disease" (al-Shāfiʿī 1996, 25.5). He advises his reader (al-Shāfiʿī 1996, 72.2):

> Wash your hands from time and the people who live in it (*al-zamāni wa-ahlihi*); face their friendship with caution, in order to receive good things from time.

Al-Shāfiʿī goes a step farther and advises his reader to remain skeptical. One should indeed have a bad opinion of people in general; such a trait is "very clever" (*min aqwā l-fiṭan*), as it is necessary for man to survive (al-Shāfiʿī 1996, 145.1–2). One should not expect from people anything else but envy and schadenfreude (al-Shāfiʿī 1996, 43.1–3). Therefore, the best reaction to such a behaviour is silence and serenity (al-Shāfiʿī 1996, 31.1–3). Silence is always a profitable trade (al-Shāfiʿī 1996, 66.1–2).[12] However, in the end, it is not time which should be blamed for human defaults and deficiencies, but the people themselves (al-Shāfiʿī 1996, 147.1–2):

> We accuse our time of having faults; we are faulty. Our time has no other fault (*ʿayb*) but us!
>
> We ridicule (*nahjū*) this time (*al-zamāna*) although it is not guilty; if time would speak, it would ridicule us!

For al-Shāfiʿī it is obvious that although time can be accused of causing pernicious events, such as death, ethical responsibility for wrongdoing lies with the people. Time can play a positive role here. Thus old age should spur people to piety, a virtuous life, and humility (al-Shāfiʿī 1996, 19.1–15, 23.1–3). Piety and knowledge together are substantial for man; deprived of them man has no dignity (al-Shāfiʿī 1996, 27.4). In particular, knowledge extracts a person's value.

---

12 Compare al-Shāfiʿī 1996, 169.1–4.

Knowledge has to be sought wherever it can be found, especially in the works of earlier scholars (*irthun qaddamathu l-awāʾilu*) (al-Shāfiʿī 1996, 122.1–4). For the wise man, troubles of time have an educational function which can be related to the Socratic idea of knowledge leading man to discover his or her ignorance (al-Shāfiʿī 1996, 131.1–2):

> Whenever time disciplines me, it shows me the deficiency of my reason;
>
> The more I know, the more I know that I know nothing.

Al-Shāfiʿī (1996, 134.1–3) considers knowledge (*ʿilm*) as a treasure which ought not be wasted upon those who are not qualified to receive it. Pearls are not to be thrown to animals.[13] On the contrary, only those who are ready to obtain knowledge should receive it; a scholar who withholds it from those who are qualified commits injustice and sin (al-Shāfiʿī 1996, 134.6–7). The reason why knowledge should be kept only for the qualified is that knowledge is power and should not be misused (al-Shāfiʿī 1996, 137.1–3):

> Among the virtues of knowledge (*al-ʿilmu min faḍlihi*) is that it makes people serve the person who serves it.
>
> It is, therefore, a duty to safeguard it in the same way people safeguard honour and blood.
>
> He who possesses knowledge and, ignorantly, conveys it to those who don't possess it (*ghayra ahlihi*), does injustice to knowledge.

Al-Shāfiʿī states that possessing knowledge affects the social state of a person: it increases the value of man and lets people follow him in the same way sheep follow the shepherd (al-Shāfiʿī 1996, 138.1–3). However, no one can know everything. For this reason, one has to pursue the best kind of knowledge (al-Shāfiʿī 1996, 151.1–2). For al-Shāfiʿī (1996, 138.4), this is the knowledge that leads him to distinguish between the permissible (*al-ḥalāl*) and the prohibited (*al-ḥarām*). More specifically (al-Shāfiʿī 1996, 164.1–2):

> All sciences except the Qur'an are distraction, save the *ḥadīth* and the deep knowledge of religion (*ʿilma l-fiqhi fī l-dīni*).
>
> Knowledge lies in that what is orally transmitted [through a chain of transmitters] (*al-ʿilmu*

13 Jesus says in Matt 7:6: "Do not give what is holy to the dogs; nor cast your pearls before swine, lest they trample them under their feet, and turn and tear you in pieces."

> *mā kāna fīhi qāla ḥaddathanā*);[14] everything else is insinuation of the devils (*waswāsu l-shayāṭīni*).

It is religious knowledge which is the most preferred field of knowledge. Al-Shāfiʿī (1996, 46.1) calls religious knowledge the "knowledge for the hereafter" (*al-ʿilma li'l-maʿādi*) and ascribes to it the ability to grant the individual reason and maturity in abundance.

Knowledge of the future is not possible, which makes concerns about the future irrelevant (al-Shāfiʿī 1996, 40.4). From an Islamic point of view, it is not possible to avoid the accidents of time, for they can destroy even powerful kings. However, people can stop embracing this vanishing world (*al-dunyā*) as a reaction to this fact. For then they can be rewarded by embracing "virgins in paradise" (*fī l-firdawsi abkārā*) (al-Shāfiʿī 1996, 53.1–5).

Al-Shāfiʿī (1996, 108.1) declares clearly that he trusts in God in regard to his sustenance:

> I trust (*tawakkaltu*) in God, my creator, in regard to my subsistence (*rizqī*), and I am sure (*wa-ayqantu*) that God, no doubt, gives me what I need (*rāziqī*).

As far as I see, this is the only occurrence of the verb "*tawakkala*" or its derivatives in the *Dīwān*. Al-Shāfiʿī certainly has trust in God; however, he calls for an active way of behaving in which one takes care of one's own life. In a statement which eventually became very famous as an Arabic epithet of wisdom, al-Shāfiʿī (1996, 111.1) recommends:

> No one would scratch your skin in the way your nails do (*mā ḥakka jildaka mithlu ẓufrik*), so take care of your own matters (*fa-tawalla anta jamīʿa amrik*).

The following verses express more explicitly the necessity of independent striving to reach goals (al-Shāfiʿī 1996, 130.1–3):

> As intensive as hard work (*al-kaddi*) is, high positions (*al-maʿālī*) can be reached; he who desires highness has to spend the nights awake (*wa-man ṭalaba l-ʿulā sahira l-layālī*).
>
> He who would aspire to highness without hard work, would waste his life seeking the impossible.
>
> You desire for glory, but you spend the night sleeping! He who searches for pearls has to dive deeply in the sea.

---

14 Al-Shāfiʿī refers in this verse to the *isnād* preceding a statement ascribed to Prophet Muḥammad and including the chain of the authorities who related the *ḥadīth* after each other.

In order to reach an elevated state, one's determination has to remain intact over a long period, metaphorically speaking, even longer than time (*khalaqa al-zamānu wa-himmatī lam takhluqi*) (al-Shāfiʿī 1996, 106.1). According to al-Shāfiʿī, success can be reached in competition with time. Besides resolution, one must have patience and endurance (al-Shāfiʿī 1996, 121.3), while being capable of grasping the right moment for fulfilling aspired achievements (al-Shāfiʿī 1996, 154.1).

The previous verses make it clear that al-Shāfiʿī does not call for a passive way of life in which man, out of piety and passive trust in God, abstains from striving towards aspired goals. For him, God's help is certainly necessary to achieve success, as God is the creator of human abilities. However, it is a human responsibility to utilise God's gifts in order to realise ambitions actively. This position might appear to contradict the aforementioned statement that events have been already written on a tablet. Both statements point towards two different categories of events in human life: those which befall man without being influenced or caused by human will; they can be considered predetermined. And those which belong to the realm of human abilities and are to be fulfilled by the people and are, thus, their responsibility.

Finally, al-Shāfiʿī pleads for a synthesis of faith and voluntary deeds, which is, in his view, not only an indispensable requirement for a successful *via activa*, but also shows how to harmonise reason and revelation. This attitude in regard to shaping one's own life corresponds with al-Shāfiʿī's combination of tradition (*al-naql*) and reason (*al-ʿaql*) in his legal theory (Schacht 1950, 6–20; Hallaq 1997, 18–32).[15] As articulated in his philosophical poetry, his position meets, to a certain extent, the position of Muslim philosophers who endeavoured via certain techniques to abolish the contradictions between their religion and rationality.

15 Mensia (2017) shows borrowings by al-Fārābī from al-Shāfiʿī's *Risāla* while philosophically dealing with the subject matter of religion.

Feriel Bouhafa

Ethics and *Fiqh* in al-Fārābī's Philosophy

1 Introduction

This volume seeks to bring together two key areas in the Arabic tradition that are most often addressed separately, philosophy and jurisprudence. Despite the profusion of philosophical discussions in Islamic legal jurisprudence, related to (among others) theory of knowledge, epistemology of evidence, aspects of logical reasoning and argumentation, and philosophy of language, many investigations of Islamic law have followed an emic approach by adhering to the scheme presented in medieval jurisprudential treatises.[1] The present chapter will instead pursue the relation between the normative system of Islamic jurisprudence and a branch of philosophy: ethics.[2] The connection seems an obvious one, given that ethics centres on gauging the moral basis of human actions and Islamic law involves determining the moral status of human actions. But what exactly is the relation between ethics and Islamic law?[3] Are laws and ethical norms identical or distinct? What is the role of *fiqh* in determining an ethical basis for human actions, and what are the methods by which the jurist discerns ethical norms? The task of answering these questions is faced with difficulties stemming from certain presumptions concerning Islamic law. Despite its argumentative discourse, Islamic law has been perceived along Ash'arite lines as a set of divine commands with no distinction between the ethical and the prescribed (Makdisi 1985, 1). To put it differently, the theistic basis of Qur'anic commands has been deemed as incompatible with a rational account of ethics, since these commands dictate on theological grounds the norms of moral conduct within the Muslim community, and therefore leave no room for an independent inquiry into the moral principles of human actions (Rahman 1985, 3). For many, Islamic ethics

1 This tendency has shifted in the recent years, with an increasing interest in philosophical questions in Islamic jurisprudence. Among others, we might here mention Hallaq 1987b, 1990; Rahman and Iqbal 2018; Arfa-Mensia 2017; Belhaj 2010; Young 2017; Kalbarczyk 2018; Bou Akl's remarks in Ibn Rushd 2015, and Bouhafa 2018a and 2018b.

2 Here I understand ethics as the practical science that concerns itself with the question of which actions should be performed or avoided. See Makdisi 1985, 47; Reinhart 1983.

3 The taxonomy of legal norms is typically a fivefold division into obligatory, proscribed, recommended, discouraged, and permitted. See Reinhart 1983, 195.

https://doi.org/10.1515/9783110552386-003

is instead rooted in the word (that is, textual authority).[4] But this perspective has been challenged in recent years.[5] A change of attitude can be sensed in Kevin Reinhart's plea to consider Islamic law as the primary domain of Islamic ethical thought. Yet, he admits the difficulty of using legal treatises to expound on such topics. Indeed, medieval legal treatises do not dwell explicitly on the question of ethics (Reinhart 1983, 187).

Responding to Reinhart's call, I would suggest that Arabic philosophical works might present an expedient alternative source of reflection on our topic. I focus on some of al-Fārābī's (d.339/950) works, mainly *Kitāb al-Milla; Nawāmīs Aflāṭūn; Fuṣūl al-madanī; and Iḥṣā' al-ʿulūm*, in which he explores the relation between ethics and Islamic law. In order to grasp this relation, a close scrutiny of his understanding of the concepts of *milla* and *fiqh* and their relation to practical philosophy is crucial. In what follows, I shall show that al-Fārābī sees lawgivers as laying down laws that do have an ethical content, and that take into consideration the requirements of justice as well as the role of emotions related to pain, pleasure, fear, and anger. These laws are restricted in their universal applications with certain conditions and also subject to a relative application. In other words, despite their substantive ethical content, laws are only particularised instances of universal ethical norms. This occasions the need for a practical art such as *fiqh*, whose role is to extend these particular instances to new cases as they arise. For this reason al-Fārābī subordinates *fiqh* to practical science and associates it with the faculty of practical reasoning (*taʿaqqul*). I shall also argue that this substantive ethical approach to law allows al-Fārābī to appropriate Aristotle's notion of *mesotes*, so that Aristotelian ethics is brought into relation to *fiqh*. Finally, my scrutiny of the relation between ethics and *fiqh* in al-Fārābī's thought will shed some light on the degree of his commitment to the Aristotelian ethical framework.

4 For instance, Brunschvig (1970, 9) remarks: "In the absence of a notion of natural law and in the negation of ethical and rational values that impose themselves upon God, or which God imposes on Himself, or which may be inherent in Him, the revealed or inspired datum, a divine phenomenon, is a priori exempt from the demands of rationality which rightly manifest themselves with regard to human law."

5 For a nuanced perspective on the Muʿtazilites and Ashʿarites debates on theological ethics see Shihadeh 2016.

2 *Milla*, Law, and Ethics

Al-Fārābī's *Kitāb al-Milla* offers us a good basis for exploring his view on law and ethics within the normative context of the Islamic community. I will focus especially on two notions used to define law and its relation to ethics, namely *milla* (usually, but rather misleadingly, translated "religion") and *taqdīr* ("measurement"), both of which are linked to the lawgiver's assessment of human actions. In *Kitāb al-Milla*, al-Fārābī defines both *milla* and law while drawing from the historical context of the development of Islam.[6] Thus Al-Fārābī begins his treatise with a succinct definition of *milla*, which might more accurately be translated as "belief-based community", for reasons that I will explain below: "*Milla* is opinions and measured actions restricted by conditions and defined for a community by the first ruler, who seeks to obtain through their practicing it a purpose specific to them or limited to them" (al-Fārābī 2001c, 93).[7] This definition underlines the importance of the first ruler as providing the foundations upon which a given community is built. This foundation hinges upon two essential components, opinions and actions, with actions being "measured" (*muqaddara*) and also occurring under varying "conditions." Before we examine the import of these qualifications, we should first discuss more generally what he understands by "opinions" and "actions."

Happily, al-Fārābī lays out a painstaking exposition to clarify these terms. All opinions, he says, fall into two categories (al-Fārābī 2001c, 94–96)[8]. The first category of opinions relates to theoretical knowledge; this would include opinions on topics such as the finiteness of the world, God and His attributes, prophecy, and this world and the hereafter. The second category of opinions relates to voluntary actions and includes accounts of good actions performed by past prophets, kings, the magnificent first ruler, and imams, as well as agreed features of good actions. Under this rubric, he also includes stories about the misdeeds of past unjust rulers, kings, and ignorant people, and the agreed features of bad actions. Aside from such historical accounts, al-Fārābī also refers to present accounts of current rulers, both just and unjust, and descriptions of good and bad actions associated with them and their shared opinions about good and

---

6 As Arfa-Mensia has noted, some studies of al-Fārābī's political writings tend to ignore the context of *fiqh* and its concrete influence on al-Fārābī's philosophy. For more on this, see Arfa-Mensia 2016, 141; Zghal 1998.

7 Here I made slight changes in Butterworth's translation; in particular, here and elsewhere I substitute "determined" with "measured" for *muqaddara*. For the Arabic see al-Fārābī 1991, 43.

8 For the Arabic see al-Fārābī 1991, 44–46.

bad deeds. So, while the first kind of opinion is linked to theological discussions that shape the beliefs of a given religious community, the second kind involves storytelling and historical reports about ethical conduct both past and present, as well as shared opinions about the good and the bad. Within al-Fārābī's own historical context, these references would encompass stories about the Prophet and his companions, past kings and rulers found in the *ḥadīth* and Qur'an, as well as references to current people including the rulers.[9] Here we see him taking a comprehensive view of what may form a basis for ethics, since we are to draw on a variety of experiences from both history and the present day.

Now turning to actions, al-Fārābī explains that these are also divided into two types:

> As for actions, they are, first of all, the actions and sayings by which God is praised and extolled. Then there are those that praise the spiritual beings and the angels. Then there are those that praise the prophets, the most virtuous kings, the righteous rulers, and the leaders of the right way from the predecessor generation. Then there are those that blame the most depraved kings, the profligate rulers, and the leaders of the errant way from the predecessor generation and denounce their activities. Then there are those that praise the most virtuous kings, the righteous rulers, and the leaders of the right way in our present time and blame those of this time who are their opposites. Then after all this, are the measured actions by which the mutual dealings of the inhabitants of cities are regulated—either regarding what a human being ought to do with respect to himself or regarding how he ought to deal with others—and bringing about the definition of what is just with respect to each particular instance of these actions (al-Fārābī 2001c, 96).[10]

Under the first category of actions, he includes deeds and sayings involving gratitude to God and to good people such as spiritual figures, angels, prophets, good kings, magnificent rulers, and imams, again both past and present.[11] Here al-Fārābī might be drawing from Porphyry's (d. 309 AD) interpretation of Aristotle which identifies the virtue of justice in relation to duties to God, our superior

9 On Islamic sources on rulership related to Prophets, kings and religious scholars see Marlow 1995.

10 For the Arabic see al-Fārābī, 1991, 46.

11 Here I agree with Germann's (2018) observation: "Thus, with God's praise one will easily connect the five daily prayers demanded of Muslims; the 'prophets', 'righteous rulers', and 'leaders of the right way' are reminiscent of the prophet Muḥammad and his predecessors; of the first four caliphs; and of either the imams of Shi'ism or other spiritual leaders of Islam (e.g., Sufis)." But it is also important to note that people from the present are also included – after all, virtuous people continue to exist, and may fall within the lineage of the Prophet or Sufis, or even be eminent *mujtahid*s and rulers, as al-Fārābī notes.

equals and ancestors.[12] A similar attribution to Aristotle is found in Miskawayh's (d.1030/420) *Tahdhīb al-akhlāq*, which discusses the importance of thanking the benefactor in relation to justice, but also specifies that Aristotle did not, like later philosophers, include rituals as part of thanking the benefactor (Miskawayh 2011, 346). Al-Fārābī clearly adopts a similar stance.

The second aspect of actions is specifically related to what he calls *taqdīr* (which is the same root as the aforementioned term *muqaddara*). Al-Fārābī distinguishes here between actions that affect agents themselves and those that affect other people. This distinction seems to parallel the two main components of law in Islamic jurisprudence, *ʿibādāt* ("ritual worship") and *muʿāmalāt* ("deeds"): the former regulates an individual person's own actions, while the latter regulate exchanges and interactions between people. Why does he speak of *taqdīr* in relation to actions? The term can mean "determination" and refer to the process of reasoning involved in establishing a legal judgement. But for al-Fārābī the term *taqdīr* reflects a process of valuation or calculation (the root *qadr* means "measure" or "amount"). Thus he explains that the *taqdīr* of actions provides a definition of justice in relation to a particular act. This implies that *taqdīr* attributes a quantifiable ethical content related to the justice of a particular act. We find a similar idea in his paraphrase of Plato's *Laws:*

> He explained in this discourse that there are in a human being certain natural things that are the causes of one's moral habits and one's actions. Therefore the lawgiver ought to reach for these natural things and set them aright. For when these natural things are set right, so will the moral habits and the actions. (I suspect that by "children" [in this connection] he means all beginners, whether in age, knowledge, or religion [*dīn*].) He explained that these natural things are based upon, and originate from, pleasure and pain; it is through these two that the virtues and the vices – and, at the end, practical judgment and the sciences – are acquired. The ordering of these two [that is, pleasure and pain] is called educating and training. Had the lawgiver commanded people to avoid the pleasures altogether, his law would not have been rightly established and people would not have followed it, because of their natural inclination to pleasures. Instead, he appointed for them certain festivals and times during which they could pursue the pleasures; for this reason these pleasures become divine. This is also the case with the various kinds of music that [the lawgivers] have permitted, knowing that people are naturally inclined toward them and in order that taking pleasure in them will be divine. He gave such examples of this as were well known among them, such as dancing and flute-playing (al-Fārābī 1963a, 91, modified).[13]
>
> Then he explained that the lawgivers turn to the means that lead to the acquisition of virtues, and they command and impress on people that they should adhere to them so that,

12 Fakhry 1998.

13 For the Arabic see al-Fārābī 1998, 130.

> through the realization of these means, the virtues would be realized. Examples of these means are legal marriage, the ordering of the appetites and pleasures, and indulging in each only in the measure (*bi'l-miqdār*) permitted by the law. The same applies to fear and anger, base and noble matters, and everything that serves as a means to the virtues (al-Fārābī 1963a, 87, modified).[14]

Employing another term that shares its root with *taqdīr* and *muqaddara*, he states that law provides a measure (*miqdār*) for determining the amount of pleasure and pain ascribed to human actions. More generally we may conclude that for al-Fārābī, law provides a certain measure that not only determines the amount of justice in relation to a specific act, but also the acceptable amount of pleasure and pain, fear, and anger.

Al-Fārābī espouses a realist, or perhaps pessimistic, view of human nature, which needs to be straightened with regard to these emotions. Thus he specifies that the lawgiver has to factor in the need of human beings for pleasure; as a concession to this need, the lawgiver should make it possible to enjoy pleasures during specific festivals observed by a given community. Yet, only the right "measure" of pleasure is provided: we see this also with marriage, where the law regulates sexual relations without entirely curtailing human pleasure, since that would be counter to human nature. The imposition of the right measures will yield virtuous people who carry out good actions. Here we see that laws do have substantive ethical content.

In his exposition of the term *milla*, al-Fārābī underlines the role of the first ruler in imparting the opinions and actions that form the normative basis for ethical knowledge in a given community. While he ascribes theoretical questions of theology to that part of *milla* called "opinions", the normative basis for assessing human actions, which is the realm of practical ethics, is assigned to the second part of *milla*, associated with the *taqdīr* of actions. As we have noted, al-Fārābī sees an important resource in stories about the deeds of successive generations of prophets, rulers, and leaders, and specifically their shared views about good and bad actions. But this is not yet sufficient. It is supplemented by the first ruler's provision of specific measures concerning actions, that is, providing a law with an ethical content assigned to voluntary actions. Could this mean that the ethical assessment of human actions can be seen to fall entirely within the realm of Islamic law? To offer a conclusive answer, we need to elucidate how al-Fārābī defines "law" (*sharʿ* or *sharīʿa*) in relation to *milla*.

First a word about this terminology. Although some scholars have attributed an Aramaic origin to *milla*, which refers to "word" or "revelation", the concept of

14 For the Arabic see al-Fārābī 1998, 126.

milla itself can also be rooted in Qur'anic discourse. The term occurs in the Qur'an to refer to the Christian and Jewish religious communities and in relation to prophets such as *millat Ibrāhīm* (Q. 3:95, 6:161 and Q.12:38) (EI2, "Milla"). Presumably then al-Fārābī's definition of *milla* implies that for him, Moses, Jesus, and Abraham were "first rulers" who provided their communities with opinions and actions. This seems to fit with al-Fārābī's own distinction between prophets and messengers in his *Min al-as'ila al-lāmiʿa wa'l-ajwiba al-jāmiʿa*, where he explains: "The difference between a messenger (*rasūl*) and prophet (*nabī*) is that the messenger is a legislator whereas the prophet is a bearer of the law already brought by someone else."[15] Adam, Noah, Abraham, Moses, Jesus, and Muḥammad are mentioned as examples of legislators.[16] In this context, *milla* would strictly be applied to prophets who were sent to communities to bring laws along with opinions. As for the term *sharīʿa*, it is often defined as the rules and regulations derived from the principles of Islamic law, as opposed to *dīn*, which signifies the discharge of debt and worship, linked to Islam as the ultimate true religion in Q. 3:19. (EI2, "Sharīʿa"). Although a closer scrutiny of the difference between these terms is beyond the scope of the chapter, I do want to draw attention to one passage in which al-Fārābī elucidates the distinction between these terms:

> *Milla* and *dīn* can almost be synonymous nouns, as are *sharīʿa* and *sunna*. For these two signify and apply to the measured actions from one part of the *milla* [the other part being the "opinions"]. It may be possible as well for the measured opinions to be called *sharīʿa*, so that *sharīʿa* and *milla* and *dīn* would be synonymous, given that *milla* consists of two parts: measured opinions and actions (al-Fārābī 2001c, 96).[17]

Here al-Fārābī remarks that *milla* is sometimes used interchangeably with other terms such as *dīn*, *sharīʿa*, and *sunna*. While this usage is, in his view, acceptable, he notes that *sharīʿa* and *sunna* are specifically linked to measured actions. This nuance is important, because it reveals that *sharīʿa* and *sunna* are specifically employed to refer to the ethical content of law, which provides a certain measured determination to actions. This is the realm in which voluntary actions are assessed, a realm circumscribed by the lawgiver who provides these specifications in the first place. But we should remember that, in his earlier definition, al-Fārābī mentioned that the lawgiver measures actions with an eye to specific goals. These measures might be specific to only one community and are often

---

15 My translation. For the Arabic see al-Fārābī 1991, 97–98.
16 Ibid.
17 For the Arabic see al-Fārābī 1991, 46.

restricted by certain conditions. Hence, different *millas* will include different measures assigned to actions. Here one can recall the example provided by Ibn Rushd (d. 1198/ 594) in his *Commentary on Aristotle's Nicomachean Ethics* on the differences of measures of justice in laws related to sacrifice and prayers imposed on various religious communities (Ibn Rushd 2018, 230). Consequently, these rites are subject to different constraints in each community. Be that as it may, one can still infer that while the term *milla* also encompasses opinions corresponding to the terrain of theoretical knowledge, the term *sharīʿa* is more specific to ethical actions and their "measurement."

We may conclude that al-Fārābī is keen to circumscribe the various realms associated with *milla*. While the theoretical part remains identified with theology, the practical part is linked to *sharʿ* or *sharīʿa*, that is, Islamic law. By equating *sharīʿa* with the practical part of *milla*, al-Fārābī effectively identifies practical ethics with *sharīʿa*.

3 Lawgivers, Laws, and Ethics

In order better to grasp the ethical content of law in al-Fārābī's thought, we should look more closely at the role of the first ruler and his successors: what are the characteristics of the lawgivers' determination of "measures" for human actions? What conditions constrain this determination, and how temporary or long-lasting are the decisions made in law? For these questions a first indication can be taken from the following passage:

> It may happen accidentally that the first ruler does not measure all of the actions and give an exhaustive account of them, but measures most of them; and with some of those he does determine, it may happen that he does not give an exhaustive account of all the conditions. On the contrary, for diverse reasons that occur, many actions such as to be measured may remain without measure: death may overtake him and carry him away before he has covered all of them; necessary occupations, such as wars and other things, may keep him from it; or it may be that he only measures actions for each incident and each occurrence he observed or is asked about, at which time he measures, legislates, and establishes a legal tradition regarding what ought to be done for that kind of incident. Since not everything that can occur does occur in his time or in his country, many things remain that could occur in another time or in another country, each needing a specifically measured and defined action. And he will have legislated nothing about them. Or else he devotes himself to those actions he presumes or knows to be principal actions which allows someone else to extrapolate the remaining ones: he legislates about the manner and amount of what ought to be done with these and leaves the rest, knowing that it will be possible for someone else to extrapolate them if he adopts his intention and following in his steps. Or he decides to begin legislating and measure actions which has most potency, benefit, value

> and use in terms of bringing coherence, bond, and order to the city: he legislates about those things alone and leaves the rest to another moment when he has time for it or so that someone else a contemporary or successor – can extrapolate then by following in his steps (al-Fārābī 2001c, 89–99). [18]

The first ruler is not in a position to determine measures for all actions, but only for most actions. This fits with a common view in *fiqh:* laws are finite whereas the situations that arise in practical affairs are infinite (Arfa-Mensia 2017, 151). Furthermore, al-Fārābī notes another difficulty, namely that even for those actions that were given a measure by the lawgiver; the conditions required for this measure may vary widely. This leads to two possible scenarios. First, a given community might end up without determined measures in relation to certain actions. Second, although the lawgiver has determined measures in relation to certain actions, the community might still lack full knowledge of all the conditions. On the other hand, the lawgiver does not leave people in a legislative void: with proper knowledge of his intention, one can discern what he would have determined in each new case. Also, the lawgiver gives priority to laws that bring most "benefit and utility", a remark we should understand as a deliberate allusion to Islamic law, where the primary approach is to extend one particular case to another through the use of analogical reasoning (*qiyās*).[19] Because the determined actions disclosed by the lawgiver have a discernible teleological design related to the benefit of the community, these measures can be extended to other cases to discern new legal rulings.

This already begins to answer the next obvious question: given that the lawgiver does not determine the ethical content of *all* laws, what should happen after his demise? Before moving on to an explicit discussion of jurisprudence, al-Fārābī alludes again to the historical context of the Muslim community, underlining the role of other leaders within the community, whom he also portrays as legislators:

> If, after his death, someone succeeds him who is like him in all respects, then the successor will be the one who measures what the first did not measure. And not only this, but it is also up to him to alter much of what the first had legislated and to measure it in another way, when he knows that this is best for his time – not because the first erred, but because the first made the measure according to what is best subsequent to the time of the first, this being the kind of thing the first would alter also, were he to observe it. It is the same if the second is followed by a third who is like the second in all respects, and the third by a fourth: it is up to the one who comes after to measure, on his own, what he does not

18 For the Arabic see al-Fārābī 1991, 48–49.

19 For a teleological understanding of law, see Ibn Rushd 1994, 49; Bouhafa 2018b, 77.

> find measured and to alter what his predecessor measured, for were his predecessor still here, he too would alter what the one who came after altered (al-Fārābī 2001c, 99).[20]

Seeing that this statement refers to the succession of lawgivers after the demise of the first, it is presumably no accident that he mentions four successors, which seems to be an allusion to the four caliphs Abū Bakr (d. 634/13), ʿUmar (d. 644/22), ʿUthmān (d. 656/35), and ʿAlī (d. 661/41). Here, then, al-Fārābī bestows the successors of the Prophet with the legislative and ethical role of determining measures to actions, especially those left undetermined by the lawgiver. The successors are also vested with the authority to alter what the first has legislated with an eye to some particular benefit once it loses its relevance. This does not mean that the first ruler erred, only that his determined measures may have been restricted to a particular time. If we do take all this to apply to the context of Islamic history, al-Fārābī would be suggesting that the four rightly guided caliphs were invested with the authority to revise laws laid down by the Prophet so as to provide a more fitting measure for their times. Such corrective actions would have been taken by the original lawgiver were he still alive. All this shows that laws are not universally valid. They have ethical content, but this content is a particular specification relevant to the particular circumstances under which the laws were promulgated. Nonetheless, laws provide a basis on which to assess the morality of human actions.

4 *Fiqh* and Ethics

It is the absence of the lawgiver and his immediate successors that warrants the emergence of jurisprudence. As Ibn Rushd will later do, al-Fārābī justifies the post-prophetic origin of jurisprudence as a guarantee for the continuity of application of Islamic norms (Bou Akl 2015, 120). Yet, al-Fārābī is not focused only on legitimising *fiqh*; he is more interested in theorising about its function and place within philosophy. Probing into the nature of jurisprudence, its principles, and its methods is central for understanding its ethical function.

Let us, therefore, first look at al-Fārābī's definition of jurisprudence. He admits that the inception of this science is necessary on the basis of the principles erected by the lawgivers, and places its emergence within the context of *milla* and political science.

---

20 For the Arabic see al-Fārābī 1991, 49–50.

> Thus, the art of jurisprudence would then be a requisite. It enables a human being to make a sound measure of each thing the lawgiver did not declare, specifically, by extrapolating it or inferring it from the things he determined by declaring them and to verify that on the basis of the lawgiver's purpose in the *milla* he legislated with respect to the nation for which it was legislated. Now, this verification is not possible unless his belief in the opinions of that religion is correct and he possesses virtues that are virtues in that religion. Whoever is like that is a jurist (al-Fārābī 2001c, 99–100).[21]
>
> Jurisprudence about the practical matters of *milla* therefore comprises only things that are particulars of universal encompassed by political science; it is, therefore, a part of political science and subordinate to practical philosophy (al-Fārābī 2001c, 101).[22]

Both passages contextualise *fiqh* within *milla* and more broadly within the scope of philosophy. First, the function of the science of *fiqh* is to extrapolate rules on the basis of the determined measures provided by the lawgivers within a *milla*. Hence a jurist is required to be cognisant of the *milla*, regarding both opinions and actions. Still it remains clear that jurisprudence is associated especially with the practical aspects of the *milla*, and is therefore linked to the assessment of voluntary actions. Thus, al-Fārābī lays down no requirement that the jurist grasp theoretical questions, a view that is also accepted in the jurisprudential tradition itself.[23] He requires merely that the jurist hold correct beliefs and possess the virtues of his *milla*. Another point, made here in the second passage, is the status of the measured actions that form the principles of *fiqh*. He specifically states that these regard particulars that fall under universals, not universals as such. This allows al-Fārābī to determine the scientific status of jurisprudence as subordinated to practical philosophy:

> The practical things in *milla* are those whose universals are in practical philosophy. That is because the practical things in *milla* are those universals measured by conditions that bind them, and what is bound with conditions is more particular than what is pronounced unqualifiedly without conditions: for instance, our saying "the human being who is writing" is more particular than our saying "the human being." Therefore, all virtuous laws are subordinate to the universals of practical philosophy. The theoretical opinions that are in *milla* have their demonstrative proofs in theoretical philosophy and are taken in *milla* without demonstrative proofs (al-Fārābī 2001c, 97).[24]

---

21 For the Arabic see al-Fārābī 1991, 50.

22 For the Arabic see al-Fārābī 1991, 52.

23 On the distinction between *fiqh* and *kalām*, see Johansen (1999, 6–7): "In its general outlines this system of theological doctrines is fully developed at the middle of the ninth century. It represents, from that period onwards, an independent discipline of thought and knowledge which is differentiated in tasks and methods from the *fiqh*."

24 For the Arabic see al-Fārābī 1991, 47.

Here al-Fārābī refers back to the now familiar point that the measured actions set up by the lawgiver are restricted by conditions. Whatever is restricted with conditions is more particular than what is not; the more specific the conditions, the less universal the prescription. This might suggest that measured actions, and the conditions attached to them, can be ranged along a spectrum where some conditions are more particular than others. Just as "writing human" is more particular than "human", so measured actions restricted by narrow conditions are less widely applicable than those that are not so restricted. So when he says that *fiqh* is subordinated to philosophy and draws its universals from practical philosophy, we should understand him to mean that jurisprudence involves a specification of universal ethical norms, tailored to particular circumstances.

For further light on the relation between *fiqh* and practical philosophy, we may turn to al-Fārābī's systematic exposition of the sciences in *Iḥṣāʾ al-ʿulūm*. There he provides a similar definition, which tasks the art of jurisprudence with inferring rulings on the basis of measured actions, concerning things that have not yet been specifically determined. He adds that this extrapolation has to be grounded on the basis of the intent of the lawgiver of the *milla* (al-Fārābī 2001b, 80). [25] In his definition of practical philosophy, specifically political philosophy, al-Fārābī underlines that the task of this science is to explore voluntary actions, dispositions and moral habits, inclinations, and states of character that lead to actions. This definition adheres to the Aristotelian understanding of the task of practical philosophy, which investigates character traits in relation to the soul and human actions that are subject to deliberation and choice (Polansky 2014, 1). He further states that the aim of political philosophy is to explain how rules arise. To establish rules, one needs two faculties. While the first is related to knowledge of universals and provides the principles of the science, the second faculty is associated with experience and observation. Al-Fārābī offers an analogy between the doctor and the ruler: both medicine and political philosophy have general principles but also call for practical experience. In the case of the doctor, the principles are learned from medical books, while experience is gained through continuous practice and exposure to large variety of medical conditions. It is the latter faculty that furnishes the doctor with the capacity to determine which treatment is needed in each particular case. Similarly, "The kingly craft is able to determine the actions with respect to each occurrence, each circumstance, and each city in each moment only by means of this faculty, which is experience" (al-Fārābī, 2001b, 78).[26] We find sim-

25 For the Arabic see al-Fārābī, 1996, 86.
26 For the Arabic see al-Fārābī 1996, 82.

ilar remarks in *Kitāb al-Milla*, which also draws a parallel between the doctor and the ruler. While the craft of ruling requires knowledge of general principles, such knowledge is insufficient without the faculty acquired through experience and observation. Furthermore, al-Fārābī provides us with a clear definition of this faculty, which he calls "prudence" (*taʿaqqul*):

> Now the faculty by means of which a human being is able to infer the stipulations with which to measure actions with respect to what he observes in each community, each city, each nation, each group, or each person, and with respect to each occurrence in a city, a nation, or a person, is what the ancients called prudence. This faculty is not required through cognisance of the universal of the art or through exhausting all of them, but through lengthy experiences with individual instances (al-Fārābī 2001c, 106).[27]

This elucidation of the faculty of prudence refers to the *taqdīr* of actions, which stands at the centre of the task of jurisprudence. The right *taqdīr* must take into account the contingent circumstances of each particular case. This is a point we already saw in the definition of *milla*, according to which the lawgiver and his successors must display prudence through their proper measure of actions and mindfulness of the various conditions.

The relation between universal rules and particular applications also appears in al-Fārābī's remarks on the relation between prudence and political science:

> First political philosophy is limited – in what it investigates of the voluntary actions, ways of life, and dispositions, and in the rest of what it investigates – to universal rules. It gives patterns for determining them with respect to each circumstance and each moment; how, by what, and to what extent they are to be determined. Then it leaves them undetermined, because determining in actuality belongs to a faculty other than this science and is such as to be added to it. Moreover, the circumstances and occurrences with respect to which determination takes place are indefinite and without limitation (al-Fārābī 2001b, 78).[28]

Political philosophy provides certain universal rules and definitions (*rusūm*) for actions, but the specific assessment of human actions, where rulings are handed down on the basis of established measures, falls outside of this science. Again, the measures and specific rulings are sensitive to the context of each action: the city or nation where it is performed, the person who acts, or the time at the action is carried out. These contextual elements call for practical prudence. Yet, prudence carries out its function under the umbrella provided by the univer-

27 For the Arabic see al-Fārābī, 1991, 58–59.
28 For the Arabic see al-Fārābī, 1996, 82–83.

sal principles discerned in political philosophy. If we take into account al-Fārābī's earlier statement that *fiqh* deals with particulars and is tasked with the function of determining particulars within a specific context, it seems plausible to identify the science of jurisprudence with the second faculty of prudence, not the first faculty exercised in political philosophy. This conclusion would also affirm the subordination of *fiqh* to practical philosophy. All this shows al-Fārābī's commitment to the scientific curriculum, which leads him to situate *fiqh* within the scope of philosophy. He is also attentive to the historical context of the emergence of *fiqh* and its autonomy, given the self-sufficiency of practical prudence.

Al-Fārābī's definition of practical reasoning in the *Fuṣūl* provides more evidence of the link between prudence and *fiqh:*

> Practical intellect (*al-ʿaql al-ʿamalī*) is the faculty by which a human being – through much experience in matters and long observation of sense-perceptible things – attains premises which he is able to seize upon what he ought to recommend or avoid with respect to each one of the matters we are to do. Some of these premises are general principles. Under each of these principles are enclosed matters we ought to recommend or avoid. Some are singular and particular; they are used as analogies (*mithālāt*) for matters a human being has not observed, and concerning which he wants to take up a position. This intellect remains a potential intellect as long as experience has not been attained. When experiences have been attained and preserved, it becomes an intellect in act. And this intellect that is in act increases along with the increase in experiences with each of the years of human being's life (al-Fārābī 2001a, 31). [29]

Al-Fārābī explains how practical intellect, which he relates to prudence, is applied to actions that are "recommended" (*yu'thar*) and "avoided" (*yujtanab*), a dichotomy that is of course taken from *fiqh*. He then explains that some of the principles employed in prudential reasoning are general, with certain particulars falling below them. These particulars are then extended to new cases as *mithālāt*. This alludes to the use of analogical reasoning to reach inferences for newly arising cases that were not determined by the lawgiver. In fact, as Lameer has shown, al-Fārābī uses the term *tamthīl* or *mithāl* (singular of *mithālāt*), *exemplum* in the Aristotelian sense, to refer to certain types of legal analogy, which also means that the second teacher deems legal analogy as pertaining to rhetorical reasoning.[30] While this discussion goes beyond our scope, the reference to *mithālāt* still affirms that al-Fārābī is drawing on his understand-

---

29 For the Arabic see al-Fārābī, 1986, 54.

30 On the relation between *qiyās* and analogy (that is, *tamthīl* or *mithālāt*), see Lameer 1994, 253 and Bou Akl 2018.

ing of *fiqh* as a science where the jurist must take into account the measured actions of particular instances, which can be extended to other acts through *qiyās*. The connection he makes between analogical reasoning and practical reasoning buttresses my contention concerning the link between the faculty of practical prudence and *fiqh*. Just as the doctor improves as he gains experience, the more particular actions the jurist has considered in the past, the greater will be his capacity to discern the norms concerning further particular actions.

Al-Fārābī's distinction between the two main faculties of practical philosophy has another consequence in relation to ethics. As I have noted, the first faculty provides definitions and general conditions, while the second faculty provides a particularised approach to human actions. This division of labour becomes clearer in his discussion of laws and virtues in the *Fuṣūl*. Here al-Fārābī adopts the Aristotelian concept of the "mean" (*mesotes*) to define good human actions and virtues (see *Nicomachean Ethics* 1106a26–b28). Al-Fārābī treats the *mesotes* as a general definition which serves as a basis for appraising human actions and virtues:

> Actions that are good deeds are mean actions, midway between two extremes both of which are bad, the one being excess and the other defect. And similarly the virtues, for they are mean states and qualities of the soul between two other states, both of which are vices, one being more excessive and the other more defective. For example, continence is a mean between greed and non-perception of pleasure, one of which, *viz.* greed, is more excessive and the other more defective. Generosity is a mean between parsimony and prodigality. Bravery is a mean between rashness and cowardice. Wit is a mean in jesting and play and so forth between impudence and unruliness, and severity. Being respectful is a middle quality between pride, and base behaviour and familiarity. Courtesy is a mean between haughtiness, boasting and swagger, and self-abasement. Forbearance is a mean between excessive anger and the state in which one never becomes angry at anything. Modesty is a mean between shamelessness and bashfulness. Friendliness is a mean between odiousness and flattery. And so on (al-Fārābī 1952,101). [31]

Adhering to Aristotle's scheme, he defines *mesotes* as a mean or middle way between two extremes, excess and defect. This fits his conception of law as a measure for controlling pain and pleasure, as well as fear and anger. The basis of good actions is provided with a measure which stands in the middle ground between two extremes. Virtues, meanwhile, are states and qualities of the soul situated between the two extremes. Al-Fārābī's example of temperance and its moderate approach to pleasure is of course an obvious one to illustrate the theory. But it should remind us of the passages we looked at earlier, where he

31 For the Arabic see al-Fārābī 1986, 36–37.

said that a need for pleasure is part of human nature and something the lawgiver must take into account when legislating. Excessive indulgence in pleasure leads to vice, and the law's role is to impose a mean that will curtail such excess. The same goes for other virtues, like generosity, courage, respect, courtesy, forbearance, modesty, and friendliness. In each case the law sets a measure that controls passions such as pleasure, pain, fear, and anger. In al-Fārābī's hands, the Aristotelian doctrine of the mean turns out to provide the jurist with a more concrete basis for identifying virtuous and vicious actions.

How then is the mean applied in concrete cases? Al-Fārābī explains this in explicitly arithmetic terms, contrasting the mean in itself (*mutawassiṭ fī nafsihi*) to the relative mean (*mutawassiṭ bi-al-'iḍāfa*):

> The expressions "mean" and "moderate" are applied in two ways: (a) the mean in itself; (b) the mean compared and related to something else. Of (a) an example is: "Six is a mean between ten and two," for the excess of ten over six is like the excess of six over two. This is a mean in itself between two extremes, and similarly for every number resembling this. It is the mean without excess or deficit, for there is not at any time a mean between ten and two other than six. (b) The relative mean is excessive and defective at different times and with reference to the difference of the things to which it is related, *e.g.*, moderate food for a boy, and moderate food for an adult, labouring man, which differs with reference to the difference of condition of the two bodies. The mean in one of them is different from the mean in the other in amount and number, in roughness and smoothness, in heaviness and lightness, and, in general, in quantity and quality. Similarly moderate desires are relative to the bodies. That is also the case of the moderate and mean in foods and medicines, for they are excessive and defective in quantity and quality according to the bodies which are treated, according to their strength at the time of year, and according to the strength of the medicine, and according to [the agent] himself, down to the individual sick man, So that what is digestible in quantity is a matter of individuals, according to the difference of the time of the year.
>
> It is this latter mean which is employed in actions and in morals. For the quantity of actions must be measured by number and amount and their quality by strength and weakness in relation to the agent and according to the purpose and cause of the action, and according to the time and place. E. g. anger, in which moderation has reference to the condition of him against whom one is angry, the cause of the anger, and the time and place involved. Similarly beating and punishments are measured in quantity and quality with reference to the beater and the beaten, the dishonesty for which the eating takes place, and the instrument which is used. The mean in every action is what is measured with reference to the things involved in the action. The things with which the different actions are compared and by which they are measured are not the same in amount in every action. On the contrary, this particular action is measured in relation to five things, for example, but sometimes the relation is to things fewer, or more, than five (al-Fārābī 1952, 101–102). [32]

32 For the Arabic see al-Fārābī 1986, 37–38.

Of particular interest here is the second sort of means, which is relative and admits of increase and decrease regarding factors, by now familiar, such as person, quantity, quality, and time. The mean required for actions and morals is relative in this sense; and the two examples provided are illuminating. Anger is relative to time, place, and action, and punishment also reflects a relative mean, for it involves measures of quantity and quality. This takes us back to al-Fārābī's definition of law. Laws are measures, with the measure corresponding to a just amount of pain and pleasure, as well as fear and anger, and these measures are subject to conditions described in terms of quantity and quality. Thus, al-Fārābī sees the ethical measure provided by the lawgiver as an application of Aristotle's general principle of the mean. A jurist must look to the *mesotes* captured in the substantive content of the law, and also the specific conditions of a given action, to reach an ethical decision.

We now have a full understanding of the ethical function of *fiqh*. Al-Fārābī holds that political philosophy provides principles governing norms of action: in particular he accepts from Aristotle the general principle that virtue lies in the mean. Yet, ethics must also take into account the specific conditions of action, and it is here that practical reasoning has a role to play. Al-Fārābī gives us a view of how this works in practice and within his own legal context. To apply laws is to gauge justice and emotion so as to reach a determination that is a particular of the universal of the mean or intermediate, specified by contingent aspects of time, place, person, quality, and quantity. This is why jurists must always consider the conditions surrounding each action, "adding" or "subtracting" as appropriate, for instance by increasing or lessening the punishment for a crime. Thus Aristotle's conception of *mesotes* is given concrete ethical content by laws understood as measures. Finally, al-Fārābī's view of law shows that he takes a practical view of ethics, in contrast to the frequent presentation of his position as being highly intellectualist. [33] As a matter of fact, al-Fārābī does not require that the jurist have any theoretical knowledge at all. After all, *fiqh* deals only with particulars of universals and calls for practical reasoning concerning contingent human actions.

---

33 For a theoretical view al-Fārābī's practical reasoning, see Black 1995. Black argues that al-Fārābī's understanding of practical reasoning does not endorse its self-sufficiency and autonomy; rather it is subordinated to theoretical wisdom. I am more inclined to accept Druart's interpretation that al-Fārābī's ethics should be understood in light of the Neoplatonic distinction between pre-philosophical and philosophical ethics, with the former, I would add, embodied by *fiqh*. See Druart (1995). Matilla (2017) has argued that the ethical development of the philosopher involves a progression similar to the Neoplatonic grades of virtue.

Hannah C. Erlwein

Ibn Sīnā's Moral Ontology and Theory of Law

1 Introduction

Among the many debates conducted in classical Islamic theology (*kalām*), the one concerned with questions of moral ontology and moral epistemology can be counted among the most vigorously debated. This debate was usually linked with the question of what theory of law should be considered the correct one. Two distinctly different positions thus developed among the *mutakallimūn* over time: on the one hand, there is the position put forward by the Ashʿarīs, which can be characterised as "theistic subjectivism" linked with a "divine command theory." They maintained that moral values, such as goodness and evil or justice and injustice, have no existence independent of the divine law (the *sharīʿa*). Moral goodness is nothing else than what God commands humans to do and what He praises, and moral evil is but what God prohibits and condemns. Values are entirely dependent on, and determined by, God's will and could theoretically take any form. There is, consequently, no way for humans to know what morality consists in and what actions are considered morally good other than through the divine law. On the other hand, there is the position adopted by the Muʿtazilīs who fundamentally disagreed with their Ashʿarī peers. Their position can be labelled "objectivism" as they maintained that moral values do in fact have a reality outside anyone's will, even God's. Moral values are objective characteristics of actions. This view entails that moral values can be known by humans through reason and their knowledge does not depend on scripture. The divine law, however, corresponds to objective notions of moral goodness and evil, and God, in being good and just, would not command what is in fact morally wrong.[1]

These debates conducted by the *mutakallimūn* have received much attention in the academic literature.[2] It might, therefore, come as a bit of a surprise that another important area of classical Islamic thought has been somewhat neglected when it comes to the aforementioned questions: this is the philosoph-

1 For the different *kalām* positions on these questions, see Hourani 1985, Chapters "Ethical Presuppositions of the Qurʾān" (23–48) and "Two Theories of Value in Early Islam" (57–66).
2 See for example Hourani 1985; Shihadeh 2006; Hallaq 2009; Emon 2010.

https://doi.org/10.1515/9783110552386-004

ical tradition (*falsafa*).[3] This might have to do with the fact that, as opposed to *kalām* works, many works of Islamic philosophy do not contain systematic discussions of these issues.[4] At the same time, however, it is not the case either that the topic is entirely absent in the writings of philosophers. A case in point is Ibn Sīnā (d. 427/1037), arguably the most influential thinker in the philosophical tradition of Islam. Despite not offering a systematic account, he does have a position on the aforementioned questions which can be distilled from various places in his writings. First and foremost is the metaphysical part of his *magnum opus*, the *Shifāʾ*, particularly the last of its ten books which contains Ibn Sīnā's political thought.

This chapter will discuss Ibn Sīnā's position on the questions of moral ontology and epistemology as well as his theory of law. Keeping in mind the debate about these questions in *kalām* as well as the different views put forward, it will be seen that not only was Ibn Sīnā very much aware of them but he actually intended to give his own views on them.[5] It would go beyond the scope of this chapter to attempt a comparative study of Ibn Sīnā's views and the views advanced by the theologians; the same would be true for the endeavour to trace the undeniable influences from Greek philosophy on Ibn Sīnā's position. The present study, therefore, has to confine itself to discussing Ibn Sīnā's position alone. In doing so, however, the intellectual context of his thought should not be forgotten, which is not least evident in the fact that he makes frequent use of terminology characteristic of these debates in the theological tradition.

2 Moral Ontology

Glimpses into Ibn Sīnā's moral ontology can be gained from his discussion of the origins and nature of evil in the context of a chapter on divine providence in the *Shifāʾ*. This discussion has received quite a bit of attention in the academic liter-

3 There are some studies dealing with aspects of Islamic political philosophy (see especially Butterworth 1983; 2000; 2011), but for the most part they do not discuss metaethical questions and legal theories, in particular not with a view to Ibn Sīnā. Butterworth (1983) discusses virtues in al-Fārābī, Ibn Sīnā, and Ibn Rushd, yet without considering metaethical questions.

4 This has also been noted by Hourani (1985, 21–22).

5 A similar point has been made by Morris (1992, 168) who states that Ibn Sīnā, like other thinkers, had to deal with these questions in view of the "many contending interpretations of Islamic law, practice, and society."

ature;[6] yet, it is worth rehearsing certain aspects of it here, since his theory of law cannot adequately be understood without his position on moral ontology.

In his discussion, Ibn Sīnā notes that the word "evil" (*al-sharr*) is used to refer to different kinds of things. Deficiencies, such as ignorance or weakness, for instance, are labelled an evil. Pains and distress are likewise called evils. To this Ibn Sīnā adds a kind of evil which can be said to correspond to what we have in mind when we speak of "moral evil": this is the evil said of "the blameworthy acts (*al-afʿāl al-madhmūma*) and (…) their principles in moral characters (*al-akhlāq*)" (Ibn Sīnā 2005, 343).[7] It is interesting and important to note that Ibn Sīnā himself does not introduce different categories of evil as when we speak of "moral evil" as opposed to, for instance, "natural evils." For him the evil that we would term "moral" is the same as the evil that we would term "natural." This is so for the following reason: generally speaking, Ibn Sīnā thinks of evil in the context of, and relating to, a thing's perfection. Everything in the cosmos, he explains, has its proper perfection, which however occurs in stages: a thing's first perfection (*al-kamāl al-awwal*) is its specific form (*ṣūra*) which makes it a member of its species. The second perfection (*al-kamāl al-thānī*) pertains to aspects that are not essential to the nature of the thing. Ibn Sīnā (1988, 14, 44) gives the example of a sword whose first perfection is its specific form as a sword, while its second perfection has to do with additional aspects such as its sharpness. Something is, then, considered an evil if it causes, or if it constitutes, a "lack of perfection" (*ʿadam kamālihi*) (Ibn Sīnā 2005, 340). This implies that the cause bringing about evil also "prevents the good" (*al-mānīʿ li'l-khayr*) which a thing could otherwise have attained and which constitutes a perfection for it (Ibn Sīnā 2005, 339). In this sense, there is no difference in category for Ibn Sīnā between the various things that might be called evil – that is to say, "moral" and "natural" evils are the same kind of evil. He thus also applies this general conception of evil as constituting the privation of a perfection, or being the cause of this privation, to what I called the category of moral evils. He here mentions, among the blameworthy actions, doing an injustice (*ẓulm*). The action of injustice can be labelled an evil insofar as it might prevent the one who suffers it from attaining a perfection, or insofar as the unjust person allows his rational soul to be controlled by his lower passions, which give rise to the impulse to do injustice, while the reverse would constitute her proper perfection (Ibn Sīnā 2005, 344). Moral evil thus relates to nothing else than the priva-

6 See especially Inati 2000; also Fontaine 2012, 161–164; Michot 1986; Steel 1999.

7 I am basing this claim on the assumption that, when Ibn Sīnā speaks of evil in actions, he can be understood to refer to the domain of morality. Compare Anzenbacher 1992, 12. All translations from the Arabic of Ibn Sīnā's works are mine (except for those from the *Risāla fī sirr al-qadar*).

tion of a perfection, and moral goodness, conversely, to the attainment of a perfection.

Ibn Sīnā's discussion of evil reveals another aspect of his moral ontology. This has to do with the question of whether the moral value of a given action is objective or relative: for instance, does Ibn Sīnā maintain that committing an injustice is inherently evil? It turns out that Ibn Sīnā holds a position according to which moral values are relative. This becomes apparent in that actions, such as doing an injustice which Ibn Sīnā previously listed among the blameworthy actions, are not *inherently* morally evil. This is so since he is adamant that, first, almost nothing in the cosmos is inherently evil without any good being found in it and, secondly, the moral value of these actions can change. The one example he gives as an exception to the rule that things are not inherently evil is blindness, whose "very existence is nothing but an evil" (Ibn Sīnā 2005, 340). Blindness constitutes the lack of a perfection that is essential for the eye by its very nature and, being nothing else but that, cannot be considered a good in any respect. This kind of evil, however, is rare and it does certainly not characterise the realm of actions and morality, as Ibn Sīnā (2005, 344) stresses: "among the actions you will not find anything called an evil which is not also a perfection in relation to its cause and agent." Ibn Sīnā here makes the crucial point that actions *can* be morally evil and this is so only *in relation* to (*bi'l-qiyās ilā*) someone. This is illustrated by the aforementioned example of the action of doing an injustice. Ibn Sīnā (2005, 343) explains: "Evil which is said of actions is also only (*innamā*) so in relation to (*bi'l-qiyās ilā*) him who loses his perfection (*kamālahu*) because of his being reached by it, such as in the case of injustice." Injustice is here considered an evil *only* insofar as it causes the sufferer of it to lose a perfection. From another point of view, however, the action of injustice is not an evil: "Injustice, for instance, proceeds from a power (*quwwa*) which seeks dominance, such as the irascible power (*al-ghaḍabiyya*), and dominance is this power's perfection – for it, it was created insofar as it is irascible, that is, it was created to direct itself towards dominance (...). Thus, this action, in relation to (*bi'l-qiyās ilā*) this power, is a good for it" (Ibn Sīnā 2005, 344). One even has to go so far as to maintain that injustice and seeking dominance are *morally good* for the irascible power as it *ought* to strive for its own perfection through these actions: "if [the irascible power] desisted from it [that is, the action of dominance], it would be, in relation to [the irascible power], an evil for it" (Ibn Sīnā 2005, 344). The only reason not to speak of striving for dominance as morally good, praiseworthy, or recommended is that in humans there is a hierarchy of powers and perfections and the irascible power belongs to those powers that have to be controlled by higher soul parts: "[dominance] is an evil only (*innamā*) for the person suffering it or for the rational soul (*al-nafs al-nāṭiqa*) whose perfection is to crush this [irascible] power and to control it. If [the rational soul] is unable to do so, it is an evil for it" (Ibn Sīnā 2005, 344).

The same logic applies to the action of adultery (*zinā*), which Ibn Sīnā (2005, 343–344) adduces as another example. It is to be regarded as evil and morally reprehensible *only* insofar as it thwarts "a perfection which has to exist in the religious regime" (since a functioning city requires clarity about family relationships, as Ibn Sīnā explains later on). From another perspective, there is consequently nothing evil or reprehensible about adultery for engaging in it means that the human reproductive faculty comes closer to reaching its perfection, which is a good (in analogy to the irascible faculty's striving for dominance). So, once more, if it were not for a hierarchy of perfections in humans, to strive for the perfection of one's reproductive faculty would be recommended and morally good.

These examples illustrate that for Ibn Sīnā the moral status of an action is not inherent to the action, but changes in relation to other things considered. This means that actions considered *in themselves* actually have no moral value. This insight should, however, be distinguished from the fact that for Ibn Sīnā actions *in themselves* are good – not in a moral sense, but in an ontological sense: existence itself is good, while non-existence or privation are evil (Inati 2000, 65–66). To the extent that actions, such as adultery and injustice, have existence, they are good, and they belong to what Ibn Sīnā calls "the order of the good" (*niẓām al-khayr*). This order permeates and characterises the whole of creation emanating from God: "[God] knows, by His essence, the [mode of] existence in the order of the good and that He is the cause, by His essence, of the good and perfection. (...) He intellectually apprehends the order of the good (...) and what He apprehends as order and good emanates from Him" (Ibn Sīnā 2005, 339). Whatever comes into existence as God's creation partakes in the goodness emanating from Him and has its place and purpose in the order, including those actions usually termed "evil."

3 The Law and Notions of Moral Goodness and Evil

The "order of the good" that emanates from God is relevant also for Ibn Sīnā's theory of law as it constitutes the foundation on which it ultimately is built. Before explaining how this is the case, a few words should be said about how the law comes under discussion for Ibn Sīnā.

The last book of the *Shifāʾ* deals with what could be labelled Ibn Sīnā's political thought. There he describes how humans come to live together in associations, what the ideal state should look like, and what laws should govern their cohabitation. In this context, Ibn Sīnā (2005, 364) remarks that "it is known that the human being differs from [all] other animals in that he cannot lead a proper life if in isolation and alone. (...) This is why [humans] have been compelled to establish cities and form associations." For their survival, humans depend on mutual relations and cooperation with others, which in turn requires the existence of laws which establish and guarantee justice in the state. Laws in turn depend on a lawgiver – and in Ibn Sīnā's ideal state it is not just any human being, however gifted, who brings these laws, but a prophet. The most general function and purpose of the law are, as Ibn Sīnā indicates, to organise human life and interaction with others in the state through prohibitions and commands. In *al-Aḍḥawiyya*, Ibn Sīnā (1962, 110) describes this function of the law thus: "the greatest objective of the law pertains to the practical aspect of human actions so that they should do what is good (*al-khayr*)." Importantly, in seeking to regulate human conduct and actions, the law is inextricably linked to notions of moral goodness and evil; the two are not independent or separable from each other. The aim of the law is to guide humans to act in a morally good way, which means that the law is informed by, and reflects, what is morally good.

The existence of this link between the law of the ideal state and notions of moral goodness and evil becomes even more evident in Ibn Sīnā's rather detailed account of the particular rules the prophet lays down. For instance, he notes that the prophet has to establish a common fund in the city, which is financed from taxes imposed on certain goods as well as war booty, serving, among other things, "as expenditure on those whom illnesses and diseases prevent from earning their livelihood." This prescription, Ibn Sīnā points out, counters the opinion of some people that these people should rather be killed – something Ibn Sīnā rejects as "evil" or "reprehensible" (*qabīḥ*) (Ibn Sīnā 2005, 371). This statement, however, implies that the rules set forth by the law are envisaged by Ibn Sīnā in terms of moral goodness and evil. The law commands actions which are associated with moral goodness. Other similar examples could be named. That the law is never divorced from considerations of morality is further shown by the following: the prophet's task of laying down particular laws has to be accompanied, so Ibn Sīnā (2005, 365), by his informing the inhabitants of the ideal state that "they have a creator, one, unique, and powerful (...) and that obedience to His command is His right (...) and that He has prepared for those who obey Him a blissful afterlife and for those who disobey Him an afterlife full of misery." Disobedience to the law, this statement indicates, is not presented as a mere violation of an obligation but is coloured in moral terms of praise, reward, blame, and punishment. In his *Risāla fī sirr al-qadar*, Ibn Sīnā (1985, 231) makes this point explicit when he says about the divine law: "As for praise and blame, these have just two objects. One is to incite a doer of good to repeat the like act which is willed to proceed from him; the second is to scare the one from whom [a reprehensible] act has occurred from repeating the like of it." Here, too, all actions are divided into morally good and evil, and the law seeks to promote nothing else than morally good actions by linking them to praise and to prevent evil actions by associating them with blame.

4 The Function of the Law

In being so closely linked to notions of moral evil and good, the law reflects nothing less than the very order of the good which underlies it. Since good and evil in general, including moral goodness and evil, are conceived of by Ibn Sīnā as the realisation of a perfection or the lack thereof, and since the law attempts to promote morally good actions, the law in fact strives to bring about humans' perfection. Ultimately, this means that the law seeks to ensure that humans can join in the all-encompassing order of the good by helping them attain their proper perfection, which constitutes the good. (It should here be noted that all other things in the cosmos, too, are so made that they strive to attain the perfection proper to them. This striving towards perfection – each thing in its own way – is part of God's arrangement of the cosmos (Ibn Sīnā 1968, 46).)

The law's endeavour to enable humans to acquire their proper perfection means the following: like everything else in the cosmos, human perfection occurs in stages. Their first perfection, Ibn Sīnā explains in his writings on psychology, consists in their human or rational soul (*al-nafs al-insāniyya* or *al-nafs al-nāṭiqa*) – as opposed to two other kinds of souls to be found in the cosmos, the animal soul (*al-nafs al-ḥayawāniyya*) and the vegetative soul (*al-nafs al-nabātiyya*). It is the rational soul that makes humans a member of the species "human." The second perfection of humans pertains to things such as their actions and desires. It is here where the law becomes relevant, for Ibn Sīnā (1962, 111–12) notes:

> when most people are called to the good (*al-khayr*) and justice, it is as if they are called to a matter that contradicts their human nature (*ṭabāʿ*) and opposes the movements of their animal soul (*nufūsihim al-ḥayawāniyya*) which is [generally] victorious over the rational soul (*al-nafs al-nāṭiqa*) – it almost seems like it [that is, the rational soul] does not exist at all or cannot act or has no power whatsoever – [and] they do not answer the call unless under force and dreading it.

It is the purpose of the law to enable the rational soul to reign over the base desires of the animal part of the human soul, so that we are made to act in accordance with our own species and thereby become perfected.[8]

The way by which the law seeks to achieve this is to teach humans proper, morally good conduct – this has become clear in Ibn Sīnā's aforementioned statement that "the greatest objective of the law pertains to the practical aspect of human actions so that they should do what is good." The law, therefore, attempts to teach the inhabitants of the ideal state what Ibn Sīnā calls "practical wisdom."

All wisdom humans can acquire, Ibn Sīnā (*Rasā'il*, 105) explains elsewhere, is divided into practical (*al-ḥikma al-ʿamaliyya*) and theoretical wisdom (*al-ḥikma al-naẓariyya*). "The aim of theoretical wisdom," he notes, "is the attainment of certain convictions concerning existents whose existence is not related to actions of humans (*bi-fiʿl al-insān*) and the aim is nothing but the attainment of an opinion, such as knowledge of God's oneness and uniqueness (*al-tawḥīd*)." Theoretical wisdom includes the sciences of physics, mathematics, and metaphysics. Practical wisdom, on the other hand, properly pertains to the domain of human actions, as already indicated, and has to do with notions of right and wrong conduct (Ibn Sīnā 1980, 16–17; *Rasā'il*, 79–81, 105–107).

All wisdom, Ibn Sīnā (1980, 16) states, constitutes a "completion (*istikmāl*) of the human soul." In seeking to teach humans practical wisdom, the law therefore endeavours to help the human soul reach its perfection – more precisely, the part of the human soul that is receptive to the practical aspect of wisdom, that is, the practical intellect (*al-ʿaql al-ʿamalī*) or the practical faculty (*al-quwwa al-ʿamaliyya*). Just like wisdom, the human soul is divided into the two faculties of the practical and theoretical (*naẓarī*) intellects (1952a, 32). The most perfect of humans are characterised as having a perfected practical intellect *as well as* a perfected theoretical intellect (2005, 358–359). Yet, the reason Ibn Sīnā presents the law as focusing, in the first place, on perfecting the *practical* intellect by teaching morally good conduct certainly has to do with his rather pessimistic view about the intellectual abilities of the majority of humans. While it is true that the prophet in his capacity as legislator has to communicate certain knowledge about God to the people, this falling under the domain of theoretical wisdom, Ibn Sīnā explicitly states that "he ought not to involve them with anything pertaining to knowledge of God (Most-High) going

8 This entails that states which significantly diverge from the law of the ideal state pose the danger that their inhabitants cannot attain their proper perfection, as Ibn Sīnā (2005, 364) himself indicates: "whoever, in establishing a state, is not familiar with the conditions [necessary for establishing] a state (...) he deprives the people of their perfections (*ʿādim li-kamālāt al-nās*)."

beyond knowledge that He is one and unique, truth, and that there is nothing similar to Him." If the prophet were to attempt to communicate metaphysical truths to them that go beyond this, "he would demand too much from them, introduce confusion into their religion, and cause them to fall into a state from which deliverance is only for him who is [divinely] helped (...) for they can conceive these states in their true form only with great strain (...) and only very few among them are able to comprehend the true nature of God's oneness, uniqueness, and transcendence" (Ibn Sīnā 2005, 365–366). It is for this reason that the law, despite seeking to perfect the inhabitants of the ideal state to the greatest degree possible, does not attempt to communicate more theoretical wisdom to them, but focuses on the practical intellect and rules that govern human interaction in the state.

The function of the practical intellect is described by Ibn Sīnā (1952a, 32) as being "the principle of movement of the human body, which urges it to particular actions." It is "a power having a certain opinion regarding particular things when it comes to what needs to be done or abstained from in terms of what is beneficial or harmful, agreeable or reprehensible (*jamīl wa-qabīḥ*), good or evil (*khayr wa-sharr*)" (Ibn Sīnā 1988, 203–204). Since this is the practical intellect's function and role, it is essential that it rules over all other motivating faculties – these being the appetitive power (*al-quwwa al-shahwāniyya*) as well as the irascible power (*al-quwwa al-ghaḍabiyya*) – so as to prevent the emergence of vices (*akhlāq radhliyya*) in humans and instead to give rise to virtuous dispositions (*akhlāq faḍīliyya*) (Ibn Sīnā 1952a, 32). It is these virtuous dispositions that give rise to morally good actions (Ibn Sīnā 2005, 354). This being the case, it is not surprising that Ibn Sīnā explicitly states that the prophet in his capacity as lawgiver has to ensure that the law is so made as to promote good dispositions in the inhabitants of the ideal state. These dispositions, Ibn Sīnā goes on to explain, correspond to the three aforementioned faculties that motivate humans to act. They constitute a mean (*wasāṭa*) between two extremes, which, were they to be adopted, would lead to the manifestation of vices in humans and to their detriment. The virtuous dispositions the law seeks to bring about in humans are, then, temperance (*ʿiffa*), which is the mean pertaining to the motivating power of the appetitive power, courage (*shajāʿa*), which pertains to the irascible power, and (practical) wisdom (*ḥikma*), which corresponds to the practical intellect. The realisation of these three virtues and means is nothing else than justice (*al-ʿadāla*) (Ibn Sīnā 2005, 378). Ibn Sīnā here seems to have come full circle: the parallel between the beginning of his discourse on the ideal state – where he introduced the prophet as lawgiver for the sake of establishing *justice* (*ʿadl*) – and his treatment of virtuous dispositions at the very end of it (this also being the very end of the *Metaphysics* of the *Shifāʾ*) – where he declared them to culminate in justice (*al-ʿadāla*) – is striking. Ibn Sīnā's ideal state is a "virtuous city" (*al-madīna al-fāḍila*) in that the virtue of justice characterises both the interaction between its inhabitants and the condition of every individual soul as well.

In teaching humans practical wisdom, the law not only seeks to perfect individuals in the manner just discussed, but also looks to the perfection of the state, with the two being interrelated. A particular prescription pertaining to the actions of individuals, but presented as having relevance for the state, is the prohibition of the aforementioned act of adultery. Adultery is not presented by Ibn Sīnā with a view to its resulting in the lack of a perfection in the individual (even though he could easily have made this point, arguing that it allows the human's animal soul to gain the upper hand over the rational soul); rather, he emphasises that it thwarts "a perfection which has to exist in the religious regime." Prescriptions pertaining to adultery are of relevance for the state and do not represent a purely private affair, as also becomes clear from what Ibn Sīnā (2005, 372) has to say about rules concerning marriage:

> then, the first thing [the prophet] has to decree regards the issue of marriage, which results in issue. He must call and urge to it, for through it comes about the endurance of the species. (...) He must organise it so that it takes place in a manifest way (*wuqūʿ ẓāhir*) so that there are no uncertainties regarding progeny causing defects in property transfer of inheritance. (...) By this – I mean the concealment of marriage – defects in [yet] other respects occur.

The issue with adultery is – and this explains why the law's prescriptions pertaining to individuals' conduct have relevance on the level of the state – that it robs the state of its very foundations that allow it to function properly. Elsewhere, Ibn Sīnā explicitly speaks of laws that facilitate "the building of the city's foundations (*arkān al-madīna*), such as marriage and communal activities" (Ibn Sīnā 2005, 375) and mentions "actions contrary to the law which bring about the corruption of the order of the city (*fasād niẓām al-madīna*), such as adultery, theft, complicity with the enemies of the city, and similar things" (Ibn Sīnā 2005, 377). Moreover, Ibn Sīnā gives individuals' actions almost cosmic relevance in that he links adultery and marriage in particular – and thereby the prescriptions of the law – to the preservation of the human species, which, it must be recalled, is part of nothing less than the order of the good. Ibn Sīnā (2005, 365) notes:

> with respect to the endurance and actual existence of the human species the need for [the prophet who brings laws to organise their cohabitation and interactions] is more pressing than the need for such benefits as the growing of hair on the eyebrows. (...) It is therefore

> impossible (...) that that whose existence in the order of the good God knows to be possible and necessary in terms of its occurrence in order to realise the order of the good should not exist. And how can it not exist if that whose existence depends on it is related to it exists?

Ibn Sīnā's concern here is the proof of the possibility of prophethood, yet his statement also makes it clear that the prophet's existence, his role as legislator, and by extension the laws themselves are connected to bringing about what the order of the good emanating from God requires to exist in actuality. Yet, the relevance of the law in bringing about the perfection of the state is expressed by Ibn Sīnā not only insofar as it is a *consequence* of the law's endeavour to teach individuals morally good conduct; Ibn Sīnā also lists among the prescriptions of the law certain commands and prohibitions which *directly* pertain to the end of making the state virtuous. "The [prophet in his function as] legislator must make obedience to whoever succeeds him an obligation," Ibn Sīnā notes, and follows this with an account of the prescribed procedures for selecting a successor. Quarrels over the issue of succession must likewise be prevented by the law: "[the prophet] has to lay down in law that, should they disagree and argue, succumbing to their passions, or should they agree on someone who is not appropriate [for the position], they have committed an act of unbelief against God" (Ibn Sīnā 2005, 374). Certain forms of usurpation and the appropriate reaction of the inhabitants of the ideal state to it are in the same manner regulated by the law: "then, [the prophet] has to decree in law that if someone secedes and claims the caliphate by virtue of power and wealth, all citizens have to fight and kill him. (...) And he has to rule that nothing brings one closer to God, after belief in the prophet, than the killing of this usurper" (Ibn Sīnā 2005, 375). Other examples could be named where Ibn Sīnā lists prescriptions of the law that regulate the way the state has to function, including state-led prayers and war against other states.

The law brought by the prophet not only contains prescriptions defining morally good conduct for individuals and proper forms of administration on the state level, but is also, and lastly, concerned with ordering family relations. (This aspect has been touched upon above when speaking about legal prescriptions concerning marriage and adultery, which Ibn Sīnā presents as serving to ensure the perfection of the *state*, yet they clearly also deal with *family* matters.) This is unsurprising, given that Ibn Sīnā presents the law as congruent with practical wisdom, which he describes as pertaining to the individual (*shakhṣ wāḥid*), the household (*ijtimāʿ manzilī*), and the state (*ijtimāʿ madanī*) (Ibn Sīnā *Rasāʾil*, 107) and which he consequently divides into "wisdom pertaining to ethical dispositions [of individuals]" (*ḥikma khuluqiyya*), "wisdom pertaining to the household" (*ḥikma manziliyya*), and "wisdom pertaining to the state" (*ḥikma *madaniyya*) (Ibn Sīnā 1980, 16). Ibn Sīnā consequently lists a number of prescriptions the prophet has to establish that evidently relate to the law's aim of perfecting individuals insofar as they are part of a household. (Ibn Sīnā (*Rasāʾil*, 107) speaks of knowledge of "how humans should arrange their household which they share with their spouse, children, and servants.") One of them is the law regarding divorce. For instance, Ibn Sīnā (2005, 372–373) states, after talking about the importance of making marriages public, that "[the prophet in his capacity as legislator] also has to ensure the permanence of the union [that is, marriage]. (...) When it comes to women, this means that the right to make a separation must not be placed in their hands as she really is of feeble intellect. (...) When it comes to men, an indemnity must be imposed on him so that he will approach separation only once he is certain." In a similar manner, the upbringing of children falls within the scope of the law: "he must legislate regarding the child that both parents must undertake his upbringing." From children the law demands subservience and obedience to the parents (Ibn Sīnā 2005, 274).

It has already become clear that Ibn Sīnā presents the most basic function of the law as organising human life in the ideal state. In teaching humans practical wisdom and thereby seeking to perfect them, the law, however, pursues another, even greater aim which transcends life in this world: it seeks to prepare humans for the hereafter. This idea is expressed by Ibn Sīnā when he says that the purpose of instilling in individuals virtuous dispositions is "that their life in this world *and* in the world to come may be happy" (Ibn Sīnā *Rasāʾil*, 107). In the same manner, the law aspires to teach wisdom that pertains to the household "so that the condition of humans [in this life] is orderly and can enable them to attain happiness" (Ibn Sīnā *Rasāʾil*, 107). Since, however, Ibn Sīnā considers true happiness attainable only in the hereafter, he emphasises the importance of gaining wisdom in this world for this ultimate aim: "all sciences [or: all knowledge] (*ʿulūm*) have one benefit in common: the attainment of the perfection (*kamāl*) of the human soul in actuality in order to prepare it for happiness in the world to come" (Ibn Sīnā 2005, 13). True happiness is of a spiritual, not of a bodily nature as most people suppose, Ibn Sīnā (1962, 113–114) explains, and it takes place when the soul has left the body behind. The greatest degree of happiness is prepared for those who had the chance to attain perfection not only of the practical but also the theoretical intellect. As noted above most people are denied this, yet they too can hope for a certain form of happiness in the hereafter if they lived a life in accordance with the rules of the law (Ibn Sīnā 1962, 164–165; Druart 2000). Ibn Sīnā emphasises in this context the importance of attaining the virtuous dispositions the law seeks to bring about in humans when he notes that "true happiness in the hereafter is achieved through the purification of the soul [which] is realised through [a virtuous] character and dispositions (*akhlāq wa-malakāt*) (...) [so that] the soul is instilled with the dispositions to control the body" (Ibn Sīnā 2005, 369). In teaching humans these dispositions, the law therefore pursues the twofold aim of, first, organising human life in a way that the superiority of the rational soul over the lower passions gives rise to morally good actions and, second thereby enabling the human soul to look as much as possible beyond its bodily sensations and prepare it for the spiritual pleasures of the world to come. This is stated in an explicit manner by Ibn Sīnā (2005, 377–78) when he notes:

> the legislator has to prescribe laws also regarding the moral dispositions (*al-akhlāq*) and customs which call to justice, which is a mean. The mean regarding moral dispositions and customs is sought in two ways: as for the one involving the breaking of the dominance of the powers [of the passions], this is for the sake of the purification of the soul in particular and for enabling it to acquire self-mastery so that it can liberate itself [in the hereafter] from the body untarnished. As for the other, which involves the use of these powers [of the passions], it is for worldly benefits.

This leads to an important insight: Ibn Sīnā's account of the function and nature of the law is nothing less than a soteriology. It is through the law that the majority of people attain the chance of salvation by escaping the fate of perpetual ignorance and the pain caused by it.

The law's characteristic of being a mirror image of the order of the good is evident not only in the particular prescriptions it contains (insofar as they reflect notions of moral goodness and evil that are inscribed in the very order of the cosmos), as has become clear, but also, and arguably even more so, in the way the prophet receives the law. Ibn Sīnā emphasises repeatedly that the law brought by the prophet is a "revealed law" (*al-sunna al-nāzila*) (Ibn Sīnā 2005, 376) and that "the prophet is from God and sent by Him (...) and all that he legislates is required by God for him to legislate" (Ibn Sīnā 2005, 369). Despite the law's being revealed to the prophet by God, Ibn Sīnā is adamant that the process of revelation is a natural cognitive process that lies within human capacity. In his works on psychology, he explains the general way in which humans acquire knowledge, which has to do with the theoretical intellect of the human rational soul whose function it is to acquire universal intelligibles, abstracted from matter, through syllogistic reasoning. The aspect that is relevant for our purposes is that the prophet is endowed with an extraordinarily strong theoretical intellect, which Ibn Sīnā calls a "holy intellect" (*ʿaql qudsī*), that enables him to grasp intuitively (that is, by way of *ḥads* or "intuition") the intelligibles without the need for a teacher (Ibn Sīnā 1952a, 36; Gutas 2000; McGinnis 2010, 147–148). The prophet's intellect reaches its most perfect developmental stage as an acquired intellect (*ʿaql mustafād*) which also implies the perfection of the prophet's rational soul. In this state, Ibn Sīnā (2005, 350) explains, his soul

> becomes an intellectual world (*ʿālaman ʿaqliyyan*) on which the form of the whole [universe] is inscribed as well as the intellected order (*al-niẓām al-maʿqūl*) in the whole [universe] and the good (*al-khayr*) emanating on the whole [universe], beginning from the principle of the whole [universe], proceeding to the noble, spiritual, absolute substances, then to the spiritual substances which are somehow connected to bodies, then to the exalted bodies (...) and so on until it [that is, the soul] completes in itself [the apprehension] of the structure (*hayʾa*) of the whole of existence. It thus becomes transformed into an intellected world that parallels the world of all existents, witnessing what is absolute righteousness (*al-ḥasan al-muṭlaq*), absolute goodness (*al-khayr al-muṭlaq*), and true absolute beauty, becoming one with it and imprinted with its like and structure.

What this implies is that by intellectually apprehending the structure of the whole of reality, which is nothing else than the order of the good emanating from God, the prophet receives his revelation. This in turn implies his understanding of the place of each thing in the order and its proper perfection. The revealed law is nothing but this grasping of the order of the good, whose mirror image it is. Or to put it in other terms, the prophet "translates," as it were, the order he apprehends into the law. This moreover means that in Ibn Sīnā's conception, (moral) goodness and evil are prior to the law as they are fixed in the very structure of the cosmos and form the law's foundation. Interestingly, this hierarchical relationship between the order of the good and the law manifests itself also in the fact that in his *magnum opus*, the *Shifāʾ*, Ibn Sīnā discusses the law only insofar as it is an extension of his account of metaphysics: without the prior analysis of God's emanation and the structure of reality, the law, its source, and function cannot be accounted for.[9]

5 The Law, Morality, and Epistemology

The fact that, for Ibn Sīnā, both the law and notions of moral goodness and evil reflect, and presuppose, an intellectual understanding of the order of the good as just described has implications for the question of whether individuals other than the prophet have access to the law and knowledge of proper moral

9 A similar point has been made by Hallaq (2009, 79) with regards to the *mutakallimūn*'s view of the *sharīʿa:* "Ultimately, law was the systematic hallmark of submission to the Lord of the Worlds (...) Technically, therefore, law becomes subservient to, and dependent on, the mother science of theology."

conduct. Ibn Sīnā appears rather sceptical as to whether most humans have the ability to discover for themselves what moral goodness and evil consist in. This is, in the first place, due to the weakness of their theoretical intellect, as noted above, which is why, according to Ibn Sīnā, the law avoids burdening the common people with matters pertaining to theoretical wisdom which they are unable to comprehend.[10] Yet, it is the theoretical intellect that facilitates grasping the *true* meaning of moral goodness and evil – "true" insofar as it understands that morality reflects perfections, which are prior to the law, and thus the order of the good. A consequence of this inability is, Ibn Sīnā suggests, that they have mistaken notions about what makes an action good or evil, which manifests itself in their practical intellect oftentimes being at fault. For instance, in discussing the need for the prophet as legislator in order to establish justice in the state, Ibn Sīnā (2005, 365) notes that most people, if left to their own opinions, "would consider what is owed them [an expression of] justice (*mā lahu ʿadl*) and what they owe [others an expression of] injustice (*mā ʿalayhi ẓulm*)." This is, arguably, a rather self-centred conception of morality and it certainly does not correspond to Ibn Sīnā's presentation of moral goodness and evil in terms of perfections or virtuous dispositions.

This then means by extension that the majority of people are oblivious to the true purpose of the law which goes beyond (the evident purpose of) organising society. They do not know of the law's ultimate aim of perfecting humans in order to facilitate for them the experience of true bliss in the hereafter. Ibn Sīnā repeatedly emphasises that the law cannot communicate the true nature of these things to the people as this would go beyond their understanding: "the law seeks to speak to the people (*al-jumhūr*) in a way they can comprehend (*yafhamūna*), approximating what they cannot comprehend. (…) [The law's] depiction of happiness as a reward is not according to its true, noble, lofty, divine form but in a form they can comprehend and they consider beautiful" (Ibn Sīnā 1962, 103, 111). To the masses the law presents itself in other terms. First and foremost among them is the law's own insistence that obedience to the law is tantamount to obedience to God – this is, as we recall, the first principle on which the law is based – and disobedience to the law is frequently framed as an act of unbelief against God. (So, for instance, in the case of the failure to obey the law which prescribes certain selection processes for whoever succeeds the prophet in his function as head of state: "if the citizens are capable of

---

10 Griffel (2012) discusses aspects of Ibn Sīnā's internal sense theory and knowledge acquisition (in particular the ways in which certain faculties may arrive at false conclusions, according to Ibn Sīnā).

[fighting a usurper] but refrain from doing so, then they disobey God and commit an act of unbelief" (Ibn Sīnā 2005, 375).) The law must not, and cannot, communicate to the people that it presents itself in these terms only in order to get them to obey the law, which they would otherwise not be inclined to do and thereby thwart the chance to attain perfection – this being the true concern of the law, as has become clear: "the first principle governing his legislation is to let them know that they have a creator, one, unique, and powerful (...) and that obedience to His command is His right (...) and that He has prepared for those who obey Him a blissful afterlife and for those who disobey Him an afterlife full of misery, *so that* (*ḥattā*) the people will hear and obey the decrees put into the prophet's mouth" (Ibn Sīnā 2005, 365). In his *Risāla fī sirr al-qadar*, Ibn Sīnā (1985, 231) states that "men must be bound by one of two bonds, either the bond of the divine Law or the bond of reason, that the order of the world may be completed," thus both indicating the objective of the law to have humans join into the order of the good through their own perfection and pointing to the notion that for many this can only be facilitated through obedience to the law, while reason, grasping the structure of existence itself, is in fact the proper way of knowing of this objective.

The quote from the *Risāla*, however, indicates something else worth noting when it comes to the question of whether humans other than the prophet have access to the true notions of moral goodness and evil as well as the law. In maintaining that it is humanly possible to know of morally good conduct and the law (since both are consequences of grasping the order of the good), Ibn Sīnā takes up an implicit position within the debate over moral epistemology pursued more explicitly by the *mutakallimūn*. Since what is required to apprehend the order of the good is a perfected theoretical intellect, the true philosopher, too, is able to do so, according to Ibn Sīnā. In the case of the prophet the grasping of the order of the good is called "revelation", while it is not so in the case of the philosopher, who lacks certain properties associated with prophethood (al-Akiti 2004; Morris 1992, 177–196). Yet, both grasp the same truth and both ways, which are in a sense one, are valid. If this is the case, it becomes evident how and why Ibn Sīnā presents himself as being able to lay out a theory of law and the particular prescriptions the law must contain in the *Metaphysics* of the *Shifāʾ*: a true philosopher like Ibn Sīnā whose theoretical intellect certainly has achieved its most perfect state has access to the same knowledge as the prophet of how humans ought to live in order for their perfection to be realised. Importantly, in discussing the law's prescriptions, Ibn Sīnā does not simply rehearse what the *sharīʿa* is already known to contain, but wants to make the point that it is possible to arrive at these insights through reason. This seems clear when, in discussing how the law's prescriptions pertaining to marriage seek to avoid defects concerning expenditure and mutual assistance, he comments that "this is something the reasonable person (*al-ʿāqil*) comes to know when he ponders over it" (Ibn Sīnā 2005, 372). In addition to this, it should be noted that Ibn Sīnā commonly introduces particular prescriptions of the law by stating that "the legislator *has to* (*yajibu*) prescribe that..." and the like. This can be seen to point to Ibn Sīnā's conviction that the law is consequent on the understanding what the order of the good entails.

6 Theory of Law

Since the function and purpose of the law have become clear as well as its connection with moral goodness and evil, a few words should be said about Ibn Sīnā's theory of law, which can be distilled from various places. Interestingly, even though Ibn Sīnā presents the law as a mirror image of the order of the good that defines the set-up of the cosmos, he does not hold – as could be expected – that the law brought by the prophet is a universal law, valid for all times and places. At the same time though he does present the law as containing certain objective, unalterable elements. His theory then is an interplay between notions of the law's objectivity and relativity. It also becomes apparent that, as an extension of this interplay, Ibn Sīnā tried to reconcile the all-important Islamic idea of a divine origin of the law and the idea of human elements in it.

Ibn Sīnā presents the divinely revealed law as relative to time and place. This means that the law brought by a particular prophet might – and according to Ibn Sīnā, in fact does – differ from the law another prophet received through revelation. This point is made in an explicit manner when Ibn Sīnā (*Rasāʾil*, 108) states that practical wisdom pertaining to the state informs humans about "those prescriptions (*ḥudūd*) which distinguish one law (*sharīʿa*) from another, one people from another, and one time from another." This relative element of the law also becomes apparent in Ibn Sīnā's enumeration in the *Shifāʾ* of the particular commands and prohibition the law of the ideal state must contain. For instance, the law's prescriptions concerning prayer have to take into account the particular customs of the people whom it addresses and may therefore vary vastly from one version of the law to another: "the legislator must prescribe for the worshippers in preparation for prayer the conditions which they *customarily* (*al-ʿāda*) adopt when they meet a human king, such as purification and cleanliness (...) reverence, calm, [and] the lowering of the eyes" (Ibn Sīnā 2005, 368). When discussing the procedures the law prescribes regarding divorce, Ibn Sīnā (2005, 373) praises Muḥammad as "the best of lawgivers" (*afḍal al-shāriʿīn*) for having decreed that a man who has pronounced the triple divorce can only remarry his former wife if she first marries another man.[11] This can be seen to imply that this Qur'anic prescription is not shared by all the different versions of the law, according to Ibn Sīnā. In *al-Aḍḥawiyya*, Ibn Sīnā (1962, 109 – 10) states in similar fashion that "the law coming by the tongue of our prophet Muḥammad contains the best and most perfect of [all] that the different versions of the law (*al-sharāʾiʿ*) can (*yumkin*) contain", thus making the point that the law can indeed take different forms. In addition to this, he presents the law itself as acknowledging that its prescriptions are relative to time and place insofar as it does not claim universal relevance. The only situation where the law, despite the relativity of its particular commands and prescriptions, may claim universality is the following, as Ibn Sīnā (2005, 376) notes:

> if another city has a praiseworthy law, the [prophet] must not interfere with it – unless the time requires the declaration that there is no law other than the revealed law. For when nations and states go astray, a law needs to be given to them. (…) If adherence to the law becomes obligatory, it might be the case that to ensure this adherence, acceptance of the law by the whole world is required. (…) [Otherwise, there appear] those who oppose [the law and its universal claim] using as an argument for their rejection that the people of another city already rejected it.

The only reason for a particular version of the law to claim universality is when a group of people who are given that law refuse obedience to it, having observed that another group of people previously rejected the law. In this situation adherence to the law needs to be ensured by proclaiming its universality and fighting anyone who opposes it.

A consequence of the law's taking into consideration the particular circumstances of the people for whom it was laid down is Ibn Sīnā's insistence that "the legislator must refer many issues, especially pertaining to transactions, to individual judgement of jurists (*ijtihād*), for different times require different rulings (*aḥkām*) which cannot possibly be predetermined" (Ibn Sīnā 2005, 377). Lastly, it has already been seen that the law speaks to the people about the hereafter and God in terms which do not correspond to their true form, but which they are able to appreciate. Just like the particular prescriptions of the law, the images it employs depend on the circumstances of its recipients and may therefore vary: "[the prophet] must let them know of God's greatness and majesty through symbols and likenesses (*rumūz wa-amthila*) derived from things which *they* consider (*ʿindahum*) great and majestic (…) and he must give them examples for happiness and misery [in the hereafter] based on what *they* understand and [are

11 This is Q. 2:229 – 230.

able to] conceive" (Ibn Sīnā 2005, 366). Ibn Sīnā (1962, 97–98) actually mentions differences in the way different versions of the revealed law depict these matters, highlighting the way the Torah (*al-Tawrāt*) (which he also labels a "law" or *sharīʿa*) employs anthropomorphic descriptions of God, which he then contrasts with the Qur'an.[12]

Yet, despite this relativity of the law and the dependence of its specific form on the circumstances of its recipients, there is an underlying objective, unchangeable aspect to it. This is, first, the fact that all versions of the law, no matter their specific prescriptions (or maybe rather: in view of the specific prescriptions they adopt), share in their ultimate purpose of perfecting humans in order to enable them to attain happiness in the hereafter. In having this common goal, however, Ibn Sīnā (*Rasā'il*, 108) can be seen to stress that there are "universal prescriptions which are shared by all versions of the law (*al-ḥudūd al-kulliyya al-mushtarika fī l-sharā'iʿ*)." Unfortunately Ibn Sīnā does not discuss which prescriptions among those he lists in the *Shifā'* fall into the category of shared universal commands and which ones he considers alterable and specific to any given law. It appears as if Ibn Sīnā believes that the law must contain certain prescriptions that are dependent on time and place and therefore differ from one law to the other, while other prescriptions simply cannot change – both, however, in order to realise human perfection. The reason for the existence of certain objective, unalterable commands and prohibitions, we may be justified to surmise, is that the law mirrors the way the cosmos is set up. This means, for instance, that certain virtues, which are a prerequisite for human perfection, can only be actualised by a certain set of rules (that is, it will always be the case that adultery has to be prohibited as it is always detrimental to the perfection of the state – while it is not a necessity that prayer, being in itself commanded by the law, take any specific form).

This interplay between the law's containing certain objective, universal aspects, on the one hand, and its being relative to time and place, on the other, manifests itself in another way, too. Ibn Sīnā is adamant that the law is of divine origins, yet he also wants to say that it contains human elements. The divine origins of the law have already been touched upon, and Ibn Sīnā (2005, 365) frequently remarks that "[the prophet] must lay down laws for the people concerning their affairs – by the permission of God, His order, His inspiration, and His sending down of the Holy Spirit on him." The law the prophet

---

12 For Muslim charges of anthropomorphist tendencies in other scriptures, such as the Bible and the Torah, see Roth 1987. For the attempt by the Jewish philosopher Saʿādia Gaon (d. 942) at reading the Torah in a non-anthropomorphic way, see Adamson 2012, 70–72.

brings is nothing but "divine law" (*al-sharīʿa al-ilāhiyya*) (Ibn Sīnā 1980, 16). He is "the one who receives revelation" (*al-mūḥā ilayhi*) (Ibn Sīnā 2005, 359) and has "divine wisdom" (Ibn Sīnā 2005, 366).

Arguably more surprising than his insistence, to be expected in an Islamic context, that the law brought by the prophet derives from God is the observation that Ibn Sīnā very much distances himself from the view traditionally held by the *mutakallimūn* that revelation is solely divine word, given to the prophets who are nothing but God's mouthpiece. Contrary to this view, Ibn Sīnā assumes, it appears, that the specific forms taken by the law make it partly a human product. This is suggested by the term *sunna* he continuously employs alongside the term *sharīʿa* to refer to the revealed law, as well as by *sānn* referring to the prophet in his capacity as lawgiver, used alongside the term *shāriʿ*. In fact, he uses the root *s-n-n* much more frequently to denote the prophet's action of legislating than the root *sh-r-ʿ*. For example, in the aforementioned quote where he stated that the prophet has to lay down laws by God's permission and revelation, Ibn Sīnā employs the terms *yasunnu* and *sunan* (pl. of *sunna*). When enumerating the particular laws the prophet has to pass, Ibn Sīnā frequently introduces them by saying "*fa-yajibu an yasunna...*" ("he has to legislate...") (Ibn Sīnā 2005, 367–374). The basic connotation of *sunna* and *sānn* in Ibn Sīnā's usage seems to be just any (human) law or lawgiver and the term does not exclusively refer to the revealed law. This becomes clear when Ibn Sīnā (2005, 364) speaks of the need of humans for a law (*sunna*) to organise their lives before actually introducing the idea of a law brought by a prophet. Likewise, he notes that cities other than the ideal state founded by the prophet might also have "a praiseworthy law" (*sunna ḥamīda*) (Ibn Sīnā 2005, 376), which is clearly not a law received through revelation. This, however, seems to imply that Ibn Sīnā understands the term *sunna* in the first instance according to its original legal meaning of a "custom" or "established way" when it had not yet become a technical term used for the Prophet's words and acts, which eventually became considered as more than "just" human actions and instead as a "second revelation."[13] In this sense, what Ibn Sīnā seems to want to express when he habitually refers to the prophet's action of legislating by the root *s-n-n* is nothing less than the idea that any prophet expresses the universal truth he has grasped in a way that is determined by circumstances and contingent. Revelation does not simply come over the prophet, he also shapes it. Yet, Ibn Sīnā does use the terms *sunna*

---

13 On the term and concept of the *sunna*, see Hallaq 2009, 39–42. It was with al-Shāfiʿī (d. 204/820) that the Prophet's *sunna* became seen as not merely human speech but a second form of revelation (Hallaq 2009, 50–51). Gurāyā (1968) draws attention to the original meaning of the term *sunna* which denoted the particular custom of a certain people or region.

and *sharīʿa* alongside each other, seemingly without conceptual distinction. For instance, in speaking about the purpose of making prayer a legal obligation, he remarks that this ensures people's continued adherence to "the *sunna* and the *sharīʿa*" (Ibn Sīnā 2005, 370). Similarly, the prophet needs to impose punishments "to prevent disobedience to the *sharīʿa*" since people commit "actions which are contrary to the *sunna*" (Ibn Sīnā 2005, 377). The prophet himself is referred to as *shāriʿ* as well as *sānn*. By using these two terms side by side, Ibn Sīnā evidently wants to stress that the commands and prohibitions brought by the prophet are not just some positive law, rather they are reflective of the universal truth revealed to the prophet when he grasps the order of the good.[14]

The fact that, according to Ibn Sīnā, all prescriptions of the law – whether they are shared by all versions of the *sharīʿa* or are specific to only one or some of them – pursue the common goal of bringing about human perfection reveals that his theory of law is teleological in nature. Whatever a prophet in his capacity as legislator commands or prohibits, he only does so because of the ability of this prescription to bring about human perfection. In this sense, the twofold nature of the law (that is, its being relative to time and place as well as its having an objective, universal aspect) is the flipside of its teleological nature. The ultimate goal or *telos* of the law is, as has become clear, humans' happiness in the hereafter, and this is the ultimate reason underlying all prescriptions. Ibn Sīnā is, as we have seen, explicit in stating this purpose of the law, and he also emphasises it time and again when he discusses, at the end of the *Shifāʾ*, the particular laws the prophet has to pass. In a great number of cases he supplies the reason why a certain prohibition or command is given. It becomes evident – not least because Ibn Sīnā himself says so explicitly – that they all have the ability to promote what is "beneficial" in attaining this goal and to avert what obstructs it. Since the law, however, also pursues certain more proximate goals, such as to teach humans virtue, to establish a just society, and to enable humans to lead a happy life in this world – all, of course, with a view to its ultimate goal – Ibn Sīnā stresses how *particular* prescriptions are "beneficial" in bringing about these goals. Prayer, for instance, is commanded by the law because it functions as a constant reminder of God and the blessings or punishments He allots in the hereafter, so as to get the inhabitants of the ideal state to adhere to the law: "the people will benefit (*yantafaʿ*) from these acts [that is, prayer] because they remember God and the resurrection, and because of this they will continue to adhere to the prescriptions and statues" (Ibn Sīnā 2005,

14 Butterworth (2000, 41–42) also touches upon Ibn Sīnā's use of terminology, but does not mention how it points to the twofold nature of the law.

368). In the same way, the reason the law makes fighting for the faith and the pilgrimage incumbent upon the inhabitants of the ideal state is that these deeds, like prayer, make them abide by the law: "these states [that is, prayer] must, if possible, be mixed with other benefits (*maṣāliḥ*) pertaining to strengthening and spreading the law, and to perform these will bring about worldly benefits (*al-munāfiʿ*) for the people, as in the case of fighting for the faith (*jihād*) and pilgrimage" (Ibn Sīnā 2005, 368). In the same manner, the law prohibits activities which are considered detrimental to facilitating its ultimate goal. This is why, according to Ibn Sīnā, certain professions, such as gambling, theft, and brigandage, are all explicitly prohibited by the law: "professions through which goods and benefits (*al-munāfiʿ*) are transferred without any benefits (*maṣāliḥ*) being rendered in exchange must be prohibited, among them gambling. (...) What one takes away must always be (...) something reckoned a human good (*al-khayrāt al-bashariyya*). Likewise, professions which bring about the opposite of welfare and usefulness (*aḍdād al-maṣāliḥ wa'l-munāfiʿ*) must be prohibited" (Ibn Sīna 2005, 371). To name a last example: the stipulations for marriage and divorce put forward by the law all have to be characterised, Ibn Sīnā points out, by their usefulness in ensuring the orderly continuation of the human species. If the law attaches certain conditions to divorce, he explains, it is so as to avert harm and bring about what is beneficial: "[the prophet] must take firm measures also regarding the permanence of the union so that not every dispute should result in separation. (...) Therein would lie many sorts of harm (*ḍarar*). The greatest cause of the general good (*al-maṣlaḥa*) is love" (Ibn Sīnā 2005, 372).[15]

In emphasising that what underlies all prescriptions contained in the law is the notion of their ability to bring about what is beneficial, Ibn Sīnā once more comes full circle: "the beneficial (*al-nāfiʿ*) is the cause which, in itself, leads to the good (*al-khayr*), and benefit (*al-munfaʿa*) is the idea (*al-maʿnā*) through which one arrives from evil (*al-sharr*) to the good (*al-khayr*)", he explains at the very beginning of the *Shifāʾ* (Ibn Sīnā 2005, 13). The beneficial nature of the law points to its promoting actions considered morally good, and this in turn contributes to humans' perfection, which is nothing else than the good. However, in being teleological and prescribing or prohibiting actions which are conducive towards facilitating its ultimate goal of perfecting humans, the law does *not* take into account that the moral status of actions is relative to

15 Butterworth (2000, 42) also discusses the law's particular prescriptions, but under the aspect of how "they have deep resonances with precepts found in the Islamic *sharīʿa* and Islamic practice," not insofar as they point to the teleological nature of the law. The same is the case with March 2015.

their agent and patient, as Ibn Sīnā actually holds. For example, the law prohibits adultery because it is detrimental to the perfection of the state and the state facilitates humans' happiness. In prohibiting adultery, the law declares it a morally blameworthy act. What the law, however, does not – and indeed cannot – take into account is that this action is, from another point of view (namely that of the animal soul which strives to satisfy the desires that arise from its very nature), not morally reprehensible, as explained above. This indicates that, in making laws, the prophet has understood the hierarchy of different perfections and imperfections not only existing in a single individual, but also among humans and on the level of the state as well as their relations to each other. The law's prescriptions then reflect the way the greatest perfection and ultimate end can be attained.

Nora Kalbarczyk

In the Footsteps of Ibn Sīnā? The Uṣūlī Debate on the *Argumentum e Contrario*

1 Introduction

Recent years have witnessed a rising interest both in the momentous philosophical oeuvre of Ibn Sīnā (d. 428/1037) and in the impact of his thinking on subsequent generations of scholars in the Islamic world. These thinkers' philosophical activities and achievements are gradually being reappraised. Ibn Sīnā's concepts and vocabulary diffused into later works and were merged into the Islamic scholarly disciplines where they had various functions to fulfil (Bauer 2011, 160; Gutas 2002b, 84–5; 2013, 33–35).

One of these disciplines was Islamic legal theory (*uṣūl al-fiqh*). For decades there has been a controversy about whether, and to which extent, one can detect Greek or Aristotelian logic in *uṣūl al-fiqh* works.[1] From al-Ghazālī (d. 505/1111) onwards we should not expect to see any direct reception of Greek logic – the question is rather in which way *uṣūl al-fiqh* texts were influenced by Avicennian philosophy of language and logic and how the two traditions interacted. In this chapter I intend to show how the debate on the *argumentum e contrario* (*mafhūm al-mukhālafa* or *dalīl al-khiṭāb*) was informed by Avicennian philosophy of language and logic.

I will start by outlining the controversial aspects of the *argumentum e contrario* in general before turning to Fakhr al-Dīn al-Rāzī's (d. 606/1210) reasoning against it, and then to the modifications of both the Avicennian position and al-Rāzī's critique in the subsequent commentary literature. We will be able to discern a shift in the *madhhab* positions on this issue: even though Fakhr al-Dīn al-

---

This article is based on my PhD thesis *Sprachphilosophie in der islamischen Rechtstheorie. Zur avicennischen Klassifikation der Bezeichnung bei Fakhr al-Dīn al-Rāzī (gest. 606/1210)* (Kalbarczyk 2018a).

1 See, for example, the following remark by Josef van Ess (1966, 382): "Die aristotelische Logik zieht ein in die Theologie; der Bereich der Jurisprudenz bleibt ihr (...) verschlossen." Ulrich Haarmann (1974, 155, 160) supports van Ess' view by saying about al-Ghazālī that he introduces "die aristotelische Logik auch in die Rechtsdogmatik – wenn auch ohne dauerhafte Wirkung." See also Weiss 2010, 23; Krawietz 1995, 144. A contrary opinion is held by Ulrich Rudolph (2005, 73): "Dass Ghazālī maßgeblich dazu beigetragen hat, die aristotelische Logik als Methodenlehre der islamischen Theologie und Rechtswissenschaft zu etablieren, ist seit langem unumstritten."

https://doi.org/10.1515/9783110552386-005

Rāzī was a Shāfiʿī scholar, Ḥanafīs standardly use a modified refutation of his criticism of the *argumentum e contrario* against its Shāfiʿī proponents.

2 Against or in Favour? The Controversial *Argumentum e Contrario*

In Islamic legal theory there are several different types of the *argumentum e contrario*, defined with regard to the element by which a statement is specified. A statement may for example be specified by a certain name (*laqab*/*ism*), a certain number (*ʿadad*), a certain condition (*sharṭ*), or a certain attribute (*ṣifa*). According to the proponents of the *argumentum e contrario*, in a case in which this specifying element is no longer present, the legal ruling (*ḥukm*) also ceases to exist.[2] The *ḥadīth* "*zakāt* is owed on sheep and goats that are free-grazing" (*fī sāʾimat al-ghanam al-zakāt*) would therefore imply that no *zakāt* needs to be paid for stall-fed (*maʿlūfa*) sheep and goats (al-Ghazālī 1993, 3:413.11).

The proponents of the *argumentum e contrario* argue that the specification "free-grazing" amounts to the *ratio legis* (*ʿilla*) of the *ḥukm*. Without the specification there would be no *ratio legis* and without the *ratio legis* the *ḥukm* that imposes the obligation to pay *zakāt* also ceases to exist.[3] Opponents, on the other hand, argue that it is not possible to draw such a general conclusion without the precise context (*qarīna*) (al-Ghazālī 1993, 3:426.ult.–427.1). "For example, it could be the case that someone had questioned the Prophet regarding free-grazing sheep in particular", Weiss remarks. The person was already certain that *zakāt* "was due upon stall-fed sheep" and "came to the Prophet to ask whether the tax was also due upon free-grazing sheep. In this context the Prophet's remark serves to clarify a particular point, not to make a statement regarding sheep in general or stall-fed sheep in particular" (Weiss 2010, 489).

The *argumentum e contrario* caused many controversies within the Shāfiʿī *madhhab* and between the different *madhāhib*. It is said that the Shāfiʿīs were more in favour of this kind of reasoning than the Ḥanafīs who opposed any

2 For a detailed enquiry into this method and an argumentation against it, see *inter alia* al-Ghazālī 1993, 3:413–149; al-Bāqillānī 1998, 3:331; al-Juwaynī 2003, 225. See also Zysow 2013, 100–109; Bernand 1986, 269–294; Weiss 2010, 482–493; Yunis Ali 2000, 192–224; Kamali 2013, 179–185; Ramić 2003, 55–60. The *argumentum e contrario* is also relevant in discussions of non-religious jurisprudential hermeneutics (as "Only S is P") (Schneider and Schnapp 2006, 156).

3 Al-Ghazālī (1993, 3:432.5–6) quotes this argument.

use of *argumentum e contrario* in legal reasoning (Zysow 2013, 101; Kamali 2013, 182; Ramić 2003, 55).[4] Yet, prominent Shāfiʿīs such as al-Ghazālī[5] and al-Āmidī (d. 631/1233) rejected its legitimacy, as did the Ḥanafī Abū l-Ḥusayn al-Baṣrī (d. 436/1044) (al-Baṣrī 1964–1965, 1:162.5–7). His work *Kitāb al-Muʿtamad* was extremely influential on the legal thinking of the Shāfiʿī Fakhr al-Dīn al-Rāzī (Ibn Khallikān 1968–1972, 2:1616.4–6; Kalbarczyk 2018a, 20); al-Rāzī subscribes to al-Baṣrī's view. However, he does not reject the *argumentum e contrario* straightaway but first reflects on its purpose: the *argumentum e contrario*, he says, informs us "that the *ḥukm* ceases to exist for that which is not mentioned (*al-maskūt ʿanhu*). However, it might be that there is an indication for the fact that the *ḥukm* of the mentioned [case] remains valid for some unmentioned [cases]" (al-Rāzī 1979, 3:11.13–15; al-Qarāfī 2000, 2:561.7; Sirāj al-Dīn al-Urmawī 1988, 1:367.9–12).

According to al-Rāzī one has to take into account several possibilities before drawing a conclusion and stating a *ḥukm* for an unmentioned case. It might be that the *ḥukm* is not applicable to other cases without the respective specification. Yet, it might also be that on the basis of other textual evidence or on the basis of a *qiyās* (analogy), one draws the conclusion that the *ḥukm* remains valid without the specification. Obviously the prohibition "do not kill your children for fear of poverty" (Q. 17:31) will not turn into a permission to kill them in a situation of wealth and affluence. The prohibition remains valid because of other textual evidence and instructions (al-Rāzī 1979, 2:138.10–139.3; 2013, 10:48; 2007, 30).

There are basically two different patterns of reasoning involved here. As Aron Zysow pointed out, the *argumentum e contrario* is based on the assumption that "since a and b are expressly regulated, but c is not, the law does not wish c to be treated in the same manner."[6] In contrast reasoning by analogy derives the same *ḥukm* for c as is regulated for a and b.[7] A false application of these two ways of deriving legal rulings and a false identification of the *ratio legis* could lead, for example, to the conclusion that while drinking grape wine is prohib-

---

4 For al-Shāfiʿī's position, see Vishanoff 2011, 60.

5 For the development of al-Ghazālī's point of view (from approving of it in his *Mankhūl* to rejecting it in his *Mustaṣfā*), see Zysow 2013, 107.

6 Oertmann 1931, 26–27 ("da a und b in bestimmter Weise geregelt sind, c aber nicht, so wünscht das Gesetz jene Regelung für den Fall c nicht eintreten zu lassen"); the (modified) English version of this quotation goes back to Zysow 2013, 103.

7 For the contrariness of these two kinds of arguments, see, for example, al-Isnawī n.d., 2:207–208; Bernand 1986, 275.

ited, drinking date wine is allowed because of the respective specification (that is, only *grape* wine would be forbidden) (al-Ghazālī 1993, 3:432).[8]

In his *Musallam al-thubūt* the Ḥanafī *uṣūlī* Muḥibb Allāh al-Bihārī (d. 1119/1707) (fol. 93v.ult) brings forward the following brief objection against the *argumentum e contrario:* "it is not among one of the three ways of signification" (*laysat bi-iḥdā al-dalālāt al-thalāth*).[9] In his commentary on the *Musallam*, Niẓām al-Dīn al-Anṣārī al-Laknawī (d. 1225/1810, also known as Baḥr al-ʿUlūm), explains this objection as follows: "[the conclusion that the *argumentum e contrario* is not valid] is drawn from this: in order to be valid the *argumentum e contrario* (*dalīl al-khiṭāb*) would have to be one of these, namely congruence (*muṭābaqa*), containment (*taḍammun*), or implication (*iltizām*). But 'it is not among one of the three ways of signification'" (al-Laknawī 2002, 1:454.9–10), therefore it cannot be valid. What is striking here is the allusion to Ibn Sīnā's threefold classification of signification. The point of departure for his reasoning is the following. In his work on legal theory *al-Maḥṣūl fī ʿilm uṣūl al-fiqh*, in a chapter on the linguistic structure and the general characteristics of the command (*amr*), al-Rāzī (1979, 2:136.3) discusses the "command (*amr*) that is qualified (*muqayyad*) by an attribute (*ṣifa*)" and in this context asks whether the aforementioned *ḥadīth* concerning *zakāt* (al-Rāzī 1979, 2:136.5–137.6):

> [1] signifies the fact that *zakāt* is not owed on [sheep] that are not free-grazing [that is, is *zakāt* also to be paid for stall-fed sheep, for example?].
>
> [1.1] The truth (*ḥaqq*) is that it does not signify this – this is the view of Abū Ḥanīfa and this view was also held by Ibn Surayj, al-Qāḍī Abū Bakr, the Imām al-Ḥaramayn, and by the majority of the Muʿtazila (*jumhūr al-Muʿtazila*).
>
> [1.2] Al-Shāfiʿī and al-Ashʿarī (...) and the majority of the *fuqahāʾ* that belong to us are of the opinion that it does signify it [that is, the *ḥadīth* signifies on the basis of the *argumentum e contrario* that no *zakāt* is to be paid for non-free-grazing sheep and goats].
>
> [2] Let us consider some aspects:
> The first is: if the speech (*khiṭāb*) that is qualified by an attribute signifies that which goes beyond it and opposes it (*mā ʿadāhu yukhālifuhū*), then it [that is, the speech] would either signify this
>
> [2.1] by means of its wording (*bi-lafẓihi*), or

8 For the debate of the opponents with the proponents of this argument, see Zysow 2013, 103. The cause of the Ḥanafī rejection lies, according to Zysow, in their "unrelenting attachment to analogy."

9 The quotation is also in al-Laknawī 2002, 1:454.10.

[2.2] by its meaning.

[Conclusion] However, it does not signify this in either way. Therefore it follows necessarily that it does not signify it at all.

In other words, the *ḥadīth* does not signify whether *zakāt* is to be paid for non-free grazing sheep; so there is no *ḥukm* derivable from this statement as regards other categories of sheep.

Thus al-Rāzī holds that a statement qualified by an attribute, and indicating a legal ruling at the same time, does not necessarily indicate the contrary legal ruling for a case that is not specified by this attribute. According to this line of reasoning – and here al-Rāzī subscribes to the exact wording of the Ḥanafī Abū l-Ḥusayn al-Baṣrī (al-Baṣrī 1964–1965, 1:162.5–7; al-Bāqillānī 1998, 2:199.19–20; al-Ghazālī 1993, 1:273; Weiss 2010, 371–373) – the ruling (*ḥukm*) must either be signified by the wording of the respective statement or must be implied by the meaning of its wording. Implied meanings are, in the Shāfiʿī tradition, those "that can be known from the expressions not with regard to their linguistic form (*ṣīgha*), but with regard to their import (*faḥwā*) and allusion (*ishāra*)" (al-Ghazālī 1993, 3:402). In other words, they can be known through an additional meaning related to the first meaning, and hinted at through contextual markers, for example. According to the Shāfiʿī classification, legal implications are subsumed under the *mafhūm*-category ("that which is understood"), which comprises different types; it is controversial whether the *argumentum e contrario* (*dalīl al-khiṭāb*/*mafhūm al-mukhālafa*) belongs to this category (Kalbarczyk 2018b). The counterpart of *mafhūm* is the *manṭūq*-category ("that which is said") in which the expression has been posited in one way or another for the respective meaning.

In his commentary on the *Maḥṣūl*, Tāj al-Dīn al-Urmawī (d. c. 656/1258) (1994, 1:440.4–8) reformulates al-Rāzī's argument:

[ad 2] If [the statement qualified by an attribute] signified that the ruling is not true for a statement with another attribute, it would signify this either

[*2.1] by congruence (*bi'l-muṭābaqa*) – and this is wrong, since it is not the same whether a legal ruling is not true for one of two attributes or whether it is true for the other attribute, or

[*2.2] by implication (*bi'l-iltizām*) – which is also wrong because the fact that a legal ruling is true for one attribute does not necessitate that it is not true for the other.

In his summary of al-Rāzī's argument al-Urmawī replaces the words "would either signify this [2.1] by means of its wording (*bi-lafẓihi*) or [2.2] by its meaning (*bi-maʿnāhu*)" with "would signify this either [*2.1] by congruence (*bi'l-muṭābaqa*) (...) or [*2.2] by implication (*bi'l-iltizām*)." This reformulation is in fact a consequence of al-Rāzī's own re-systematisation of *uṣūlī* hermeneutics.

3 The threefold classification of signification

Al-Rāzī does not use the dichotomy between *manṭūq* and *mafhūm*, but integrates this classification into a broader hermeneutical conception, which is based upon the threefold classification of signification: by congruence (*muṭābaqa*), by containment (*taḍammun*), and by implication (*iltizām*). His work in law encompasses both legal hermeneutics and logical propaedeutics. It would go beyond the scope of this chapter to delve into the nature of this broader project, which would merit a paper in its own right. I will therefore only outline his use of the classification of signification taken from Ibn Sīnā.

In his own logical propaedeutics, when dealing with misconceptions about the signification of the five predicables, especially of the differentiae, Ibn Sīnā (1952b, hereafter *Madkhal*, 42.19–43.1) elaborates on "what we mean when we say 'an expression signifies a meaning'." He then distinguishes between a primary (*awwal*), secondary (*thānī*), and extrinsic (*khārijī*) way of signification. In this context, the primary way of signification is a case where an expression is taken to signify the complete definition: "as for the primary [way], it is as when we say 'animal'; for it signifies [primarily] 'body having a soul' as a whole (*yadullu ʿalā jumlat al-jism dhī al-nafs*)" (*Madkhal*, 43.6–7). The secondary way is the signification of intrinsic and essential constituents, that is, the species signifies its genus or its differentia: "as for the secondary [way], it is for example when [the expression 'animal'] signifies 'body' [alone], since the meaning of body is necessarily included (*muḍamman*) in the meaning of animality; for what signifies 'animality' comprises (*ishtamala*) the meaning of body – not in such a way that it would indicate it extrinsically (*lā ʿalā annahū yushīru ilayhi min khārij*)" (*Madkhal*, 43.7–9). This way of signification signifies a notion by containment; it amounts to the signification of the shared quiddity (*māhiyya mushtaraka*). Finally, when an expression signifies a meaning which corresponds neither to its definition nor to a part of it, but which is somehow attached to this meaning, this is called the extrinsic way of signification (*dalāla khārijiyya*) (*Madkhal*, 43.9–11). The differentia "rational" (*nāṭiq*), for example, does not signify in a primary way "substance," "body," or "endowed with sensation," but "rational" does imply these predicates. Ibn Sīnā (*Madkhal*, 43.1–3) describes its relation to the primary way of signification as follows: "if there is another meaning which is associated with it [that is, the meaning signified by the primary way of signification] in terms of an extrinsic association by which the mind notices this other meaning just at the same moment in which it notices the first meaning, then the expression does not signify this [second meaning] primarily." The description of this way of signification as a kind of transfer from a first to a second meaning is reminiscent of the way in which rhetoricians and philologians define tropes: "you first understand a meaning from an expression, then this meaning indicates a further meaning to you" (al-Jurjānī 1969, 263.2–3). This is what ʿAbd al-Qāhir al-Jurjānī (d. 471/1078) calls the meaning of the meaning (*maʿnā al-maʿnā*).

After having introduced these distinctions, Ibn Sīnā (*Madkhal*, 43.12–15) coins specific technical terms for the primary, secondary and extrinsic modes of signification:

> If we intended to condense and summarise all this [that is, the discussion about the division of signification], we would take the signification of expressions to occur in three modes:
>
> signification by congruence (*dalālat muṭābaqa*), just like "animal" signifies the totality of "sensitive body having a soul" (*kamā yadullu al-ḥayawān ʿalā jumlat al-jism dhī al-nafs al-ḥassās*);
>
> signification by containment (*dalālat taḍammun*), just like the expression "animal" signifies "body"; and
>
> signification by implication (*dalālat luzūm*), as "roof" signifies "foundation."

Ibn Sīnā assigns the term *muṭābaqa* – which is a technical term used in several disciplines[10] – to the primary way of signification in order to underline the

10 Depending on the context, *muṭābaqa* can be translated as "commensuration", "equality", "correspondence" etc. (Lane 1968, 5:1825a; Ibn Manẓūr 1883–1890, 12:78. The Latin translation of the *Madkhal* of the *Shifāʾ* has *significatio parilitatis* for *dalālat al-muṭābaqa* (Ibn Sīnā 1508 [1961], fol. 5vb.1–2). Al-Fārābī (1956–1957, 123–124, §11) uses the term *muṭābiq* (not a *terminus technicus*) as a synonym for *musāwiyan* in the context of relations of equivalence, such as the complete and adequate definition of a species. In the context of the *Burhān* complex, *muṭābaqa* expresses "the 'correspondence' of one's belief whether affirmative or negative, with the state of affairs that obtains externally" (Black 2006, 17–18). Since in the context of the *Madkhal* complex *muṭābaqa* is used in a different sense, namely to express the congruence between a word and its concept, I prefer to translate *muṭābaqa* here as "congruence." In Arabic grammar theory, *muṭābaqa* is used for different kinds of syntactic congruence (Sinnū and Jihāmī 2010, 3:4675–4676). It is also a *terminus technicus* in *ʿilm al-badīʿ* for a chiastic or antithetic word or sentence order (alongside *ṭibāq* und *taṭbīq*) (al-Rāzī 1985, 285; al-Sakkākī 2011, 533; Simon 1993, 6; Mehren 1853, 97).

semantic equivalence between a universal expression and its signified quiddity, or to be more precise, to highlight the equivalence and convertibility between the species and its complete definition. The second mode is labelled *taḍammun*[11] in order to stress the intrinsic relation at stake, as in the relation of the species to its constituting differentia or to its genus. The inverse direction, namely the relation of the differentia to the species constituted by it, is emphasised by the term *luzūm* which was already used as the technical term for several types of implication.[12] In his later works this semantic implication receives its own technical term, namely *iltizām*.[13] Ibn Sīnā's theory is in fact far more elaborate than what has been outlined here and it is of course part of a broader logical and ontological system, but the above suffices for our purposes.

Al-Rāzī revisits and elaborates on the threefold classification of signification in numerous instances. In his legal work *al-Maḥṣūl* he combines logical and legal terminology with hermeneutical issues, and brings them together mainly under the two categories of *muṭābaqa* and *iltizām*. Under *muṭābaqa* he subsumes four main relationships:

1. a word that corresponds to exactly one meaning;
2. several words that are loosely connected to several meanings;
3. different words signifying one and the same meaning;
4. inversely, one expression that signifies several different meanings at the same time; this last case is a real hermeneutical challenge.

Here he systematically discusses aspects of the Avicennian logical tradition, mainly from the *Isagoge*, *Categories*, and *On Interpretation*, alongside what the *uṣūlīs* previously discussed under the *manṭūq*-category. That is to say, he arranges the various technical terms used to designate a scriptural expression

11 For the term *taḍammun* I adopt Riccardo Strobino's (2016) convention of translating it by "containment" and by using the expression "entailment" to include both kinds of implications, namely *taḍammun* and *iltizām*. See also Lane 1968, 5:1804c; Ibn Manẓūr 1883–1890, 17:126. The Latin translation of the *Madkhal* of the *Shifāʾ* has *significatio continentie for dalālat al-taḍammun* (Ibn Sīnā 1508 [1961], fol. 5vb.3–4).

12 Especially in hypothetical propositions and syllogisms (Jabr and al-ʿAjam 1996, 773–774). On al-Fārābī's and Ibn Sīnā's accounts of *luzūm*, see Karimullah 2014; 2015, 250; Schöck 2007, 67–68; 2006, 83; Street 1995.

13 On this issue, see Kalbarczyk 2018a, 86–87. The logic of the *Kitāb al-Najāt* is a special case: it is based on passages of Ibn Sīnā's earlier works (namely on the *Mukhtaṣar al-aṣghar fī l-manṭiq*, written in the year 1013/1014) and was written "practically without composing a single line anew" (Gutas 2014, 116) in his "middle period" (c. 411–418/1020–1027), to be more precise, in the year 417/1026 or 418/1027. However, its late date of composition might explain the use of the term *iltizām*, which is only attested in later works.

as being clear or unclear, as being unambiguous or polysemic, and as being plain or in need of explanation, and combines this terminology used for classifying divine language with technical terms that classify words that are, for example, used in a syllogism or other kinds of universal speech, that is, logical terminology. He does the same when it comes to the overall topic of implication, which is relevant for both logic and *uṣūl al-fiqh* (Kalbarczyk 2018b, 194–196).

Fakhr al-Dīn al-Rāzī's new systematisation explains why Tāj al-Dīn al-Urmawī chooses to reformulate the argument against the *argumentum e contrario*. Generations of opponents of the *argumentum e contrario* would consequently refer to this line of reasoning (with the addition of the *taḍammun*-way of signification). This, however, goes along with a shift of the *madhhab* position on the issue, as I want to illustrate in the following. The Ḥanafīs, being opponents of the *argumentum e contrario*, use it against the Shāfiʿīs, the majority of whom (after al-Rāzī) become proponents of the argument.

4 Challenging the Legitimacy of the *Argumentum e Contrario* on the Basis of the Threefold Classification

It is not long after Tāj al-Dīn al-Urmawī's commentary that we can detect a shift in the Shāfiʿī reasoning. In contrast to al-Urmawī, who states that the *argumentum e contrario* is neither a congruent signification nor an implication, al-Bayḍāwī (d. 685/1286)[14] in his *Minhāj al-wuṣūl ilā ʿilm al-uṣūl* (which is based on the commentaries on the *Maḥṣūl* by the two al-Urmawīs, Tāj al-Dīn and Sirāj al-Dīn) states that the *argumentum e contrario* is indeed a valid implication (al-Bayḍāwī 1989, 69.6–8):

> If it signified it [that is, if the statement signified a ruling for an unmentioned case], it would do so either by congruence (*muṭābaqa*) or by implication (*iltizām*). We say that it signifies by implication, since it is proven that order (*tartīb*) signifies causality (*ʿilliyya*): when the cause (*ʿilla*) ceases to exist, that which is caused likewise ceases to exist.

According to the proponents of the *argumentum e contrario* the fact that a statement is specified by a certain attribute must have a specific reason – therefore,

14 His date of death is a controversial issue: this is the date given by al-Suyūṭī (1908, 1:286.5). For the controversy, see EI2, "al-Bayḍāwī"; al-Suyūṭī 1908, 1:286.6; EI3, "al-Bayḍāwī" (Walid Saleh argues for the year 719/1319).

they deem this attribute to be the *ratio legis* (*ʿilla*) of the legal ruling. When the *ratio legis* no longer exists the legal ruling also ceases to exist. The *argumentum e contrario* is as simple as that.

In his commentary on al-Bayḍāwī's *Minhāj al-wuṣūl ilā ʿilm al-uṣūl*, the Shāfiʿī Shams al-Dīn al-Iṣfahānī (d. 749/1348) first cites an opponent of the *argumentum e contrario* who argues in a familiar fashion, but with an additional element. Then al-Iṣfahānī expresses his support for al-Bayḍāwī's viewpoint and refutes the opponent's arguments. He begins by putting the case for the opponent of the *argumentum e contrario* (Shams al-Dīn al-Iṣfahānī 1999 [1420], 1:292.10 – 293.5):[15]

> If the attachment (*taʿlīq*) of the legal ruling to one of two essential attributes were to signify the negation of that ruling which goes beyond [one of the essential attributes], it would signify this either by congruence (*muṭābaqa*), by containment (*taḍammun*), or by implication (*iltizām*). But the conclusion is wrong, so the antecedent must also be wrong. (...) As for the falsity of the conclusion: signification of congruence and containment obviously play no role here, since it is not the same whether a legal ruling for something unmentioned is negated or whether a mentioned legal ruling or its part is affirmed. Implication also plays no role here, because it is a condition for implication that the mind (*dhihn*) turns from the meaning (*al-musammā*) itself to that which is signified by implication (*ilā ʾl-madlūl al-iltizāmī*). But in our case [that is, the *argumentum e contrario*] the mind does not turn to it, since whoever conceptualises that which is signified by congruence by his saying "*zakāt* is owed on sheep and goats that are free-grazing" (*fī sāʾimat al-ghanam zakāt*) has paid no attention whatsoever to stall-fed (*maʿlūfa*) sheep and the non-obligation to pay *zakāt* for them.

Al-Iṣfāḥānī then responds:

> The author [of the *Minhāj*, that is, al-Bayḍāwī] responds to the question at stake that [the legal ruling regarding the unmentioned case] is indeed signified by implication, since it is proven that the attachment of the legal ruling to the attribute indicates the causality (*ʿilliyya*) of the attribute (*waṣf*) with regard to the legal ruling. The non-existence of the cause necessitates with certainty the non-existence of that which is caused. As for [the opponent's] words, "the mind does not turn to it", this is impossible and not admitted. To be a signification of implication, for the *uṣūlīs* it is sufficient that certainty about the *implicans* (*jazm biʾl-malzūm*) is gained by conceptualising simultaneously both the implicate (*lāzim*) and the *implicans* (*malzūm*); it [that is, implication in the view of the *uṣūlīs*] does not depend on the mind turning from the *implicans* to the implicate.

The opponent of the *argumentum e contrario* brings forward the argument that the initial statement is to signify the ruling of the unmentioned case by one of

15 See also al-Isnawī n.d., 2:215.

the three ways of signification, namely congruence, containment, and implication (Ibn al-Ḥājib 2006, 2:668; al-Bābartī 2005, 2:58; al-Ījī 2000, 170–172, 256; Taqī al-Dīn al-Subkī and Tāj al-Dīn al-Subkī 1981, 1:374–376). The opponent then seeks to rule out each way of signification. Congruence and containment are eliminated together on the basis that one cannot signify something unmentioned in this way without laying down a relation between the verbal expression and the signified meaning. In other words, the command to fulfil a specific action is not equivalent to a command not to fulfil the contrary action or some other unmentioned action. But implication is also ruled out, since the *argumentum e contrario* fails to meet a prerequisite for this form of signification, namely that the mind must necessarily turn sequentially from the first meaning to the implied second meaning. There is no inner relationship between the meaning of the first sentence and the meaning of the unmentioned second sentence. Since the initial conclusion that the ruling of the unmentioned sentence is signified by one of three kinds is – according to this opponent – untenable, the antecedent, that is, the ruling of an unmentioned sentence is signified at all, is also false. This argument is a *modus tollendo tollens:* if p, then q; not q; therefore not p.

Al-Iṣfahānī refutes this argument with al-Bayḍāwī's reasoning: the kind of signification at stake here is indeed implication, since the specific attribute in the initial statement is considered to be the cause of the legal ruling. A statement without this specific attribute would not trigger the legal ruling. The opponent's objection that for it to be an implication the mind would first need to grasp the first meaning and then the second, implied one, is met with a distinction between degrees of immediacy in implication. As al-Iṣfahānī (Shams al-Dīn al-Iṣfahānī 1986, 1:155.10–15) concedes in a different passage, it is true that this would not be a real implication in the narrow sense of an inner relationship between two sentences, where the mind grasps two notions simultaneously:

> The *uṣūlīs* did not make mental implication (*luzūm dhihnī*) a prerequisite for signification by implication (*dalālat al-iltizām*). Instead they use the expression [sc. "implication"] for that which is attached to the meaning (*lāzim al-musammā*), no matter whether it is attached extrinsically (*khārijī*) or mentally (*dhihnī*). [By contrast,] the logicians did make mental implication a condition [for this sort of signification], that is, the conceptualisation of the [first] meaning is necessarily followed by the conceptualisation of the extrinsic [second] meaning. Otherwise no understanding will be reached, since understanding is based upon the fact that an expression is posited for the relevant meaning, or that after grasping the first meaning the second meaning follows.

According to al-Iṣfahānī, implication in the strict sense is mental implication (*luzūm dhihnī*). The *uṣūlī*, however, does not require this kind of implication.

He is content with extrinsic implication (*luzūm khārijī*). Thus, in the logical context we would say that a ban on X would signify a ban on Y only if the former immediately calls the latter to mind; in the legal context, though, signification requires only that there be some extramental link between the two. The differentiation between *luzūm dhihnī* and *luzūm khārijī* corresponds to that between different kinds of necessity and inseparability, which have been elaborated in logical texts (Kalbarczyk 2018a, 157–158). Ibn Sīnā (1956, 50.6–7) describes extrinsic implication in his *Burhān* as follows: "Things are necessary in two ways: either necessary in implication (*fī luzūm*), without being necessary to one another in essence and nature (*fī jawhar wa-ṭabīʿa*) – these are external implicates (*lawāzim khārija*) and we have explained earlier that they are not useful to obtain certain knowledge – or necessary in essence and nature, i.e. the things that are *per se* (*al-umūr al-mawjūda bi-dhātihā*)."[16] Extrinsic properties are necessary in the sense of "inseparability" in existence (like the relation between the terms "black" and "crow", for example), but there is no "definitional connection with their subjects." In essential implication the properties are necessary in relation to that of what they hold (Strobino 2016, 262).

Fakhr al-Dīn al-Rāzī coins the term *luzūm dhihnī* for the essential implication. This is based on Ibn Sīnā's characterisation of the implication as a signification in which the mind (*dhihn*) turns from a primary, congruent meaning to an implied one (Ibn Sīnā 1910, 15.1–2). Take for example the expression "rational" (*nāṭiq*) which is congruent to "something that has rationality" (*shayʾ lahu nuṭq*). It does not say "whether this thing is a substance or not a substance; however it implies (*illā annahū yalzamu*) that this thing must be a substance, a body, and sensitive" (Ibn Sīnā 1960, 33.1–4). For the differentia "rational" implies the genus "animal", which it divides.

The refutation of the argument that the *argumentum e contrario* is not an implication, on the basis of the differentiation between two different types of implication, goes back to the Mālikī jurist Shihāb al-Dīn al-Qarāfī (d. 684/1285). One must distinguish between an implication (*mulāzama*) by which one gains certain knowledge and an implication by which one obtains only presumption (*ẓann*), and not certain knowledge. An example of the first is the relation of evenness to four, while the second is illustrated by "impurity (*najāsa*) in relation to the cup of the barber (*kaʾs al-ḥajjām*)" (al-Qarāfī 2000, 2:218.14). The *argumentum e contrario* – or to be precise: this particular kind of the *argumentum e contrario* – is equivalent to the second kind of implication (al-

16 Translated in Strobino 2016, 261.

Qarāfī 2000, 2:218.10 – 14), which is a mere inseparability in imagination or existence, but not in definition.

Although one might be willing to lower the epistemological requirements in the legal disciplines,[17] Fakhr al-Dīn al-Rāzī in his *Maḥṣūl* made his more demanding position clear: "signification by implication does not consider the external implication (*al-luzūm al-khārijī*)"! The *argumentum e contrario* could not, in other words, be taken as a valid implication. This is the rationale behind al-Bihārī's words in the early eighteenth century AD: "[the *argumentum e contrario*] is not among one of the three ways of signification (*laysat bi-iḥdā al-dalālāt al-thalāth*)."[18]

5 Conclusion

Both the proponents and the opponents of the *argumentum e contrario* draw in their reasoning upon the Avicennian threefold classification of signification. The modified argument of Fakhr al-Dīn al-Rāzī against the *argumentum e contrario* evolves into a standard argument used by Ḥanafī opponents against Shāfiʿī proponents. This debate gives a hint at the significance of Avicennian logic, in general, and the relevance of the classification of signification, in particular, for *uṣūl al-fiqh* methodology. Furthermore, by looking at the different commentary traditions, such as exegesis of the *Mahṣūl*, of Ibn al-Ḥājib's *Mukhtaṣar*, or of al-Bayḍāwī's *Minḥāj*, it becomes clear that the initial lines of reasoning were transformed and elaborated upon in a fruitful and productive manner.

---

17 See, for example, van Ess 1966, 382: "im juristischen *ictihād* genügte überzeugende Wahrscheinlichkeit, im *kalām* strebte man nach unzweifelhafter Gewissheit."
18 See note 10.

Ulrich Rudolph

Al-Ghazālī on Philosophy and Jurisprudence

1 Introduction

As is well-known, al-Ghazālī (d. 505/1111) was an excellent scholar in various sciences. Moreover, he is renowned for having combined several disciplines in new and ingenious ways, a fact expressed, for instance, by Marie Bernand by calling him "un artisan de la fusion des systèmes de pensée" (1991). It thus seems legitimate to expect that al-Ghazālī would have something important to say about the combination of sciences which is at the centre of this volume, namely philosophy and jurisprudence, all the more as he wrote important works in both fields.

On closer inspection, though, things turn out to be more complicated. There are good reasons to suppose that his contribution to jurisprudence, or rather to the relation between jurisprudence and philosophy, does not really match his accomplishments in other domains. When we talk about Sufism, for instance, it is obvious that his approach was innovative, if not revolutionary, combining classical Sufism with elements taken from other disciplines, in particular philosophy. Moreover, al-Ghazālī himself stressed the original character of his writings on Sufism, entitling the most important amongst them *The Revival of the Religious Sciences* (*Iḥyāʾ ʿulūm al-dīn*).[1] The same applies to theology. In this case, his works may have been more conventional than in Sufism, but his impact on the field was nonetheless considerable and in many respects innovative. This has already been emphasised by Muslim historiographers such as Ibn Khaldūn (d. 808/1406) (1958a, 3:27–43, esp. 41; 1958b, 3:34–55, esp. 52),[2] and it is confirmed by modern scholarship which has long focused on al-Ghazālī's accomplishments in *kalām* and philosophy, producing numerous articles and passionate debates on the topic.[3]

When it comes to jurisprudence, however, the situation is different. Of course, al-Ghazālī's contribution to this field has been acknowledged, too, but

1 Al-Ghazālī's reflections on Sufism (and philosophy) have been discussed regularly in modern scholarship. See among many others the recent publications by Gianotti 2001; Treiger 2012; Abrahamov 2015.

2 See also Ibn Khaldūn 1958a, 3:113–116; 1958b, 3:143–146.

3 Among the numerous publications which could be mentioned in this respect see in particular Frank 1992, 1994; Griffel 2009; Shihadeh 2016a; Rudolph forthcoming.

https://doi.org/10.1515/9783110552386-006

it has never raised the same kind of enthusiasm among scholars, either in the Muslim tradition or in modern academia. Ibn Khaldūn, to quote him again, has devoted just one line to al-Ghazālī when describing the science of "the principles of jurisprudence" (*uṣūl al-fiqh*) in his *Muqaddima* (1958a, 3:22; 1958b, 3:28–29). In the chapter on "jurisprudence" (*fiqh*) he does not even mention his name (1958a, 3:1–14; 1958b, 3:3–23). Modern scholars, in their turn, pay more attention to al-Ghazālī's accomplishments in both fields but their output on the matter is limited, too. To illustrate this it may suffice to call to mind the two volumes on *Islam and Rationality: The Impact of al-Ghazālī*, recently edited by Georges Tamer and Frank Griffel in commemoration of his 900th anniversary. They contain numerous articles dealing with Sufism, theology, and philosophy but not a single chapter on jurisprudence, let alone its relationship to philosophy (Tamer 2015; Griffel 2016).

As compared to other topics, al-Ghazālī's reflections on philosophy and jurisprudence seem thus to be less prominent and less striking. So far, they have neither been at the centre of interest nor generated any extensive academic debate. As a consequence, my own contribution will not focus on a specific, disputed problem. I will rather try to give a general outline of the topic and the main questions which are at stake. In order to do so, three points will be raised under the headings of "Philosophy and Jurisprudence", "Logic and Jurisprudence", and "Philosophical Ethics and Jurisprudence" before arriving at a final section in which we will look at a fifteenth century scholar who seems to have taken al-Ghazālī's project further than al-Ghazālī did himself.

2 Philosophy and Jurisprudence – or: the Theoretical Background of the Topic

First we have to examine how al-Ghazālī conceived of philosophy and jurisprudence and how he connected them to each other and to further disciplines. This is a question about taxonomy and the classification of sciences to be answered by looking into the texts which he has especially devoted to this topic. As a matter of fact, al-Ghazālī liked classifying the sciences. He has written no fewer than eight times on this matter. The series of presentations starts with *Maqāṣid al-falāsifa* (*The Intentions of the Philosophers*), continues with *Faḍā'iḥ al-Bāṭiniyya* (*The Disgraces of the Batinites*), *Jawāhir al-Qur'ān* (*The Jewels of the Qur'an*), *Iḥyā' 'ulūm al-dīn* containing two classifications, *Mīzān al-'amal* (*The Scale of Action*) including another two, and finally ends with *al-Mustaṣfā min 'ilm al-uṣūl* (*The Distillation of the Science of the Principles* [*of Jurisprudence*]).[4] Each of these different taxonomies reveals a certain facet of his approach to the topic, but for our purpose it is sufficient to examine two of them: the classification given in Book One of the *Iḥyā'*, that is, the *Kitāb al-'Ilm* (*The Book of Knowledge*), and the one given in the *Mustaṣfā*. The first classification is the most elaborate ever presented by al-Ghazālī, the second the only one given in a work on jurisprudence, which makes it particularly interesting for us.

To begin with the *Kitāb al-'Ilm*:[5] as al-Ghazālī explains in this book, there are two classes of sciences which are incumbent on the community as a whole (*farḍ al-kifāya*), one of them being (I) the non-religious (*ghayr shar'iyya*) and the other (II) the religious (*shar'iyya*) sciences. The first class, that is, the non-religious sciences, can be divided into three categories: (1) praiseworthy disciplines (*maḥmūda*) such as medicine, mathematics, and politics (*siyāsa*); (2) blameworthy disciplines (*madhmūma*) such as magic and the science of talismans; and (3) permissible disciplines (*mubāḥ*) such as poetics and history. In contrast to that, all religious sciences are praiseworthy, at least in principle, because they are "learned from the prophets." In practice, it may have happened that scholars have introduced some doubtful and blameworthy elements into these disciplines, too (al-Ghazālī 1403/1982, 1:16.7–23, 2009, 59–60 (French)).

The praiseworthy among the religious sciences comprise a whole range of disciplines, presented by al-Ghazālī in a complex order of categories and subdivisions. The first category (1) is constituted by sciences dealing with the principles or sources (*uṣūl*), that is, the Qur'an, the Sunna of the Prophet, the consensus of the community (*ijmā'*), and the traditions of the Prophet's companions (*āthār al-ṣaḥāba*). The second (2) comprises the sciences of the branches (*furū'*) which are divided into (a) the science of this world (*'ilm al-dunyā*), namely jurisprudence (*fiqh*), and (b) the science of the path to the hereafter (*'ilm ṭarīq al-ākhira*). The latter is subdivided into (i) the science of unveiling (*'ilm al-mukāshafa*), which is the knowledge of the righteous (*al-ṣiddīqūn*) and those close to God (*al-muqarrabūn*), essentially the apex of the sciences (*ghāyat al-'ulūm*), according to al-Ghazālī, and (ii) the science of [right] practice (*'ilm al-mu'āmala*), also called the science of the states of the heart (*'ilm aḥwāl al-qalb*), which constitutes the topic of the *Iḥyā'*. The third category (3) deals with preliminaries (*muqaddimāt*) such as lexicography (*lugha*) and grammar (*naḥw*); the fourth category (4) with supplementary disciplines (*mutammimāt*),

4 An overview of these classifications with special attention to the "science of unveiling" (*'ilm al-mukāshafa*) is given by Treiger 2011.

5 For the following, see Table 1 in the Appendix. Compare Treiger 2011, 6–10.

including again a number of divisions and subdivisions. This time the main division is into (a) sciences related to the Qur'an and (b) sciences related to the Sunna. The former are subdivided into (i) disciplines dealing with the expression (*lafẓ*) of the Qur'an like the Qur'anic readings (*qirā'āt*) and letters (*ḥurūf*) and (ii) disciplines dealing with its meaning (*ma'nā*) such as exegesis (*tafsīr*) and *nota bene* the principles of jurisprudence (*uṣūl*). The latter comprise the science of the transmitters (*'ilm al-rijāl*) and again the principles of jurisprudence (*uṣūl al-fiqh*) because the Sunna is, next to the Qur'an, the most important source of Islamic law (al-Ghazālī 1403/1982, 1:16.23–17.15, 2009, 60–62 (French)).

All in all, the classification is sophisticated, and it is admittedly interesting and instructive, but does not appear to supply the information we would actually like to have. In particular, the text says not a word about philosophy nor about theology, which is surprising, to say the least, in a classification including non-religious as well as religious sciences.

Al-Ghazālī must have been aware of these difficulties for, having finished his presentation, he adds some further information. It concerns partly the absence of theology, partly the absence of philosophy within the classification, both explanations being of interest for us. Regarding theology, we are told that its main arguments are already to be found in the Qur'an and the Sunna. Apart from that, theology has nothing to offer but dialectical exercise and the inclination to quarrel with opponents. Therefore, *kalām* may be helpful in protecting the community against the sophistries of heretics and unbelievers, but it is certainly not the right way to obtain knowledge about God's essence and His attributes (al-Ghazālī 1403/1982, 1:22.4–13, 2009, 74–75 (French)).[6] Regarding philosophy, al-Ghazālī's assessment is even harsher. As he tells us, it does not constitute a science in its own right (*'ilm bi-ra'sihā*), but a conglomerate of four genuinely different disciplines. These are (1) mathematics, (2) logic, that is, the investigation of proofs and definitions, which is actually part of theology, according to al-Ghazālī, (3) metaphysics (*ilāhiyyāt*), that is, the investigation of God's essence and attributes, which he also considers to be part of theology, and (4) physics (*ṭabī'iyyāt*). The latter aims at investigating the material bodies and as such may be compared to medicine, but medicine is indispensable for humans whereas physics is not (al-Ghazālī 1403/1982, 1:22.13–24, 2009, 75–76 (French)).

These explanations are astonishing and would certainly deserve a detailed discussion. Yet, for our purpose, it is sufficient to realise that, despite their explicit character, they do not help us to answer the questions we have. It appears that the elaborate classification of the sciences presented in the *Kitāb*

6 Compare al-Ghazālī 1403/1982, 1:22.24–24.14; 2009, 76–80 (French).

al-ʿIlm recognises logic as both legitimate and relevant to the religious sciences, including *kalām* and *(uṣūl al-) fiqh*. But apart from that, it is silent about the relationship between philosophy and jurisprudence. This makes it all the more important to proceed to our next text. That is the *Mustaṣfā min ʿilm al-uṣūl*.

Of course, the *Mustaṣfā* is not about the question of how to classify and organise the sciences. Nevertheless, it can be useful for our purpose, as it contains three pieces of information which might be relevant to us, one in the Exordium of the book (*Khuṭbat al-kitāb*), one in its Preface (*Ṣadr al-kitāb*), the third one being the structure of the book itself.

To start with the exordium:[7] as al-Ghazālī explains at the very beginning, there are three classes of sciences: (I) the purely rational disciplines (*ʿaqlī maḥḍ*); (II) the purely traditional disciplines (*naqlī maḥd*); and (III) the disciplines combining reason and revelation (*mā izdawaja fīhi al-ʿaql wa'l-samʿ*), which are the most exalted of all. The examples given in this context are mathematics and astronomy for the first class, *ḥadīth* and *tafsīr* for the second, and *fiqh* as well as *uṣūl al-fiqh* for the third (al-Ghazālī 1971, 9.5 – 14).

Three pages later, al-Ghazālī picks up the same topic, this time in the preface to his book.[8] Here we are told that the sciences are divided into two classes: (I) the rational sciences (*ʿaqliyya*) and (II) the religious sciences (*dīniyya*), both of which can be subdivided into universal and particular disciplines. In case of the religious sciences, (1) the universal disciplines are identified as theology (*kalām*) and the science of the hidden, also known as the science of the heart (*ʿilm al-bāṭin*/*al-qalb*), whereas (2) the category of particular disciplines is constituted by the sciences dealing with *fiqh*, *uṣūl al-fiqh*, *ḥadīth*, and *tafsīr* (al-Ghazālī 1971, 12.10 – 13.8).[9]

Another two pages later, al-Ghazālī comes to explaining the structure of his book,[10] and there we learn that the *Mustaṣfā* consists of an Introduction (*Muqaddima*) and four major parts. The Introduction is devoted to the epistemological fundaments of the theoretical sciences (*madārik al-ʿulūm al-naẓariyya*), whereas the four parts of the book deal with (I) legal assessments (*al-aḥkām*); (II) the sources of legal assessments (*uṣul al-aḥkām*); (III) the proofs for legal assessments (*adillat al-aḥkām*); and (IV) the conditions for being a *mujtahid* (al-Ghazālī 1971, 15.5 – 18.9).

---

7 See Table 2 in the Appendix; compare Treiger 2011, 17.

8 See Table 3 in the Appendix; compare Treiger 2011, 17.

9 The long elaboration on *kalām* as presented by al-Ghazālī in this context has been translated and analysed by Treiger 2011, 18 – 22.

10 See Table 4 in the Appendix.

Again, one might wonder what all of this has to do with our topic. Throughout the introductory pages of the *Mustaṣfā*, al-Ghazālī does not mention philosophy nor does he refer to its relationship to jurisprudence. Despite this fact, however, it is possible to establish a connection between these two realms proceeding from the passages just quoted. One approach would involve turning from al-Ghazālī himself to the way later authors such as Ibn Rushd (d. 595/1198) understood his text. As is well known, Ibn Rushd wrote an epitome of his book entitled *Mukhtaṣar al-Mustaṣfā*.[11] Its main goal is to summarise the content of the *Mustaṣfā*. In doing so, Ibn Rushd presents a keen analysis of the intentions expressed in the text, touching on both juridical and philosophical aspects.

At the very beginning of his *Mukhtaṣar*, Ibn Rushd discusses the classification of the sciences given by al-Ghazālī, but not by simply repeating the same content in other words; his intention is rather to elucidate the background and the structure of al-Ghazālī's argument by presenting his points and his reflections in a new arrangement. This arrangement runs as follows: in terms of their objects and their goals, we have to distinguish three classes of sciences. (I) The first investigates theoretical issues such as the existence of atoms or the question of whether the world has been created in time (*ḥudūth al-ʿālam*). Consequently, its goal is to create reasoned beliefs (*iʿtiqādāt*) on these issues in our souls. (II) The second class is practical science which consists of two categories. One of them is dealing with universals such as legal assessments (*al-aḥkām*), the sources of legal assessments (*uṣūl al-aḥkām*), and the conditions of being a *mujtahid*. The other one is devoted to particular questions such as the correct way of praying or fasting which can be summarised as the duties incumbent on every believer (*al-farāʾiḍ*). (III) The third and final class is the instrumental sciences. They deal with the rules (*qawānīn*) and the conditions of how to obtain knowledge, among them the proofs (*adilla*) to be used in both classes mentioned before (Bou Akl 2015, 118.8–17 (Arabic), 119.17–35 (French)).

So far, the discourse has been about goals and objects. Ibn Rushd has characterised the sciences under discussion by referring to their subject-matters. However, we need not stay at this provisional point but can identify every science he alluded to, and this at two different levels. The first level is more or less self-explanatory because it remains within the conceptual framework of the religious sciences shared by the *Mustaṣfā* and the *Mukhtaṣar*. On this level, it is quite easy to identify the disciplines intended by Ibn Rushd when he mentions their respective goals and objects. The theoretical science dealing with topics such as the

11 The text has recently been edited and investigated by Ziad Bou Akl (2015). The following owes much to his observations.

generation of the world in time is to be identified with theology (*kalām*). The universal practical science dealing with legal assessments and their sources can be equated with the principles of jurisprudence (*uṣūl al-fiqh*). The particular practical science dealing with our concrete duties corresponds to jurisprudence (*fiqh*). And the instrumental science dealing with the rules and the conditions of cognition is nothing but another part of the *uṣūl al-fiqh*, that is, the part which is devoted to the proofs of the legal assessments (*adillat al-aḥkām*).

In addition to these assignments, there is yet another possibility of identifying the sciences which are at stake here. This becomes evident when we dispense with the level of religious disciplines and turn to the level of philosophy. Within the conceptual framework of philosophy, the correspondence between the objects of knowledge and their respective disciplines runs as follows – and this is confirmed by other texts written by Ibn Rushd: the sciences dealing with God and the structure of this world are metaphysics and physics. The universal practical science is ethics, the particular practical science politics, and the science dealing with the rules and the conditions of cognition cannot be but logic.[12]

As a result, there are two lists. Following Ibn Rushd we have recognised the parallels between rational and religious sciences and we have finally succeeded in establishing a relationship between philosophy and the principles of jurisprudence. As it turned out, some parts of the *uṣūl al-fiqh* correspond to logic, whereas another part of it corresponds to philosophical ethics. I will therefore focus on these two issues in the following.

3 Logic and Jurisprudence

Of the aspects related to our topic, logic is probably the one which has received the bulk of scholarly attention (Brunschvig 1971; Hana 1974; Marmura 1975; al-ʿAjam 1989; Street 2004, 555–559; Rudolph 2005; El-Rouayheb 2016, 411–416).[13] Al-Ghazālī himself promoted this interest by stressing the importance of Aristotelian logic in several contexts, the most prominent of them being probably the unconditioned appraisal of the science of logic in his autobiographical writ-

---

12 See Table 5 in the Appendix; compare Bou Akl 2015, 7–8 and the references to other texts by Ibn Rushd given by Bou Akl 2015, 331–332.

13 Compare also the unpublished PhD dissertations by al-Sayyed Ahmad 1981 and Becheri 2009.

ing, *The Deliverer from Error* (*al-Munqidh min al-ḍalāl*).[14] Furthermore, he wrote a number of introductory works on logic such as *The Standard of Knowledge* (*Miʿyār al-ʿilm*), *The Touchstone for Speculation* (*Miḥakk al-naẓar*), and the first part of the *Mustaṣfā*, not to mention *The Straight Balance* (*al-Qisṭās al-mustaqīm*), which is rather an apology of syllogistic reasoning than an exposition of it.[15]

The goal of these introductory writings was twofold. First, they were meant to explain the logical terminology al-Ghazālī himself had used in *The Incoherence of the Philosophers* (*Tahāfut al-falāsifa*). This is one of the purposes explicitly mentioned in the preface to his *Miʿyār al-ʿilm* (al-Ghazālī 1961, 60.7–9). Second and more important, they were supposed to teach religious scholars how to apply Aristotelian logic within their own disciplines. Apparently, al-Ghazālī was convinced that everybody working in the religious sciences had to learn the methods of proof and the conditions of demonstration. This seems to be the reason why he explained these rules in more than one introductory writing and why his various explanations were situated on different intellectual levels. *Miʿyār al-ʿilm*, for instance, presents the important elements of Aristotelian logic in a detailed manner, using broadly philosophical terminology. In addition, its examples are often taken from metaphysical issues, which gives reason to believe that its addressees were mainly theologians.[16] By contrast, *Miḥakk al-naẓar* and the Introduction to the *Mustaṣfā* (which heavily draws on the *Miḥakk*) are confined to the basics of logic. They avoid philosophical language, replace it, if possible, by the terminology of the religious sciences,[17] and focus on examples taken from jurisprudence. In all probability its addressees thus were the *fuqahāʾ*.[18]

---

14 Containing sentences such as: "There is nothing in this [i.e. logic] which must be rejected. On the contrary, it is the sort of thing mentioned by the *mutakallimūn* and the partisans of reason (*ahl al-naẓar*) in connection with the proof they use" (al-Ghazālī 1969, 22.13–14; McCarthy 2000, 65 (English)).

15 Edition of the text by Chelhot; for a short description of the contents, see Rudolph 2005, 86–88; compare also Kleinknecht 1972.

16 This is confirmed by the fact that the text was written immediately after and in close connection to the *Tahāfut*; compare also my remarks in Rudolph 2005, 85.

17 The relationship between philosophical and juridical terminology is explicitly addressed in the last chapter of the *Miḥakk* where al-Ghazālī discusses various ways of defining *ḥadd* ("definition"), *ʿilm* ("knowledge"), *ʿaraḍ* ("accident"), *ḥādith* ("created in time"), *mutaḍādd* ("contrary"), *ḥayāt* ("life"), *ḥaraka* ("motion"), and *wājib* ("necessary") (al-Ghazālī 1994, 145–161; compare also al-Ghazālī 1971, 31.9–39.22).

18 Additional evidence is given by the fact that al-Ghazālī distinguishes in the *Miḥakk* three types of scholars: the theologians (*al-mutakallimūn*), the logicians (*al-manṭiqiyyūn*), and "us"

The theoretical background of al-Ghazālī's commitment to logic consists of two basic assumptions. One of them is his conviction that all kinds of valid proofs, as applied in the sciences, are nothing but variations of the same logical structure. Consequently, they all can be converted into their basic pattern which is the syllogistic form (Rudolph 2005, 77–79, 89–90).[19] The second assumption is even more general. According to al-Ghazālī, syllogistic reasoning cannot be reduced to its scientific applications. In its basic elements, it is rather the common way used by all human beings when they speculate and try to discover new insights. Thus he writes in Book 39 of the *Iḥyā'*, that is, *The Book about Thinking* (*Kitāb al-Taffakur*): "The meaning of 'thinking' (*ma'nā al-fikr*) is to bring two pieces of knowledge into the heart [of a human being] in order to conclude a third piece of knowledge" (al-Ghazālī 1403/1982, 4:425.16, 2012, 37).[20] Afterwards, this definition is illustrated by a syllogism and repeated in several variations, all of them stressing its evidential and universal validity.

As a consequence, every scholar should learn how to use syllogisms correctly. In order to do so, he should study Aristotelian logic, which is the authoritative and unsurpassed presentation of syllogistic reasoning. By stressing this argument again and again, al-Ghazālī established a link between logic and jurisprudence declaring the first to be an indispensable propaedeutics to the second.[21] However, his optimism concerning the learning abilities of the *fuqahā'* and the actual applicability of syllogisms to *fiqh* was not unconditional. On a close reading of his manuals on logic, one can find a couple of passages which come across as more sceptical and thus uncover the limits of his own methodological programme.

One of these passages is a chapter devoted to the shortcomings of religious scholars. As al-Ghazālī explains, many of them tend to use arguments which are neither correct nor reliable, for a variety of reasons. One is simply the scholars' lack of knowledge about methodological questions (*quṣūr al-'ilm*) (al-Ghazālī 1994, 109.7, 1971, 62.15), another their tendency to mingle several types of arguments, thereby combining what should be kept strictly separate (al-Ghazālī

(*naḥnu*), that is, apparently, the *fuqahā'* (al-Ghazālī 1994, 97.24–25; compare also al-Ghazālī 1971, 54.19–20).

19 The same conviction lies behind al-Ghazālī's assumption that analogical argumentation is inconclusive unless it can be regimented into syllogistic form (El-Rouayheb 2016, 412).

20 *I'lam anna ma'nā al-fikr huwa iḥḍār ma'rifatayn fī l-qalb li-yustathmara minhumā ma'rifa thālitha.*

21 Al-'Ajam 1989, 93–99 emphasises that al-Ghazālī used Aristotelian logic in order to enrich Islamic jurisprudence; compare also Said 2013, 78–79.

1994, 109.9–10, 1971, 62.16–17).[22] The third problem consists of the fact that many scholars treat the premises to be used in syllogisms in a careless and incorrect way. Sometimes they do not reveal their premises, allegedly because they are evident (*wāḍiḥ*) (al-Ghazālī 1994, 109.7–8, 1971, 62.15).[23] Sometimes they accept premises which are not proven at all but only generally accepted and well-known (*mashhūr*) (al-Ghazālī 1994, 108.6–9, 1971, 61:19–21). And sometimes they even hide their premises in order to intentionally deceive (*talbīs*) their opponents. This is due to the fact that religious scholars, as a rule, adhere to the doctrines of their own school, trying to justify and defend them at any cost (al-Ghazālī 1994, 109.8–9, 1971, 62.16).[24]

The list of shortcomings which are common among scholars is long but it has to be completed by another problem. It does not concern the personal (in)capacities of the *fuqahāʾ* but the structure of their discipline, that is, jurisprudence itself. Of course, jurisprudence is a science based on reasoning. As such it is open to methodological reflections as presented by al-Ghazālī in the *Miʿyār*, the *Miḥakk*, and the *Mustaṣfā*. However, jurisprudence and in particular its sources cannot be submitted to rationalisation in every respect as they include elements which are based on tradition and have to be accepted necessarily, even if they are not compatible with philosophical logic.

One of the difficulties to be mentioned in this context is the status of the propositions used in jurisprudence. Most of them have to be taken from the Qur'an and the Sunna, both of which constitute the uncontroversial material sources of Islamic law. As a consequence, many premises accepted by the *fuqahāʾ* are not compatible with the rules of demonstrative logic. They are neither universally valid nor do they meet the conditions of certainty (*yaqīn*),[25] which would be the prerequisites of being a premise in a demonstrative syllogism. Instead, jurists often argue on the basis of propositions which are nothing but commonly accepted (*mashhūrāt*), adopted from trustworthy people

22 Compare also al-Ghazālī 1994, 111.11–ult.; 1971, 64.1–8.

23 Compare also al-Ghazālī 1994, 109.13–110.1; 1971, 62.17–63.5.

24 Compare also al-Ghazālī 1994, 110.1–111.11; 1971, 63.5–64.1.

25 According to al-Ghazālī (1994, 102–108; 1971, 57–62), who follows essentially al-Fārābī and Avicenna in this respect, six classes of premises can be characterised as certain (*yaqīn*): (1) primary propositions (*awwaliyyāt*) such as the axiom of contradiction; (2) self-perceptions (*mushāhadāt bāṭina*) as, for instance, "I am hungry"; (3) sense perceptions (*maḥsūsāt ẓāhira*) as, for instance, "Salt is white"; (4) experiences (*tajribiyyāt*) as, for instance, "Fire is burning"; (5) safe traditions (*mutawātirāt*) as, for instance, "Mecca exists"; (6) indubitable conceptions of the imaginative faculty (*wahmiyyāt*) as, for instance, "A body has six sides" (meaning: it has three dimensions). Compare also al-Ghazālī 1961, 186–193 where the classification and the terminology are slightly different. For al-Fārābī's treatment of the topic, see Black 2006.

(*maqbūlāt*) or expressing a wide-spread belief (*maẓnūnāt*) (al-Ghazālī 1961, 193.7–198.18). More than that: they are actually justified to do so because preponderant belief (*ẓann*) is all that is needed in the legal sciences (*al-fiqhiyyāt*) in contrast to the rational sciences (*al-ʿaqliyyāt*) which have to be based on certain premises (al-Ghazālī 1961, 176.7–177.12).

Another difficulty applies to the argument which is at the core of legal reasoning, that is, analogy or the *qiyās* of the *fuqahāʾ*. As mentioned above, al-Ghazālī was convinced that it can be converted into a syllogism. As a consequence, he acknowledged its general validity and assumed it to be equivalent to philosophical logic, at least in theory. When it comes to practice, however, al-Ghazālī adds an important qualification. According to him, jurists at work should not refer to syllogisms but keep analogy as the standard form of their reasoning. Apparently, this fits better to the requirements of Islamic law, which is based not upon universally valid premises but particular propositions.

The point is explained in a chapter of the *Miʿyār* entitled "The Paradigm" (*al-tamthīl*) (al-Ghazālī 1961, 165–177).[26] It investigates the analogy of the jurists (*al-qiyās al-fiqhī*) as well as the inference from the visible to the invisible (*al-istidlāl bi'l-shāhid ʿalā l-ghāʾib* and *radd al-ghāʾib ʿalā l-shāhid*, respectively) commonly used in Islamic theology. Both of them correspond *formaliter* to the argument called "paradigm" (*tamthīl*) in the Aristotelian tradition. This had already been demonstrated by Abū Naṣr al-Fārābī (d. 339/950 or 951)[27] whose logical writings were in more than one respect a source of inspiration for al-Ghazālī (Street 2004, 559). As a matter of fact al-Ghazālī follows al-Fārābī in equating the *qiyās* of the jurists and the *istidlāl* of the theologians with the *tamthīl* of the philosophers (al-Ghazālī 1961, 165.8–10). Furthermore, he insists on the fact that all three of them can be converted into syllogistic form.[28] Yet, in practice, his advice is nuanced.

26 The chapter has been analysed by El-Rouayheb 2016, 412–414 (who refers to a different edition of the *Miʿyār*). The following remarks of mine are heavily indebted to his observations and results.

27 The topic is discussed in the last two chapters of al-Fārābī's *Short Book on the Syllogism* (*Kitāb al-Qiyās al-ṣaghīr*), also known as *Short Summary of Logic as Practiced by the Theologians* (*al-Mukhtaṣar al-ṣaghīr fī l-manṭiq ʿalā ṭarīqat al-mutakallimīn*). The Arabic text is available in two editions, one of them prepared by Dānishpazhūh and the other one by al-ʿAjam (who erroneously printed these two chapters at the end of another book by al-Fārābī, that is, his *Kitāb* [or: *al-Madkhal ilā*] *al-Qiyās*). An English translation is given by Rescher 1963. For a short description of the work, see Rudolph 2017, 557–558. A detailed examination of al-Fārābī's analysis of the *tamthīl*, the *istidlāl*, and the *qiyās fiqhī* is to be found in Lameer 1994, 40–42, 176–258.

28 For the examples given in the *Miʿyār*, see below. Another important source would be al-Ghazālī's *The Balanced Book of What-to-Believe* (*al-Iqtiṣād fī l-iʿtiqād*) which contains a number

While recommending the *mutakallimūn* to actually make use of syllogisms in their writings, he tells the *fuqahā'* that they would do better to stick with their traditional analogical arguments instead of replacing them by syllogisms.

This advice is illustrated by several concrete examples. The first example raises an issue often discussed in Islamic theology, that is, the question of whether – or rather, for which reason – we may assume that the heavens are not eternal but created in time. The traditional argument used by the *mutakallimūn* in this respect is an *istidlāl* running as follows: "The heavens are created in time since they are composite bodies like animals and plants and these are created in time" (al-Ghazālī 1961, 165.14–15).[29] Yet, this argument is inconclusive, as al-Ghazālī explains. Presented in this form, its validity depends on the assumption that being composite is the "cause" of the judgement that animals and plants are created in time. This assumption, in its turn, can only be taken for granted if we know for sure that anything composite (including animals and plants) must be created in time. The crucial element of the entire proof is thus the universal premise "Everything composite is created in time." Yet, if this is the case, we should mention it explicitly by constructing a different argument. This argument should be a demonstrative syllogism in the first figure running as follows: "The heavens are composite. Everything composite is created in time. The heavens are created in time." Presented in this form, our proof has become conclusive, according to al-Ghazālī. Hence it follows that syllogisms are superior to traditional analogies as far as theological issues are concerned (al-Ghazālī 1961, 165.16–166.2).[30]

The case is different when it comes to juridical issues. This is illustrated by another example raising the famous problem whether – or rather, for which reason – consuming date wine is prohibited. Traditionally, the prohibition was justified by an analogy. It can be formulated in various ways, one of them being: "If we know that grape wine (*khamr*) is prohibited and we have a preponderant belief (*ẓann*) that the cause (*'illa*) for the prohibition is that it is intoxicating, then we are justified in concluding that date wine (*nabīdh*), which is also intoxicating, is also prohibited."[31] In principle, this *qiyās* can be transformed into a categorical syllogism just like the theological *istidlāl* mentioned before. The appropriate syllogism would run something like "Every date wine is an intoxicant. Every intoxicant is prohibited. Every date wine is prohibited" (al-Ghazālī

of categorical syllogisms serving as arguments in the theological discussion; compare my preliminary remarks on the topic in Rudolph 2005, 88–91.

29 Compare El-Rouayheb 2016, 412.

30 Compare El-Rouayheb 2016, 412.

31 The wording is taken from El-Rouayheb 2016, 413; compare al-Ghazālī 1961, 171.17.

1994, 90.9–10, 1971, 50.1–2),[32] which seems to be perfect, at least on formal grounds. In this case, however, al-Ghazālī prefers keeping the analogical form of the argument. Obviously, he is convinced that, whereas syllogistic reasoning fits better to theological issues, the *qiyās* is better adapted to the requirements of legal decisions. One reason might be that when it comes to juridical matters like the prohibition of consuming wine, analogical reasoning is more explicit and more transparent: it mentions all the relevant elements of the argument including its root (*aṣl*) and the judgement (*ḥukm*) attributed to the root. In contrast to that, the syllogism omits both the root and its judgement replacing them by an allegedly universal premise ("Every intoxicant is prohibited"), the status of which is not actually confirmed.

We may thus conclude that the connection between logic and jurisprudence as established by al-Ghazālī is less firm than we might have expected. In this respect his goal seems to have been theoretical rather than practical. The *fuqahā'* should know the general rules of Aristotelian logic but they were not expected to apply them to every legal question. All in all it appears very likely that al-Ghazālī deemed the ties between *manṭiq* and *fiqh* to be less strong than those between *manṭiq* and *kalām*. He is not very explicit on this point but his reason may have been that jurisprudence was an area where preponderant belief and non-certain premises were sufficient, whereas theology, seeking knowledge of God and His creation, was viewed as a rational science (*ʿilm ʿaqlī*) striving for certainty (El-Rouayheb 2016, 414).[33]

4 Philosophical Ethics and Jurisprudence

As mentioned before, Ibn Rushd was convinced that there are structural parallels between *uṣūl al-fiqh* and philosophical ethics. It thus seems appropriate to examine these parallels by asking what al-Ghazālī has to say about them. The best way to do so appears to be to address his major writings in these two fields, that is, the *Mustaṣfā* in jurisprudence and the *Mīzān al-ʿamal* in ethics. In both cases, we want to know if they contain reflections and arguments referring to the field of the other. So, we will ask whether al-Ghazālī discusses issues of ethics in the *Mustaṣfā* and issues of jurisprudence in the *Mīzān*.

To start with the latter: as an attentive reading of the *Mīzān* reveals, the term *fiqh* is actually mentioned several times within the book. However, none of these

32 Compare El-Rouayheb 2016, 413.
33 Compare al-Ghazālī's entire discussion of the *fiqhiyyāt* at 1961, 170.22–177.12.

passages gives us a systematic account of what jurisprudence actually is and what its relationship to ethics might be. They rather consist of scattered remarks about *fiqh* and about the *fuqahā'*, some of which seem to be completely accidental whereas others betray an ironic, if not extremely critical, tone.

To give just two examples: in one passage of the *Mīzān*, *fiqh* is assigned to the sphere of politics, that is, the art of governing people (*siyāsa*). This was the usual way of locating it, as we have already been told by Ibn Rushd. Yet, al-Ghazālī for his part adds a further qualification to this general statement. According to him, the *fuqahā'* as well as the theologians, who are called *wu''āẓ* ("preachers") in this context, are only in the position to govern ordinary people (*al-'awāmm*). The governance of the elite (*al-khawāṣṣ*) cannot be their task but must be delegated to real scholars and sages (*al-'ulamā' wa'l-ḥukamā'*) (al-Ghazālī 1964, 329.17–18, 2006, 184 (German)).

The second critique goes in the same direction. It focuses on the question of how we obtain knowledge and whether knowledge is attainable by everybody and in any scientific discipline. Here again, al-Ghazālī's position is very clear. For him, real insight is only accessible to those who have cleansed their souls and opened their minds in order to understand the intelligible structure of the world and the divine realities (*al-ḥaqā'iq al-ilāhiyya*) (al-Ghazālī 1964, 218.ult.–219.4, 2006, 109 (German)). Throughout the *Mīzān*, this way of gaining knowledge is stressed by him,[34] which demonstrates that the epistemology presented in this text combines both Sufi convictions and philosophical elements.[35] As a consequence, the knowledge al-Ghazālī is talking about is not attainable by jurists; their arguments can at best play a secondary role in this context. This is illustrated by two plays on words, obviously meant to mock the doctors of law and their ignorance. The first says that the *fuqahā'* often teach persons who possess more insight (*afqah*) than themselves (al-Ghazālī 1964, 220.12, 2006, 110). The second affirms that everybody who makes just a little effort (*al-qalīl bi'l-ijtihād*) in order to obtain real knowledge will easily surpass the *mujtahidūn*, that is, the official representatives of *ijtihād* (al-Ghazālī 1964, 219.11, 2006, 109).

In short, when writing the *Mīzān al-'amal*, al-Ghazālī was not interested in connecting ethics and jurisprudence. Whatever he says about *fiqh* or *uṣūl al-fiqh* in this book demonstrates that he did not consider it the right way to examine ethical problems and to form our character, both of which are the goals of

---

34 Compare, for instance, al-Ghazālī 1964, 240–246; 2006, 126–129 and al-Ghazālī 1964, 251–254; 2006, 133–135.

35 For a general introduction to al-Ghazālī's ethics, see Sherif 1975. The fact that *Mīzān al-'amal* presents both philosophy and Sufism as paths to the highest felicity has often been stressed, recently by Garden 2015, 210–228 and Mohamed 2015, 188–193; compare also Said 2013, 92–113.

akhlāq. This is confirmed by another passage from the *Mīzān* worth mentioning here. It deals with the fundamental question of all ethics, namely: "How can we know what is good and what is bad?" Al-Ghazālī's answer refers to neither the Qur'an nor to legal assessments but simply to human intellect. As he explains, it is our intellect that enables us to solve this problem and to distinguish what has to be distinguished, namely "true" and "false" in propositions or beliefs (*al-ḥaqq wa'l-bāṭil fī l-iʿtiqādāt*), sincerity and lies in speech (*al-ṣidq wa'l-kidhb fī l-maqāl*), and "good" and "bad" in our acts (*al-jamīl wa'l-qabīḥ fī l-afʿāl*) (al-Ghazālī 1964, 233.7–10, 2006, 120–121).[36]

Having arrived at this point we have to admit that the results obtained so far do not encourage us to continue our investigation. What al-Ghazālī explains in the *Mīzān* seems to exclude any serious relationship between the science of ethics and *uṣūl al-fiqh*. However, we still have to cross-check this result by turning to other writings and changing our perspective. So, our last question is whether the *Mustaṣfā* contains anything relevant about ethics.

Unsurprisingly, the answer is no. Throughout the *Mustaṣfā*, al-Ghazālī does not address ethical questions, at least not in an explicit manner. The only exception to be mentioned in this context is a section from the first part of the book discussing the nature and the constituent elements of legal assessments (*aḥkām*) (al-Ghazālī 1971, 69–80; Reinhart 1995, 87–104 (English)). This section was examined, some years ago, in a book by A. Kevin Reinhart entitled *Before Revelation*.[37] As we learn from his book, it was part of a lengthy controversy in Muslim religious thought focusing on the problem of how we know about moral judgements. The controversial question which was at stake can be summarised as follows: what is the assessment (if any) for useful and beneficial human acts before revelation comes to assign their value? Are useful acts before revelation proscribed, permitted, obligatory, or something else (Reinhart 1995, 29–31, 38, 62)?[38]

In principle, this question is highly relevant in the context of philosophical ethics. However, the way al-Ghazālī discusses it in the *Mustaṣfā* ignores this relevance, and that for two reasons: first, throughout the section devoted to this question he does not mention philosophy. All his arguments, objections, and explanations remain within the conceptual framework of jurisprudence and

36 For the Arabic reception of the late ancient motto that logic is a tool for distinguishing true from false and good from bad, see Adamson 2011.

37 The most relevant passages are to be found in Reinhart 1995, 70–75, 115–117. Reinhart's analysis of al-Ghazālī's arguments is diligent and convincing despite the scholarly debate provoked by his book (see Ormsby 1998, 1999; Reinhart 1999).

38 Compare Ormsby 1998, 119.

Islamic theology, his main opponents apparently being the school of the Muʿtazila.[39] Second, al-Ghazālī's position in the *Mustaṣfā* is completely different from what he had advocated in the *Mīzān*. Furthermore, he nowhere mentions these differences explicitly nor does he try to discuss the reasons behind them.

This is not the place for a detailed description of the arguments given in the *Mustaṣfā*. They are extensively discussed by Reinhart[40] and can easily be followed in his translation of the relevant passages of the Arabic text. In our context, it suffices to say that al-Ghazālī, in the *Mustaṣfā*, maintains an orthodox Ashʿarī position. According to this position, any kind of moral assessments must be based on revelation because our intellect, although having some vague estimations of what might be recommended and what is to be avoided (arising from our self-interest) (Reinhart 1995, 171),[41] is not able to decide independently what is right and what is wrong. This is expressed in a whole series of affirmations and arguments, including the following particularly unequivocal statement: "Therefore we say: the intellect neither commends nor detests nor does it make thanking the benefactor obligatory nor is there any assessment for acts before the arrival of the revelation" (al-Ghazālī 1971, 69.10 – 11).[42]

5 Final Remarks: al-Ghazālī and Beyond

This result is surprising to say the least. The same scholar who told us that everybody should follow the universally valid rules of Aristotelian logic and that our intellect enables us to distinguish between "good" and "bad" ends up with a statement on the intellect (and thus on rationality) which seems to be opposite, if not contradictory, to what he himself affirmed elsewhere. Of course, there may be several ways of explaining the manifest differences between al-Ghazālī's statements. One way, for instance, would be to suppose that his views on the topic developed during his lifetime.[43] As far as we know, he wrote the *Mīzān*

---

39 Al-Ghazālī's discussion in the *Mustaṣfā* focuses on the positions and the arguments of the Muʿtazila; see Reinhart 1995, 88, 90 – 95, 97, 101, 103. Apart from the Muʿtazilīs he mentions the Ashʿarīs as well as the Ḥanbalīs, but not a single philosopher.

40 See the arguments summarised by Reinhart 1995, 71 – 75.

41 Compare Said 2013, 83.

42 *Fa-li-hādhā qulnā al-ʿaql lā yuḥassinu wa-lā yuqabbiḥu wa-lā yūjibu shukr al-munʿim wa-lā ḥukm li'l-afʿāl qabla wurūd al-sharʿ*. Compare the English translation by Reinhart 1995, 87.

43 The developmental hypothesis which has a long history in scholarship has been stressed again recently by Madelung 2015 and Garden 2015, 208 – 210, 227 – 228.

in 488/1095, whereas the *Mustaṣfā* was finished nearly fifteen years later.[44] It is thus not impossible that his ideas may have changed during all these years.[45] Another possibility to explain the divergence would be to say that he adapted his doctrine to the audience he was addressing. As we have seen, he considered *fiqh* only to be the right way of governing ordinary people, whereas the elite should be guided by real scholars and sages (*al-ʿulamāʾ wa'l-ḥukamāʾ*) (El-Rouayheb 2016, 414).[46] We could thus argue that the *Mustaṣfā* contains the doctrine for the *ʿawāmm*, whereas the *Mīzān*, addressing the *khawāṣṣ*, must argue on a different level.[47] In either case, however, we cannot help conceding that

---

44 Although there is still some debate about the time of origin of the *Mīzān*, most scholars agree that it was written in 488/1095 as a sequel to the *Miʿyār* and earlier than the *Iḥyāʾ* (Bouyges 1959, 28–29; Treiger 2012, 12; Garden 2015, 208–209). In the case of the *Mustaṣfā* we know for sure that it originated in 503/1109. Several manuscripts and Ibn Khallikān's testimony confirm that the text was completed on 6 Muḥarram 503/5 August 1109 (Bouyges 1959, 73–74; Treiger 2013, 14).

45 However, when we follow the developmental hypothesis assuming that the doctrine of the *Mīzān* was superseded in later writings, we face a problem: there may be some evidence that the *Mīzān* "shows al-Ghazālī in a very different frame of mind" than the one depicted in later texts (Garden 2015, 208–209), but it would be extremely difficult to argue that the entire ethical doctrine as exposed in it was superseded later on. Several parts of the *Iḥyāʾ* draw heavily on the *Mīzān* (see in particular *Kitāb ʿAjāʾib al-qalb* [Book 21] and *Kitāb Riyāḍat al-nafs* [Book 22]). And even *al-Munqidh min al-ḍalāl*, written probably in 501/1107 (Bouyges 1959, 70–71; compare Treiger 2012, 14 who assumes a slightly earlier date of origin), is in some respect close to the ideas of the *Mīzān*. The famous passage at the beginning of the *Munqidh* where al-Ghazālī describes his doubts and his quest for an indisputable foundation of all knowledge (see Rudolph 2018, 4–11 with further references) can be interpreted as a distant echo of the very last sentences of the *Mīzān* which run as follows: "Those who do not doubt do not reflect. Those who do not reflect do not see. And those who do not see remain in blindness and error" (al-Ghazālī 1964, 409.21–22; 2006, 238 (German): *fa-man lam yashukk lam yanẓur wa-man lam yanẓur lam yabṣur wa-man lam yabṣur baqiya fī l-ʿamā wa'l-ḍalāl*).

46 Compare above n. 33.

47 When following this hypothesis we face the problem of how to explain the conflicting statements about the *ʿaql* to be found in the *Mīzān* and in the *Mustāṣfā*. One solution would be that the word *ʿaql* which is equivocal was used in different ways by al-Ghazālī. In the *Mustaṣfā* he argues against the Muʿtazila and their understanding of moral reasoning. In this context *ʿaql* could be rendered as "reason" (which would fit the doctrine of the Muʿtazila) meaning a purely human capacity as opposed to sense perception. According to al-Ghazālī, this capacity is not able to really distinguish between "good" and "bad" because it lacks divine assistance and is always restrained to self-interest. In contrast, the argument of the *Mīzān* seems to be developed within the philosophical tradition. In this context, *ʿaql* may best be rendered as "intellect" meaning a faculty shared by human beings and several higher entities (that is, the cosmic intellects and ultimately God) and thus transcending the realm of anthropology. Endowed with this faculty, humans are supposed to have access to knowledge about "true" and "false" as well as

the connection between *falsafa* and (*uṣūl al-*) *fiqh* as established by al-Ghazālī is precarious. Regardless of *how* we explain the difference between his philosophical reflections as presented in the *Mīzān* and his legal reasoning as presented in the *Mustaṣfā*, the fact remains that there *is* a considerable difference between the two which cannot be bridged by rhetorical efforts.

In sum, we thus have to admit that al-Ghazālī's contribution to our topic was rather limited and oddly vague. It is true, he identified the major points of convergence between philosophy and jurisprudence, or logic and ethics (including the theory of intellect). Furthermore, he was working on these points in particular when reflecting on the relation between Aristotelian logic and legal reasoning. Despite these efforts, however, al-Ghazālī did not succeed in establishing a systematic and consistent link between the two disciplines. This applies to the field of logic where he taught syllogisms but preferred using analogies when it came to juridical reasoning. And it applies to the domain of ethics and noetics where he presented his readers with conflicting statements about the role of the intellect (*al-ʿaql*).

Does this mean that our investigation ends up with a conclusion which is entirely negative, if not frustrating? Although it may seem so at first sight, this is not necessarily the case. At least not if we are ready to enlarge our perspective, and go beyond the scope of questions which have been asked so far. Until now, we have mainly focused on al-Ghazālī's own achievements by following what he has expressed in his own writings. There is, however, another possible approach to our topic, and the example of Ibn Rushd's *Mukhtaṣar al-Mustaṣfā* given above has already shown that this approach may be successful. It does not focus on what al-Ghazālī *himself* has written but on what he has *initiated* by his writings. In other words, it asks for his impact on the field and his possible influence on later reflections about philosophy and jurisprudence.

Seen from this angle, the picture changes considerably. Without elaborating systematically on our topic, al-Ghazālī seems to have opened a gate to it, thereby inciting other authors to go further in this direction. This is at least the impression we get when reading later works on *uṣūl al-fiqh*, for they include numerous passages discussing philosophical issues both in logic and in the field of ethics and noetics. As far as logic is concerned, this is easily demonstrated. From the sixth/twelfth century onward, many influential *fuqahāʾ* such as Ibn Qudāma (d. 620/1223), Sayf al-Dīn al-Āmidī (d. 631/1233), and Ibn al-Ḥājib (d. 646/1248)

"good" and "bad." The only requirement would be that they cleanse their souls and thereby enable their intellects to be enlightened from "above" which is more or less the thematic focus of the *Mīzān*.

introduced Aristotelian logic into legal theory, thereby following the example of al-Ghazālī's *Mustaṣfā*. Thus a long tradition of logical studies emerged amongst Islamic jurists, which was admittedly not uncontested but remained one of the characteristic features of later *uṣūl al-fiqh* works.[48]

When it comes to ethics and noetics, the situation is different. In their case, it is more difficult to discern al-Ghazālī's impact on the field. This is all the more true as the study of these topics and their possible interaction with legal reasoning, in particular in the later period, is not even in its infancy. There is, however, an interesting textual example worth mentioning here. It cannot be assigned to al-Ghazālī directly but might be related in some way to the intellectual activities initiated by him. It reveals that later jurists accepted the integration of philosophical noetics into their own reflections, thereby connecting legal theory with the long tradition of reasoning about the intellect, which was ultimately rooted in Avicenna (Davidson 1992, 83–94; McGinnis 2010, 117–130)[49] but also shared by al-Ghazālī (Davidson 1992, 129–144; Treiger 2012, 18–29).[50]

The example is taken from a text written by the Ottoman author Mullā Khusraw (d. 885/1480 or 1481). He was one of the eminent scholars working under the patronage of Meḥmed II and was appointed by him *qāḍī* of Constantinople as well as professor at the Ayasofya *madrasa*, to mention only his most prestigious positions.[51] Mullā Khusraw wrote several works on *uṣūl al-fiqh*, among them a handbook called *The Stairs to Arriving* (*Mirqāt al-wuṣūl*) and a commentary on it entitled *The Mirror of the Principles on Commenting The Stairs to Arriving* (*Mir'āt al-uṣūl fī sharḥ Mirqāt al-wuṣūl*). Whereas the former is an extremely short *aide mémoire* to the standard issues to be taught in classes about *uṣūl*

---

48 See Hallaq 1990, 372 who emphasises that later scholars went several steps beyond al-Ghazālī in integrating the formal precepts of logic into the body of legal theory; compare Street 2004, 558–559; El-Rouayheb 2016, 414, 416–424.

49 For a more detailed account of Avicenna's epistemology, see Gutas 2000. Of course, important reflections on the intellect were already presented by earlier philosophers such as al-Kindī and al-Fārābī, but the terminology of the text to be discussed in the following is unequivocally Avicennan.

50 As mentioned, this does not apply to the *Mustaṣfā* but to other writings by al-Ghazālī such as the *Mīzān* and the *Iḥyā'* (compare above n. 45).

51 For biographical details, see Repp 1986, 128–137, 154–166; Reinhart 2007, 2–13; Arslan 2016, 39–46. On Mullā Khusraw's writings and his doctrine, see the proceedings of the symposium held at Bursa in 2011 which have been edited by Yücedoğru 2013.

al-fiqh, the latter gives an elaborate account of the same topics,[52] containing a number of inspiring and unexpected reflections.[53]

One of these reflections focuses on the question of how to define a legal subject (*al-mukallaf*) or, as the text puts it, how to define "someone to whom the assessment applies" (*al-maḥkūm ʿalayhi*) (Mullā Khusraw 1307, 2:239.2, 1309, 2:432.10). Since this topic had already been treated numerous times in former *uṣūl al-fiqh* writings, one would not expect anything unconventional under this title. Despite being perfectly aware of the scholarly tradition, Mullā Khusraw nonetheless prefers to address the issue in a new way. This becomes evident from the very beginning of his presentation. In the *Mirqāt*, that is, the handbook, he introduces the topic as follows: "[Chapter] On someone to whom the assessment applies, that is, a legal subject: the fact of being a legal subject (*al-taklīf*) depends on the basic legal capacity (*al-ahliyya*) [of a person] which in turn depends on the [fact that he possesses a] dispositional intellect (*al-ʿaql bi'l-malaka*)."[54]

Presented in this terse form the statement would probably have been incomprehensible to his readers. Therefore Mullā Khusraw hastens to explain it by proffering a long commentary, this time in the *Mirʾāt:* his explanation starts with a rough exposition of the philosophical or, more precisely, Avicennan theory of intellect. Accordingly we are told that the term *ʿaql*, as used in philosophical language, points to a faculty of the soul which enables us to gain knowledge and to act according to our deliberations. As Mullā Khusraw (1307, 2:239.6 – 12; 1309, 2:432.12 – 23) explains, this faculty comprises two aspects which may be called "theoretical intellect" (*ʿaql naẓarī*) and "practical intellect" (*ʿaql ʿamalī*). The theoretical intellect in its turn is not uniform but exists in four different stages (*marātib*) depending upon the degree to which our soul has been able to receive abstracted forms and to grasp the intelligibles. These stages are called: (1) "material intellect'" (*ʿaql hayūlānī*), meaning the rational soul at the

52 On both texts, see Reinhart 2007, 14 – 15; Arslan 2016, 51 – 54. Arslan 2016, 85 – 261 gives a partial German translation of the *Mirqāt* but his translation does not cover the part which is of particular interest for us.

53 The text was available to me in two versions: (1) a facsimile of a manuscript of the *Mirʾāt* published in Istanbul in 1307 AH; and (2) on the margin of Sulaymān b. ʿAbdallāh al-Izmīrī's glosses (*ḥāshiya*) on the *Mirʾāt* printed in Istanbul in 1309 AH. I owe both these versions to A. Kevin Reinhart who presented the text at a workshop on "Islamic Legal Theories in the Late Post-Classical Period" convened by Asad Q. Ahmed at UC Berkeley on September 29–October 1, 2017. I want to express my thanks to Asad Ahmed for inviting me to the workshop and to Kevin Reinhard for providing me with copies of the text and sharing with me important information about Mullā Khusraw.

54 *Mirqāt al-wuṣūl* as quoted in brackets in Mullā Khusraw 1307, 2:239.3 – 6; 1309, 2:432.10 – 12.

very beginning of its created nature (*fī mabdaʾ al-fiṭra*) when it is still devoid of any object of knowledge; (2) "dispositional intellect" (*ʿaql biʾl-malaka*), the stage when our intellect has grasped those objects of knowledge which are self-evident (like the so-called "laws of thought") and is thus disposed to attain further theoretical knowledge (*istaʿaddat li-taḥṣīl al-naẓariyyāt*); (3) "actual intellect" (*ʿaql biʾl-fiʿl*), the intellect that has acquired theoretical knowledge and has access to it whenever it wants but does not consider it at the moment; and (4) "acquired intellect" (*ʿaql mustafād*), the highest stage of human intellect, coming about when the intelligible forms are actually present in the soul (Mullā Khusraw 1307, 2:239.12–240.6; 1309, 2:432.23–32).[55]

Having accomplished this exposition, Mullā Khusraw continues his presentation by emphasising the parallels between philosophical noetics and juridical theory. His elaboration on this point is long and multifarious, evoking several concepts such as *dhimma* ("legal protection") and the Qur'anic *amāna* ("trust") which need not be explained here in detail. However, the major point of his argument seems to be clear. It consists of declaring that two stages of (the philosophical theory of) the intellect just mentioned are relevant within the conceptual framework of jurisprudence: the "material intellect" and the "dispositional intellect".

Both of them are somehow connected to our legal capacity, named in Arabic by the generic term *ahliyya*. The *ahliyya* exists in two forms (*nawʿāni*) which are to be understood as two stages: (a) a kind of necessary or basic capacity (*ahliyyat al-wujūb*) and (b) the capacity to act (*ahliyyat al-adāʾ*) (Mullā Khusraw 1307, 2:243.4–8; 1309, 2:434.4–6). The first one applies to human beings from the very beginning of their existence, that is, already in their embryonic state (*janīn*) (Mullā Khusraw 1307, 2:244.10; 1309, 2:434.29). It entails certain basic rights such as the right of inheriting (*irth*) (Mullā Khusraw 1307, 2:244.12–13; 1309, 2:434.31) and is itself related to the fact that we are rational beings. This does not mean that the *ahliyyat al-wujūb* is to be identified with our intellect but it *relies* on the intellect because the fact that human beings are endowed with a (material) intellect is a necessary condition (*sharṭ*) of its existence (Mullā Khusraw 1307, 2:243.18–244.4; 1309, 2:434.14–24). By contrast, the second *ahliyya* is the characteristic feature of a legal subject (*mukallaf*). It is our capacity of acting according to moral obligations and of being responsible for our own acts (Mullā Khusraw 1307, 2:243.7–8; 1309, 2:434.6). This capacity presupposes that, having grasped the basic laws of thought, we have become able to reflect

55 For Avicenna's theory which is the model of Mullā Khusraw's exposition, see Davidson 1992, 83–87; McGinnis 2010, 118–120.

on our own and to attain knowledge. In other words, *ahliyyat al-adāʾ* is, in philosophical terminology, nothing but our dispositional intellect (*ʿaql biʾl-malaka*) (Mullā Khusraw 1307, 2:240.6–241.8; 1309, 2:432.32–433.8). This may be surprising for religious scholars and certainly hard to accept. However, Mullā Khusraw (1307, 2:241.8–10; 1309, 2:433.8–9) insists on this identification by telling his colleagues that "even if something just mentioned may be taken from the teaching of the philosophers, it obviously does not contradict the doctrine of the *ahl al-sunna* as expressed by the theologians (*al-mutakallimūn*)."

Without doubt Mullā Khusraw's reflections on legal capacity and the stages of human intellect need further investigation. So far, we lack several pieces of information which would allow us to better understand his argument and situate it within the context both of his own doctrine and the legal discourse of his time. What we do know, however, is that he merged philosophy with jurisprudence. And, as we have just seen, his way of combining the two went far beyond any of al-Ghazālī's attempts in this field. These observations are instructive all the more as both of them confirm the twofold conclusion already expressed before: al-Ghazālī seems to have been successful in promoting the merging of philosophical with juridical reasoning, but later scholars seem to have been more successful in realising this goal.

Appendix

Table 1: The classification of the sciences according to Book One of *Iḥyāʾ ʿulūm al-dīn* (*The Revival of the Sciences of Religion*), that is, *Kitāb al-ʿIlm* (*The Book of Knowledge*); the classification comprises the sciences characterised by al-Ghazālī as incumbent on the community as a whole (*farḍ al-kifāya*).

I. Non-religious (*ghayr sharʿiyya*) sciences:
   1. Praiseworthy (*maḥmūda*): medicine, arithmetic, agriculture, weaving, politics etc.
   2. Blameworthy (*madhmūma*): magic, science of the talismans, science of trickery and deception
   3. Permissible (*mubāḥ*): science of poetry, historiography etc.

II. Religious (*sharʿiyya*) sciences (which are all praiseworthy because of their prophetic origin but may contain blameworthy elements in practice introduced at a later stage):
   1. Principles/Sources (*uṣūl*): Qur'an, Sunna, consensus of the community (*ijmāʿ*), traditions of the Prophet's companions (*āthār al-ṣaḥāba*)

2. Branches (*furūʿ*):
   a. Science of this world (*ʿilm al-dunyā*): jurisprudence (*fiqh*)
   b. Science of the path to the hereafter (*ʿilm ṭarīq al-ākhira*)
      i. Science of unveiling (*ʿilm al-mukāshafa*)
      ii. Science of [right] practice (*ʿilm al-muʿāmala*) or science of the states of the heart (*ʿilm aḥwāl al-qalb*)
3. Preliminaries (*muqadimmāt*): lexicography (*lugha*), grammar (*naḥw*)
4. Supplements (*mutammimāt*):
   a. Related to the Qur'an:
      i. Concerning its expression (*lafẓ*): readings (*qirāʾāt*), letters (*ḥurūf*)
      ii. Concerning its meaning (*maʿnā*): exegesis (*tafsīr*), principles of jurisprudence (*uṣūl al-fiqh*)
   b. Related to the Sunna: science of the transmitters (*ʿilm al-rijāl*), principles of jurisprudence (*uṣūl al-fiqh*)

Table 2: The classification of the sciences according to the Exordium (*Khuṭba*) of *al-Mustaṣfā min ʿilm al-uṣūl* (*The Distillation of the Science of the Principles* [*of Jurisprudence*])

I. Purely rational (*ʿaqlī maḥḍ*) sciences:
arithmetic, geometry, astronomy etc.

II. Purely traditional (*naqlī maḥḍ*) sciences:
exegesis (*tafsīr*) of the Qur'an, sciences of the *ḥadīth* etc.

III. Combined (*mā izdawaja fīhi al-ʿaql wa-l-samʿ*) sciences:
jurisprudence (*fiqh*), principles of jurisprudence (*uṣūl al-fiqh*) etc.

Table 3: The classification of the sciences according to the Preface (*Ṣadr*) of *al-Mustaṣfā min ʿilm al-uṣūl* (*The Distillation of the Science of the Principles* [*of Jurisprudence*])

I. Rational (*ʿaqliyya*) sciences:
medicine, arithmetic, geometry etc.

II. Religious (*dīniyya*) sciences:
   1. Universal (*kulliyya*): theology (*kalām*), science of the hidden (*ʿilm al-bāṭin*) or science of the heart (*ʿilm al-qalb*)

2. Particular (*juzʾiyya*): jurisprudence (*fiqh*), principles of jurisprudence (*uṣūl al-fiqh*), sciences of the *ḥadīth*, exegesis (*tafsīr*) of the Qur'an etc.

Table 4: The structure of *al-Mustaṣfā min ʿilm al-uṣūl* (*The Distillation of the Science of the Principles [of Jurisprudence]*)

Introduction (*Muqaddima*): The epistemological fundaments of the theoretical sciences (*madārik al-ʿulūm al-naẓariyya*)

Part 1: Legal assessment (*al-ḥukm*)
Part 2: The sources of legal assessments (*uṣūl al-aḥkām*)
Part 3: The proofs for legal assessments (*adillat al-aḥkām*)
Part 3: The conditions for being a legal scholar (*mujtahid*)

Table 5: Description and classification of the sciences according to the Introduction of Ibn Rushd's *Epitome of the "Distillation"* (*Mukhtaṣar al-Mustaṣfā*)

I. Theoretical Science:
   Its goal (*ghāya*) is a belief (*iʿtiqād*) emerging in the soul; it deals with questions such as atoms (*al-juzʾ alladhī lā yatajazzaʾ*) and the creation of the world in time (*ḥudūth al-ʿālam*).

   [Identification:
   a. Within the religious sciences: *kalām*
   b. Within philosophy (as mentioned in further classifications of the sciences by Ibn Rushd): metaphysics and physics]

II. Practical Science:
   Its goal is action (*ʿamal*).
   1. Universal:
      It deals with legal assessments (*al-aḥkām*), the sources of legal assessments (*uṣūl al-aḥkām*) such as the Qur'an, the Sunna, and the consensus of the community, as well as the conditions for being a legal scholar (*al-mujtahid*).

      [Identification:
      a. Within the religious sciences: *uṣūl al-fiqh*
      b. Within philosophy: ethics]

2. Particular:
   It deals with the *furūʿ* and the duties (*al-farāʾiḍ*) incumbent on every believer.

   [Identification:
   a. Within the religious sciences: *fiqh*
   b. Within philosophy: politics]

III. Instrumental Sciences:
It deals with the rules of reasoning as applied in theoretical and practical science, e. g. the proofs for legal assessments (*adillat al-aḥkām*).

[Identification:
a. Within the religious sciences: *uṣūl al-fiqh*
b. Within philosophy: logic]

Felicitas Opwis

Syllogistic Logic in Islamic Legal Theory: al-Ghazālī's Arguments for the Certainty of Legal Analogy (*Qiyās*)

1 Why Law Needs Logic

In his introduction to the *Mustaṣfā*, Abū Ḥāmid al-Ghazālī (d. 505/1111) (1993, 1:30) clearly expresses the view that thorough knowledge of logic is requisite to evaluate the correctness of someone's arguments; the science of legal theory (*uṣūl al-fiqh*), he notes, is no exception. That logic, by which I mean syllogistic logic, is essential for legal reasoning is, however, not self-evident. While these two sciences are not in conflict, they do not necessarily pursue the same goals. Logic, one may say, is the systematic study of the forms of reasoning, with the aim to obtain arguments in which a specific relation of logical support exists between the assumptions of the argument and its conclusion.

Where logic as a science theorises about the correct procedures of arguments and patterns of argumentation, and, thus, partakes in the debate over how to discern fallacy from truth, Islamic jurisprudence theorises about the correct way to infer from the statements found in the sacred sources of the law, which for the believer is Truth, the correct conduct of the faithful. The aim of legal reasoning is not to establish the truth-value of a legal statement in the sources of law per se,[1] but the correct action that is inferred therefrom. Jurisprudents infer (*istadalla*) from the language and wording of the Qur'an and *ḥadīth* legal conclusions, that is, rulings (*aḥkām*). The correctness of the inference confers validity upon the legal ruling and, thus, upon the conduct prescribed. The role of jurisprudence, thus, is one of verifying and legitimising a particular way of doing things, be that how sale transactions are contracted, family relations ordered, or religious rituals performed; it partakes in ordering and shaping society.

Another difference between logical arguments and legal reasoning is that the former, when correctly structured, lead to certainty, whereas the latter

1 Al-Ghazālī points out that it is the science of theology (*kalām*) which establishes that the sayings of the Prophet are authoritative proof (*ḥujja*) and an indicant necessitating truthfulness (*dalīl wājib al-ṣidq*); the jurisprudent, in contrast, investigates the aspects of their indicants and the condition of their soundness (al-Ghazālī 1993, 1:17).

https://doi.org/10.1515/9783110552386-007

leads to validity (Brunschvig 1970, 12–13). Law does not have to be logically correct to confer validity upon a legal ruling.[2] A rational system that results in predictable law is desired, though the rationality does not have to be logical.[3] Rather, a completely logical legal system with inferences that are certain is not actually the aim of legal reasoning, as such a system prevents the flexibility needed to address the myriad legal instances and contingencies of life. If fact A always necessarily leads to ruling B, there is no room for mitigating circumstances or considerations of justice and fairness.[4] Hence, from a practical perspective, it is undesirable to have a logical, and thus rigid, legal system because it does not validate exceptions and departures from logically arrived at rulings. For theoreticians of law, however, the practical considerations are not decisive. Their concern is to construct a coherent legal system in which legal inferences display a valid relation between the indicant, that is, the textual statement, and its indicated, that is, the ruling inferred from it (van Ess 1970, 26). This validity is strongest when one can demonstrate a rational relationship between the text and the legal act related to it to the point that the latter is a consequence of the former. For example, the Qur'anic statement (Q. 4:92) "whosoever kills a believer by mistake should free a believing slave" is translated into law in that when a homicide is found to have been unintentional, the perpetrator is not liable to retaliation (*qiṣāṣ*) but expiates by freeing a Muslim slave. Qur'an 4:11 says about inheritance that "if [a man] has no son, and his parents are his heirs, a third [of the inheritance goes] to his mother." This statement results in the legal ruling that under these circumstances the deceased's father receives two-thirds of the inheritance, even though the text itself is silent about the father's share.[5] The often ambiguous wording of the Qur'an and Prophetic reports leads to much debate over how to correctly infer rulings from them.

A ruling's correctness depends on the strength of the connection between text and ruling inferred from it. The strongest form of relationship between indicant/text and indicated/ruling is a logical one. Demonstrative proof (*burhān*), in particular the categorical syllogism that is based on epistemologically certain premises, leads to a definite conclusion. Syllogistic demonstration, thus, leads to the truth-value of the conclusion. Translated into the realm of Islamic law, this means that legal reasoning that follows the form of syllogistic logic leads

---

2 For example, in Islamic law oaths are deemed legal evidence that convey validity on particular legal acts, yet they have no logical relation to the act.

3 For different types of legal rationality, see Weber 1978, 656–657, 810–821.

4 Legal procedures such as juristic preference (*istiḥsān*), license (*rukhṣa*), and consideration of well-being (*istiṣlāḥ*) serve to circumvent undesired outcomes that lead to hardship and injustice.

5 For examples of transforming textual statements into legal acts, see Kamali 2003, 166–201.

to rulings that are certain – and, hence, irrefutable. Ordering society on the basis of such logically correct rulings is, thus, intellectually beyond challenge.

Logic as a science, in particular Aristotelian syllogistic reasoning, has been known among Muslim scholars since at least the early third/ninth century. Most Greek works on logic were translated into Arabic by the end of the third/ninth century. Al-Fārābī (d. 339/950) commented extensively on them (EI2, "Manṭiḳ"), and Ibn Sīnā's (d. 428/1037) writings on logic were well-absorbed in Islamic scholarship, not only in philosophy but also in theology (Rescher 1964, 15–18, 29, 40, 46, 51–53). Nevertheless, in jurisprudential writings, Aristotelian syllogistic logic was somewhat of a late-comer, not making itself felt much before the fifth/eleventh century. This is not to say that Islamic law was illogical or irrational nor that Greek logic had no impact on the articulation of legal theory prior to the late fifth/eleventh century. Al-Shāfiʿī's (d. 204/820) discussion of analogy (*qiyās*) was influenced by Aristotle's *Topics* (EI2, "Manṭiḳ"). Yet, by the end of the fourth/tenth century, one finds little use made of logic in legal arguments beyond the conjunctive and disjunctive syllogism (Hallaq 1990, 316–318). Among the first jurisprudents to thoroughly engage with logic was Ibn Ḥazm (d. 456/1062). The Andalusian Ẓāhirī scholar expounded its utility for the religious sciences, including law. He emphasised that through the study of logic the student is able to distinguish between proof (*burhān*) and falsehood. Logic, according to Ibn Ḥazm, brought one closer to the revealed Truth (Chejne 1984, 62–63):

> All experts should know that the individual who does not understand the value of logic is at a distance from what Almighty God and His Prophet – may God pray for him and give him peace – had prescribed; that such an individual should not be permitted to pass legal judgment [on a dispute] between two individuals because of his ignorance of definitions of words (*ḥudūd al-kalām*), their structure, the formulation of premises, and the drawing of conclusions on which rests the proof that is always certain; nor will he be able to discern between true and false premises.

2 Logic in Islamic Legal Reasoning

The conscious and deliberate application of Aristotelian syllogistic logic in legal reasoning reaches a new stage around the time of al-Ghazālī, who can be credited with a major role in this shift. Endreß (2005, 132) remarks that al-Ghazālī was to jurists what Ibn Sīnā was to philosophers in applying logical methods to the subject matter of Islamic law. When comparing the works on legal theory of illustrious jurists such as al-Jaṣṣāṣ (d. 370/980), Abū l-Ḥusayn al-Baṣrī (d. 436/

1044), and al-Juwaynī (d. 478/1085)[6] with those of al-Ghazālī, it is apparent that the latter is purposefully structuring his legal arguments in the syllogistic form of demonstrative proof (*burhān*); his predecessors are much less concerned about arranging their arguments in a logically correct fashion.[7] Al-Ghazālī is usually credited as the first jurist introducing his legal work with a chapter on logic (Hallaq 1997, 39; 1989, 318–319).[8] His insistence on the need of logic as a propaedeutic to all disciplines disengaged logic from philosophy, and the taint of being a "foreign" science (Rescher 1964, 59–61). By the time of Fakhr al-Dīn al-Rāzī (d. 606/1210), Ibn Qudāma (d. 620/1223), al-Āmidī (d. 631/1234), and Ibn al-Ḥājib (d. 646/1248) logic is deemed an integral part of *uṣūl al-fiqh* and part of the *madrasa* curriculum (Hallaq 1990, 315–358; Endreß 2005, 129).[9]

While the precise course of and the exact reasons for integrating syllogistic logic into Islamic legal theory have not yet been sufficiently studied to allow for a detailed and comprehensive account,[10] two interrelated factors seem to be driving the process: the quest for legal certainty amid competition over the authoritative interpretation of God's law. As stated above, the language of the material sources of Islamic law is often ambiguous. The result is a variety of competing interpretations of what God wants the believers to do and not to do. However, since there is general agreement among Muslims that God is perfect, His law, by extension, is also perfect and, thus, needs to be free from contradictions. In practice, however, Muslims rarely agreed upon the interpretation of any particular legal instance – to the point that the existence of different interpretations (*ikhtilāf*) was used, for example, by the Shīʿī scholar Qāḍī Nuʿmān (d. 363/973) to discredit the whole Sunnī enterprise (Hallaq 1987, 67, n. 84).

One tool to reduce such differences was dialectic (*jadal*) by showing that one opinion was more valid than another. Aristotelian dialectic, absorbed into Islamic thought no later than the early third/ninth century, was the dominant

6 Al-Juwaynī was obviously familiar with syllogistic logic. His theological arguments display the change from reasoning based on two terms to the three terms of syllogistic reasoning with a universal middle term (EI2, "ʿIlm al-kalām").

7 The late fifth/eleventh century is characterised by efforts to make Islamic legal theory more coherent. This leads, for example, to scrutinising the rationality of law-finding procedures such as the *a contrario* argument (*mafhūm al-mukhālafa*), rationalising it in a manner that allows its integration into legal analogy (*qiyās*) (Opwis 2011, 77–84).

8 Chehata (1965, 14) states that it was al-Juwaynī who for the first time tried to introduce Aristotelian logic into legal theory in his work *al-Burhān*.

9 For example, in his work *al-Maḥṣūl* al-Rāzī argues almost exclusively in syllogistic structures with three terms.

10 Hallaq (1997, 134–143) provides a concise account of the development of logic in Islamic law, which is based on his many studies of the subject matter.

method of legal argumentation, in particular in the procedure of analogy (*qiyās*) (Hallaq 1997, 136–137).[11] Next to consensus (*ijmāʿ*), analogy (*qiyās*) is accepted as a non-textual source of law in Sunnī Islam. The importance of analogical reasoning results from its ability to extend the revealed law to new legal situations, thereby laying claim to the applicability of the divine law to legal situations not directly expressed in the material sources of the law. A textually-attested ruling is extended to a new, undecided case on account of a legal reason (*ʿilla*) common to both situations. The method of question and answer, characteristic of juridical dialectic, is used to identify the *ratio legis* (*ʿilla*) through arguments such as co-presence and co-absence (*ṭard wa-ʿaks*) and sorting and eliminating (*sabr wa-taqsīm*) (Hallaq 1987, 199–201, 205). Testing of formal consistency was deemed a reliable tool in verifying the *ratio legis* (El Shamsy 2014, 29–30, 34).[12]

Although dialectical methods to identify the *ratio legis* are used to this day, *jadal* was not without its detractors (Mahdi 1970, 59). Already al-Ḥakīm al-Tirmidhī (d. *c.* 300/917) questioned the reliability of the method of *jadal*. Likewise, the Ashʿarī Mālikī scholar Abū Bakr al-Bāqillānī (d. 403/1013) rejected the claim that *jadal* could produce proof of legal causes (El Shamsy 2014, 29, n. 49). The criticism directed against dialectic demonstratively to prove the conclusion of legal analogy reflects jurists' quest for certainty in law, that is, to arrive at rulings that are authoritative and not challengeable. Yet, the question arises, whether it is possible at all to have demonstrative proof for rulings arrived at by legal analogy? Legal propositions in Islamic law are, by nature of their sources, imprecise, usually not articulated in a general and absolute manner that permits an uncontroversial syllogistic argument (Hallaq 1985–1986, 96).

Al-Ghazālī's claim that legal analogy is the same as the Aristotelian syllogism (see below), both termed *qiyās*, was, prior to his time, rather contested. For example, the Ḥanafī Muʿtazilī al-Jaṣṣāṣ differentiates between legal analogy and the Aristotelian syllogism, saying that the relationship between the ruling of the new case (*ḥukm al-farʿ*) and that of the original case (*ḥukm al-aṣl*) is not the same as in demonstrative proof. New rulings arrived at by legal analogy are only probable (not certain), and hence open to debate and to finding different, potentially inconsistent solutions (Shehaby 1982, 41–45). Furthermore, he distin-

---

11 According to Young (2017, in particular chapters 2 and 3), who provides a detailed account of the development of dialectic in Islamic law, Muslim scholars employed dialectical methods since early Islam; he provides evidence from the second/eighth century.

12 El Shamsy suggests that applying rational as opposed to linguistic standards to the *ratio legis* may have contributed to the shift in its terminology from *maʿnā* to *ʿilla*, and from understanding the *ratio legis* as a "sign" for the ruling toward considering it a "motive" for the ruling (Zysow 1984, 374–394).

guishes the *ratio legis* in legal analogy (*qiyās sharʿī*) from the cause in syllogistic analogy (*qiyās ʿaqlī*), which he understands as the efficient cause that determines the existence of effects, whereas a legal cause (*ʿilla sharʿiyya*) does not necessitate the ruling but is only an indication or a signal for it (Bernand 1985, 632). That the causal quality of analogy and syllogism are different is also maintained by the Muʿtazilī ʿAbd al-Jabbār (d. 415/1024). He additionally points out that *qiyās sharʿī* belongs epistemologically to the realm of acquired knowledge (*ʿilm muktasab*), not necessary knowledge, and hence is uncertain and cannot lead to one, single truth (Brunschvig 1976, 2:398, 400). Abū Bakr al-Bāqillānī (d. 403/1013) similarly understands the aim of analogical reasoning in law to know something that is not known by necessity or by the senses; legal analogy, thus, results in acquired, non-necessary knowledge (Shehaby 1973, 69). Going further in denying a similarity between legal analogy and syllogistic reasoning, Ibn Ḥazm rejects the use of legal analogy (*qiyās*) altogether, saying that it cannot substitute for proof (*burhān*). The way jurists and theologians practice *qiyās*, he maintains, that is, arriving at knowledge of the hidden on the basis of the visible (*istidlāl bi'l-shāhid ʿalā'l-ghā'ib*), is simply invalid (Chejne 1984, 64–68). The logical coherence of such arguments is also questioned by Ibn Sīnā, who criticises those who think it is valid to analogise from the seen to the unseen based on signs (*ʿalāma*) (Shehaby 1973, 70).[13]

In short, the criticism levelled against legal analogy is primarily based on the epistemology of its bases as well as the structure of the procedure. Not only are the sources of analogy, that is, the premises, not certain but the inferential arguments are not fashioned along the Aristotelian syllogistic forms with three terms. As long as the conclusions of legal analogy, that is, legal rulings, are not derived according to the rules of demonstrative proof, they are not certain but contestable and revocable (van Ess 1970, 23; Brunschvig 1970, 19).[14]

The sphere of law is, however, an important arena of ordering society and a reflection of its norms and values. It therefore provides a suitable stage for the contestation over how society ought to be. In the competing world views on

---

13 Gutas' (2012, 419–420) presentation of Ibn Sīnā's understanding of such analogies seems to point to the insufficiency of "signs" to lead to conclusions, not the analogy itself. Black (2013, 120) sees Ibn Sīnā's articulation of the principles of knowledge in light of his disputes with dialectical theologians, who typically make arguments about the world of the divine in analogy to the observable world.

14 Syllogistic arguments are, however, not completely missing from the authoritative sources of the law. Gwynne (2016, 20–30, 2004, 152–169, 170–191) presents ample evidence that revelation contains arguments that can be translated into formal logical structures, in particular into the three figures of the Aristotelian syllogism as well as conjunctive and disjunctive syllogisms.

Islam of the fifth/eleventh century, one way to get the upper hand was by integrating syllogistic logic into law-finding. Providing methods of proof that are independent, logic provides instruments of thinking that are always valid (Rudolph 2005, 76, 80, 88–91). As Gutas (2002a, 281) observes, “all the sciences which actually used [logical proof] gained in respect in the eyes of the learned.” The epistemological certainty provided by syllogistic logic makes Islamic law a rational system that all reasonable people can agree upon (Carter 1997, 109). If legal analogy, the mainstay of law-finding, is structured like a syllogism, then the conclusion, namely the ruling of the undecided case (*ḥukm al-farʿ*) is (potentially) certain – and thus unassailable. The ability of Sunnī Ashʿarī jurisprudents to prove with certainty that their way of deriving law is logically sound and, thus, unchallengeable means victory against competing visions of society by detractors from among the ranks of philosophers, Muʿtazilīs, Ismāʿīlīs, and political authorities alike.[15] In this endeavour, Aristotelian syllogistic logic provided the intellectual tools. Syllogism, in Carter's words, authenticates analogy as a technique that is able to infinitely extend the finite sources of the law to meet new circumstances (Carter 1997, 104). It enables the success of the Sunnī Ashʿarī worldview of Islam and the claim that their way of law-finding[16] is certain, authoritative, and a correct representation of the divine will.

In what follows, I present how the leading Ashʿarī Shāfiʿī jurisprudent of his time, al-Ghazālī, accomplishes this feat. He employs syllogistic reasoning to establish the logical validity of legal analogy (*qiyās*), which, he maintains, is epistemologically as certain as syllogistic reasoning (*burhān*); rulings arrived in analogy to scripture are logically sound and irrefutable.

15 For examples of the challenges to Sunnī Ashʿarī legal thought from various sectarian, philosophical, and political sides, see El Shamsy 2014, 25–26; al-Ghazālī 1383/1964, 1991; Glassen (1981, 161) explicitly states that al-Ghazālī introduced logic in order to equip scholars with a weapon against the Ismāʿīlīs; Hallaq 1990, 315–319, 335; 1987b, 44, 66–67; 1984b, 685–686; Niẓām al-Mulk 1960, 208–227; Opwis 2011, 71–77, 86–92; van Ess 1970, 46–47.

16 Al-Ghazālī champions syllogistic logic not only in the discipline of law. His use of logic aimed at showing the harmony between the intellect and revelation through the methodological rapprochement between theology, jurisprudence, and philosophy, which he considers complementary to one another (Rudolph 2004, 92–93).

3 Al-Ghazālī: Demonstrating the Certainty of Legal Analogy

3.1 Legal Analogy Is Equivalent to Syllogistic Reasoning

In his final work on legal theory, *al-Mustaṣfā min ʿilm al-uṣūl*, al-Ghazālī (1993, 1:18) states that the objective of legal theory is to know how to obtain legal rulings from indicants (*iqtibās al-aḥkām min al-adilla*), namely from the Qur'an, the Sunna, and consensus. He prefaces the work with a brief introductory chapter on logical arguments.[17] One of al-Ghazālī's aims in this summary of logic is to show that legal analogy (*qiyās*) is transformable into syllogistic arguments (*barāhīn ʿaqliyya*), namely into arguments that are based on two premises (*muqaddimatān*) from which the conclusion (*natīja*) (that is, the ruling of the "new case" or the *farʿ*) logically follows.[18] Al-Ghazālī (1993, 1:117) acknowledges that jurists customarily do not structure their analogies syllogistically but instead say "date wine is inebriant, so it is prohibited in analogy to grape wine." But he insists that legal analogy nevertheless is on par with demonstrative syllogism in that both are arguments in which a specific is subsumed under a general. Like the demonstrative syllogism, legal analogy is based on two premises, each of which is composed of two parts (*juzʾān*), namely a subject (*mubtadaʾ*) and a predicate (*khabar*). The subject is what in legal terminology is the ruled upon (*maḥkūm ʿalayhi*) and the predicate is the ruling (*ḥukm*). In order to engender a demonstrative conclusion (*natīja*), one of the parts necessarily has to be repeated in both premises. The repeated element is the middle term, or in legal parlance the *ratio legis* (*ʿilla*), which answers the question "why?" in the conclusion (al-Ghazālī 1993, 1:118–119; 1390/1971, 435, 441).[19] Al-Ghazālī presents a few examples of how to structure legal analogy syllogistically. The legal ruling that date wine (*nabīdh*) is prohibited in analogy to grape wine

---

17 Although al-Ghazālī (1993, 1:30) insists upon the need to know the rules of logical arguments, he, nevertheless, understands that not everyone is interested in reading his *Introduction on Logic*, and, without further comment, tells such readers to skip ahead to the main chapters on legal theory.

18 Al-Ghazālī (1390/1971, 435–438) also addresses this topic in *Shifāʾ al-ghalīl*, in which he provides several examples, some of which I mention here. My analysis in this paper is, however, primarily based on al-Ghazālī's last work on legal theory, *al-Mustaṣfā*. Rudolph (2005, 73–97) provides a comprehensive analysis of al-Ghazālī's attitude toward logic, drawing on a much broader range of his writings than attempted here.

19 For further references on where al-Ghazālī makes the same argument, see Rudolph 2005, 78.

(*khamr*) can be expressed as a first figure syllogism (al-Ghazālī 1993, 1:116–117):[20]

I	every date wine is inebriant	← sense perception/empirical knowledge
II	every inebriant is prohibited	← text[21]
III	every date wine is prohibited[22]	

Similarly, al-Ghazālī (1993, 1:124–125) argues that the ruling that edibles are prohibited to be traded usuriously in analogy to the prohibition of quantitative increase in trading wheat (*burr*) can be expressed as:[23]

I	every wheat is edible	← sense perception/empirical knowledge
II	every wheat is usurious	← text
III	some edibles are usurious	

Not all legal analogies, however, are transformable into categorical syllogisms, especially when the premises are not formulated as universal statements, as is the case with the analogy from theft to grave robbery (al-Ghazālī 1390/1971, 435):

I	the grave robber is a thief	← experience
II	the thief's hand is cut	← text
III	the grave robber's hand is cut	

Al-Ghazālī (1390/1971, 436) admits that there is debate over the correctness of the first premise that the grave robber is a thief. In order to be an admissible premise from which a conclusion derives, it needs further support. Support for this case comes from a report by the Prophet's wife, ʿĀʾisha, who says "the thief of our dead is like the thief of our living" (al-Ghazālī 1390/1971, 437).

20 I use the Roman numerals I and II to refer to the two premises, and III to refer to the conclusion; the arrows indicate the sources of knowledge about a premise.
21 Namely the Prophetic *ḥadith* "*kull muskir ḥarām*" (al-Ghazālī 1993, 1:117). One notices that al-Ghazālī here does not need the Qur'anic prohibition of grape wine to arrive at the prohibition of date wine.
22 Al-Ghazālī (1993, 1:116) likens this syllogism to the categorical syllogism of: I every body is composite; II every composite is created in time (*ḥādith*); III every body is created in time.
23 While this syllogism leads to a valid conclusion, it does not lend itself to juridical analogy, that is, the conclusion is not logically extendable to bring forth a ruling on anything other than wheat. For ruling other edibles to be prohibited, additional evidence is needed.

In his summary of logical arguments, al-Ghazālī (1390/1971, 1:133) presents five forms of demonstrative proof (*burhān*), namely the three figures of the Aristotelian syllogism plus the conjunctive and disjunctive syllogism, saying that "any indicant (*dalīl*) that cannot be reverted to one of these five types of proof, does not produce a conclusion." As his examples in *al-Mustaṣfā*[24] illustrate, it is possible to construct legal analogy in the forms of demonstrative proof with three terms, so that the ruling for the new case is a logical conclusion of the two premises. The procedure of legal analogy is therefore established as logically valid and correct. Yet, although the structure may be the same, the conclusions of legal analogies and syllogisms differ epistemologically. Al-Ghazālī (1993, 1:120, 134; 1390/1971, 441) states that the proof (*burhān*) is certain (*qaṭʿī*) if the premises are known (*maʿlūma*); and if they are probable (*maẓnūna*), then the proof is what is accepted in law (*fiqhī*).

Legal analogy, al-Ghazālī admits, does not usually lead to certain conclusions because it is based on probable premises (al-Ghazālī 1993, 1:116–117, 134; Rudolph 2005, 77). As his examples show, one of the premises is usually known by sense perception (*ḥiss*) and experience (*tajriba*), and the other on the basis of authoritative texts that are not "objective" truths, and hence only of probable value. Al-Ghazālī (1993, 1:134) clearly expresses that conclusive proof (*burhān muntij*) can only be fashioned from definite premises (*muqaddimāt yaqīniyya*). In order for legal analogy to obtain certain, unassailable conclusions, al-Ghazālī has to prove that the authoritative bases of Islamic law, the Qur'an and *ḥadīth*, are known with certainty. For this purpose, he re-visits the epistemological status of the type of evidence that provides the basis of legal arguments. Using the tools expounded in his summary of logic, that is, definition and demonstration, al-Ghazālī presents a typology of knowledge and means of discernment that lead to necessary knowledge. He includes in the category of certain knowledge also knowledge arrived at through reflection as well as recurrent transmission (*tawātur*). In this, he departs from the view commonly held among Muslim theologians (*mutakallimūn*) that acquired knowledge (*muktasab*) is not necessary (*ḍarūrī*) and, hence, not certain (Abrahamov 1993, 20–21).[25] Instead, al-Ghazālī's theory of knowledge is heavily indebted to Ibn

24 The problematic nature of the premises of the examples listed in *Shifāʾ al-ghalīl* does not seem to be lost on al-Ghazālī. The examples of the syllogistic structure of legal analogies that he gives in *Shifāʾ al-ghalīl* generally do not show up in *al-Mustaṣfā*, where al-Ghazālī uses predominantly universal first premises.

25 Some theologians, such as the Ashʿarī Shāfiʿī al-Juwaynī, hold knowledge that results from speculation to be certain (Abrahamov 1993, 21, n. 11, 24–25). Abrahamov's detailed account of

Sīnā and the importance the latter gives to psychological factors in attaining certainty.[26]

3.2 The Premises of Legal Analogy Are Known with Certainty

Al-Ghazālī starts by looking at the meaning of certainty. Certainty (*yaqīn*), he says, is established when the soul willingly concedes veracity to a proposition (*qaḍiya*) (al-Ghazālī 1993, 1:135).[27] He distinguishes between three states of certainty: first, certainty that is safe from error,[28] such as the indisputable fact that 3 is smaller than 6, and that one person cannot be in two places simultaneously (al-Ghazālī 1993, 1:135, 138). Second, certainty that the soul verifies with decisive assent or conviction (*taṣdīq jazm, iʿtiqād jazm*), in the sense that one is confident about its correctness and feels no need for further inquiry. For example, the conviction of Muslims, Jews, and Christians that their creed and religion are true (al-Ghazālī 1993, 1:136). The third state of certainty that al-Ghazālī lists is probability (*ẓann*), namely when one feels confident about the veracity of something (al-Ghazālī 1993, 1:136–137). Al-Ghazālī concedes that in Islamic law categories two and three are deemed to constitute certain knowledge, but in reality only the first is certain, because the other two types of knowledge admit error (*ghalaṭ*) (al-Ghazālī 1993, 1:137). Knowledge that is based on matters belonging to one's religious creed or those that are only probable do not constitute premises from which immediate certain conclusions obtain (al-Ghazālī 1993, 1:138). This means that the premises used in Islamic legal analogy, that is, statements from the Qur'an and Prophetic reports, do not lead to irrefutable conclusions. Rulings (conclusions) pronounced by Islamic law on the basis of analogical reasoning are, thus, inferior in their truth-value to demonstrative truth used in philosophy and, moreover, of no higher validity than rulings (conclusions) put forward by non-Sunnī sects.

---

different theologians' typologies of necessary knowledge shows a wide variety of views, with few commonalities.

26 Rudolph (2004, 76) also points toward the affinity between al-Ghazālī and Ibn Sīnā. Gutas' (2012, 396–398) and Black's (2013, 120–142) presentation of Ibn Sīnā's categories of knowledge indicates that Ibn Sīnā obviously provides the blueprint for al-Ghazālī's interpretation, though he does not follow them precisely.

27 In legal discourse, the term *qaḍiya* is also used in reference to a legal case and its ruling.

28 Al-Ghazālī (1993, 1:135, 138) does not use a specific term apart from saying that one has certainty in the soul about the knowledge (*nafs al-yaqīn*).

Yet, when looking at the way certain knowledge is reached, one arrives at a different division of knowledge, a typology that is divided according to decisive conviction (*iʿtiqād jazm*). It is here that al-Ghazālī's epistemology displays his indebtedness to Ibn Sīnā, who, according to Black (2013, 120), "develops new accounts of the ways in which sources of cognition as diverse as sensation, introspective reflection, experience, and testimony, are able to produce certitude." Decisive conviction, al-Ghazālī (1993, 1:138) states, falls into seven divisions:[29]

1) Axiomatic knowledge (*awwaliyyāt*): certain
2) Self-awareness/internal observation (*mushāhadāt bāṭina*): certain
3) Sense perception/external observation (*maḥsūsāt ẓāhira*): certain
4) Experience/empirical knowledge (*tajriba*): certain
5) Recurrent transmission (*mutawātirāt*): certain
6) Estimations (*wahmiyyāt*): not certain
7) Widely known knowledge (*mushāharāt*): not certain

Into the first category falls axiomatic, self-evident knowledge (*awwaliyyāt*). This type of knowledge, al-Ghazālī states, is purely rational knowledge; no sense perception is involved. As an example he mentions knowledge of one's own existence; knowledge of the impossibility that two contradictory statements are both true; the knowledge that 2 is bigger than 1 (al-Ghazālī 1993, 1:138–139). The second type of conviction is obtained through inner observations or self-awareness (*al-mushāhadāt al-bāṭina*). A person knows that she is hungry, thirsty, happy, and so on – no rational investigation is needed to know it (al-Ghazālī 1993, 1:139).[30] The third category of conviction is arrived at by external sense perception or sense perception of things external to oneself (*al-maḥsūsāt al-ẓāhira*), for example, that snow is white or that the sun is shining (al-Ghazālī 1993, 1:139–141). Into the fourth category falls experience or empirical knowledge (*tajriba*),[31] such as the knowledge that fire burns and that bread satiates. Empirical knowledge is, according to al-Ghazālī, obtained from repeated observation or perception that there is an inseparable relation (*talāzum*) between the occurrences, a cause and effect (*sabab wa-musabbab*) in the sense that there is a regularity

29 When comparing al-Ghazālī's list of sources of knowledge with that of Ibn Sīnā, the affinity is apparent (Black 2013, 124; Gutas 2012, 396–398). For a detailed account of Ibn Sīnā's understanding of *awwaliyyāt*, see Gutas 2012, 397, 404–408.

30 For Ibn Sīnā's understanding of this category, which can be called self-awareness, see Gutas 2012, 402–404.

31 Al-Ghazālī expresses his arguments for empirical observation leading to certainty similarly to Ibn Sīnā (Black 2013, 128–130; Gutas 2012, 396, 398–400).

and consistency of how things customarily occur (*iṭṭirād al-ʿādāt*).[32] However, al-Ghazālī points out that since people differ in their experiences, there may be disagreement over the certainty of this type of knowledge;[33] it is often only certain to the one experiencing it (al-Ghazālī 1993, 1:141–44).[34] As the fifth type of conviction, al-Ghazālī lists recurrent transmissions (*mutawātirāt*). The existence of Mecca or of al-Shāfiʿī, or that the number of daily prayers is five are examples of such widely transmitted information. Ruling the information truthful goes beyond sense perception but is based on both sense perception and the intellect. Only with repeated instances of hearing, each instance in itself being one piece of probable evidence, is knowledge (*ʿilm*) obtained; that is, probability about the veracity of what one hears turns into knowledge (al-Ghazālī 1993, 1:144).[35]

Al-Ghazālī (1993, 1:145–153) lists two additional types of knowledge – estimations (*wahmiyyāt*) and widely accepted views (*mushāharāt*) – which he, however, disqualifies arguing that neither actually imparts knowledge.[36] In contrast, the first five modes of cognition are, according to al-Ghazālī, ways to attain true, certain knowledge, namely knowledge that is valid to be used as premises of demonstrative proofs (*muqaddimāt al-barāhīn*) (al-Ghazālī 1993, 1:154). One may say that by looking at how knowledge is obtained, al-Ghazālī provides an alternative to dividing knowledge into certainty, conviction, and probable knowledge and instead proposes that five of the seven modes of conviction lead, or have the potential to lead, to certain knowledge. Certain knowledge is not exclu-

---

32 Elsewhere, al-Ghazālī (1390/1971, 441) argues against a necessary causality between cause and effect, emphasising that while the effect (*maʿlūl*) indicates the existence of the cause (*ʿilla*), the latter does not necessitate it. In *al-Mustaṣfā*, he refers the reader to his *Tahāfut al-falāsifa*. He also uses the concept of custom to support the correctness of consensus (*ijmāʿ*) as a source of law (Hallaq 1986). For detailed analyses of al-Ghazālī's denial of necessary causality, see Dutton 2001, 30–35; Alon 1980, 397–405.

33 As Gutas (2002a, 281) points out, it was widely accepted in the medieval Arabic sciences that experience leads to certainty. Theologians, such as ʿAbd al-Jabbār and Muḥammad b. Ḥasan al-Ṭūsī (d. 460/1067), likewise consider experience part of necessary knowledge (Abrahamov 1993, 22–23).

34 See also Black 2013, 129–130.

35 Ibn Sīnā differentiates between recurrent transmission (*mutawātirāt*) and authoritative statements (*maqbūlāt*), such as Prophetic reports. This latter category of knowledge is acknowledged as truth without mediation because the adherents of that religion accept them; no syllogism can be constructed to prove a Prophetic statement (Gutas 2012, 396, 401). See also Black 2013, 132–134. Many Muslim theologians likewise considered recurrent transmission to lead to certainty, so for example al-Baghdādī (d. 428/1037) and al-Bāqillānī. They believe that the necessary knowledge of recurrent transmission is created in the person by God (Abrahamov 1993, 21–22).

36 Ibn Sīnā likewise exempts widely accepted knowledge from necessary knowledge and from being able to serve as a premise in syllogistic arguments (Black 2013, 134–136).

sively necessary (*ḍarūrī*), immediate knowledge, as many theologians hold, but includes knowledge that is arrived at by experience and observation as well as inductively gathered knowledge.

So far, al-Ghazālī has argued that legal analogy, at least in principle if not in every instance, is translatable into syllogistically structured arguments and that there are five modes of discernment that lead to certain knowledge, which include experience and recurrent knowledge. Hence, the premises used in legal analogy, namely Qur'anic statements[37] and recurrent *ḥadīth*s, constitute certain premises from which certain conclusions obtain.

Yet, the dilemma persists that most of the textual bases of analogy are not known with certainty. Rather, the majority of *ḥadīth*s, which make up the bulk of the source material of Islamic law, are classified as isolated or singular (*āḥād*) reports; only a handful of Prophetic sayings are deemed to belong to the category of recurrent *ḥadīth*s. By looking closely at how recurrent knowledge is acquired, al-Ghazālī, making use of Ibn Sīnā's epistemological system, overcomes this dilemma and in the process enlarges the scope of *tawātur* to include what customarily among jurists are considered isolated *ḥadīth*s. He does so with the following arguments, which are structured in syllogisms. It is here that we see al-Ghazālī applying syllogistic logic to render Islamic law irrefutable.

3.3 Conviction (*I'tiqād*) Leads to Certainty about Recurrent Transmission (*Tawātur*)

The discussion of *tawātur* starts with the statement, which al-Ghazālī subsequently seeks to prove, that recurrent transmission imparts knowledge (*al-tawātur yufīd al-'ilm*) (al-Ghazālī 1993, 2:131–132).[38] The first thing that he clarifies is which type of knowledge recurrent transmission (*tawātur*) engenders – is it necessary (*ḍarūrī*) or speculative (*naẓarī*) knowledge? In other words, can knowledge that is not axiomatic (*awwalī*), such as knowledge obtained through rational reflection (*naẓar*), be classified among necessary knowledge? (al-Ghazālī 1993, 2:136)

Speculative knowledge, al-Ghazālī (1993, 2:134) points out, is often thought of as allowing for probability, and hence not part of necessary, certain knowledge. Yet, contrary to common claims (al-Ghazālī 1993, 2:136), necessary knowledge, according to al-Ghazālī, is not only axiomatic or self-evident but includes

37 The Qur'an as a whole is deemed to be recurrently transmitted.

38 See also Weiss 1985, 81–105.

knowledge that is obtained through intermediary means, that is, it is acquired and needs reflection. Al-Ghazālī maintains that most mathematical knowledge, though considered immediate, is actually acquired through intermediaries. For example, knowledge of the fact that 2 equals one half of 4 is known only through an intermediary, namely the knowledge that one half equals one part of a whole, with each part being equal to the other.[39] Hence, he argues, restricting necessary knowledge to a priori knowledge, or knowledge obtained without an intermediary, is incorrect (al-Ghazālī 1993, 2:135–136). Necessary knowledge, thus, encompasses both immediate (*awwalī*) knowledge and knowledge that is arrived at through speculation (*naẓar*). Al-Ghazālī's line of reasoning can be expressed with the following syllogism:

I all necessary knowledge is certain
II some necessary knowledge is speculative knowledge
III some speculative knowledge is certain

Having established that some speculative knowledge is classifiable among necessary certain knowledge, al-Ghazālī turns his attention to the claim that recurrent transmission imparts knowledge, namely speculative knowledge obtained through intermediaries. He states that just as mathematics belongs to the category of necessary knowledge, even though it is speculative (as opposed to self-evident knowledge), so does knowledge about the veracity of recurrent reports (al-Ghazālī 1993, 2:136). And this, he says, is akin to knowledge imparted by empirical observation or experience (*tajriba*), which is based on regularity of custom (*iṭṭirād al-ʿādāt*), such as that water quenches thirst and wine inebriates (al-Ghazālī 1993, 2:136). In other words, al-Ghazālī argues that knowledge obtained from mathematical calculations, recurrent reports, and experience all impart certainty even though it is obtained through reflection.

Al-Ghazālī's line of reasoning can be expressed in the following modal syllogism. It needs to be noted that al-Ghazālī does not mention these relations as possibilities, apart from saying that the certainty obtained by experience (al-Ghazālī 1993, 1:141–144) and recurrent transmission (al-Ghazālī 1993, 2:146) may vary according to the person experiencing it.

39 The same example is used by Ibn Sīnā to differentiate between immediate, self-evident truths (*awwaliyyāt*) and principles that, as Gutas (2012, 497, 408–410) calls it, have a built-in syllogism (*muqaddamāt fiṭriyyat al-qiyās*). See also Black 2013, 125–127. Al-Ghazālī builds on Ibn Sīnā's differentiation to argue instead that some types of knowledge deemed necessary are in fact only obtained through reflection.

I speculative knowledge is possibly necessary knowledge
II recurrent transmission is speculative knowledge
III recurrent transmission is possibly necessary knowledge

The next step in al-Ghazālī's argument is to prove that recurrent transmission leads to knowledge that is on par with knowledge obtained by mathematical calculations or empirical evidence. To this end, al-Ghazālī discusses the conditions by which recurrent transmission is established.

Al-Ghazālī (1993, 2:138 – 141), building on the science of *ḥadīth* criticism, lists four conditions for considering a transmission recurrent:[40] first, the reported has to be based on knowledge (*ʿilm*), not on probability (*ẓann*). Second, the knowledge about the reported has to be necessary (*ḍarūrī*) in that it is based on sense perception (that is, hearing or *samʿ*).[41] Third, the number of people transmitting the report has to be complete (*kāmil*), or, following Weiss' translation, adequate (Weiss 1985, 88 – 89). Fourth, these three conditions have to be fulfilled at every stage of the transmission and in every generation. The first two conditions are unproblematic and agreed upon. However, there is a long-standing debate in *ḥadīth* studies and law over how many transmitters are required to establish recurrence (Hallaq 2005, 60 – 63; Kamali 2003, 94 – 95). What is an adequate or complete number? Al-Ghazālī claims that there is no specific number that engenders this knowledge. Rather, building on his above-mentioned division of sources of cognition that lead to certainty, al-Ghazālī states (1993, 2:141, 146) that a person finds in herself when completeness or adequacy of information has been reached to impart knowledge.[42] This type of knowledge, he states, although not reached through the five senses, is similar to knowledge reached about another person loving, hating, or being afraid of someone, in that it is knowledge based on indications, while each individual indication is not certain but with repetition, and when they are taken all together, conviction (*iʿtiqād*) about its truthfulness obtains (al-Ghazālī 1993, 2:142 – 143). The inner

40 See also Weiss 1985, 88 – 95.

41 Al-Ghazālī follows here the more stringent conditions for *ḥadīth* transmission that require a direct hearing (*samāʿa*). The commonly used term *ʿan* for receiving a *ḥadīth* "on the authority of" someone is ambiguous about the actual way of transmission; for details, see, for example, al-Shahrazūrī 2006, 95 – 127. Ibn Sīnā includes in the category of recurrent transmission also knowledge of historical figures and geographical facts not directly observed (Black 2013, 132).

42 Ibn Sīnā also refrains from specifying a number of transmissions that lead to certainty because "[t]he evidence that certitude has been achieved rests primarily on the psychological state of the knower – the tranquillity of her mind [...]. It is the certitude which decides the completeness of the observations, not the number of the observations" (Black 2013, 133).

conviction that knowledge about the truthfulness of a recurrent report obtains, al-Ghazālī adds, is often supported by contextual evidence (*qarīna*, pl. *qarā'in*). Contextual evidence by itself, al-Ghazālī emphasises, can engender knowledge (such as knowing that another person is afraid of someone else). Hence, hearing repeatedly a report, with or without contextual evidence to the veracity of the reported, leads to certain knowledge (al-Ghazālī 1993, 2:141–147), though how many instances of hearing a report and/or how many pieces of supportive evidence are needed to reach the state of knowledge may vary from person to person (al-Ghazālī 1993, 2:146). In short, the number of reports that impart certain knowledge differs according to situation, person, and circumstantial evidence, and it is known when one knows it.

Translated into syllogistic form, al-Ghazālī's argument would look like this:

I adequate information leads to inner conviction (*iʿtiqād*)
II inner conviction leads to certainty
III adequate information leads to certainty

Al-Ghazālī (1993, 2:141) defends the logical correctness of his argument that hearing something for an unspecified but adequate number leads to certain knowledge with the following conjunctive syllogism, saying that:

I	if an adequate number has been reached, knowledge obtains	← experience
II	we know that knowledge has been obtained	← conviction/internal observation
III	an adequate number has been reached	

Al-Ghazālī here follows closely Ibn Sīnā's understanding of the role of self-awareness or consciousness to produce certain knowledge. The role of the intellect is decisive in transforming experience and recurrent transmission into certain knowledge. As Black (2013, 140) puts it, "Avicenna suggests that certitude is always marked by an inner feeling of confidence or conviction that functions as the primary indicator that actual knowledge has been attained." She calls it second-order belief, or "knowing that one knows" (Black 2013, 122). For Ibn Sīnā, the mental state of certainty means that it is certainty of something, namely an intelligible already present in the knower.[43] This state of certainty does not

43 Gutas interprets Ibn Sīnā's epistemology not so much in terms of the psychological state of the person but emphasises the role of experience, that is, testing and proving. Through testing

depend on any articulation of why one is certain but only that it is so – and this is known through self-awareness (Black 2013, 138–141).

In his discussion of certainty and *tawātur*, al-Ghazālī adopts a definition[44] of what belongs to the category of certain knowledge that enables him to include in it not only axiomatic or self-evident knowledge but also speculative knowledge (*naẓarī*). Knowledge arrived at by recurrent transmission is based on some form of inductive accumulation of evidence upon which one has to reflect. It is not tied to a specific number of pieces of evidence[45] but rather is obtained by reaching internal conviction, namely conviction that one knows with certainty the truth-value of the reported.[46] In al-Ghazālī's typology, knowledge reached by recurrent transmission (*tawātur*) is incorporated into internal observation (*mushāhadāt bāṭina*) and is epistemologically as certain as the knowledge that one is hungry or angry. Being certain, knowledge obtained on account of recurrent reports is, thus, unassailable.

Although al-Ghazālī does not explicitly say so, his argument has far-reaching implications in the area of law-finding. His definition of certain knowledge affects the epistemological status of the sources of law and the rulings derived therefrom. In al-Ghazālī's interpretation, the Qur'an and recurrent *ḥadīth*s as sources of knowledge lead to certain, necessary knowledge (*tawātur* yields *ʿilm ḍarūrī yaqīnī*), the truthfulness of which is not objectively verifiable but determined in the mind (soul) of a person, subjectively.[47] It is reached upon a person's "knowledge" or "conviction" that a report is true.

---

and proving one attributes to the observed occurrence an intrinsic cause (Gutas 2012, 399). Hence, one may say, the knowledge arrived at through experience (*tajriba*) is verified through syllogistic reasoning, though one may not be aware of it, but one knows that one knows. McGinnis emphasises that for Ibn Sīnā experience (*tajriba*) leads to certain knowledge on account of knowing the intrinsic relationship that belongs to the nature of the thing observed, such as purging belonging to the nature of scammony. Experience does not explain why the relationship is as it is, only that it is such (McGinnis 2003, 320–325).

44 Al-Ghazālī (1993, 2:135–136) points out that depending on one's definition of *ḍarūrī* and *naẓarī* one arrives at a different understanding of these matters.

45 Al-Ghazālī's argument means that incomplete induction can lead to definite conclusions.

46 Ibn Ḥazm has a similar typology of necessary knowledge, in which conviction that something is according to its real state constitutes certainty. Certainty is reached by immediate understanding, sense perception, demonstration, and beliefs that God enjoins one to follow; the latter include transmitted reports (Abrahamov 1993, 24–25).

47 Nuseibeh (1989, 39, 52–53) argues that Ibn Sīnā's theory of knowledge is fundamentally subjective and unverifiable, though not anti-empiricist or anti-inductivist. He also points out the similarities between the epistemology of Ibn Sīnā and al-Ghazālī. Black (2013, 122–123, 140–141) stresses that for Ibn Sīnā the conviction that knowledge or certainty exists is not just a subjective belief but that Ibn Sīnā holds that there must be something present in the intellect,

Taken to its logical conclusion, even a single instance of hearing a report can engender certainty about its veracity in the hearer.[48] As mentioned above, in his analysis of certainty al-Ghazālī proclaimed that experience (*tajriba*) may lead to certain knowledge, even if only certain to the person experiencing it. Hence, if my experience tells me that a particular person only tells the truth, I believe her report with certainty. Certainty and truth is thus no longer objectively verifiable but a subjective "feeling."

Moreover, without having a specific requirement for when recurrent reports are deemed certain, other than the fact that a person evaluating them obtains certain knowledge through inner conviction that the report is true, a Prophetic report that some designate as a singular *ḥadīth* of probable knowledge may be deemed by others to be certain, as long as that person knows or has conviction that it is certain. This means that legal analogies, such as prohibiting date wine in analogy to grape wine, are based on certain knowledge, that is, on *ḥadīth*s or statements that in the mind of the examiner are certain, irrespective of whether they are recurrent (*mutawātir*) or singular (*aḥad*).[49] The two premises of legal analogy – one based on a text, the other on empirical observation or sense perception – are thus both certain and yield a certain conclusion. Al-Ghazālī, thus, demonstrates that legal analogical reasoning, just as syllogistic arguments, leads to certain knowledge. Rulings arrived at in analogy to the authoritative sources are irrefutable. In his case for the certainty of legal analogy, al-Ghazālī successfully accomplishes his aim to use logic in the defence of religion (Marmura 1975, 101). The Sunnī Ashʿarī interpretation of the law is logically sound and safe from challenges, and the jurists' position as shapers of society is thereby successfully defended.

4 Concluding Reflections

Syllogistic logic was integrated into Islamic legal theory in the fifth/eleventh century. This process is associated in particular with al-Ghazālī, though he clearly had predecessors. There is no single causal explanation of why it hap-

namely a first-order belief, on which this second-order belief is based. This concurs with Gutas' (2012, 399–400) finding that the truth-value of empirical observation is based on "a syllogism which attributes the observed repeated occurrence to an intrinsic cause."

48 This could be made by a syllogism such as the following: I: People know with certainty that recurrent reports are true; II: This is a recurrent report; III: This report is true with certainty.

49 Ibn Ḥazm also holds that even singular *ḥadīth*s are necessary knowledge (Abrahamov 1993, 25).

pened at this point in time. Yet, some light is shed by looking at how syllogistic logic was used and to what end. Syllogistic logic produces certain conclusions. The quest for arriving at certain, rationally unchallengeable answers is evident in many of the intellectual debates of the time. Al-Ghazālī employs logical arguments to fend off claims and challenges by Ismāʿīlīs as well as to contradict the claims of the philosophers; Ibn Ḥazm similarly uses logic as a tool in his polemics with other Muslims as well as Jews and Christians (Chejne 1984, 58, 62). Both deemed syllogistics superior to the dialectical method. In addition, the political situation of the time of al-Ghazālī was such that the *ʿulamāʾ* had to push back against claims by secular authorities (a still strong Seljuk empire) over the sphere of law. Al-Juwaynī's discussion on the existence of *mujtahids* fits into that intellectual environment as well (Hallaq 1984a, 26–41). With logic as their tool, jurists are able to independently verify the premises of legal analogy without having to take recourse to already established doctrines. Logic, thus, becomes a means to shun *taqlīd* (Rudolph 2005, 80) and is, not surprisingly, championed by proponents of *ijtihād*, such as Ibn Ḥazm and al-Ghazālī (Chejne 1984, 62, 68). While the aim of employing logic in legal reasoning lies in ascertaining its conclusions, it also served to prove the validity of the sources of the law. Al-Ghazālī enlarges the subject matter of legal analogy that leads to valid results by arguing for the certainty, or potential certainty, of the premises, namely the individual *ḥadīth*s. His emphasis on the psychological factors of establishing certainty puts the focus not so much on the source of law itself as on the interpreters of the sources, the *ʿulamāʾ*. They are the ones who know with certainty that the sources of the law and the analogies derived therefrom are true. Combining logic and Ibn Sīnā's theory of knowledge, al-Ghazālī proved that the Ashʿarī Sunnī interpretation of the divine will for Muslim society leads to irrefutable knowledge. Yet, the effects of integrating logic into Islamic law are mainly felt in the area of legal theory. Legal practice remains largely untouched. As Hallaq (1997, 142) says, "it is hard to discern the presence of formal logic in the reasoning exercised by judges and jurisconsults with regard to ordinary, day-to-day problems arising in Muslim societies." The practical application of law does not seem to need logic after all.

Joep Lameer

Deontic Modalities in Ibn Ḥazm

1 Introduction

To this day, not much has been written about obligations, permissions, and prohibitions in Islamic law and their place in medieval Arabic logic.[1] As is well known, Aristotelian modal logic centres around the concepts of necessity, possibility, and impossibility, whereas in deontic (normative) logic the key notions are obligation, permission, and prohibition:[2]

Aristotelian modal logic	Necessary	(N)	"Modalities"
	Possible	(P)	Qualify propositions, e.g. "Np", "IMp"
	Impossible	(I)	
Deontic logic	Obligatory	(OB)	
	Permissible	(PE)	
	Impermissible	(IM)	

Fig. 1: Aristotelian vs. deontic modalities.

This is an enlarged version of a lecture given in January 2017 in the Médiathèque Marguerite Duras in Paris. I hereby thank Ali Benmakhlouf of Université Paris-Est Créteil and Marc Pavlopoulos of the Collège International de Philosophie for kindly allowing me to publish this lecture in the present volume. I should also like to thank Peter Adamson for his important comments on an earlier version.

1 The only relevant publications that I know of are Mikhail 2004, referred to in note 33 below; Auda 1428/2007, 237, where he says that Georg H. von Wright's "law of commitment" which states that "If doing what we ought to do commits us to do something else, then this new act is also something that we ought to do" is identical to the rule stating "*mā lā yatimmu al-wājib illā bihi fa-huwa wājib*" in Islamic law; Lameer 1994, 239–256, mentioned below in reference to al-Fārābī.

2 For a general outline of deontic logic and its relation to classical modal logic, see McNamara 2014. It should be noted that Ibn Ḥazm would not recognise the normative statuses of "permissible" (PE) and "omissible" (OM) as defined in section 1.2 of that article; on permission in Ibn Ḥazm see also below.

https://doi.org/10.1515/9783110552386-008

In contradistinction to Aristotelian modal logic, deontic logic is a relative newcomer in the field. According to the Finnish philosopher and logician Georg Henrik von Wright (1916 – 2003), the Austrian Ernst Mally (1879 – 1944) must be considered the first to have taken upon himself the task of a systematic exploration and development of its rules, even if some of its elements are already to be found in the work of the British philosopher Jeremy Bentham (1748 – 1832). Yet, as also stated by von Wright, contemporary deontic logic is not founded upon the works of either Bentham or Mally. Rather, it is based on the idea that a comparison can be made between the concepts of necessity, possibility, and impossibility as operative in modal logic and the notions of obligation, permission, and prohibition that are at the heart of a logic of norms. In the view of von Wright, Gottfried Wilhelm Leibniz (1646 – 1716) deserves the credit for having been the first to suggest collating the Aristotelian modalities with the modalities as operative in a system of natural law, making him the first representative of an approach to the logic of norms that led to the emergence of modern deontic logic as an offshoot of modal logic. Nevertheless, contemporary deontic logic developed independently from the work of Leibniz; indeed, its founding fathers appear to have been unaware even of the existence of his views (von Wright 1981, 3).

In his article "The Emergence of Deontic Logic in the Fourteenth Century", another Finnish philosopher and logician, Simo Knuuttila, traces the beginnings of deontic logic as an offshoot of modal logic still further back in time. He does this by drawing attention to a number of fourteenth-century writers such as Robert Holcot (d. 1349) and Roger Rosetus (fl. c. 1335), who discussed problems concerning conditional obligations and permissions in a way similar to Aristotle's statements on the basic rules of inference in modal logic as found in the *Prior Analytics* and the *Metaphysics*. Indeed, Robert Holcot even explicitly raises the question of whether or not the rule of inference concerning necessity statements de dicto $(p \rightarrow q) \rightarrow (Np \rightarrow Nq)$ also applies in the case of obligations. In other words: $(p \rightarrow q) \rightarrow (Op \rightarrow Oq)$? (Knuuttila 1981, 225 – 226, 240).

According to Knuuttila, this emerging interest in deontic theory was the result of a change in ethical paradigm, which from the end of the thirteenth century onwards came to be based on the assertion of free will, leading to a need to investigate how to direct one's will in such a way as to live in accordance with the divine law and thereby secure one's place in the hereafter. Before then, thinkers such as Thomas Aquinas (d. 1274) were of the opinion that what the virtuous man wills is an immutable dictate of practical reason as a function of a disposition to being virtuous, a dictate which the virtuous man, qua being virtuous, cannot possibly overrule. In other words: where in the days of Aquinas virtuous conduct was regarded as a function of moral *dispositions* as immanent in the individual, from the end of the thirteenth century it came to be looked upon as a function of one's observation of an external set of *rules* on the basis of *free choice*. And it is this change of focus from living according to one's moral dispositions to acting voluntarily in accordance with a code of norms, which according to Knuuttila led to a rising interest in what exactly this code of norms *implies*, an interest that is reflected in the writings of Robert Holcot and Roger Rosetus referred to earlier (Knuuttila 1981, 232–235).

2 Deontic Modalities in Medieval Islam

2.1 Earliest mention in al-Fārābī

In view of these considerations, it might seem that there is little hope of moving the beginnings of deontic logic as an offshoot of modal logic further back in time to a period in which the aforementioned change in ethical paradigm had not yet come about, which is, roughly speaking, to a period before the end of the thirteenth century. It is therefore not without significance that contrary to the situation in medieval Christian thought, it is already as early as the first half of the tenth century that we find the Islamic philosopher Abū Naṣr al-Fārābī (d. c. 339/950) drawing a parallel between the Aristotelian modalities and the deontic modalities of Islamic law.[3] But in his case it was not a change of ethical paradigm, but rather his commentary on Aristotle's *De Interpretatione* which made him briefly refer to the subject. Unfortunately, his remarks, made in the opening lines of his commentary on *De Interpretatione* 12 21a 34–37,[4] are very concise and limited to the suggestion that obligation, permission, and prohibition are somehow on a par with necessity, possibility, and impossibility:[5]

3 This means that Ibn Ḥazm was not the first to discuss this matter, as claimed in Auda 1428/2007, 207. His suggestion there that Ibn Ḥazm could have borrowed from al-Ghazālī (d. 505/1111) ignores the fact that when Ibn Ḥazm passed away in 456/1064, al-Ghazālī was just six years old.

4 For the Greek text, see Aristotle 1974, 49–72; for the English translation, see Aristotle 1963, 59: "Having cleared up these points, we must consider how negations and affirmations of the possible to be and the not possible are related to one another, and of the admissible and not admissible, and about the impossible and the necessary. For there are some puzzles here." In the Arabic logical tradition from al-Fārābī onward, the term "admissible" (*yaḥtamil*, for Aristotle's *endechomenon*) plays no role in discussions on the possible as a modal concept, which limit themselves to the use of *mumkin* ("possible", Arist. *dynaton*), and concerning which Aristotle had also said: "From 'possible to be' follow 'admissible to be' (and, reciprocally, the former from the latter)" (Aristotle 1974, 13 22a 15–16; Aristotle 1963, 61 (English)).

5 Al-Fārābī 1960, 163.8–164.1; al-Fārābī 1981, 158 (English), here quoted with some changes and the addition of Arabic terminology between brackets.

> Aristotle now begins to examine modal statements (*al-qaḍāyā dhawāt al-jihāt*). Modes are expressions which, when linked with the hyparctic verb (*kalima wujūdiyya*) or verb containing the force of the hyparctic verb, signify how the predicate holds of the subject. For there are many ways in which a predicate can hold of a subject, as in "laudably (*jamīl*), Zayd is just" (...) – "deplorably (*qabīḥ*), 'Amr is unjust" (...) "Laudably" and "deplorably" signify how the predicate holds of the subject. Similarly words expressing "impermissible" (*ḥarām*) and "permissible" (*ḥalāl*), as in "It is impermissible (*ḥarām 'alayhi*) that Zayd take away someone else's money" and "It is permissible (*ḥalāl lahu*) or allowed (*mubāḥ lahu*) that Zayd do this or that". Similarly words like "ought to" (*yanbaghī*), "must" (*yajib*), "makes a good job of" (*yuḥsin*). For all these are modes added to verbs.
>
> There are primary and secondary modes. Examples of the secondary modes are the ones we have just enumerated. Of primary modes there are two: the possible (*al-mumkin*) and the necessary (*al-ḍarūrī*). There are many things related either to the possible – such as "it is admissible" (*yaḥtamil*), "it is conceivable" (*yajūzu*) – or to the necessary – such as "impossible" (*mumtani'*), "absurd" (*muḥāl*) and the like.
>
> Since it is Aristotle's aim to consider modal statements, he makes it his principal purpose to examine the primary modes, namely the possible (*al-mumkin*) with its concomitants and the necessary (*al-ḍarūrī*) with its concomitants and correlates. He omits to enumerate the secondary modes because the same account holds of them as of the primary modes.

So, in the above, there is a suggestion of a parallel between the deontic modalities of "permissible" and "impermissible", on the one hand, and what is possible or necessary, on the other. But I do not think that al-Fārābī's broad remark that of "the secondary modes (...) the same account holds (...) as of the primary modes", is by itself enough to posit a system of deontic modalities and their relations that would mimic the modalities of the *De Interpretatione* and their relations. Also, in his commentary, al-Fārābī understands possibility in a way that is not compatible with the common understanding of permission in Islamic law. This is because, as we shall see below, for Aristotle – and with him, al-Fārābī – what is possible to be is equivalent to that which is not impossible to be,[6] which, in Islamic law, then would mean that the permissible stands for all that which is not impermissible, the obligatory included. Such an understanding of permission, however, goes against the very nature of permission in Islamic law (explicit or implicit), which stands for the optional alone. Furthermore, in the one place where one would have hoped to find al-Fārābī elaborate,

6 See below Table 2 and Figure 3, with Aristotle 1974, 13 22b 10–28, 1963, 63; al-Fārābī 1960, 179.18–28, 190.8–191.2; al-Fārābī 1981, 173, 183–184. In his short treatise on the *De Interpretatione* called *Kitāb al-'Ibāra*, al-Fārābī (1985, 133–163, at 155.9) mentions the deontic *yanbaghī* ("ought") among the modalities, while prohibition and permission are left unmentioned. Also, nothing is said about modal relations other than that some senses of the possible comprise the necessary and vice versa (al-Fārābī 1985, 162.15–163.5). This being so, not much can be deduced from this treatise.

which is his discussion of legal inferences in his *Kitāb al-Qiyās al-ṣaghīr*, nothing is said at all (Lameer 1994, 233–258). On the contrary, legal inferences are treated there as if they follow the rules of Aristotelian predicate logic – which they do not[7] – while the discussions do not go beyond literal, amplified, or restricted applications of individual legal norms, without informing us in any way about the interdefinability of obligations, permissions, and prohibitions. So, at the time when he wrote his *Kitāb al-Qiyās al-ṣaghīr*, al-Fārābī did not have the deontic modalities in mind, while his commentary on Aristotle's *De Interpretatione* does not allow us to go beyond his rather broad statement that of "the secondary modes (...) the same account holds (...) as of the primary modes."[8]

It seems that al-Fārābī came to make the comparison between the Aristotelian and the deontic modalites by interpolation of Ammonius' use of the adverb *kalōs* ("well", adj. *kalos*, "good") as an example of a modal qualification in the latter's commentary on *De Int.* 12 21a 34–37 (Ammonius 1897, 214.27), a commentary which al-Fārābī knew at least indirectly.[9] For in the above quotation from his commentary on this same passage, al-Fārābī uses the words *jamīl* ("good")[10] and its opposite *qabīḥ* ("bad") side by side with the juridical concepts of *ḥalāl* ("permissible") and *ḥarām* ("impermissible"). On the other hand, there is also a possible influence from the occurrence of the term *wājib* for *anagkaion* ("necessary") in the Arabic translation of the *De Interpretatione*, for instance at *De Int.* 12 21b 26 (Aristotle 1948–1952, 1:87.18).[11] This is because in Islamic law *wājib* is one of the terms – the other being *farḍ* – used for "obligatory" (EI2, "Farḍ"). This may then also explain how, at the end of the first paragraph of the above quotation from

7 See Lameer 1994, 244–245 for a critical discussion of this matter, the basic point being that propositions in predicate logic have a truth value (true/false), while deontic propositions have none. Also, the deontic modalities are to be understood as logical operators which qualify propositions as a whole, just like the traditional modalities do, and are therefore not predicates, as believed by al-Fārābī.

8 Unfortunately, the part on modal syllogistics of al-Fārābī's large commentary on Aristotle's *Prior Analytics* is lost, so that we do not know if he brought up the parallel between the deontic and the Aristotelian modalities there. Still, his commentary on the *De Interpretatione* gives no reason to suspect that he treated the matter any different in that work. On this commentary and some surviving quotations from the lost part on modal syllogistics, see Lameer 1994, 7–9.

9 On al-Fārābī's partial and indirect dependence on the commentary by Ammonius, see al-Fārābī 1981, xcii–xcv.

10 In the Arabic translations of Greek philosophical works available to me, the connection *jamīl–kalōs* (adverb) could not be documented. But the connection *jamīl–kalos* (adjective) is for instance found in the Arabic translation of Aristotle's *Rhetoric* (Aristotle 1982, 2:80).

11 See also Aristotle 1913, 25.17.

his commentary, al-Fārābī came to use a deontic *yajib* ("must") and *yanbaghī* ("ought") as secondary modes that come under the primary mode *ḍarūrī* ("necessary"). However this may be, I think that the influence from Ammonius, even if indirect, was decisive here.

2.2 Ibn Ḥazm: a Ẓāhirī account

After al-Fārābī, the second earliest Muslim author known to have suggested that a parallel might be drawn between the modalities of Aristotelian logic and the deontic qualifications of "obligatory", "permissible", and "impermissible" is the Andalusian polymath Ibn Ḥazm (d. 456/1064), who earned his fame as a poet, historian, theologian, jurist, and minor philosopher (EI2, "Ibn Ḥazm").[12] The comparison in question is found in his treatise on Aristotelian logic, *al-Taqrīb li-ḥadd al-manṭiq* (*A Clarification of the Essence of Logic*).[13] Even if he did study logic in the tradition of the Baghdad school in logic as represented by Abū Bishr Mattā b. Yūnus and al-Fārābī (Lameer 2013, 417–428), Ibn Ḥazm was not a logician, but mostly a jurist and theologian. As such, he is especially known as a representative of the Ẓāhirī school, which propagated a literal interpretation of the Qur'an and the traditions (EI2 "al-Ẓāhiriyya").

Before going into Ibn Ḥazm and the deontic modalities, it may be helpful to first cast Aristotle's statements on the modalities into a number of tables and figures. Aristotle discusses the modalites in various places, one of them being his *De Interpretatione* 12 and 13. As this is the only work to be linked to statements associating the deontic with the Aristotelian modalities in al-Fārābī and Ibn Ḥazm, this is the only text by Aristotle that I shall refer to in what follows. Aristotle's initial representation of the modalities there is as shown below:

12 See also Adang, Fierro, and Schmidtke 2013, with a bibliography of secondary sources by Leigh Chipman on pages 761–787.

13 Ibn Ḥazm 1980–1983, 4:93–356: *Kitāb al-Taqrīb li-ḥadd al-manṭiq wa'l-mudkhal ilayhi bi'l-alfāẓ al-ʿāmmiyya wa'l-amthila al-fiqhiyya*. I have not seen the edition by ʿAbd al-Ḥaqq al-Turkumānī (Beirut: Dār Ibn Ḥazm, 2007).

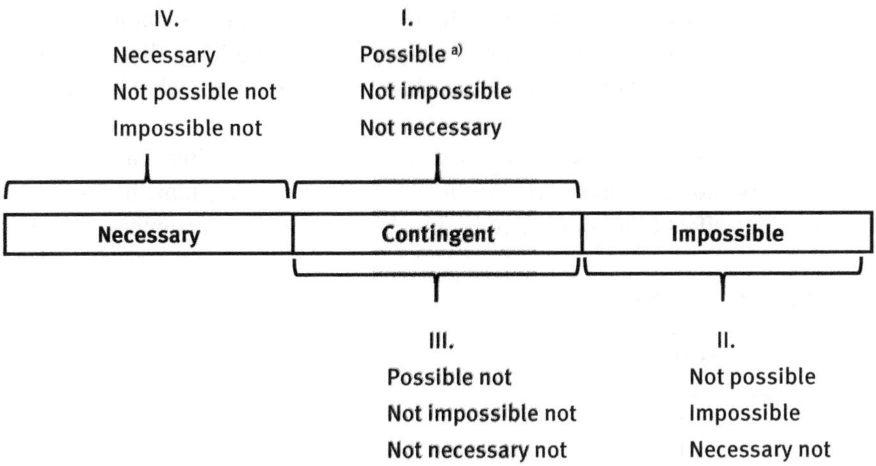

[a] Comprises both the possible (*dynaton*) and the admissible (*endechomenon*), which Aristotle uses side by side in *De Int.* 13 22a 14–34, after which they coalesce into the possible (*dynaton*) in the remainder of that chapter.

Fig. 2: Modalities in *De Int.* 13 22a 14–22b 10.

The above figure is based on the following table of equivalences, cited and explained in *De Int.* 13 22a 14–22b 10 (with the sign "=" denoting equivalence and "~" denoting negation):[14]

Tab. 1: Equivalences between the modalities in *De Int.* 13 22a 14–22b 10; possible = not impossible = not necessary.

I.	P	=	~I	=	~N
II.	~P	=	I	=	N~
III.	P~	=	~I~	=	~N~
IV.	~P~	=	I~	=	N

In the above table, "possible to be" in row I is equivalent with "not impossible to be" and also with "not necessary to be", and thus only comprises contingent relations, as is also shown in Figure 2. Similarly for what is "possible not to be" in row III and for their negations in rows II and IV, respectively. This understanding of possibility is called "two-sided" possibility. It should be noted that possibility as

14 For the English, see Aristotle 1963, 61–62.

the negation of necessity and impossibility is based on the assumption that if someone says that something is "not impossible" without adding that it is necessary, such a state of affairs is simply possible; and similarly for what is "not necessary."[15]

The above representation conflicted with Aristotle's earlier statements on contradictory modal propositions in *De Int.* 12,[16] prompting him, in *De Int.* 13 22b 10–28, to effect a minor change in the above table of equivalences, like so:[17]

Tab. 2: Equivalences between the modalities in *De Int.* 13 22b 10–28; possible = not impossible.

I.	P	=	~I	=	~N~
II.	~P	=	I	=	N~
III.	P~	=	~I~	=	~N
IV.	~P~	=	I~	=	N

In this arrangement, in which ~N~ and ~N of rows I and III have changed places, rows I and II and rows III and IV now contain three pairs of opposites, in addition to each of them representing a series of equivalences. In the above table, "possible to be" is equivalent with "not impossible to be" (that is, "not necessary not to be") and thus accommodates contingent and necessary relations. Similarly, for what is "possible not to be", which accommodates contingent and impossible relations. This understanding of possibility is called "one-sided" possibility and can be represented as follows:

15 See Jaakko Hintikka, *Time and Necessity: Studies in Aristotle's Theory of Modality* (Oxford: Clarendon Press, 1973), 47 § 5.

16 For the English, see Aristotle 1963, 59–61.

17 For the English, see Aristotle 1963, 63.

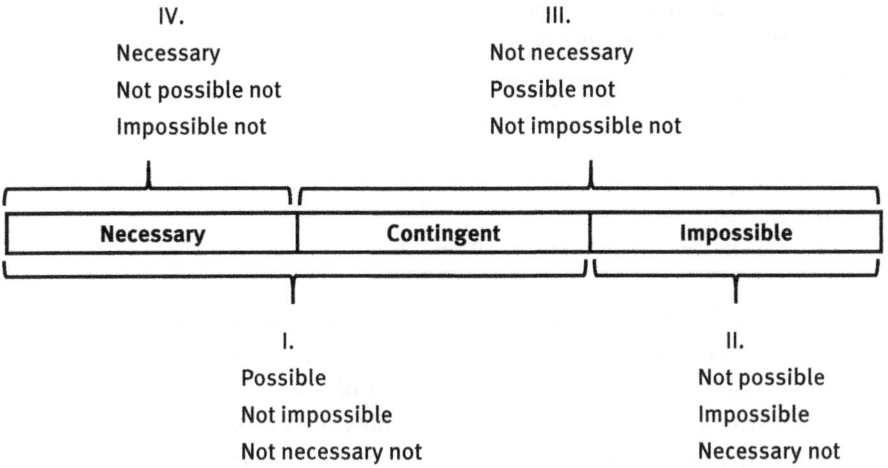

Fig. 3: Modalities in *De Int.* 13 22b 10–28; possible = not impossible.

This much for a very basic outline of the relations between necessity, possibility, and impossibility in Aristotle's *De Interpretatione*. Let us now turn to Ibn Ḥazm. In the *De Interpretatione* part of the *Taqrīb*, Ibn Ḥazm (1980–1983, 4:195.12, 15, 17) makes a distinction between statements regarding possible (*mumkin*), necessary (*wājib*), and impossible (*mumtaniʿ*) relations. For him, the possible stands for that which may or may not be, but which as yet has not come to be (Ibn Ḥazm 1980–1983, 4:195.15, 196.17–18),[18] which comprises both the future being (or not-being) of what currently *is not*, and the future not-being (or being) of what currently *is*. This possibility corresponds to two-sided possibility of Table 1 and Figure 2.

Ibn Ḥazm (1980–1983, 4:214.10–18) posits the following equivalences (*mutalāʾimāt*) between the modalities, where the members of each row are said to be compatible in meaning (*muttafiqāt al-maʿānī*):[19]

18 195.15: "*wa-immā mumkin, wa-huwa alladhī qad yakūnu wa-qad lā yakūnu*", "or possible, which is that which may or may not be"; 4: 196.17–18: "*al-mumkin fa-lam yaʾti baʿd*", "the possible [is that which] has not yet come to be."

19 The division of the table into six lines merely copies the layout of the edition.

Tab. 3: Equivalences between the modalities according to Ibn Ḥazm; possible = contingent.

1.	P	=	~I	=	~N	=	~N~				
2.	N~	=	I	=	~P						
3.	~N	=	~N~								
4.	~I	=	~I~								
5.	P	=	P~								
6.	~N	=	~N~	=	~I	=	~I~	=	P	=	P~

Even if the way of presentation is different, one can see that there is a partial overlap with Table 1. Lines 1 and 2 of Table 3 coincide with rows I and II of Table 1, the only difference being the addition of ~N~ in line 1. However, given that, on a two-sided interpretation of possibility, P is taken to connote P~ and vice versa, this is certainly permissible.[20] Lines 3 to 5 in Table 3 are nothing but a listing of the connoted equivalences between the members of rows I and III of Table 1. Line 6, finally, is a statement on the connoted equivalences between the members of all of lines 3 to 5; that is, between the members of rows I and III of Table 1. Ibn Ḥazm makes no separate mention of the members of row III in Table 1. Also, the members of row IV in Table 1 are entirely absent from Table 3. These two matters will be discussed presently.

In addition to the above, Ibn Ḥazm (1980 – 1983, 4:195.12 – 19) also posits the following parallels between the Aristotelian and the deontic modalities:[21]

(1) Necessary (N) (*wājib*) – Obligatory (OB) (*farḍ, lāzim*)
(2) Possible (P) (*mumkin*) – Permissible (PE) (*ḥalāl, mubāḥ*)
(3) Impossible (I) (*mumtaniʿ*) – Impermissible (IM) (*ḥarām, maḥẓūr*)

He further states very clearly that the relation between obligations, permissions, and prohibitions is a relation of exclusive disjunction, that is, a disjunction of

20 See also Aristotle 1974, 12 21b 35 – 37 (Aristotle 1963, 61: "'possible to be' and 'possible not to be' may be thought to actually follow from one another. For it is possible for the same thing to be and not to be").

21 From among the legal qualifications, *mubāḥ* is further subdivided into *mubāḥ mustaḥabb* ("recommended"), *mubāḥ mustawin* ("indifferent") and *mubāḥ makrūh* ("disapproved"), which are then compared with the probable (*mumkin qarīb*), possibility proper (*mumkin maḥḍ*), and the improbable (*mumkin baʿīd*) (Ibn Ḥazm 1980 – 1983, 4: 195.20 – 196.5). This latter distinction appears to go back (via the Baghdad school in logic; see al-Fārābī 1960, 95.1 – 5, with al-Fārābī 1981, 89 – 90) to Ammonius 1897, 142.1 – 5, where the distinction is between the possible "for the most part" (*hōs epi to polu*), the "equally" (*epi isēs*) possible, and a "minor" possibility (*ep' elatton*).

which only one member can be true at any one time (Ibn Ḥazm 1980 – 1983, 4:250.5 – 8).[22] This disjunction can be symbolised as follows, although its being exclusive is not implied in the formula, deriving as it does from "additional information" (with the sign "v" for "or"):

(4) (OB v PE v IM)

Also, in his discussion of the various ways of taking an indication (*dalīl*) from the texts (*naṣṣ*, that is, the Qur'an or the Prophetic traditions) in his *al-Iḥkām fī uṣūl al-aḥkām* (1345 – 1347, 5:106.18 – 21), Ibn Ḥazm says the following:

> Fourthly, there is the case in which all the members [of a division] are false, save one, which therefore is the one that holds. For instance, a particular thing is prohibited, obligatory, or permitted, each with its own legal consequences. Now, if it is neither obligatory nor prohibited, it must be permitted and have the applicable legal consequence, or else his [that is, the Prophet's] words would allow for a disjunction all of whose members are false, and thus be false [themselves].[23]

In my view, this means that the disjunction (OB v PE v IM) is proven to be exhaustive by means of a dogmatic *reductio ad impossibile*.

So, according to Ibn Ḥazm, OB, PE, and IM are all the legal qualifications that we have; also, they stand in a relation of exclusive disjunction, which means that only one member can be true at any one time. If we assert PE, for instance, this means that the other two disjuncts must be negated, while the joint negation of those two disjuncts too, implies the assertion of PE, implying that they are equivalent (with the sign "&" for "and"):

(5) PE = (~OB & ~IM)

---

22 The disjuncts are described as being in "complete opposition" (*tāmma al-taʿānud*), which implies that they are mutually exclusive. Note that Ibn Ḥazm explicitly declares that this disjunction is complete (*tāmma mustawfāh*), that is, that there are no alternatives other than the three qualifications mentioned. In the passage concerned he divides *mubāḥ* into its three subcategories of *mubāḥ mustawin*, *mubāḥ mustaḥabb*, and *mubāḥ makrūh* (see previous footnote); for the purposes of the above discussions, however, this makes no difference, the general idea being one of an exclusive disjunction between OB, PE, and IM. That the five qualifications that result if we subdivide *mubāḥ* into its subcategories are all in exclusive conjunction is confirmed by Ibn Ḥazm 1980 – 1983, 4:250.5 – 8.

23 In the edition, the text is given as follows:

ورابعها اقسام تبطل كلها الا واحداً فيصح ذلک الواحد مثل ان يكون هذا الشيء اما حرام فله حكم كذا، واما فرض فله حكم كذا،
واما مباح فله حكم كذا، فليس فرضا ولا حراما فهو مباح له حكم كذا او يكون قوله يقتضى اقساما كلها فاسد فهو قول فاسد.

This means that the kind of possibility of Table 1 is no longer valid. For according to the above, we should *not* write, after Table 1, rows I and III, Table 3, line 6, and the stated correspondences between P, N, I and PE, OB, and IM:

(6) PE = ~OB = ~IM
(7) PE~ = ~OB~ = ~IM~

But rather:

(8) PE = (~OB & ~IM)
(9) PE~ = (~OB~ & ~IM~)

In other words, each of PE, ~OB, and ~IM would no longer be equivalent with each of the other two separately; rather, in each case and more generally speaking, one of PE, OB, or IM would only be equivalent with the conjunction of the negations of the other two. And similarly for PE~, OB~, and IM~ and their negations. This would mean that Ibn Ḥazm's understanding of permission would not adequately reflect his earlier understanding of possibility in Aristotle. But is this so? I think the answer to this question must be in the negative. This is so because in his *al-Iḥkām fī uṣūl al-aḥkām* mentioned earlier and written after the *Taqrīb*,[24] Ibn Ḥazm says, in his extensive discussion of *ijmāʿ* (legal consensus): "their claim that this matter receives no mention in the texts, is void of meaning (...) because all that which the Almighty God has not declared forbidden through the mouth of His Prophet, He actually permitted" (Ibn Ḥazm 1345–1347, 4:140.13–14). This means that, if there is no rule by which a particular thing is forbidden (~IM), this must be taken to imply that it is (implicitly) permitted (PE), without there being a need to first establish that it is not obligatory (~OB) either. And similarly for obligations; at least, this is how I think that the following statement, made just after the former, should be understood: "and everything which he (that is, the Prophet), may peace be upon him, did not command, was not rendered obligatory by Him [either]" (Ibn Ḥazm 1345–1347, 4:140.16). This Ẓāhirī reading of the absence of obligations and prohibitions, a reading that was the logical consequence of his rejection of the use of analogy (*qiyās*) in Islamic law, stands out even more clearly in his short treatise on legal theory, called *al-Nubadh fī uṣūl al-fiqh al-Ẓāhirī*, where he says: "(W)hatever is not commanded or not forbidden is licit, due to His saying, may He be exalted,

24 Ibn Ḥazm 1345–1347, 5:107.10–12: "In our book called *al-Taqrīb*, these things were already explained at length, which is why we limit ourselves to the amount of detail provided here."

'He created for you all that is in the earth.' (Qur'an 2:229) [The Prophet] (pbuh) commands us to refrain from doing only that which he has forbidden, and only that which he has commanded are we obliged to do, the best way we can" (Ibn Ḥazm 1431/2010, 81.6–9).[25] In other words: we only must *do* what was commanded and *not do* what was prohibited, the rest being merely optional and licit. Such being the case, row I of Table 1 applies after all:

(10) PE = ~OB = ~IM

This means that Ibn Ḥazm's understanding of the negation of obligations and prohibitions (~OB and ~IM) is the same as his understanding of the negation of necessity and impossibility (~N and ~I) which, on a two-sided interpretation of possibility (see Table 1 and Figure 2), each imply an affirmation of possibility (P): if something is said to be not prohibited, this simply means that it is (implicitly) permitted, and likewise, if it is not obligatory, it is simply (implicitly) permitted. Also, in the *Taqrīb*, Ibn Ḥazm (1980–1983, 4:263.15) says that what is forbidden, is not permitted. This means that a statement on the absence of a permission (~PE) is taken in the everyday rather than in a strictly logical sense, so that ~PE = IM, rather than (IM v OB). In other words: ~PE does not refer to the absence of a permission, but rather to the presence of a prohibition (IM). All this is consistent with Figures 2 and 3 and Tables 1, 2, and 3.

Earlier, it was stated that row III of Table 1 was not mentioned separately by Ibn Ḥazm like rows I and II, although its members *are* mentioned separately in their relation to the members of row I (Table 3, lines 3, 4, 5). Even if we cannot be sure why row III was not mentioned separately, it is conceivable that, as a jurist, Ibn Ḥazm regarded the possibility of something's not being the case (P~) more as a negation of the necessity of its being the case (~N) than as an independent possibility, in the same way in which he must have regarded a permission for some action to be omitted (PE~) as the negation of some positive obligation (~OB). But in that case he still needed the connoted equivalences between rows I and III that would allow for this, which may have prompted the inclusion of lines 3, 4, 5 (and 6) in Table 3.

As for the absence of row IV of Table 1 from Table 3, we should ask ourselves what would happen if we were to affirm the first member of the disjunction (OB v

---

25 In the edition, the text is given as follows:
وما لم يأت به أمر ولا نهي فهو مباح لقوله تعالى "خَلَقَ لَكُم مَّا فِي الْأَرْضِ جَمِيعًا" (البقرة : 29)، ويأمرنا عليه السلام أن لا نترك منه إلّا ما نهانا عنه ولا يلزمنا إلّا ما استطعناه ممّا أمرنا به.
For the English, see Sabra 2013, 153 last paragraph, with substantial changes in the last sentence. This work by Ibn Ḥazm is referred to by Sabra as *al-Nubdha al-kāfiya fī uṣūl aḥkām al-dīn*.

PE v IM). Does this lead to OB = (~PE & ~IM)? In other words: when something is obligatory, is it then at the same time not permissible and not impermissible? I think not for Ibn Ḥazm. The equivalence seems formally correct, but earlier it has been said that for Ibn Ḥazm, ~PE = IM and ~IM = PE. If we substitute ~PE and ~IM by their equivalents, we get: OB = (IM & PE), which is plainly absurd. I think therefore that Ibn Ḥazm's silence, in the *Taqrīb*, on row IV of Table 1 (~P~ = I~ = N) may have been motivated by his intuition as a jurist.[26]

Another matter concerns Ibn Ḥazm's objection to those who interpret some commands as obligations and others as mere recommendations (*mubāḥ mandūb*), and some proscriptions as prohibitions and others as mere dissuasions (*mubāḥ makrūh*). This is because, being a Ẓāhirī, Ibn Ḥazm believed in a literal interpretation of the texts, so that any deviation from their apparent meaning had to be founded on textual evidence or consensus (Ibn Ḥazm 1431/2010, 38.7–15, 46.3–5).[27] Also, the meaning of dissuasion and recommendation in both cases being that one is free to either engage in or abstain from a certain action, the contested interpretation of commands and prohibitions is counterintuitive and at odds with linguistic practice and consensus (Ibn Ḥazm 1431/2010, 46.9–12).[28]

Convincing though it is from his own point of view, I think that those criticised by Ibn Ḥazm may not have regarded permission in its relation to obligation and prohibition as referring equally to PE and PE~. Indeed, in the context of obligations and prohibitions, permission for them appears to have been limited to what is permissible *to be* in the case of obligations, and to what is permissible *not to be* in the case of prohibitions. And this is more like one-sided possibility

---

26 Interestingly, Ibn Ḥazm (1980–1983, 4:198.6–7) does mention the equivalence N = I~, but I still believe that my explanation for the absence of row IV of Table 1 from Table 3 is correct. The above means that the deontic equivalences (6) and (9) cited by Knuuttila (1981, 236) as being among the ones that are presupposed in the works of William Ockham (d. 1347), Robert Holcot, and Roger Rosetus, were not meaningful for Ibn Ḥazm. From among the other equivalences mentioned there, (7) is implied by the sum total of a) Table 3 line 1, b) the stated correspondences between the Aristotelian and the deontic modalities, c) the connoted equivalence between P and P~, and d) the stated equivalence between ~OB and P. And although (5), (8), and (10) are one way or the other all implied by Table 3 and the stated correspondences between the Aristotelian and the deontic modalities, their reference to obligations to abstain from doing certain things (OB~p) instead of to prohibitions to engage in such things (IMp) probably explains why I did not come across any of them during my readings in Ibn Ḥazm.

27 For the English, see Sabra 2013, 129 first paragraph, 134.2–7.

28 With Sabra 2013, 134.10–14. The text of the *Nubadh* being somewhat ambiguous, see also Ibn Ḥazm 1345–1347, 3:8.4–12 where the double-sidedness of recommendations and dissuasions is spelled out more clearly.

in Figure 3 than like two-sided possibility in Figure 2. But it also introduces a difficulty inasmuch as there would be two-sided permissions in the case of true permissions (explicit or implicit), and one-sided permissions in the case of some obligations and prohibitions, which would certainly complicate matters significantly if one should wish to give a consistent account of these modalities and their relations.

In the part of the *Taqrīb* which treats of syllogistic, Ibn Ḥazm (1980 – 1983, 4: 240.2 – 243.2) also mentions legal arguments. Unfortunately, the Aristotelian and deontic modalities are not associated there. Instead, the latter are treated as if they were terms of predicate logic rather than logical operators.[29] This is also shown by the conversion of a proposition like "Some infidels, it is permitted to kill" to "Some of those whose killing is permitted are infidels" (Ibn Ḥazm 1980 – 1983, 4:226.1 – 2), while there is no talk of the much more interesting "Some infidels, it is permitted not to kill", which one would expect on the basis of Table 3, line 5. Ibn Ḥazm's legal syllogistic is almost certainly derived from the legal syllogistic of al-Fārābī's *Kitāb al-Qiyās al-ṣaghīr* mentioned earlier, in which legal and modal discourse are not associated either. The fact that he stuck to a format like al-Fārābī's rather than applying his earlier statements on the deontic modalities to legal syllogistic, seems to indicate that he was not aware of the implications that the former should have for the latter.[30]

3 Conclusion

According to the Spanish biographer Ṣāʿid al-Andalusī (d. 462/1070), Ibn Ḥazm, in his *Taqrīb*, deviates in many places from the logical teachings of Aristotle, leaving the impression that he had not really understood it. This is also why Ṣāʿid (1912, 76.5 – 8) rejected this work as being full of mistakes and aberrations. This is not the place to pass judgement on Ibn Ḥazm's understanding of Aristotelian logic as a whole. But if one looks at his – admittedly concise – statements on the Aristotelian modalities and their relations, one gains the impression that he viewed these modalities through the prism of a Ẓāhirī jurist, which might explain some of his apparent "mistakes" or "aberrations." More important, because unprecedented, are the implications of his remarks on the equivalences between the Aristotelian modalities and the modal qualifications of Islamic law.

---

29 See also note 7 above.

30 This approach to legal syllogistic had apparently not changed when he came to write his *al-Iḥkām fī uṣūl al-aḥkām*, as may be inferred from Ibn Ḥazm 1345 – 1347, 5:106.10.

His ideas in both fields being well-documented,[31] it was possible to spell out the consequences of his words when he associates the deontic with the Aristotelian modalities, even if not all possible parallels yield meaningful statements from the point of view of Islamic law.[32] In this connection it is important to note that Ibn Ḥazm, in his *al-Iḥkām fī uṣūl al-aḥkām*, still subscribes to the ideas of the *Taqrīb*; important, as it is the basis that allows for a joint reading of these works, leading to the various deontic equivalences discussed in this chapter. Unfortunately, Ibn Ḥazm himself does not seem to have been fully aware of the combined importance of his statements in one place and the other. The only explanation that I can offer is that the level of the courses in logic that he took was never high enough to reach that amount of detail.

In the end, it can be stated that Ibn Ḥazm's works contain sufficient information to conclude that he must have had a Ẓāhirī reading of the modalities – Aristotelian and deontic – and their interrelations. While this in itself is important and new information, it is of course not enough to call this a "system" of deontic logic as an offshoot of Aristotelian modal logic. But some very basic considerations are there, which Ibn Ḥazm then did not follow up, a fact that is probably due to his limited formation as a logician. Unfortunately, I have so far not come across any author from after the time of Ibn Ḥazm who elaborated on his ideas, either in a work on logic or in some legal text. It is to be hoped that future research will change this situation.[33]

---

31 Which is not always the same as well-developed.

32 See the absence of Table 1 line IV from Table 3, and of obligations involving omissions mentioned above in note 26.

33 I think that John Mikhail's claim that "the discoveries in deontic logic attributed to Western philosophers like Ockham and Leibniz were anticipated by earlier Islamic thinkers", while not entirely wrong, is vindicated through a mistaken, "one-sided" reading of permission in Islamic law. Also, his claim that "of every conceivable act, either its performance or its non-performance is permissible" appears based on the erroneous assumption that obligations imply permissions of performance in Islamic law, and prohibitions permissions of non-performance (Mikhail 2004, 66).

Ziad Bou Akl

Splitting the Process and the Result: Philosophy from a Legal Perspective in Averroes' *Decisive Treatise*

1 Introduction

Philosophy has a lot to say about jurisprudence. As al-Fārābī (d. 339/950) does in his *Iḥṣā'*, it can assign a place to this discipline within a general framework, by determining its object and purpose and comparing it to other disciplines, such as theology and the rational sciences. After all, the nature of philosophical concepts is to encompass the whole of reality. From this philosophical perspective, jurisprudence seems to be a rhetorical discipline, founded on merely endoxic premises which lack scientific certainty and reasoning, and supported by weak epistemic tools such as analogy. Yet the converse is also true, for legal discourse has a lot to say about philosophy. Law governs a whole range of human activities, and philosophy, like medicine or law itself, is a social activity that can be submitted to legal analysis and examined through the lens of the concepts and principles of jurisprudence. Legal discourse can determine the purpose of philosophy and its social utility. It can address concerns about its social consequences by determining whether this activity has harmful consequences, whether essentially or accidentally, and if so how to deal with this fact.

In the Islamic tradition, the need for a thorough legal investigation of philosophy stems from the notorious attacks on philosophy found in al-Ghazālī's (d. 505/1111) *Tahāfut al-falāsifa*. In a rationalist vein, the great Ash'arī theologian argues in this book, first, that certain claims made by the philosophers are false or lack demonstrative criteria, and second, that they diverge from the Islamic community's true religious teachings concerning three theses (the eternity of the world; God's knowledge of particulars; and the resurrection of the body). The first argument occupies nearly the entire work, and presents a type of criticism that can be addressed, on rational grounds, to any philosophical system. The second point, by contrast, appears very briefly. It occupies the last page of the book and serves as both consequence and conclusion of what preceded. Here al-Ghazālī is guided by a religious and social preoccupation. Besides being wrong or inadequate by their own rational standards, the philosophers

I thank Peter Adamson for his comments on an earlier version of this chapter.

https://doi.org/10.1515/9783110552386-009

lay down three teachings that are also dangerous for society. In an unprecedented attack, the philosophers are accused of apostasy and held responsible for leading their followers astray.[1]

These manifold accusations provoked several responses from Averroes (d. 595/1198): one as a philosopher responding to the criticism, argument against argument, as he does in the *Tahāfut al-Tahāfut*; the other from a religious and theological standpoint, showing that contrary to al-Ghazālī's claim, the theses of the Aristotelians are much more compatible with revelation than the theologian's own system. This is the aim of the *Kashf*, which has been rightly described as a "counter treatise" of theology (Geoffroy 1999, 25). The first book is a response to the rational arguments of the *Tahāfut*, the second one a reaction inspired by the last page of the *Tahāfut* which had questioned the harmony of philosophical conclusions and religious truth. In both cases, Averroes presents philosophy as a complete set of correct doctrines free of error and in accordance with the standards of reason itself (by showing that it is internally coherent and based on true, rationally defensible premises) or with those of revelation (by demonstrating truth's compatibility with truth, so long as the religious texts are correctly understood).

Faṣl al-maqāl, the third book of the tryptic, tackles the problem from yet another angle. In a way, it is not primarily concerned with the content of the last page of the *Tahāfut* but questions more radically al-Ghazālī's inference from scientific error to juridical accusation of apostasy. Averroes is not so much out to establish the truth – even if he does this, too, in the *Faṣl* – as to invalidate the general principle of legal accusation when applied to philosophy. By doing so, he can secure once and for all the possibility of practicing philosophy without external interventions at each new conclusion and for each particular system.

Since this is his aim, the argument cannot merely cover a singular philosophical system, the correct one which is composed of a set of true propositions compatible with revelation. It must be situated on a more general level, encompassing philosophy as a whole in all its evolution and diversity. If Averroes endeavours to show that the accusation of apostasy cannot be applied to philosophy, he must prove this with regard to both correct and incorrect philosophical solutions. Otherwise, unless we assume that all philosophical speculations necessarily lead to one set of conclusions – a claim obviously invalidated by the diversity of philosophical systems – he would not be defending the obligation to practice philosophy in an absolute sense, but only the correct philosophical

1 On these issues, see Griffel 2009.

system. The very idea of philosophical practice or quest regardless of the truth to which it leads would be rendered senseless. In other words, if only one specific system of thought were compatible with religious truth and all others were harmful and subject to legal accusation, the harmony between philosophy and religion would be purely incidental. If, on the contrary, philosophical enquiry itself were compatible with religion, their harmony would be necessary and their opposition merely accidental. That is precisely what Averroes wants to demonstrate in the text.

Philosophy is thus defined as a process, guided by a method and oriented towards an end.[2] This is the unusual and interesting description Averroes gives us in the first part of the *Decisive Treatise*: philosophy is not described backwards, once the quest is completed and with the demonstrated propositions to be presented to the reader, but is rather forward-looking. It is more reminiscent of the process of reasoning and the making of syllogisms as described in Aristotle's *Topics* with its gymnastic role, than the *Analytics* with its already grasped method. Philosophy becomes a practice that precedes its results, just like medicine and law. As such, it can be compared, not to the theoretical side of religion as is the case in the *Kashf*, but to its practical side, that is jurisprudence. From this perspective the jurist, who is neither a professional philosopher nor addresses his answer to such professionals, has something to say about philosophy.

Of course, in an activity whose ultimate product is propositions, theory cannot be totally dismissed from the process and should ultimately be investigated for a full examination of the discipline. This is mirrored by the interrelatedness of the practical and the theoretical sides of religion, which are likewise inextricably intertwined.[3] As is evident in the *Faṣl*, the law is concerned with human acts. These include mental acts, such as assent, which are related to propositional truths and thus to the theoretical aspect of religion, and could become the object of legal enquiry. In those cases, the objective of the laws is to protect what al-Ghāzālī labels the "religion" (*dīn*) of people from apostates and threats to their beliefs.[4] The end of the *Tahāfut* serves this very goal.

---

2 In a certain way, every defense of philosophy against an external attack should be situated at a level of generality beyond the particular allegiance of the philosopher. Compare, for instance, the way Abū Bakr al-Rāzī (d. 313 or 323/925 or 935) defends philosophy in *Aʿlām al-nubuwwa* (Abū Ḥātim al-Rāzī 2003, 22–23; English text in Gutas 2014, 237–238).

3 As mentioned by Hourani in the introduction to his translation, the term *sharʿ* encompasses those two sides of religion in the *Faṣl*, and is translated by "Law" when it refers to a source of commands and prohibitions, and as "Scripture" whenever it refers to a text (Ibn Rushd 2012, 19).

4 "Religion" is one of the five objectives the law seeks to protect. On this issue, see Opwis 2010.

Although theoretical and practical aspects are mingled in both philosophy and religion, the shift from theory to practice, which is justified by the legal nature of the *Faṣl*, allows for a separation of these two aspects of philosophy from each other, and an initial focus on the process before reintroducing the result. Besides its strategic and rhetorical virtue, persuading the reader of the benefits of a speculative process before dealing with any problematic conclusions, this separation also influences the way the result is presented. Averroes reinstates philosophical conclusions to the extent they are relevant to a jurist, and not in the manner they are lengthily discussed in the *Kashf* or the *Tahāfut*. He reintroduces them from outside the profession, not to defend the correct answer in a theoretical debate, as a seeker of truth, but to show that the whole range of philosophical answers is legally acceptable and does not lead to apostasy. This point of view opens a breach between what can legally be said and the truth. It does not seek to identify the true answer in a theory-based approach in order to dismiss all others, but to set, in a practice-based approach, the legal boundaries of the theoretical debate and the limits that seekers of truth cannot cross. As we will see below, this whole operation is possible mainly because of the input of the Islamic legal tradition. It provided Averroes with the necessary tools to investigate philosophy in continuity with legal science, and to persuade his readership of the validity of his reasoning by resorting to concepts and proofs that were familiar to them.

The Islamic legal tradition, alongside its interest in legal norms found in positive law or books on the *furūʿ* (first-order legal norms), from early on developed a reflexive discourse oriented towards legal activity, and itself became an object of investigation. This meta-discourse evolved as an independent genre, that of legal theory (*uṣūl al-fiqh*), fixing the norms that should be respected in arriving at the *furūʿ*, debating the hermeneutical tools at hand (the validity of the *a fortiori* argument and the *a contrario* argument, analogy, etc.), and subsequently extracted material (the validity of solitary reports (*āḥād*), the legal value of the Prophet's deeds, etc.). Most importantly for us, legal theory developed a set of questions surrounding the concept of *ijtihād*, which is generally treated in its own right in a separate chapter. This central concept of *ijtihād*, as every legal theorist reminds us, contains in its very lexical meaning the idea of effort (*juhd*). This effort is exerted by a *mujtahid* and oriented towards a goal, which is extracting a legal status from problematic material. Apart from its ethical and deontological aspects, effort plays a concrete methodological role in regard to the juridical responsibility of a *mujtahid* in the case of an error. It could be used to emphasise, within the whole juridical operation, the process, regardless of the result, in determining the *mujtahid*'s responsibility: has he done everything he can, and if so can he nonetheless be blamed for his errors? It is this interstice between juridical process and result, evident and well-established for every *mujtahid*, that Averroes applies in his legal investigation of philosophy.

2 Philosophy as a Practice

The law deals primarily with human actions, and the object of investigation announced in the beginning of the *Decisive Treatise* is an action: practising philosophy (*fiʿl al-falsafa*). Philosophy is defined as an activity consisting in "the study of existing beings and reflection on them (*iʿtibārihim*) as proofs of the Artisan." The fulfilment of this activity is achieved in three steps or actions which are developed in the first part of the treatise: (1) engaging in the philosophical quest; (2) acquiring the specific tools to fulfil the activity; and finally (3) reaching a conclusion, which can be considered as the end of a unified philosophical sequence. Averroes submits all three actions to juridical examination.

(1) Engaging in the philosophical quest is a voluntary action driven by the aim of this practice, which is reflection (*iʿtibār*) upon beings as proofs of God. Its legal foundation rests on a main scriptural argument, the Qur'anic injunction in favour of *iʿtibār* cited at the beginning of the treatise: "Reflect, you who have vision" (*iʿtabirū yā ūlī 'l-abṣār*, Q. 59:2). Averroes uses it to support his assertion that philosophy is not only permitted by the law, but mandatory for those who can perform it. This somehow odd "obligation" to practice philosophy would have appeared to Averroes' readership as a valid and persuasive argument, given the history of this verse in legal theory debates, to which Averroes alludes in the text.

The verse was not always a clear juridical norm. It was first used in legal discourse to establish the validity of analogy (*ḥujjiyyat al-qiyās*) when this operation was faced by a strong anti-analogist movement. Around the ninth century AD, it started to be cited as a key scriptural proof to be used alongside rational arguments in favour of the obligation of using *qiyās* to extend the law to unprecedented new cases.[5] Subsequent debates transformed the function of this verse and elevated it, in the eyes of scholars, to the status of a meta-legal norm that

5 The anti-analogist movement was divided between the traditionalists who rejected all types of *qiyās* and reasoning, in the midst of a general suspicion towards reason, and rational theologians like al-Naẓẓām (d. 220-30/835-45), who rejected what they deemed a weak epistemic tool that could only provide mere opinion. Ibn ʿUlayya (d. 218/832) is considered the first scholar to use this verse in order to establish the validity of *qiyās*. On this issue, see Zysow 2013, 163–191.

was widely cited in *uṣūlī* literature. With this newfound function, the imperative "Reflect!" now bore the weight of a legal norm, that is, an obligation, which in this technical context superseded its initial illocutionary force, that of a concluding sentence that exhorts the reader to reflect upon the fate of the Jewish rebel tribe of Banū Naḍīr.[6]

Recalling the history of this verse allows us to measure the input of the legal tradition on Averroes' argumentation, and the rhetorical weight it gives to his initial argument. Legal theory gave him a scriptural foundation that could support theoretical reasoning. More importantly, thanks to the peculiar nature of its object, it gave him what positive law (*furūʿ*) could not provide him with: a juridical tool to deal with mental operations. Since *iʿtibār* had succeeded in imposing legal analogy on the mainstream Sunnī legal schools, it should be able to establish syllogism or "rational *qiyās*."

Indeed, as he puts it, rational *qiyās* used in theoretical speculation is more fittingly called "*iʿtibār*" than "legal *qiyās*" used in its practical counterpart. This *a fortiori* argumentation, which regards theory as superior to practice, can also be traced back to a well-established theme in legal theory, at least among *uṣūlī* theologians like al-Ghazālī, who ascribes higher epistemic standards to *ʿilm* ("theory") than to *ʿamal* ("practice"). While theory (that is, knowledge of God's nature or His attributes) should be certain and founded on authentic, unequivocal reports, practice can settle for weaker and presumptive (*ẓannī*) premises, founded on solitary reports (*āḥād*) and probable expressions (*ẓawāhir*). This epistemic tolerance towards practice is generally justified by the rarity of unequivocal premises that necessitate dealing with presumptive data. This hierarchy enables Averroes to frame his argument: if practical reasoning, with all its unanimously agreed upon epistemic imperfection, is legally obligatory, theoretical reasoning is *a fortiori* obligatory as well. To this epistemic hierarchy one can add a comparison between the ends of the two sciences: whereas law studies God's command, philosophy enquires into His very nature (Ibn Rushd 2012, 46 [3.1–10]).

(2) Theoretical reasoning, however, is not yet philosophy, because speculative theology (*kalām*) is also a rational investigation leading to knowledge of God. In fact, for a theologian like al-Ghazālī, the superiority of *ʿilm* over *ʿamal* is meant to place theology, founded on rational premises and dealing with the existent (*al-mawjūd*), at a higher rank than *fiqh*, which is satisfied with presumption. Drawing upon this epistemic hierarchy, Averroes substitutes *falsafa* with

6 On which see *Encyclopedia of the Qur'ān*, "Naḍīr (banū al-)."

kalām by focussing on the utmost importance of acquiring the right philosophical method, that is, Greek logic and its pinnacle, the theory of demonstration. This amounts to the second step of philosophical activity, following on the initial engagement in the philosophical quest. The superiority of *burhān* ("demonstration") is admitted even by al-Ghazālī, according to whom logic is a neutral and universal tool that he himself introduced into Islamic sciences such as *uṣūl al-fiqh*.[7] The aforementioned distinction between process and result allows Averroes to identify the former with the proper tool of the philosophical quest, that is, logic, in order to establish the superiority of philosophical activity in theoretical reasoning before dealing with any problematic conclusions of the latter.

Thus far, there is no real divergence between Averroes and al-Ghazālī. They both praise theoretical speculation and the superiority of the logical method. The only difference between the two lies in the fact that, unlike al-Ghazālī whose logic is a universal and decontextualised tool with no essential link to the culture of the Greeks or other parts of their philosophy,[8] Averroes insists on the necessity of delving into the books of the ancients (*kutub al-qudamāʾ*) in order to study logic, and specifically defends this enterprise against those who criticise the importation of foreign sciences. Being a foreign science is a peculiarity that logic does not share with legal *qiyās*, since the latter is considered a rational and hence a universal process. The analogy with legal *qiyās* is not helpful in this particular case, and the jurist must search elsewhere in order to resolve this problem. Interestingly, in order to give a legal answer to this issue, Averroes resorts for once to positive law. He draws an analogy between logic as an instrument for the mind and the material instrument used in ritual slaughtering. Since the origin of the latter has never been an issue, then that of the former should likewise be unproblematic.[9]

(3) But it is really with the third step in the philosophical process that Averroes deviates from al-Ghazālī and opposes the very idea of the *takfīr* of the philosophers (that is, al-Ghazālī's declaring them unbelievers). This final step is the action of assenting (*taṣdīq*) to a given philosophical conclusion, after a process of reflection that follows the right method. Along with the concept of conceptualisation (*taṣawwur*), assent is one of the two pillars of all mental operations,

7 See further Ulrich Rudolph's paper in the present volume.
8 On this issue, see Gutas 2014, 320–322.
9 Indeed, in his *Bidāya*, the origin of the *ālat al-dhakāt* is not an issue. See Ibn Rushd 2003, vol. I, 675–6.

and as such it belongs as much to psychology as it does to logic.[10] Within the former science, this concept refers to the mental operation of assenting to a proposition. It is therefore an action, and as such could be submitted to the *sharʿ* which in this context is considered as the law governing human actions (*afʿāl*). Yet, as part of logic, this concept refers to the result, or the content, of a mental operation. Unlike conceptualisation, assent has to do with propositions: it is the conviction that a certain proposition is true. In this latter sense, assent falls under opinions (*ārāʾ*), and insofar as those opinions concern religious truth, assent could be concerned with the *sharʿ* here considered as a revealed text.

In the *Decisive Treatise*, the act of assenting is dealt with after the presentation of the question of the eternity of the world: "For assent to a thing as a result of an indication [of it] arising in the soul is something compulsory (*iḍṭirārī*), not voluntary (*ikhtiyārī*); i.e. it is not for us [to choose] not to assent or to assent, as it is to stand up or not to stand up" (Ibn Rushd 2012, 57 [13.15–20]).[11] From a juridical perspective, compulsory acts are not part of the legal charge (*taklīf*). Indeed, as stated in the *uṣūlī* sections on *taklīf*, free choice (*ikhtiyār*) is one of the conditions of legal acts.[12] Thus the main challenge for Averroes is to build his theory of juridical error without undermining the principle of the compulsiveness of assent, on which the necessity of scientific conclusions is founded.

The first and main problem this principle raises is that, if assenting to any given proposition is a compulsory act, and since compulsory acts cannot be part of the legal charge, there will be no opinion that revelation could impose

10 On this subject, see Black 1990, 71–78. On the problem of its Greek origins, see Lameer 2006, 3–35.

11 Hourani wonders about the Aristotelian source of this doctrine and, following Wolfson, suggests linking it to the doctrine of *pistis*, which does not depend on free choice and will (he cites *Eth. Nic.* VI 2 on the necessary character of the object of science). However, it seems to refer more directly to the Aristotelian definition of the syllogism, whose characteristic is to produce the conclusion *by necessity* from what is posited (*Top.* I.1 1001a25–27; *Pr. An.* I.1 24b18–20). ἐξ ἀνάγκης is rendered by *min al-iḍṭirār* both in al-Dimashqī's translation of *Topics I–VII* (Aristotle 1980, 2:489.25–26) and in Tadhārī's translation of the *Prior Analytics* (Aristotle 1980, 1:142.4–5). While in the context of the *Analytics*, it refers to formal necessity, in the dialectical context of the *Topics*, it refers to the compulsion of a conclusion that a questioner imposes upon the respondent. It is in this latter sense that it is used by Averroes, namely that of an assent that imposes itself upon the practitioner of philosophy as a compulsory action. On necessity as a distinctive feature of the Aristotelian syllogism and a comparison between the *Topics* and the *Analytics*, see Crubellier 2011.

12 On this issue in al-Ghazālī's *Mustaṣfā* and short commentary on the topic by Averroes, see Bou Akl 2012.

upon its followers. First of all, it would fail to lay down its own foundation, or what *uṣūlīs* call "the first obligation" (*al-wājib al-awwal*), that is, the decision following from the assent that this *sharīʿa* is the law of God that one should obey.[13] It will also fail to impose upon its followers the main propositions shared by the community, like the existence of God and of the prophets, known to the legal tradition under the name of *dīn* ("religious belief"), one of the five main points every law should protect. If someone, after having thoroughly examined the core Islamic teaching, fails to assent to it, would it be possible to sanction him in the afterlife? According to al-Ghazālī (1997, 2:401.8–10), al-Jāḥiẓ (d. 255/868) for instance deemed this impossible, if the person sincerely exerted his maximum effort in examining those propositions. This extreme position on the compulsion of assent is presented as a minority view, since mainstream scholars such as al-Ghazālī tried to draw a line between the main religious propositions to which everybody should assent – and in which he included the three crucial theses denied by the philosophers – and the minor propositions which call for different solutions.

Consequently, assent is legally problematic. In a way, it is a compulsory act independent of our will and as such it cannot be part of the legal charge. Yet, as a mental act, it produces propositions that can conflict with the revealed truth protected by the law. In order to do justice to both its compulsory character and its capacity to impose a set of common values on society as a whole, Averroes distinguishes assent with respect to two types of questions (*masāʾil*): on the one hand, difficult questions (*al-ʿawīṣa*), such as the question of the eternity of the world and, on the other, easy ones the knowledge of which is possible for everybody (*mumkina li'l-jamīʿ*). This distinction, which is neither modal (dividing propositions into the necessary and the possible) nor epistemic (dividing them into certain and presumptive), concerns the process of reaching the solution of a given problem by questioning its difficulty. This echoes a point made by Aristotle at the very beginning of the *Topics* when he explains what dialectical problems are: only problems that provoke puzzlement (*shakka fīhi shākk*, ἀπορήσειεν ἄν τις) ought to be investigated.[14] Conversely, evident questions should not be an object of investigation. Those who raise practical problems such as "Should the gods be honoured?" ought simply to be punished, while those who wonder about theoretical problems such as "Is snow white?" should go have a look.[15]

---

13 On this first obligation, see Bou Akl 2012.

14 *Top.* I 11, 105a5.

15 In the Arabic translation of Tadhārī: "For those who puzzle over whether one must adore God and care for one's parents or not need punishment, while those who puzzle over whether snow is white or not need perception" (Aristotle 1980, 2:507.1–5). As mentioned by Brunschwig,

Following a general trend in the Arabic tradition, Averroes finds a socio-political application for this distinction, seeing it as a reflection of the social division between the masses and the elite. Knowledge that is possible for everybody can be found in classes of cognition, since all types of premises, whether demonstrative, dialectical, or rhetorical, lead to such knowledge. This is possible because of the clarity and evidentness of those propositions, founded on the miraculous character of the Qur'anic message which guarantees a determined and systematic assent regardless of one's cognitive class. Averroes cites the "acknowledgment of God, of the prophetic missions, and of happiness and misery in the next life" (Ibn Rushd 2012, 58 [14.20–23]). Because of their clarity, any failure to assent to such propositions can only be explained by a voluntary action, either negligence (*ghafla*) in looking at those propositions despite the miracle inciting us to do it or obstinacy (*ʿinād*) in refusing to admit the assent once it has happened (Ibn Rushd 2012, 58 [15.2–3]). The first occurs before the act of assenting, the second after it; in both cases law can intervene, in this world or in the next, to condemn this type of error.

By contrast, solutions for the difficult questions are not reached systematically. This makes them apt for scientific investigation and explains the fact that thinkers disagree about them. Averroes sees the question of the eternity of the world as an example. Accordingly, for this type of proposition assenting is not determined but rather aleatory: while some philosophers reach the true answer, others could be misled during their reasoning by a fallacy (*shubha*) (Ibn Rushd 2012, 57 [13.22]).[16] Therefore, unlike with the first type of question, here the absence of assent is not to be explained by a voluntary act that obstructs the systematic reception of a clear message; it is more likely to be involuntary or constrained. For this reason, errors with regard to such questions lie totally outside the sphere of legal acts and cannot be condemned. This class includes the demonstrative propositions concerning the eternity of the world, God's knowledge of particulars, and the resurrection of the bodies in the afterlife, the very issues that incurred al-Ghazālī's denunciation of the philosophers.[17]

Aristotelian dialectic thus distances itself from both cynism and skepticism (Aristote 2009, xxvii).

16 Hourani translates *shubha* with "consideration."

17 Unlike those that are accessible to everyone, these propositions, like philosophical problems, are not part of the Qur'anic message. Revelation makes only allusions (*tanbīhāt*) to them. One may observe that these three problems that divide the philosophers and theologians are the "demonstrative versions" of the three basic truths to which all cognitive classes should agree: the eternity of the world corresponds to the question of God as the Creator of the universe; His knowledge of particulars to prophetic knowledge of the contingent future; and the resurrec-

In sum, Averroes distinguishes between a clear and, thus, determined assent, the absence of which is necessarily a voluntary act that can be condemned by the law, and an involuntary and aleatory one, reserved for difficult questions and thus safe from any accusation of error. Without abandoning the main principle of the constraining character of assent, he succeeds in protecting a basic truth that should be universally agreed upon, and in absolving the philosophers from any accusation of error. What the law can and should control is not, as al-Ghazālī pretends, the conclusion of a chain of philosophical argument, but the very beginning of the quest. Instead of imposing a solution to some philosophical questions, it should select those who can enquire and protect others from the harmful consequences of such an investigation. By organising the practice of philosophy in society, the law decides *who* should be thinking about theoretical questions instead of interfering, as al-Ghazālī does, in *what* should be said about them.

3 Philosophers as *mujtahids*

The restriction of philosophy to an elite goes back to a tradition that predates Arabic philosophy (Gutas 2014, 256–266). However, the social organisation of its practice as described in the *Faṣl* explicitly parallels that of the law found in the theoretical legal literature and, to a lesser degree, that of medicine. Philosophers, like *mujtahid*s, are entitled to commit errors because of the difficulty of their task, while others are not allowed to delve into these questions. The relation of both philosophers and the *ʿāmma* towards philosophy is that of *mujtahids* and *muqallid*s towards the law. Just as the *muqallid* in law is the one who is unqualified to produce *ijtihād* by himself, and who should therefore follow the *ijtihād* of professionals, the *ʿāmmī* in philosophy is the one who lacks the natural and acquired skills to become a philosopher. The practice of philosophy is prohibited to him because of its dangers for both him and society (Ibn Rushd 2012, 48 [6.1–5]).

As a result, from a juridical perspective the dichotomy between the elite and the masses characterises two groups of people specifically in terms of the relation each group bears towards a particular discipline. This relational definition of *mujtahid* and *muqallid* is supported by the Ghazālian distinction between

---

tion of the bodies to the afterlife. Al-Ghazālī, in his legal distinction between belief and unbelief, should have kept to these general truths (God; His prophets; the afterlife) to which all classes assent, instead of imposing upon everybody the dialectical solutions of the theologians.

the *mujtahid* simpliciter and the *mujtahid* in relation to a specific field. In light of this distinction, the same person can be a *mujtahid* in a certain sub-field of law and a *muqallid* in another.[18] From this perspective, speaking of the masses and the elite refers less to social status, as is the case in political philosophy, and more to the relation anyone can have to a specific set of knowledge. The *ʿāmmī* in relation to philosophy is the layman, while the philosopher is the professional.

This description of the philosopher as *mujtahid* in theoretical matters allows Averroes to extend to the philosophical practice the whole reflection conducted by legal theory on legal practice itself, in order to define the legal consequences of error in theoretical questions. His main argument relies on a Prophetic tradition: "If the judge (*al-ḥākim*) after exerting his mind (*idhā ijtahada*) hits the point (*aṣāba*), he will have a double reward, and if he misses it (*akhṭaʾa*), he will still have a single reward" (Ibn Rushd 2012, 57 [13]).[19] This *ḥadīth* allows him to establish, against al-Ghazālī's accusation, the well-known idea of forgiveness (*maʿdhūr, maṣfūḥ*) for philosophers in case of error. Once we have conceded their legitimacy as judges in theoretical matters, this *ḥadīth* allows us to draw an analogy between theory and practice. The legal obligation to engage in philosophical activity is grounded in a set of preconditions restricting its practice, regardless of the validity of every single result that might stray from revelation.

Similarly to the verse on *iʿtibār*, the persuasive force of this Prophetic tradition as an argument for forgiveness towards philosophers relies on one of the most important debates in legal theory, regarding *ijtihād*.[20] This Prophetic tradition is no mere decontextualised or isolated justification of error, but evokes for the audience of the *fatwā* a whole set of arguments of an important group of scholars to whom Averroes belongs: the *muḥaqqiqa* ("the fallibilists"). In what follows, I will briefly highlight the main issues of this debate as it appears primarily in the *Mustaṣfā*, as well as its short commentary by Averroes, and then present the positions of Averroes and al-Ghazālī on this matter.[21]

18 Al-Ghazālī 1997, 2:389.1–17: "*ijtihād* is not, according to me, an indivisible status." See also this remark: "As for the grammarians and the theologians, we cannot count on them because they are, in relation to that science, like the masses, unless there is a question involving grammar and theology" (al-Ghazālī 1997, 1:343.6–7). See also Hallaq 1984c, 6.

19 Slightly modified translation.

20 Zysow recalls two anecdotes to illustrate the importance of this issue in legal theory. On this whole question, see Zysow 2013, chapter 5.

21 A full presentation of the arguments and the references can be found in Ibn Rushd 2015, 88–106.

This issue arises in the sections devoted to *ijtihād*. Truth and error are designated by the two verbs we find in the aforementioned *ḥadīth: aṣāba*, to "hit", and *akhṭa'a*, to "miss", like an archer with a target. Two levels of error should be distinguished in this question. First, the alethic level, that of scientific error (*khaṭa'*), when one misses the truth and, second, the juridical level, when one misses the truth and is held responsible for his action by an accusation of error (*takhṭi'a*).

For this reason, the famous saying analysed in this section, "Every *mujtahid* is right" (*kull mujtahid muṣīb*), can mean two different things. On a juridical level, it means that no *mujtahid* will be held responsible for his errors; while admitting the existence of truth and error, this reading forgives the error of the *mujtahid* by denying the existence of any accusation of error. But on an alethic level, the saying means that every *mujtahid* is right because there is no pre-established truth to find in those juridical questions, and whatever the *mujtahid* decides becomes the true answer. In consequence, the very possibility of error is excluded and, of course, any possible accusation of error. In the texts, both positions are called *muṣawwiba* ("infallibilist"). We can distinguish between them by labelling the first position "juridical infallibilism" (where the law protects all specialists even when they are wrong), and the second position "alethic infallibilism" (characterised more radically by the absence of just one good answer when it comes to juridical matters), sometimes called "radical infallibilism" (*al-mu'ammima fī l-taṣwīb*).[22] The other position is that of the *muḥaqqiqa* or the *mukhaṭṭi'a* ("fallibilist"). Again, we can contrast two varieties: "alethic fallibilism", meaning that there is only one true solution but no legal consequences for those who are wrong, and a more radical interpretation, "juridical fallibilism", where the existence of one true solution entails legal consequences for those who miss it.

In a way, alethic fallibilism and juridical infallibilism are similar. In both cases, the principle of non-contradiction is maintained in juridical matters and the accusation of error excluded, as the juridical and alethic levels are explicitly separated. This is not the case in the two other positions. Alethic infallibilism denies that there is only ever one good answer in juridical matters and, naturally, the accusation of error, while juridical fallibilism, represented by a minority (like Bishr al-Marīsī (d. 218/833), who is cited by al-Ghazālī), maintains it along with its legal consequences (al-Ghazālī 1997, 2:401.1, 405.6–10). The first position denies both levels and the second one maintains both. What matters

22 Zysow 2013, 261.

though is that neither of these two positions separate alethic and juridical levels and both establish between them a relation of inference.

Al-Ghazālī, for instance, holds an alethic infallibilist position for juridical questions. According to him, in the case of theology, which belongs to the realm of reason (*al-aḥkām al-ʿaqliyya*), or in the case of categorical (*qaṭʿiyya*) legal issues supported by a clear and certain text, the principle of non-contradiction does apply: in theology, because its absence leads to sophistry,[23] and in categorical legal issues, because the certainty of the text excludes the opposite solution. By virtue of this principle, an accusation of error may be levelled at those who miss the right solution. For al-Ghazālī, the juridical level is inferred from the alethic one. On the other hand, when it comes to presumptive juridical matters, which have as their basis only equivocal texts, two contradictory solutions coming from two different *mujtahid*s are right,[24] because those matters do not pertain to a determined legal status (*laysa fīhā dalīl qāṭiʿ wa-lā fīhā ḥukm muʿayyan*) (al-Ghazālī 1997, 2:410.11–12). Therefore, there is no error and no accusation of error. In neither case is the alethic level dissociated from the juridical one. Its presence entails legal consequences, in a *modus ponens* type of reasoning, similar to the case of philosophers and their problematic teachings. Furthermore, its absence negates any accusation of error, as in the case of *mujtahid*s making pronouncements on presumptive legal matters.[25]

Averroes, who discusses this question at length in his short commentary on al-Ghazālī's *Mustaṣfā*, criticises the radical alethic infallibilism of al-Ghazālī in favour of an alethic fallibilist position, hence maintaining both the existence of a truth and the forgiveness for those who miss it. If no *mujtahid* will be incriminated, this is not because there is no possibility of error, but rather because the alethic and the juridical level should be dissociated. According to Averroes, the possibility of error applies everywhere, because we have in each case a good and true answer to seek: in rational and theoretical questions as

23 Al-ʿAnbarī (d. 168/785), according to the tradition, held an infaillibilist solution even for theoretical questions (al-Ghazālī 1997, 2:402.14), a position that has been qualified as sophistical (al-Ghazālī 1997, 2:403.8).

24 Those matters concern only positive law (*furūʿ*) and not the meta-norms of legal theory which are considered as categorical. Thus, in addition to the principles upholding the validity of *ijmāʿ*, *qiyās*, *khabar al-wāḥid*, etc., the meta-norm according to which every *mujtahid* is right *cannot* be both true according to a *mujtahid* and wrong according to another one. Otherwise, its relativism will turn against it.

25 More precisely, it is the absence of any accusation of error in presumptive legal matters, founded on a scriptural basis, that entails the impossibility of error (a reasoning by *modus tollens* that corroborates the inference from the alethic to the juridical level). See al-Ghazālī 1997, 2:414.20–23.

well as juridical matters. In the legal sphere, the existence of a good answer rests on the unequivocal character of the intention of the Lawgiver, even when the texts are presumptive. Denying it in this last case, as al-Ghazālī proposes to do, is an act of sophistry with dangerous social consequences.

On these grounds, for Averroes error does not automatically lead to an accusation of error. And contrary to what al-Ghazālī says in his aforementioned *modus tollens* argument, the absence of any incrimination does not lead to an absence of any possibility of error: "the invalidation of the accusation of error does not imply the absence of error, because the unintentional error (*al-khaṭa' al-ghayr muta'ammad*) is forgiven by the law."[26] This is possible because the *mujtahid* is under no obligation to find the right answer, only to be fully willing to do so. This is the methodological role of effort (*juhd*), which emphasises the process regardless of the result. One's legal obligation is not hitting upon the right answer but only full deployment of the process. In a way, the very concept of forgiveness is based on this dissociation of alethic and deontic levels, for it presupposes a right answer that one can miss without being incriminated.[27]

In order to define this qualification of "unintentional", Averroes reframes al-Ghazālī's distinction between "categorical" and "presumptive" propositions by applying the same criteria he will later use in the *Decisive Treatise*, that is, by classifying these two types of propositions in terms of their level of difficulty. On the one hand, we have legal categorical questions which are easy to understand ("the way leading to them is wide"). Thus, missing the mark concerning these, especially for *mujtahid*s, is a sign of passion or bias (*hawā*, *hawāda*) troubling the assent. These states of mind are for legal deliberation what negligence and stubbornness are in the case of assent to basic theological matters: they involve voluntary acts that interfere with a determined action and prevent it from happening normally. Accordingly, they belong to the realm of legal acts for which one is held responsible.

On the other hand, presumptive legal questions are difficult ones, much like the difficult questions of philosophy. Assent in their case is not determined, and a *mujtahid* who misses the truth when dealing with them cannot be incriminated, exactly like the philosophers when dealing with difficult questions. In both cases they are allowed to commit unintentional errors because of the difficulty of the questions. This permission is based on the dissociation of the alethic and juridical levels which benefits both philosophers and *mujtahid*s.

---

26 *Short Commentary on the* Mustaṣfā, § 295, Arabic edition with French translation in Ibn Rushd 2015.

27 This idea of emphasising the process is also present in the radical infaillibilist position, characterised by an absence of result (Zysow 2013, 259).

These analogies with the law enable Averroes to persuade his readership of the legal validity of philosophical practice. In order to defend philosophers from the accusation of *takfīr*, he reflects on the role of error in different philosophical systems, with an eye to explaining how it has arisen in the reasoning that gave rise to those systems. Along these lines, when examined from a juridical perspective, the practice of philosophy in the *Decisive Treatise* appears to be akin to dialectic and seems to belong to the group of arts that the Aristotelian tradition calls stochastic. It includes dialectic and rhetoric, but also medicine and navigation. In those arts, as opposed to productive ones (like house-building), *ergon* and *telos* are dissociated. Hence, the objective of their practitioners is less to reach the goal in every single instance, than to have a complete command of the method or capacity.[28] When it comes to non-determined sciences (in which we can include jurisprudence as described by legal theorists in the chapters on *ijtihād*), individual failures thwart neither their validity as sciences nor the legitimacy of their practitioners.[29] Confronted with the accusations of al-Ghazālī, who questions the validity of the philosophical method and the coherence of its different systems, Averroes seeks to safeguard its scientific status and the professional authority of its practitioners, despite occasional failures.

---

28 See Alexander, *In Top.* 1.3, 32.10–34.5, commenting on *Top.* I.3 101b5–10. See also Aristotle, *Rhet.* I.1, 1355b10 – 11.

29 For a presentation of stochastic arts and of the Galen-Alexander debate on the status of medicine as an art despite its failures, see Ierodiakonou 1995.

Jon Hoover

Foundations of Ibn Taymiyya's Religious Utilitarianism

1 Introduction

Sophia Vasalou (2016, 171–172) in her recent monograph on the theological ethics of the Damascene theologian Ibn Taymiyya (d. 728/1328) insightfully observes that his view of God's morality resembles the utilitarianism of the English philosopher Jeremy Bentham (d. 1832). According to Ibn Taymiyya, God in His wise purpose weighs up the good and the evil in order to choose the preponderant good, and the good that God does in the world far exceeds the evil. Vasalou (2016, 172) writes, "Ibn Taymiyya's account of God's morality echoes nothing if not the axiom of utilitarianism articulated by Bentham: 'It is the greatest happiness of the greatest number that is the measure of right and wrong'." Findings of my own work on Ibn Taymiyya's theology reinforce and extend the aptness of Vasalou's assessment: God creates the world in the best possible way; God creates evil and metes out punishment to deter, instruct, purify, and spur on to repentance; and God's mercy and wise purpose preclude chastising anyone in hellfire forever. The goal towards which God creates and commands is universal human salvation and total worship of God that gives God His full due as God (Hoover 2007, 26–29, 190–206, 211–228; 2009; 2015; 2018).[1] The greatest happiness that God maximises for the greatest number is fundamentally religious in character.

Utilitarian thinking has also been observed in Ibn Taymiyya's ethical and jurisprudential deliberation. Michael Cook notes Ibn Taymiyya's exhortation to weigh up the benefits (*maṣāliḥ*) and detriments (*mafāsid*) of acts in order to choose the greater of two goods or the lesser of two evils. Cook relates an anecdote to illustrate the point. During a Mongol invasion of Syria, Ibn Taymiyya vis-

I am grateful to Ali-Reza Bhojani and Christopher Woodard for their insightful comments on earlier drafts of this chapter. The research for this chapter was funded by the British Academy.

1 Vasalou (2016, 137–196) correctly highlights the centrality for Ibn Taymiyya of wise purpose, benefit, and God's right to worship in giving rise to God's commands, but she incorrectly concludes that he does not explain why God punishes. While Ibn Taymiyya does sometimes says that God's wise purposes cannot be known, he does in other places give reasons, and the fundamental aim of punishment is engendering religious devotion.

https://doi.org/10.1515/9783110552386-010

ited the camp of the Mongols and found them drunk. One of his comrades wanted to rebuke the Mongols for drinking alcohol, but Ibn Taymiyya countered that they should be left to drink. If the Mongols were to stop drinking, they would be able to inflict even more harm on the Muslims. Cook also observes that Ibn Taymiyya has none of the traditional Ḥanbalī uneasiness about political power. Public offices are fundamentally religious in character, and Ibn Taymiyya insists that these offices be given to the candidates best able to do the job, neither those too scrupulous to engage political reality effectively, nor those who ignore morality in the name of political expediency (Cook 2000, 154 – 157).[2]

Yahya Michot has highlighted and translated a number of texts bringing out utilitarian reasoning in Ibn Taymiyya. In a study of texts on the ethics of quitting bad company, Michot (2006, 20) speaks of Ibn Taymiyya's "profound utilitarianism" and shows how he calls for weighing up the benefits and detriments in each situation. One should ordinarily abandon the company of the disobedient and the perverse to avoid corruption, but not if there is preponderant benefit in staying in contact, or if even greater detriment would ensue from leaving (Michot 2006, 14 – 17, 20, 85 – 100).[3] In other passages translated by Michot, Ibn Taymiyya argues against insurrection because the detriment entailed always exceeds the detriment of leaving an unjust ruler in office, and, in the course of discussing the prophet Joseph in Egypt, he gives instruction on choosing the preponderant benefit when faced with competing obligations (Michot 2012a, 222 and 263 – 264). Also, at the end of a treatise on the caliphate, Ibn Taymiyya identifies benefit-detriment analysis and adapting the law to circumstances as the way of the Prophet himself (Michot 2006, 50 – 53, n. 3).[4] We will return to this treatise below.

The consistency of Ibn Taymiyya's utilitarianism across the divine and human levels is remarkable within the Ashʿarī-dominated context of his time because Ashʿarī voluntarism does not admit of God acting for purposes or according to any recognisable moral criteria. The aim of the present investigation

2 On Ibn Taymiyya's counsel not to forbid wine to the Mongols, see further Michot 2006, 96 – 97, n. 2. Vasalou (2016, 92) hesitates to call Ibn Taymiyya's ethics on the human level "utilitarian", explaining that he does not frame his concern as the greatest good for the greatest number in the fashion of Jeremy Bentham and John Stuart Mill (d. 1873). However, Vasalou undermines this caution elsewhere by noting that Ibn Taymiyya frequently has the benefit of the community or the world as a whole in view such "that it is public interest rather than individual self-interest that Ibn Taymiyya isolates as the ultimate foundation for ethical norms" (Vasalou 2016, 101; also 23, 45 – 46, 48 – 52, 100 – 102).

3 Michot (2006, 20) also takes Ibn Taymiyya's utilitarianism, prudence, and pragmatism as evidence that he is a "theologian of moderation." I evaluate this portrayal in Hoover 2016.

4 Michot does not mention the fact that the treatise from which he translates deals with the caliphate. Caterina Bori (2016, 7, 23) also speaks of Ibn Taymiyya's "highly utilitarian" stance.

is to explore the conceptual foundations of utilitarianism in Ibn Taymiyya's theology, jurisprudence, and ethics: first how he overcomes Ash'arī voluntarist objections to formulate a coherent theology of a God acting toward utilitarian ends, and then how he justifies utilitarian ethical and jurisprudential deliberation at the human level, especially in view of his conviction that revelation has already indicated everything of human benefit.

I will consider how Ibn Taymiyya upholds God's purposive activity against Ash'arī voluntarism through exposition of his treatise *al-Irāda wa'l-amr* dating to 714/1315. This treatise has the advantage of tackling the major issues directly and comprehensively, even if not as fully as in some of Ibn Taymiyya's other works. This study of *Irāda* will show that Ibn Taymiyya's divine utilitarianism is grounded in a perpetually dynamic vision of God that is made conceptually possible by integrating features of the medieval Islamic philosophical tradition (*falsafa*).[5]

The second part of the study takes up Ibn Taymiyya's ethics and jurisprudence. Vasalou argues in her recent monograph that Ibn Taymiyya's claims to rational discernment of ethical value are very thin because revelation in fact specifies the full range of human benefit. The centrality of *maṣlaḥa* – benefit, utility, and welfare – in Ibn Taymiyya's ethics is ultimately a rationalisation of the revealed law in the interest of piety that flows out of the belief that reason and revelation coincide. While Vasalou is correct on this key point, she does not push through to Ibn Taymiyya's conviction that utilitarianism itself is the way of the Prophet, as noted already by Michot, and that this opens the door to substantive ethical and jurisprudential reflection in the face of dilemmas thrown up by sin and human weakness. I will illustrate this through exposition of Ibn Taymiyya's treatise on the caliphate. This will make apparent that the character of human utilitarianism is in certain respects similar to the utilitarianism of God.

5 For discussion of the issues in other Taymiyyan works in addition to *Irāda* and references to competing voluntarist Ash'arī views, see Hoover 2010b, 116–119; 2010a; 2007, 70–102.

2 God's Utilitarianism Rooted in God's Perpetual Dynamism

Ibn Taymiyya's *al-Irāda wa'l-amr* runs to 78 printed pages in the eighth volume of the large collection of his works *Majmūʿ al-fatāwā*.[6] Ibn Taymiyya says that the focus of this treatise – causality (*taʿlīl*) in the will of God – encompasses everything theological, jurisprudential, and eschatological. It relates to theological issues of God's names and attributes and God's creation and determination of all things, to legal and moral questions surrounding God's command and prohibition, and to eschatological matters of reward and punishment. It is also at the core of controversies over God's power, justice, and love in theology and whether legal rulings derive from a wise purpose (*ḥikma*), a benefit (*maṣlaḥa*), and a cause (*ʿilla*), or from God's sheer will (Ibn Taymiyya 1961–1967, 8:81–82).

The occasion of *Irāda* is a trilemma presented to Ibn Taymiyya in the year 714/1315. The three prongs of the trilemma are as follows. First, if God created without cause, God would be aimless, which cannot be true. Second, if God created for a cause and this cause were eternal, then the effect would likewise be eternal. That would mean that the world is eternal, which is also problematic. On the other hand, and third, if God created for a cause and this cause were originated in time, then it would follow that this cause must itself have a cause, and so forth into an infinite regress. However, the trilemma asserts, an infinite regress is impossible. Here is the trilemma given to Ibn Taymiyya in direct quotation (Ibn Taymiyya 1961–1967, 8:81):

> Concerning the goodness of the will of God – Exalted is He – in creating creatures and bringing forth the human race. Does He create for a cause (*ʿilla*) or for other than a cause?
>
> 1) If it is said, "not for a cause", He is aimless – Exalted is God above that.
> 2) If it is said, "for a cause", and if you say that it is eternal (*lam tazal*), it follows necessarily that the effect is eternal.
> 3) And if you say that it is temporally originated (*muḥdatha*), it follows necessarily that it had a cause, but an endless chain is absurd.

6 In Ibn Taymiyya 1961–1967, 8:81–158 and Ibn Taymiyya 1341–1349/1922–1930, 5:113–170. In both editions, the treatise is titled *Aqwam mā qīla fī l-qaḍāʾ wa'l-qadar wa'l-ḥikma wa'l-taʿlīl*. It appears under the title *al-Irāda wa'l-amr* in Ibn Taymiyya 1323/1905, 1:318–386. In continuity with previous scholarship I use the title *al-Irāda wa'l-amr*, but cite it from Ibn Taymiyya 1961–1967.

At the end of *Irāda*, Ibn Taymiyya (1961–1967, 8:155–158) observes that not all three prongs of the trilemma can be false. At least one of the following must be true: 1) God is aimless; 2) the world is eternal; or 3) an infinite regress is possible. Ibn Taymiyya explicitly rejects the eternity of the world, but beyond that he is uncharacteristically reticent. He does not come down firmly in favour of God's aimlessness – an unflattering description of Ashʿarī voluntarism – or for an infinite regress. Instead, he concludes that such questions must be approached gradually and investigated from all sides until the truth appears "to whomever God wills to guide" (Ibn Taymiyya 1961–1967, 8:158). Perhaps Ibn Taymiyya was wary of repercussions from the Ashʿarī-dominated establishment, should he come out firmly against the first view. Nevertheless, the body of *Irāda* makes eminently clear that his sympathies lie with an infinite regress.

Early in the treatise, Ibn Taymiyya (1961–1967, 8:83–93) outlines the three groups that correspond to the three prongs of the opening trilemma. These are 1) the voluntarists who deny causality in God's will, which is the view of the Ashʿarī *kalām* theologians, 2) the philosophers who affirm the eternity of the world, and 3) those who affirm that God creates and commands for a praiseworthy purpose. Among this last group are the Muʿtazilīs. We will start with the philosophers.

Ibn Taymiyya does not mention any philosophers by name, but he clearly has in view philosophers of a post-Avicennan ilk who think in terms of complete causality.[7] He explains that the philosophers affirm both the eternity of the final cause of the world and the eternity of the efficient cause. The Originator of the world is thus a complete cause (*ʿilla tāmma*), which means that it necessitates its effect without any delay in time. Otherwise, if the cause were not present in eternity in all its fullness, another cause would have been required to bring about the world. Then, another cause prior to that cause would have been required to bring it into existence, and so on in an infinite regress. Otherwise, the effect would have originated without a cause or a preponderator (*murajjiḥ*), and for the philosophers preponderance without a preponderator is absurd.

Ibn Taymiyya retorts in *Irāda* that the philosophers' notion of a complete cause necessitates that nothing occur in time at all and that this is even more obviously false than an infinite regress of causes or preponderance without a preponderator. The philosophers' God as complete cause could never originate

7 Lukas Muehlethaler (2012) notes that usage of the term "complete cause" is well established by the thirteenth century and he discusses evidence from Abū l-Barakāt al-Baghdādī (d. c. 560/1165), Athīr al-Dīn al-Abharī (d. 663/1264), and Ibn Kammūna (d. 683/1284).

temporal events. This is because the effect of a complete cause can never lag behind that cause in time. If something were to occur in time, it would originate without cause or something to originate it. To Ibn Taymiyya (1961–1967, 8:84–87), this is absurd, and no attempt to introduce intermediaries into the system, as the philosophers do, will alleviate the problem. In making God a complete cause, the philosophers cannot explain how events occur in time.

Moreover, Ibn Taymiyya argues, an infinite regress of temporally originating events should pose no difficulties to the philosophers because they posit the similar notion of eternal motion in the heavenly spheres. He also claims that an infinite regress of events fits better with divine revelation, as revelation indicates that the origination of the heavens and the earth in six days followed on from prior events and causes. Moreover, it is in fact better to say that God created this world for a prior cause that originated in time than to say that this world is eternal and devoid of originating events. Ibn Taymiyya claims that reason as well finds this more plausible. Reason also affirms that nothing occurs in time without a prior cause, but it does not assert that an effect must proceed from its cause without any delay in time (Ibn Taymiyya 1961–1967, 8:87–88).

On this question of the infinite regress, Ibn Taymiyya opposes *kalām* theologians who insist that events must have a beginning. On causal priority, however, he comes down on the side of *kalām* against *falsafa* by insisting that God has a real will. He complains that the philosophers reduce God's will to God's knowledge even though they affirm divine final causality. For Ibn Taymiyya, a God who acts on behalf of a final cause (*ʿilla ghāʾiyya*), or what he calls a desired wise purpose (*ḥikma maṭlūba*), must necessarily be possessed of a will (Ibn Taymiyya 1961–1967, 8:88). The final causality of God for Ibn Taymiyya is not merely a causality drawing creatures to God; it is also a causality orienting the operation of God's own will.

We now shift to the group affirming that God creates and commands for a cause or praiseworthy wise purpose. Ibn Taymiyya says that this view is held by Muslims from each of the four Sunnī law schools, as well as Muʿtazilīs, Karrāmīs, *ḥadīth* experts, Sufis, Qur'an exegetes, most of the ancient philosophers, and even some later philosophers like Abū l-Barakāt al-Baghdādī (d. c. 560/1165). Ibn Taymiyya's sympathies clearly lie with this group. Nonetheless, he singles out the Muʿtazilīs for censure. He criticises the Muʿtazilīs for imposing human standards of good and bad on God, obligating God to do the best (*al-aṣlāḥ*) for humans, and limiting God's power and will (Ibn Taymiyya 1961–1967, 8:91–92). He also denounces the Muʿtazilīs for maintaining that God's wise purpose is something "created and disjoined from Him" (*makhlūqa munfaṣila ʿanhu*) (Ibn Taymiyya 1961–1967, 8:89) and that God created the world for the wise purpose of benefiting creatures "without any judgement redounding from that to Him and without any act or attribute subsisting in Him" (Ibn Taymiyya 1961–1967, 8:89).

The Muʿtazilīs are concerned to protect God's absolute unity, and, like the Ashʿarīs, they hold that God cannot be a locus or substrate for temporal origination. Thus, the Muʿtazilīs locate God's purpose, which is temporally originated, outside God's essence. God's purpose is disjoined from God, and it does not subsist in Him. Furthermore, according to the Muʿtazilīs, God cannot gain anything from acting for a purpose because God has no need of anything. Ibn Taymiyya rejects this Muʿtazilī God as indifferent and disinterested and therefore imperfect. For Ibn Taymiyya, acting well toward others is praiseworthy, and praise and benefit naturally redound to agents of good acts. Moreover, Ibn Taymiyya (1961–1967, 8:89–90) writes, "anyone who commits an act in which there is neither pleasure, nor benefit, nor profit for himself in any respect, neither sooner nor later, is aimless, and he is not praised for this." Pure altruism is irrational; the only acts that are rational are those that involve some kind of benefit and profit for the agent of the act, and not just the recipient (Ibn Taymiyya 1961–1967, 8:89–91, 125–126, 149–151). The full theological import of this ethical egoism becomes more apparent in Ibn Taymiyya's comments on his third group, the voluntarists.

In *Irāda* Ibn Taymiyya identifies the voluntarists as those who affirm that God creates and commands out of sheer will without cause. Ibn Taymiyya tells us that this position is held widely among Sunnī *kalām* theologians and legal scholars, among them al-Ashʿarī (d. 324/935) and his followers, and Ibn Ḥazm (d. 456/1064) and the Ẓāhirīs. Ibn Taymiyya outlines the main voluntarist arguments near the beginning of *Irāda* and provides counterarguments later in the treatise. The first voluntarist argument is as follows. If God had created the world for a cause, He would have been imperfect beforehand, and creating on account of that cause would have perfected Him. Putting it another way, positing a cause for creation implies that God was perfected by that cause, which means that He was previously imperfect (Ibn Taymiyya 1961–1967, 8:83). Ibn Taymiyya counters that it is in fact rational that an agent be perfected by His act. To say that God is perfected by His acts is no different from saying that God is perfected by His attributes or His essence. Moreover, an agent who brings things into existence with a wise purpose, that is, a cause, is in fact more perfect than one who does not, and it is the essence of perfection that things come into existence at their proper time, not before (Ibn Taymiyya 1961–1967, 8:146–147).[8] With this, Ibn Taymiyya defangs the voluntarist argument by turn-

8 A fuller description of these arguments is given in Hoover 2007, 100–101.

ing an alleged imperfection into a perfection. A God who acts for causes and wise purposes is eminently more perfect than one who does not. Nonetheless, this would still appear to imply need in God inasmuch as He acts to gain benefits that He did not previously enjoy. Also, it would seem to make God dependent on creatures and created things for the expression of His perfection through wise acts. I will take up these problems further below.

The second voluntarist argument expands on the latter two positions in the opening trilemma of *Irāda*. If God had created for a cause that was eternal, the effect would have been eternal as well. The *kalām* theologians deny that the relation between God and the world is that of an eternal cause with its eternal effect. Conversely, if God had created for a cause that originated in time, this would cause two problems. First, it would entail some kind of temporal change in God, and it would turn God into a locus or substrate (*maḥall*) for temporarily originating events (*ḥawādith*). Second, it would entail an infinite regress of causes because each originated cause would require a prior cause to bring it into existence and so on into the infinite past (Ibn Taymiyya 1961–1967, 8:83–84). Ashʿarīs and others seek to avoid these problems by positing God's will as a single eternal attribute whose very nature it is to specify one thing over another and to bring the world into existence at the appointed moment. Ibn Taymiyya sets out arguments against this. An eternal divine will simply cannot specify one thing over another without a cause giving rise to that specification (*takhṣīṣ*). To deny specifying causes is to throw causality in general into doubt, and that would undermine cosmological proofs for the existence of God (Ibn Taymiyya 1961–1967, 8:147–148). The alternative view, explains Ibn Taymiyya (1961–1967, 8:149), is that God's wise purpose and God's act occur by means of God's will and God's power, and all of these things – God's wise purpose, God's acts, God's will, and God's power – subsist in God's essence just as all other divine attributes subsist in God's essence.

On the question of the infinite regress, Ibn Taymiyya (1961–1967, 8:152, 154–155) asserts that everyone agrees that causes cannot regress forever. However, an infinite regress of conditions and effects (*al-shurūṭ wa'l-āthār*), that is, an infinite regress of temporally originating events, is permitted. According to Ibn Taymiyya, this is in fact equivalent to the statement of the *salaf*, the early Muslims, that "God has been speaking from eternity when He wills. Acts and other [things] linked to His will and His power have been subsisting in Him from eternity" (Ibn Taymiyya 1961–1967, 8:152). In *Irāda* Ibn Taymiyya also notes that people holding this view say that *kalām* arguments against an infinite regress are weak (Ibn Taymiyya 1961–1967, 8:152–153). Ibn Taymiyya does not provide detailed refutations of these arguments in *Irāda*, but he does do so in his later work *Minhāj al-sunna* (Ibn Taymiyya 1406/1986, 1:432–438).[9]

By now, it is clear that Ibn Taymiyya in *Irāda* favours a dynamic view of God in which it is of God's perfection to act by will and power for wise purposes from eternity. All of these elements – God's act, God's will, God's power, and God's wise purpose – subsist in God's essence, and God's acts and wise purposes regress into the past without beginning. These are equivalent to events (*ḥawādith*) subsisting in God's essence, which in other texts Ibn Taymiyya prefers to call God's voluntary acts and attributes.[10] Also, in other texts, Ibn Taymiyya works out the implications of this theology for creation. Since God has been creating one thing or another from eternity, there has always been one created thing or another in existence. No single created thing is eternal without beginning. However, the genus of created things has no beginning (Hoover 2004, 287–329; 2007, 88–91).

Back in *Irāda*, a good part of the middle of the treatise is devoted to the problem of evil, God's creation of the human act, and the interplay between human responsibility and God's predetermination of all things. Ibn Taymiyya's reflections on evil clarify the utilitarian character of God's acts as he underlines that God sends messengers to bring preponderant benefit. Ibn Taymiyya writes (1961–1967, 8:93–94), "The messengers – God bless them – were raised up to obtain benefits and perfect them and to strip away detriments and reduce them to the extent possible."[11] Similar logic also applies more broadly to things like rain. Rain is certainly profitable overall even if it sometimes destroys homes and disrupts travellers. Ibn Taymiyya (1961–1967, 8:94) states the general rule as follows: "Something whose profit and benefit is general is an intended good and beloved mercy even if some people are harmed by it."[12] In short, God in His wise purpose maximises benefit in all that He does. Ibn Taymiyya affirms in texts that are probably later than *Irāda* that God creates this world in the best possible way and that evil is essentially non-existent – it is nothing but the lack of good.[13] This approach to theodicy is distinctively Neoplatonic and Avicennan, and further resonances with Avicennism become even more apparent when we move to Ibn Taymiyya's attempt to ward off the charge that God needs creatures in order to be perfect.

---

9 The arguments are exposited in Hoover 2007, 91–95.

10 For elaboration, see Hoover 2010a, 2007, 84–88, 95–96.

11 As translated in Hoover 2007, 186.

12 As translated in Hoover 2007, 186.

13 For elaboration, see Hoover 2007, 224–228.

The context is a passage toward the end of *Irāda* discussing God's love for humans and human love for God. Ibn Taymiyya (1961–1967, 8:140–145) links love to obedience, praise, and worship. Humans express love for God by doing what God commands, and God in turn loves humans who obey Him, praise Him, and laud Him. However, God's love, praise, and laudation of Himself are always far greater than any love, praise, and laudation that humans could give Him. In fact, they are so much greater that God ultimately has no need of the human contribution. Ibn Taymiyya (1961–1967, 8:145) writes, "[God] praises Himself, lauds Himself, and glorifies Himself – Glory be to Him, Exalted is He. He is the Sufficient-in-Himself (*al-ghanī bi-nafsihī*). He does not need anyone else. On the contrary, everything other than Him is in want of Him." When God rejoices, loves, and is well pleased with His servants, it does not mean that God needs them. On the contrary, it is in fact God who created in them what He loves. Ibn Taymiyya (1961–1967, 8:145) puts it this way: "[God] is not perfected by another. It is He who created them, and He it is who guided them and helped them so that they did what He loves, is well pleased with, and rejoices at. These beloved things occurred only by His power, His will, and His creation." Focusing on God's self-love, Ibn Taymiyya (1961–1967, 8:144) writes, "what God loves of worship of Him and obedience to Him follows from love for Himself, and love of that is the cause of [His] love for His believing servants. His love for believers follows from love for Himself."[14]

Joseph Bell in his book *Love Theory in Ḥanbalite Islam* noted already in 1979 that Ibn Taymiyya's impulse here is Neoplatonic and finds much resonance within Sufism. We may add that it is also Avicennan inasmuch as God's self-love gives rise to the world as a necessary concomitant (Bell 1979, 71–73; Hoover 2007, 70–76). The similarities, however, end there. Whereas the First Principle of Avicenna (Ibn Sīnā, d. 428/1037) is eternal in a timeless sense, Ibn Taymiyya envisions the life of God as profoundly historical. God by virtue of His perfection is ever active without beginning and without end. Yet, Ibn Taymiyya's theology is not the modern process philosophy of Alfred North Whitehead and Charles Hartshorne in which the fate of God is dependent upon the fate of the world.[15] For Ibn Taymiyya, God is the indestructible creator of all things. The perfect and self-sufficient historical process of God's inner life has as its necessary concomitant the best possible creaturely history, a drama in which God is always maximising human benefit through what He creates and what He commands. This is furthermore the vision of God supported by both revelation and reason.

14 For further discussion of these texts, see Hoover 2007, 99–100.
15 For an introduction to process philosophy's theological aspects, see Viney 2014.

All considered, Ibn Taymiyya's theology is highly successful at rooting the utilitarian rationality of both God's creation and God's revelation all the way down into God's essence, and it is his temporalisation of the Avicennan notion of God's self-love that makes this possible. Additionally, Ibn Taymiyya at the beginning of *Irāda* indicates that considerations of cause and benefit pervade theological, ethical, and legal discourse, and the body of *Irāda* illustrates this in theology. This provides Ibn Taymiyya's own warrant for looking to utilitarianism as a key to his thought more generally. The question now is how Ibn Taymiyya integrates utilitarian reasoning into the derivation of God's law.

3 Religious Utilitarianism as the Way of the Prophet

Given that Ibn Taymiyya clearly differs from Ashʿarīs over the roles that purpose, benefit, and causality play in the will of God, it is curious that his views on ethical value are in fact very close to those of later Ashʿarism. As Vasalou explains, Ibn Taymiyya sidelines both the Muʿtazilī deontology in which good and bad are objective qualities of acts themselves and the subjectivist aspect of Ashʿarī ethics that conceives good and bad as functions of God's command and prohibition. Instead, acts are good or bad and just or unjust by virtue of their outcomes, that is, whether they yield pleasure or pain, benefit or harm. Ibn Taymiyya's approach to ethical value is decidedly consequentialist, and he is indebted in this directly to the later Ashʿarī Fakhr al-Dīn al-Rāzī (d. 606/1210) and more distantly to al-Ghazālī (d. 505/1111) and Avicenna (Vasalou 2016, 11–136; Hoover 2007, 34–44).[16]

We first take up the puzzle of how later Ashʿarīs fit ethical and legal consequentialism together with denial of purpose in God's will. To address this and to fill in important background to Ibn Taymiyya, I turn to an essay by Ahmed El Shamsy (2014) on wisdom in God's law. El Shamsy explores the paradox that Shāfiʿī jurists of Muʿtazilī inclination do not draw on benefit to derive legal rulings while those of Ashʿarī proclivity do.

El Shamsy (2014, 22–25) identifies two tenth-century Shāfiʿī jurists influenced by Muʿtazilism: al-Qaffāl al-Shāshī (d. 365/976) and Abū Bakr Aḥmad b. ʿUmar b. Yūsuf al-Khaffāf (death date unknown). Al-Qaffāl and al-Khaffāf adopt the Muʿtazilī notion that God's purpose in the law is to promote human

16 For an overview of Muʿtazilī and Ashʿarī ethical theory and especially Fakhr al-Din al-Rāzī, see Shihadeh 2016b; and more fully Shihadeh 2006, 45–107.

benefit (*maṣlaḥa*), effectively embedding the law within theology. For these Muʿtazilī-inspired Shāfiʿīs, reason knows acts to be obligatory, forbidden, or permissible. Acts that fall within the category of the permissible in reason may be further specified by the revealed law, and such legal rulings follow deductively from God's wisdom. A God who is wise and powerful will realise human benefit, and human benefit is then the cause of those factors or causes that give rise to specific legal rulings. In other words, "God's wisdom gives rise to laws that serve the benefit of His creatures" (El Shamsy 2014, 25).

El Shamsy explains that these tenth-century Shāfiʿīs justify the validity of legal analogy with benefit but do not use their theories of benefit to derive new legal rulings. Their aim is simply to provide an apologetic against those who would denigrate the rationality of God's law. The precise benefits of specific rulings are not knowable even though the law is known to be beneficial in general. This reminds El Shamsy of the tenth-century Ḥanafī jurists Abū l-Ḥasan al-Karkhī (d. 340/952) and Abū Bakr al-Jaṣṣāṣ (d. 370/980) and their distinction between the cause of a specific ruling, on the one hand, and the cause of benefit (al-Jaṣṣāṣ) or the wise purpose (al-Karkhī), on the other. The cause of benefit or the wise purpose in a rule is not known in detail and cannot be used to establish the rule. The rule is established only by the legal cause, which is merely a sign or marker that God has given to indicate His ruling. Even though benefit is not considered when deriving specific rulings, the theological conviction remains that God in His wisdom brings about human benefit through the law (El Shamsy 2014, 27–29).

El Shamsy (2014, 30–34) then takes up al-Ghazālī who turns the tables to integrate benefit into legal theory by moving it "out of the realm of theology and into the realm of law" (El Shamsy 2014, 34). Unlike his Muʿtazilī-inspired Shāfiʿī predecessors, al-Ghazālī does not deduce the beneficial character of the law from God's attribute of wisdom. Rather he derives it inductively from the existing rulings of the divine law itself. In other words, he works from the bottom up instead of the top down. For al-Ghazālī as an Ashʿarī theologian, God is not subject to objective ethical standards, and God's actions are not motivated by purposes or considerations of benefit. However, this does not prevent human beings from using reason to study the law and to infer that it promotes benefit.[17]

17 El Shamsy (2014, 32–33) suggests that al-Ghazālī's empirical and inductive approach to discerning benefit in the divine law takes inspiration from his interaction with Galen's elaboration of the usefulness of the various parts of the human body. Rather than asserting that God in His wisdom necessarily created the parts of the human body to be useful, al-Ghazālī works inductively from the beneficial design of the human body to elucidate God's wisdom. El Shamsy works out the methodological parallel between al-Ghazālī's ethics and teleological proof for God

With this in mind, al-Ghazālī examines the rulings established in the law to discern its fundamental principles, and then he uses these principles to extend the law to other cases. For example, al-Ghazālī investigates the purpose of prohibiting intoxicants and discerns that it is protection of the intellect. Protecting the intellect is then taken to be one of the fundamental purposes of the law (*maqāṣid al-sharīʿa*); the other four purposes are protecting life, progeny, property, and religion. When the various purposes of the law have been established, they may be used as criteria to judge the suitability or appropriateness (*munāsaba*) of particular characteristics to be legal causes and then draw these causes into a coherent framework of human benefit. According to El Shamsy (2014, 30–32), al-Ghazālī successfully turns benefit into an instrument of legal reasoning by banishing considerations of benefit from the realm of theology.[18]

El Shamsy stops with al-Ghazālī, but if we move forward another century, we find that Fakhr al-Dīn al-Rāzī elaborates much the same approach. Al-Rāzī in his *al-Maḥṣūl fī ʿilm uṣūl al-fiqh* concedes that God's acts and rulings are not "caused by motives and purposes" (*muʿallala bi'l-dawāʿī wa'l-aghrāḍ*). Nonetheless, al-Rāzī contends that there is a certain regularity about the revolutions of the celestial spheres, the movements of the constellations, and the fact that fire burns what it contacts. The repetition of these movements and events is not necessary (*wājib*) but rather a matter of God's custom (*ʿāda*). In all probability (*ẓann*) these movements and patterns of activity will continue on in the future as they have in the past. In a similar manner, inductive examination of God's law reveals regular patterns of coincidence between rulings and benefits that will in all probability remain stable so as to form the basis for determining the suitability of various characteristics to be legal causes. However, these legal causes are in no way caused by divine purposes. Moreover, al-Rāzī (1992, 5:172–179, especially 179) argues, it is sufficient to have only probable knowledge of the suitability of legal causes since probability is sufficient to establish a point of law. Certainty is not required.[19]

---

directly elsewhere (El Shamsy 2016). Similarly, Frank Griffel (2009, 225–234) shows that al-Ghazālī in his *Iḥyāʾ ʿulūm al-dīn* does not derive the goodness of the world from the nature of God. Instead, he examines the wonders of the created world to arrive at the conclusion that this is the most wonderful world possible and that this reveals God's wisdom.

18 See also the discussion of "suitability" in al-Ghazālī in Opwis 2010, 80–88.

19 See also the discussions of this text in Shihadeh 2006, 99–101 (with translation of al-Rāzī 1992, 5:179); Opwis 2010, 118–121; Vasalou 2016, 163–164. The classic study on the requirement of only probability to establish points of law is Zysow 2013.

We are now in a position to examine Ibn Taymiyya's critique of later Ashʿarīs like al-Ghazālī and al-Rāzī. His deductive and theological approach to the rationality of the law stands behind his accusation that the later Ashʿarīs contradict themselves: they detect benefit in God's law inductively but deny that it derives from purpose in God's will.[20] Ibn Taymiyya also criticises the Ashʿarīs for grounding the suitability of the legal causes in God's custom rather than God's direct legislation, and he maintains that God explicitly legislates in order to attract benefit and repel detriment. Benefit and purpose in the law are not merely coincidences of God's legislative custom. Ibn Taymiyya (1961–1967, 17:200) writes, "those among the later [Ashʿarīs] who uphold suitability (*munāsaba*) say that what is suitable is taken into consideration in the revelation. They draw inferences on the basis of coincidence (*iqtirān*) only, not on the grounds that the Legislator ruled what He ruled in order to obtain benefit sought by means of the ruling or to repel detriment."[21]

Ibn Taymiyya also rejects a further feature of later Ashʿarī legal theory: the unattested or unstated benefit (*al-maṣlaḥa al-mursala*). Al-Ghazālī developed the category of unstated benefit to indicate benefits not mentioned in the revelation. This would appear to expand the use of benefit to derive new law extensively. However, not just any unstated benefit is suitable to be a legal cause. Al-Ghazālī restricts suitability to those unstated benefits that conform to the five purposes of the law, namely, preservation of religion, life, intellect, progeny, and property.[22] Ibn Taymiyya criticises the concept of unstated benefit from two directions. From one direction, deriving new law on the basis of unstated benefits is tantamount to legislating rulings that God did not authorise – this is unacceptable. From the other, legally sanctioned benefit is not limited to the so-called five purposes of the law. According to Ibn Taymiyya, many people working within this narrow framework neglect other legally prescribed benefits. The law includes all real benefits in both worldly and religious affairs, and there are in fact no benefits left unstated in revelation. If a benefit is a true benefit, revelation will have indicated it, and those who think otherwise are unaware.[23] Ibn Taymiyya (1961–1967, 11:344–345) expresses the principle thus:[24]

---

20 See, for example, Ibn Taymiyya 1961–1967, "Jawāb ahl al-ʿilm wa'l-īmān anna 'qul huwa Allāh aḥad' taʿdilu thulth al-Qur'ān", 17:5–205, at 177.

21 See further Zysow 2013, 196–204, for the doctrine of *munāsaba* and brief mention of Ibn Taymiyya's criticism of it.

22 See Opwis 2010, 67–88, on al-Ghazālī and unattested or unstated *maṣlaḥa*.

23 Ibn Taymiyya 1961–1967, *Qāʿida fī l-muʿjizāt wa'l-karāmāt*, 11:311–362, at 342–346; 1341–1349/1922–1930, *Qāʿida sharīfa fī l-muʿjizāt wa-l-karāmāt*, 5:3–36, at 22–24. Discussions of Ibn Taymiyya's views on unstated or unattested benefit include Vasalou 2016, 202–205, 209–

> The principle overall is that the law (*sharīʿa*) never neglects a benefit (*maṣlaḥa*). Indeed, God – Exalted is He – has perfected the religion for us and completed the blessing. The Prophet – May God bless him and give him peace – has indeed spoken about everything that will bring us closer to the Garden of Paradise. (...) One of two possibilities must obtain for the rational person who believes that something is a benefit even though the revelation (*sharʿ*) does not relate it. Either the revelation indicates it and the person looking into it does not know it, or it is not a benefit even though he believes it to be a benefit. Benefit is profit that accrues and predominates, and often people imagine that something is profitable in religion and in this world, when in fact its profit is outweighed by harm. As He – Exalted is He – said about wine and gambling, "Say! In these two is a great sin and profits for the people. Their sin is greater than their profit" [Q. 2:219].

This passage makes readily apparent that Ibn Taymiyya is an apologist for the all-encompassing rationality of the law. The question then is whether Ibn Taymiyya's deductive approach to benefit in God's law and his claim that the law encompasses all benefits obviate substantive appeal to benefit in deriving specific rulings, much as it did for tenth-century Muʿtazilī-inspired Shāfiʿīs. Does Ibn Taymiyya merely comb the revelation for all possible indications of benefit and not think substantively beyond the text? Felicitas Opwis and Sophia Vasalou present opposing views on the question.

In a monograph on benefit (*maṣlaḥa*) in the Islamic tradition, Opwis (2010, 185–190) outlines Ibn Taymiyya's rejection of unstated benefit, and she clarifies that he does not follow later Ashʿarīs in using benefit to identify causes in legal analogies. However, she also notices that Ibn Taymiyya permits anything not prohibited to meet the needs of humans for their livelihoods and that he sometimes sets aside prohibitions on the basis of benefit, need, and necessity. For example, carrion is normally forbidden, but he allows a Muslim to eat it if necessary to avoid starvation. He also permits risk in sales to avoid the greater detriment of usury; thus, a pregnant animal may be sold even though the value of the offspring is not yet known. Opwis (2010, 184–185) concludes from such examples that Ibn Taymiyya uses benefit in a substantive manner to derive new rulings. She sums up, "Ibn Taymiyya's interpretation of *maṣlaḥa* follows a substantive rationality that is more inclusive than that of al-Ghazālī and includes

211; Opwis 2010, 186–190; Rapoport 2010, 198–199; Al-Matroudi 2006, 78–80; and Laoust 1939, 245–250. Opwis (2010, 187) translates the beginning of Ibn Taymiyya's discussion of unstated benefit from 1341–1349/1922–1930, 5:22, and, as she notes (187, n. 46), Laoust (1939, 246–247) also translates parts of this text but garbles the translation and says incorrectly that Ibn Taymiyya affirms the existence of unstated benefits.

24 Ibn Taymiyya (1961–1967, 19:308) writes elsewhere, "The law (*sharīʿa*) (...) encompasses the benefits of this world and the hereafter."

anything that brings about benefit and averts harm; every benefit that is not prohibited in the law is permitted; and in cases of need, *maṣlaḥa* can even overrule explicit prohibitions" (Opwis 2010, 198). Opwis furthermore perceives danger in Ibn Taymiyya's method, as his "reasoning lacks guidelines which assure some measure of accountability in the law-finding procedure." This results in an "intellectual elitism" that criticises the rulings of others but provides no criteria by which to measure its own (Opwis 2010, 198 – 199).

In contrast to Opwis, Vasalou finds claims to substantive legal rationality in Ibn Taymiyya very thin. She explains that, in the majority of his examples illustrating the need to weigh up benefit and harm, "the preferred action has been established on scriptural grounds" (Vasalou 2016, 207) and that consideration of benefit occurs "within the regulating framework of scripture" (Vasalou 2016, 209). Vasalou does note that Ibn Taymiyya presumes permissibility in customary acts when no textual indicants prohibit them, but she counters that he also requires positive demonstration that no prohibition exists. In the end, it is the revealed law that determines what is beneficial for human beings (Vasalou 2016, 207 – 220). Vasalou (2016, 221 – 229) argues that this is indeed the way it has to be in light of Ibn Taymiyya's theology. God in His wise purpose and justice sought to benefit humankind with prophecy, and we humans "should be able to believe that *our* sense of good and the *Lawgiver's* sense of good coincide" (Vasalou 2016, 228). In other words, it is Ibn Taymiyya's faith conviction that the revealed law encompasses all human benefit, and he takes it upon himself to buttress this conviction with rational argument. Vasalou (2016, 229 – 250) observes that Ibn Taymiyya's legal reflection uses reason to defend the all-encompassing benefit of the law much as his theological production is an apologetic for the rationality of revelation.[25]

Vasalou would appear to bring us back to viewing Ibn Taymiyya after the fashion of the tenth-century Shāfiʿīs al-Qaffāl and al-Khaffāf, with benefit playing no substantive role in the derivation of legal rulings. It is certainly clear that Ibn Taymiyya does not integrate benefit into a formal system of legal cause derivation along the lines of al-Ghazālī and al-Rāzī. However, there is more to Ibn Taymiyya's legal discourse on benefit than apologetics, and taking the perspectives of both Opwis and Vasalou together provides important insights. They are two sides of the same coin of a revelation-based authorisation to engage in utilitarian ethical and jurisprudential reasoning.

---

25 Rapoport (2010, 193 – 199) also underlines the parallels between Ibn Taymiyya's insistence that human benefit and the rulings of the law coincide, his assertion that a legal analogy never contradicts a revealed text, and his claim that reason and revelation never contradict in matters of theological doctrine.

To unpack this, I first revisit a passage that Vasalou uses to show how Ibn Taymiyya retains the priority of scriptural texts even while speaking directly about weighing up benefits and detriments. The text is found in Ibn Taymiyya's treatise on commanding the right and forbidding the wrong,[26] and the question at hand is whether to intervene in the moral affairs of others. Here are the key parts of the passage in translation. It is divided into four paragraphs to facilitate reference (Ibn Taymiyya 1961–1967, 28:129–131):[27]

> If benefits and detriments and good things and evil things contradict or compete with each other, then it is necessary to give preponderance to the preponderant of them. (...) If commanding and prohibiting involve obtaining benefit and repelling detriment, what opposes [carrying out this obligation] must also be examined. If the benefits lost or the detriments obtained are greater, it is no longer commanded. On the contrary, it is forbidden if its detriment is greater than its benefit.
>
> However, the extent of the benefits and the detriments must be considered according to the scale of the law (*sharīʿa*). When someone can follow the texts, he should not deviate from them. If not, he should exercise independent reasoning (*ijtahada bi-raʾyihi*) to come to a knowledge of similar and corresponding cases. However, it is rare that texts will be lacking for those who are expert in them and their indications of legal rulings.
>
> If, therefore, an individual or a group [faces a situation] combining right and wrong such that they cannot differentiate between the two and such that they have to do both or omit doing both, it is not permissible to command [only] the right and prohibit [only] the wrong. On the contrary, one has to investigate. If the right is greater, it is commanded, even if it necessarily entails wrong of lesser import. Wrong is not prohibited if it necessarily entails losing right greater than it. Indeed, prohibiting in that case would be tantamount to blocking the way of God. (...)
>
> Falling under this category is the indulgence of the Prophet – God bless him and give him peace – toward ʿAbd Allāh b. Ubayy and his like from among the leaders of hypocrisy and immorality, in view of their supporters [being large in number]. Putting an end to [Ibn Ubayy's] wrong by punishing him would necessarily have entailed putting an end to something right that was greater than that, namely, the fury and fervour of his people [for advancing the cause of religion]. People would also have found it distasteful had they heard that Muḥammad had killed one of his Companions [in punishment].

---

26 I will cite the treatise from Ibn Taymiyya 1961–1967, *al-Ḥisba*, 28:60–178, of which it forms a part (that is, 121–178); *Ḥisba* is translated in Ibn Taymiya 1985. The treatise has also been published separately as Ibn Taymiyya 1984, and it appears as well in Ibn Taymiyya 1420/2000, 2:198–311. Cook (2000, 151, n. 48) examines the complex textual history of the treatise in detail and suggests that it may have originally been part of *al-Istiqāma* although, as Cook explains, this suggestion is not without difficulties.

27 Ibn Taymiyya 1985, 80–81 (my translation differs). The first part of this text is translated in Johansen 2008, 283–284.

Vasalou (2016, 207) in her argument draws only on the first two paragraphs above. She quotes most of the first paragraph as a "remarkable methodological statement" of Ibn Taymiyya's call to use one's own judgement in balancing utility in commanding and forbidding. She then quotes much of the second paragraph to show that Ibn Taymiyya closes the door on "the prospect of a more substantive evaluative judgement." Texts are decisive in weighing up benefit and detriment, and those who know the texts well will not be lacking for guidance (Vasalou 2016, 209).

Reading all four paragraphs together adds nuance. The structure of the passage does indeed express Ibn Taymiyya's confidence that the law encompasses all benefits, but in a certain fashion. Twice over, in the first and third paragraphs, Ibn Taymiyya instructs readers to weigh up benefits and detriments before commanding or prohibiting an action. After the first instruction, he directs readers to subject their actions to the scale of the law, as there will almost always be a relevant text. Yet, if they cannot find a text, they should resort to independent reasoning on the basis of similar cases. Then, in the fourth paragraph, Ibn Taymiyya grounds the instruction to weigh up benefit and detriment in the precedent of the Prophet's indulgent dealings with ʿAbd Allāh b. Ubayy. Here, the precedent simply establishes the utilitarian principle. It does not indicate the ruling for a specific case in Ibn Taymiyya's time and place. The import of this passage is both that the revealed law is the measure of true benefit and that the law provides a principle for ethical and jurisprudential reasoning in utilitarian calculation. Textual indicants may not be clear or ready to hand for every specific situation, and this requires weighing up the benefit and detriment of an action for religion.[28]

The centrality of utilitarian reasoning to Ibn Taymiyya's ethics and jurisprudence becomes even clearer in a text that Vasalou does not consider: his treatise on the caliphate, which I will dub *Khilāfa* and which runs to 15 pages in volume 35 of *Majmūʿ al-fatāwā*.[29] In *Khilāfa*, Ibn Taymiyya joins together substantive and

---

28 Michot (2012b, 263–266), translates passages from *Minhāj al-sunna*, 6:410–416, in which Ibn Taymiyya distinguishes between universals, such as the commands to pray and give alms, and particulars, such as the direction of prayer in a specific place and the alms due on a specific item. Texts, according to Ibn Taymiyya, cannot rule on particulars, only on universals; analogy (*qiyās*) and independent reasoning (*ijtihād*) are required to ascertain the rulings on specific instances. This dovetails with the distinction I am making here between utilitarianism as an ethical and jurisprudential principle rooted in the revealed texts and the need to weigh up benefits and detriments in the conduct of day-to-day affairs.

29 Ibn Taymiyya 1961–1967, *Khilāfa*, 35:18–32. Mona Hassan (2010, 339–346, which is reprised in Hassan 2016, 111–114) and Ovamir Anjum (2012, 252–259) draw on this treatise to correct Henri Laoust's assertion, often repeated in secondary literature on Islamic political theory,

apologetic aspects of his legal methodology, and a review of this treatise will serve to illustrate how he both deploys the weighing up of benefit and detriment as a substantive legal and ethical source and then again grounds such utilitarian reasoning in the practice of the Prophet. This treatise is also of interest because it shows how Ibn Taymiyya addresses the difficulty that the ideal caliphate of the "rightly guided" no longer existed in his time. It will become apparent that part of Ibn Taymiyya's resort to utilitarian reasoning stems from his conviction that sin and weakness plague the human condition and must be taken into account.

Ibn Taymiyya begins *Khilāfa* with a Prophetic tradition stating that "the caliphate of prophecy" (*khilāfat al-nubuwwa*) will last thirty years before kingship (*mulk*) sets in. He links the "caliphate of prophecy" to the four "rightly guided caliphs" (*al-khulafāʾ al-rāshidūn*) – Abū Bakr, ʿUmar, ʿUthmān, and ʿAlī – and the beginning of kingship to the reign of Muʿāwiya. Ibn Taymiyya allows that there were more caliphs than just the first four "rightly guided", and he permits calling kings "caliphs" as well, even if they do not attain the perfection of the prophetic caliphate (Ibn Taymiyya 1961–1967, 35:18–20). Ibn Taymiyya maintains that the "caliphate of prophecy", or what he also calls the "practice of the caliphs" (*sunnat al-khulafāʾ*), is fundamentally a matter of obligation for the Muslim community. Kingship is only permissible in case of need (*ḥāja*) deriving from a lack of knowledge or power. Kingship is not permissible in itself, and it involves a failure to uphold part of the religion. Ibn Taymiyya also mentions the view that a caliphate tarnished by kingship (*shawb al-khilāfa bi'l-mulk*) is permissible and two extreme positions that he clearly rejects. One is that of the Khārijīs, Muʿtazilīs, and others for whom kingship is never permissible, even in case of need. The other extreme is to permit kingship absolutely without reference to the practice of the caliphs (Ibn Taymiyya 1961–1967, 35:22, 24–27).

The challenge facing Ibn Taymiyya is bridging the moral distance between the continuing obligation of the "caliphate of prophecy" and the reality of kingship in his day. He observes that omitting the "caliphate of prophecy" when it is in fact possible is blameworthy and subject to punishment, but, he asks, is it a major sin (*kabīra*) or a minor sin (*ṣaghīra*)? Ibn Taymiyya claims that the texts of the Qur'an and the Sunna favour the view that this depends on whether the king's good deeds outweigh his evil deeds and whether his good deeds exceed the good deeds of someone who commits no evil deeds at all. Failure to fulfil

---

that Ibn Taymiyya denied the obligatory character of the caliphate. For Laoust's view, see Laoust 1939, 281–283.

the obligation of the "caliphate of prophecy" is not necessarily a major sin (Ibn Taymiyya 1961–1967, 35:27–28).[30]

This matter of weighing up the good deeds and the evil deeds of those exercising kingship leads Ibn Taymiyya to the broader question of how to assess good deeds that will not be committed unless accompanied by evil deeds. This phenomenon, he says, appears in two forms. In the first, the good deed is impossible without the evil deed, in which case the evil deed is in fact no longer evil. This so-called evil deed is obligatory or recommended if it is essential to the performance of another obligatory or recommended deed. If the detriment of the so-called evil deed is less than the benefit of the good deed, then the so-called evil deed is not forbidden, as when someone eats carrion to survive or wears silk to protect against the cold.[31] Ibn Taymiyya complains that many people fail to understand the logic of needs and detriments. They ignore the needs that make some forbidden acts permitted, or they fail to see that detriment may render recommended or obligatory acts forbidden, as in the case of ritual prayer for someone who is ill or ritual purification for someone on the verge of death. Ibn Taymiyya applies this reasoning to restate the permissibility of deviation from the prophetic caliphate in case of inability to adhere to some of its practices. Sometimes the obligations of political or administrative authority can only be fulfilled by means of some lesser harm (Ibn Taymiyya 1961–1967, 35:28–29).

The second form in which good and evil deeds mix, according to Ibn Taymiyya, is when a good deed could be committed without an evil deed but only with difficulty. In reality people cannot bring themselves to commit this good deed without also engaging in something prohibited to help them through, something "whose sinfulness is less than the profit (*manfaʿa*) of the good deed" (Ibn Taymiyya 1961–1967, 35:30). Ibn Taymiyya observes that this form of good deed occurs frequently across all sectors of society ranging from rulers and scholars to Sufis and the general populace. He cites a number of examples (Ibn Taymiyya 1961–1967, 35:30):

---

30 For elaboration of Ibn Taymiyya's view that a politically and militarily potent leader who commits some injustices and sins is better than a supposedly upright but impotent leader, see Michot 2014.

31 Anjum (2012, 126–127, 188) argues that al-Ghazālī's attitude to politics is pessimistic and cynical for accepting the legitimacy of imperfect rulers to avoid anarchy by analogy to the necessity of eating carrion to avoid death, whereas Ibn Taymiyya's approach is optimistic and "as far as it could be from Ghazālī's attitude of 'eating carrion'" (Anjum 2012, 188). Given that Ibn Taymiyya also invokes eating carrion as an analogy for thinking about political ethics, as here in *Khilāfa*, Anjum clearly overstates his case.

> An example is someone who cannot bring himself to achieve the benefits of administrative authority in commanding the right and prohibiting the wrong, carrying out the prescribed punishments (*ḥudūd*), securing the roads, undertaking *jihād* against the enemy, and distributing resources, without engaging in some prohibited things like expropriating some of the resources, domineering the people, showing favouritism in distribution, and other such capricious behaviours. It is likewise in *jihād*. He is not able to bring himself to undertake *jihād* without a certain kind of rashness. In scholarship he is not able to bring himself to study the science of jurisprudence and the foundations of religion without certain kinds of prohibited things like [exercising his own] opinion (*ra'y*) and [engaging in] rationalist theology (*kalām*), and he cannot bring himself to study the science of the legislated rites of worship and the knowledge that is commanded without a certain kind of monkishness (*rahbāniyya*).

With this last example – the scholar who indulges in a bit of monkishness – Ibn Taymiyya may well have himself in mind, and Yahya Michot takes this passage to be the key to unlocking the mystery of his celibacy. Ibn Taymiyya never married even though he believed that a Muslim man should do so, and Michot (2001, 186–187) suggests that he saw this as a perverse side effect of his devotion to piety and scholarship.[32]

Ibn Taymiyya continues in *Khilāfa* explaining that this phenomenon of indulging in evil deeds to make more beneficial deeds bearable is widespread among kings and others and that it has caused considerable strife and confusion. However, even though the revealed law does not authorise or excuse such evil deeds, it does command rulers to do good deeds, and they should do those good deeds even if that involves committing evil deeds of lesser import. Ibn Taymiyya (1961–1967, 35:31) gives the example of *jihād:* "Emirs are commanded to undertake *jihād*, even if it is known that they will not undertake *jihād* without a certain kind of injustice whose detriment is less in comparison to the benefit of *jihād*." Moreover, explains Ibn Taymiyya, rulers should not be prohibited from evil deeds if prohibition might dissuade them from performing good deeds that yield benefit outweighing the detriment of those evil deeds. Sometimes permitting an evil deed leads to greater good all around. Ibn Taymiyya (1961–1967, 35:31–32) cites an example concerning the second Sunnī caliph: "'Umar b. al-Khaṭṭāb employed an immoral person because of the preponderance of benefit in using him, and he put an end to his immorality through his strength and justice." At other times, omitting prohibition of a wrong averts another wrong that would be even more detrimental. As an example, Ibn Taymiyya notes that a king who converts to Islam should not be prohibited from drinking wine if prohibition would lead him to apostatise. Nevertheless, Ibn Tay-

32 Ibn Taymiyya 1961–1967, 35:30 is translated into French in Michot 2001, 186.

miyya observes, there will also be times when prohibitions must be made plain to achieve other ends. It all depends on the circumstances, and for Ibn Taymiyya the precedent for such prudent discernment is found in the Prophet: "Because of [the diversity of the circumstances], the position of the Prophet – May God bless him and give him peace – varied regarding his command, his prohibition, his *jihād*, his pardon, his carrying out of the prescribed punishments, his harshness, and his mercy" (Ibn Taymiyya 1961–1967, 35:32).[33]

This final appeal to the Prophet in *Khilāfa* could be interpreted to give divine sanction to unbridled utilitarianism as normative Islam: the commands and prohibitions of the law are subject to prudential strategising and even expendable. This is the worry of Opwis. However, such a reading misses the role of human failure in Ibn Taymiyya's deliberations. The Muslim community is indeed obligated to fulfil the "caliphate of prophecy" and prohibited from eating carrion and drinking wine. The greatest benefit is to be found in observing such obligations and prohibitions. However, Ibn Taymiyya in *Khilāfa* discusses what to do when that is not possible due to sin and human weakness. What is to be done is to make the best of a sinful world by weighing up benefits versus detriments in order to advance the cause of religion and draw closer to the revealed law in the best way possible. This too finds its support in revelation: it is the way of Prophet. Opwis is right that Ibn Taymiyya deploys benefit substantively in his juristic and ethical reasoning, and Vasalou is also correct that Ibn Taymiyya traces all benefit back to revelation. Their two views may be reconciled by seeing that for Ibn Taymiyya revelation sanctions substantive utilitarian reasoning oriented toward the greater good of the Muslim community and ever fuller obedience to the commands of God. This utilitarian reasoning is not independent of an ultimate aim revealed by God, but it does require making substantive judgments about the relative benefit of adhering to legal rulings in the many circumstances that fall short of that ultimate aim. It is the rule for how to proceed when following God's law is not fully possible.

4 Conclusion

Our study of Ibn Taymiyya's *Irāda* has yielded two major results concerning his theology. First, the Avicennan notion of God's self-love giving rise to the world as a necessary concomitant provides Ibn Taymiyya with the philosophical resources

---

33 Michot (2006, 52–53) translates and comments upon the last three paragraphs of Ibn Taymiyya 1961–1967, 35:31–32.

to portray God as the self-interested, perpetual creator of the world. Second, his temporalisation of the essence of this God enables him to depict Him as a dynamic utilitarian agent maximising benefit for both Himself and human beings through the historical process. Some things like rain may cause harm to some people for a time, but God creates preponderant good and the best possible world overall.

Shifting to Ibn Taymiyya's ethics and legal reflection, he affirms that God's revealed law encompasses all human benefit pertaining to both this world and the hereafter and that maximum human benefit is to be found in total obedience to the law. However, human ignorance of relevant revealed texts and human sin and weakness mean that it is not always possible to adhere to the law perfectly, and so utilitarian calculations must be made between competing courses of action to ascertain the best way to advance religion. Ibn Taymiyya in his treatise on the caliphate and his treatise on commanding the right and forbidding the wrong stipulates weighing up the benefits and detriments of acts so as to attain the greatest benefit or avert the greatest detriment, and he grounds this in the example of the Prophet.

Ibn Taymiyya states at the beginning of *Irāda* that the issue of causality pervades everything to do with theology and law. Moreover, the treatise makes apparent that his view of causality is utilitarian in orientation, and it rejects Ashʿarī voluntarism in God's will. It thus comes as no surprise that we can observe marked parallels between God and humans in their utilitarian agency. Ibn Taymiyya's God does the best possible creating and commanding in a world beset with evils. Likewise, humans should follow the Prophet in choosing preponderant benefit for religion as they act in a world beset by ignorance, sin, and weakness. Ibn Taymiyya does not resolve the problems of evil, sin, and human weakness in the texts considered in this study, but, if we fill out the implications of his arguments for universal salvation, these problems will find ultimate resolution in the hereafter when God will bring everyone to obey and worship Him alone, when benefit will be full and complete for all.

As a theologian, ethicist, and jurist, Ibn Taymiyya provides an Avicennan-informed apology for the utilitarian rationality of God's creation and God's command. What God creates is the best possible, and what God commands through the revealed law encompasses all benefit. This law not only specifies obligations and prohibitions; it also provides the Prophet's exemplary utilitarianism as the operative principle when perfect obedience to obligations and prohibitions is too difficult or impossible. Ibn Taymiyya thus places great weight on human calculation for ascertaining the best course of action in everyday circumstances. Such calculations are of course subject to the limitations of human knowledge of both texts and actual benefits and thus lead to differing judgements about the most beneficial way to promote religious flourishing.[34] This observation applies even to Ibn Taymiyya's own corpus, as it has often been noted that his writings are occasional and circumstantial in character and that his views are not easily systematised.[35] Nonetheless, modern research is increasingly bringing out consistencies of theme, purpose, and vision in his thought. Ibn Taymiyya's diverse interventions reflect a religious utilitarianism ever seeking the most effective way to point readers toward what he believed to be in everyone's best interest – full obedience to God – and he supports this with a theology of God's utilitarian activity working toward that same goal.

34 Ibn Taymiyya urged respect for difference in independent reasoning in some texts. See especially Ibn Taymiyya 1961–1967, *Rafʿ al-malām ʿan al-aʾimma al-aʿlām*, 20:231–290; translated in al-Matroudi 2007; Michot 2012b.

35 See Vasalou 2016, 16–19, for a full discussion of the circumstantial character of Ibn Taymiyya's writings with references to other voices on the issue. Vasalou also seeks explicitly to highlight the diversity and seeming inconsistency of Ibn Taymiyya's various claims and formulations through the dialectical rhetorical strategy of her presentation (Vasalou 2016, 6–7). Nonetheless, she rightly discerns through the course of her monograph recurring themes and consistent patterns of thought in Ibn Taymiyya's writings on ethics.

Robert Gleave

Value Ontology and the Assumption of Non-Assessment in Postclassical Shīʿī Legal Theory

1 Introduction

Postclassical Twelver Shīʿī legal theory (*uṣūl al-fiqh*) was characterised by a series of internal debates, which occasionally spilled over into political and social tensions.[1] The most prominent of these was the so-called Akhbārī-Uṣūlī debate, in which two "schools" of jurisprudence emerged – the Akhbāriyya and the Uṣūliyya. The Akhbāriyya were suspicious of the expansion of the role of so-called rational interpretive techniques in Shīʿī jurisprudence. They saw this as Sunnī methods infecting the Shīʿī sphere of legal derivation; the Akhbāriyya considered themselves as loyal to the original impetus of Shīʿism, and thought of the Uṣūliyya as deviants. On the other hand, the Uṣūliyya, commonly labelled the *mujtahidūn* (that is, those who support the exercise of personal juristic reasoning, or *ijtihād*) considered these techniques to be promoted by the Shīʿī Imāms themselves, and essential to operating the legal framework the Imāms instituted. For the *mujtahidūn*, it was the Akhbāriyya who were deviants, influenced as they were by Sunnī trends – the *ahl al-ḥadīth* and Ashʿarism – in which reason is demoted to a subservient status, and revelation is the ultimate source of legal truth. Another, linked, internal Shīʿī debate concerned the emergence of a vibrant Shīʿī theological-philosophical school, particularly in Safavid Iran. The

1 By "postclassical", I am referring to the period between the later fifteenth and early nineteenth centuries CE. See Ahmed and Gleave 2018, 1–5. The term is supposed to be a little more than a convenient time marker. In Shīʿī jurisprudence, the period can be characterised by an elaboration of the intellectual structures established during the period up to the work of al-ʿAllāma al-Ḥillī (d. 726/1325). See Calder 1989. Work after al-ʿAllāma can be characterised as an elaboration of, and reaction to, the framework which, by his time, had become stabilised in Shīʿī works of both *fiqh* and *uṣūl*. The Akhbārī school, of course, based much of its doctrine on the vilification of the achievements of al-ʿAllāma al-Ḥillī, and a return to the uncorrupted pre-ʿAllāma period. From a historical perspective, their analysis is party accurate: al-ʿAllāma did, indeed, bring in a series of terminological and intellectual changes which formed the basis for later Shīʿī legal discussion. But it is typical of a legal polemic to lay the blame for deviation at the doorstep of an individual. The Akhbārīs see al-ʿAllāma as their bête noir – but in fact his work emerges as one (possible but not inevitable) avenue of development from earlier Shīʿī jurisprudence. See Gleave 2007a and the secondary literature cited therein.

https://doi.org/10.1515/9783110552386-011

Safavids conquered a land in which philosophical and theological enquiry was already thriving, much of which building on the ideas of Shihāb al-Dīn al-Suhrawardī (d. 587/1191) and Fakhr al-Dīn al-Rāzī (d. 606/1210). The focus of the activity was in Shīrāz, with the most prominent writers being Jalāl al-Dīn al-Dawānī (d. 908/1502) and the father and son, Ṣadr al-Dīn (d. 903/1498) and Ghiyāth al-Dīn al-Dashtakī (d. 949/1542). The philosophical discussions were not explicitly Shīʿī, and the sectarian or theological allegiance of these writers is not always explicit, or indeed necessarily important for assessing their philosophical output (Bdaiwi 2014). Shīʿī Safavid political control inevitably led to philosophical discussions becoming more explicitly Shīʿī, eventually leading to the emergence of a distinctly Shīʿī form of mystical philosophy initiated by Mīr Dāmād (d. 1040/1631) and continued to even greater acclaim and influence by his student Mullā Ṣadrā (Ṣadr al-Dīn al-Shīrāzī, d. 1050/1640). The legitimacy of this sort of intellectual enquiry was the subject of much internal debate with many (both Akhbārīs and Uṣūlīs) viewing this philosophical/theological form of enquiry as not only irreligious, but also dangerous for the faith of Twelver Shīʿism. Internal debate on both these issues possibly demonstrates how the emergence of a Shīʿī political power had led to intellectual discussions over which position was the most authentically "Shīʿī", and which was heretical.

It is against this background – first the Akhbārī-Uṣūlī conflict, and second the flourishing of a distinctly Shīʿī Safavid philosophical school – that developments in Safavid *uṣūl al-fiqh* can be usefully analysed. The intrusion of these two debates into the expositions of Shīʿī legal theory could be illustrated by a number of the standard discussions in legal theory (*uṣūl*) works. In this chapter, my focus is on the "assumption of fundamental non-assessment" (*al-barāʾa al-aṣliyya*), the debate around which had become so involved that, by Safavid times, it merited its own discrete chapter in *uṣūl* works.

2 Fundamental Non-Assessment (*al-barāʾa al-aṣliyya*) in Islamic Legal Theory

In its mature elaboration, the term *al-barāʾa al-aṣliyya* (literally "fundamental licence" or "basic freedom") referred to the doctrine that, in the absence of explicit regulation, all "things" (*ashyāʾ* – encompassing both actions and substances) are free of legal categorisation (on the categorisation schema in Islamic legal discussions: obligatory to prohibited, pure to impure, valid to invalid, permitted to forbidden). The issue of legal situations which appear unregulated by the existing sources was naturally one that arose very soon in Islamic legal discussions. The various solutions to this problem are well-mapped in the secondary literature. They include:[2]

1. extension of linguistic reference. Word meaning is expanded to cover instances not normally thought to be the reference of a legal ruling – including implication (*mafhūm*) and similar processes;
2. analogical reasoning. By transferring the ruling for a known case to an unknown case through discovering a common factor;
3. independent rational discovery. That is, human reason's ability to determine moral/legal properties, that is, to supplement the textual supply of evidence with the "rational" discovery or determination of these properties;
4. discovery (or invention) of general legal principles which bypass the above interpretive mechanisms and provide a legal assessment. These include appeals to "legal maxims" – *qawāʿid fiqhiyya* – and the general "aims of the law" – *maqāṣid al-sharīʿa*, which have become particularly popular in the contemporary period.

All of these were controversial and debated, both in principle and in substance. It is the third of these – the identification of moral properties through the human faculty of reason – that relates most directly with the assumption of non-assessment in the absence of revelatory indication. The discussion was both a theological debate concerning the ability of the rational faculty to discover religious truths, and a legal dispute concerning the correct procedure for the qualified jurist confronted by silence in the indicators on a particular circumstance.

In tracing the history of *al-barāʾa al-aṣliyya* (or *aṣālat al-barāʾa*) in Muslim legal literature, one needs to distinguish between the technical term (*al-barāʾa al-aṣliyya*) and the discussion around the legal principle (non-assessment in the absence of legislation). The term *al-barāʾa al-aṣliyya* was not used in the earliest texts of legal theory; the earliest specific use of the term I have identified is *al-Mustaṣfā* of al-Ghazālī (d. 505/1111).[3] However, the *uṣūl* discussion of the issue before al-Ghazālī was extensive, under the rubric of *al-ḥaẓr wa'l-ibāḥa* ("proscription and permission"). In these discussions, there is a dispute around the fundamental nature of things/actions (*aṣl*): are they permitted or proscribed? The early history of the discussion is yet to be written, and is not our direct concern here – but the technical terminology (*al-ḥaẓr wa'l-ibāḥa*), if not the issue itself, appears first in Muʿtazilī writings and is soon taken up by non-Muʿtazilī

2 For a description of these various mechanisms of extending the text, see Hallaq 1998; Weiss 1998. For a summary of the debates in secondary literature, see Gleave 2014.

3 Al-Ghaẓālī 1996; it is regularly cited by al-Ghazālī, and is clearly a technical term, see, for example, pages 97, 101, 103, 117, 121, 159, and 160 amongst others.

uṣūlīs until it becomes a standard point of discussion.[4] Writers of *uṣūl* identify various different opinions on the issue of whether "things" (*al-ashyā'*) are essentially – or in their fundamental nature – permitted or forbidden. The issue is discussed in the very earliest work of legal theory, *al-Fuṣūl fī' l-uṣūl* of al-Jaṣṣāṣ (d. 370/981), who identifies three positions, though he does not identify names of those who hold them (al-Jaṣṣāṣ 1994, 3:247). The three camps are:

1. those who say that unless reason identifies something to be evil (*qabīḥ*) or obligatory (*wājib*), then these things are permitted (*mubāḥ*);
2. those who say that unless reason decrees something to be obligatory, then all things are considered prohibited (*maḥẓūr*);
3. those who say one cannot say anything about these things – whether they are permitted or proscribed without a revelatory indicator.

The first two positions outlined by al-Jaṣṣāṣ have specifically Muʿtazilī underpinnings, in that the assessments of an action as bad or obligatory are made by reason (*ʿaql*). His own opinion is a variation on the first of these (that is, permission), and this was indeed a popular Muʿtazilī view. Crucial to the presentation here is that, for al-Jaṣṣāṣ and for subsequent Muʿtazilī *uṣūl* writers, the assessments of bad or obligatory cannot change or be replaced (*lā yajūz fīhi al-taghyīr wa'l-tabdīl*). The unchanging nature of these assessments means that, ontologically speaking, they are qualities an action might have "in itself" (*li-nafsihi*). The actions which are not categorised as evil or obligatory by reason are, according to al-Jaṣṣāṣ, assessed as permitted by reason; but this assessment, unlike the other two, is changeable. If the Lawgiver decrees differently, these items can be made obligatory, or forbidden or some other of the categorisations.

The difference between al-Jaṣṣāṣ's position and those of the second view is not based on the fundamental Muʿtazilī principle that reason is capable of identifying assessments; rather the distinction lies in the fact that, for the second view, reason decrees the action prohibited based on the following argumentation. (1) It is a principle, established by reason independently, that no one is permitted to make use of an item unless the item's owner has given permission to that person specifically, or to people generally; (2) everything on earth belongs to God; (3) if God has not given an assessment, then he has not given permission, so things are fundamentally forbidden unless reason declares them to be permitted.

4 The debate around *al-ḥiẓr wa'l-ibāḥa* was effectively the debate around the status of rules derieved distinct from revelatory sources ("before revelation" as Reinhart (1995) puts it).

The discussion between the first two positions is, then, primarily an internal Muʿtazilī debate. The third opinion – that it is not possible to say whether something is permitted or proscribed without a revelatory assessment – is associated with the Ashʿarī Sunnīs in subsequent *uṣūl* works. However, as the argument developed in *uṣūl* works, the first and third positions began to draw closer together: those who argued that the fundamental ruling was one of permission unless there was a rational indicator that it was proscribed or obligatory (position 1 above) had a certain overlap in argumentation with those who argued that one cannot say what the assessment is until revelation reveals it (position 3). Both positions develop out of the view that assessments of both prohibition or proscription requires evidence; these assessments can never be deduced from a lack of evidence. The two positions differ, of course, over what a lack of evidence in itself indicates. Does it indicate permission (often characterised as a Muʿtazilī position), or does it indicate nothing (and in such circumstances, a secondary rule kicks in, which equates to a non-declaration of any rule, ontologically speaking, but a pragmatic acceptance of expedient permission)? One sees, for example, in the work of Fakhr al-Dīn al-Rāzī, a certain melding of these two positions.[5]

From these initial discussions in *uṣūl* works, a set of principles emerges, linked to the principle that until there is a revelatory indicator that the assessment is something new, the assessment remains with its "original/fundamental state" (*aṣl*). For al-Jaṣṣāṣ, and eventually for nearly all Muʿtazilīs (including the Imāmiyya), the "original state" of an action is that it is "disassociated" or "free" (*barāʾa*) from any legal requirement. Whether this equated to a legal assessment of permission *(ibāḥa)* was the subject of much subsequent debate. It is in this complex that *al-barāʾa al-aṣliyya* emerges as a technical term. Al-Ghazālī often employs it in conjunction with the larger issue of "continuance" (*istiṣḥāb*) – that is, the notion that once an assessment has been established, it is assumed to continue as enforced until a credible piece of evidence establishes it to have changed. Al-Ghazālī's use of the term seems not always to refer to the original assessment of an item in the absence of revelation, but rather the established assessment of an item by revelation which remains as it is (i.e. is "free" of change rather than free of assessment). For example, he states "If an act of worship is made obligatory at one point in time, the legal requirement (*al-dhimma*) remains in place after the elapse of that time, in accordance with *al-barāʾa al-aṣliyya*" (al-Ghazālī 1996, 159). Here the term refers not to the state of an action

5 See, for example, al-Rāzī's discussion of the principle that you should take the minimum of what is said, where he employs *al-barāʾa al-aṣliyya* extensively (al-Rāzī 1991, 6: 154–155).

before any revelatory intervention, but rather the ability of an assessment, once established, to remain in force despite the change of time. That is, *al-barāʾa al-aṣliyya* here appears to be very close (if not identical) to the notion of continuance (*istṣḥāb*) in al-Ghazālī's usage. This is most likely due to the fact that al-Ghazālī proposes a position roughly equivalent to the third of al-Jaṣṣāṣ's schema (namely one can say nothing about categorisation until there is some form of divine decree).

The history of both the term and the idea of *al-barāʾa al-aṣliyya* in Shīʿī legal theory is not, it should be stated, separate from its development in Sunnī works (Muʿtazilī or otherwise). In the earliest surviving works of *uṣūl* one finds discussions of "proscription and permission" along similar lines to those discussed by al-Jaṣṣāṣ. Al-Ṭūṣī, in his *al-ʿUdda fī uṣūl al-fiqh*, argues for fundamental permission (al-Ṭūṣī 1997, 2:737); al-Sharīf al-Murtaḍā adopts the minority position of proscription (al-Sharīf al-Murtaḍā 1996, 2:805). It is al-Ṭūsī's position that proves dominant in subsequent tradition, laying the groundwork of a full-blown theory of *al-barāʾa al-aṣliyya* in later Imāmī *uṣūl*. The term itself appears for the first time in al-Muḥaqqiq's (d. 676/1277) *uṣūl* work *Maʿārij al-uṣūl*, appearing in relation to abrogation (*naskh*) (al-Muḥaqqiq al-Ḥillī 1983, 164) and "isolated traditions" (*al-khabar al-wāḥid*). In a section on the principle that "there is no assessment" (*aṣālat al-nafy*), he writes (al-Muḥaqqiq al-Ḥillī 1983, 212–213):

> know that the original state (*al-aṣl*) is that the requirement (*al-dhimma*) does not require any legal acts [to be fulfilled]. When a claimant makes a claim that there is a legal assessment, he can be refuted by adopting *al-barāʾa al-aṣliyya* in asserting the non-existence [of the legal assessment]. One could say: if that assessment [which he is claiming] was secure, then there would be a legal indication of it. But this is not the case, entailing that one deny [the assessment's existence].

Certainly, the Arabic phrasing is allusive and technical, but the message is clearly discernible. For al-Muḥaqqiq, the fundamental nature of things – the "original state" – is that there is no legal requirement to perform or avoid performing an action. For someone to propose an assessment, they need evidence (that is, an indication – *dalīl*). In the absence of evidence, there is no assessment and an action can be performed without any consequences (legal or otherwise). The assessment proposed by the claimant is therefore denied.

The use of the court-room terminology (claim, claimant etc.) is no accident. Court-room practice dictates, of course, that the burden of proof was on the claimant, not on the defendant. The court protects the *status quo ante*, and needs a good reason to overturn it. In this sense the two parties to a dispute are not equal; in the same way, the one arguing for an assessment is not equal to the one defending the lack of an assessment. The former has to do more work than the latter, because the former has the presumption of no assessment (that is, *al-barāʾa al-aṣliyya*) on her side.

Al-Muḥaqqiq mentions two caveats to his assertion that *al-barāʾa al-aṣliyya* can guard against unjustified assessments. First, one has to be sure that there is no indication of an assessment. This requires a thorough search through the various mechanisms for acquiring indications (*ḍabṭ turuq al-istidlālāt*), and it being clear (*bayyin*) that there are no indications. Second, the issue or action for which there is supposed to be no indication must be the sort of thing that if it were regulated, the assessment would be well-known. This is the link with the mechanisms of "general harm" (*ʿumūm al-balwā*) – if the action under examination is a commonly accepted element of the daily life of the community, and it forms a community need or requirement. Prohibiting the action in question, or imposing a different set of rules for its regulation, would impose unjustified hardship on the community.

As one can see, *al-barāʾa al-aṣliyya* entered Shīʿī *uṣūl* discussions (in the work of al-Muḥaqqiq) already with a complex and sophisticated set of legal ideas around it. The passage just described formed the bedrock of subsequent discussions of *al-barāʾa al-aṣliyya*, as subsequent *uṣūl* writers drew on this framework (and often this specific passage) for their own elaboration of the principle. The most important work of postclassical Shīʿī *uṣūl* was probably the *Maʿālim al-uṣūl* of Ḥasan b. al-Shahīd al-Thānī (d. 1030/1621). He employs the term *al-barāʾa al-aṣliyya* in his discussion of *istiṣḥāb* ("continuance"). The reference is not fully explored, but it appears as if he conceives of *al-barāʾa al-aṣliyya* as the principle underlying the validity of *istiṣḥāb:*

> the scholars agree that an assessment must remain in place if there is no legal indication [of change]; this is in accordance with *al-barāʾa al-aṣliyya*, and there is no meaning to *istiṣḥāb* other than this.[6]

That is, *al-barāʾa al-aṣliyya* – that is, the notion that things are fundamentally free of assessment until there is evidence of a change – establishes the basis of the principle of *istiṣḥāb* – that is, that an assessment once in place remains there until there is an indication of change. In this sense, *al-barāʾa al-aṣliyya* appears more fundamental than *istiṣḥāb* in the legal theory espoused by Ḥasan b. al-Shahīd al-Thānī. Similarly, *al-barāʾa al-aṣliyya* is referred to in relation to two equally powerful indications of contradictory rulings. Some scholars,

6 Al-Shahīd al-Thānī 1995, 234. This work was the introduction to a work of *fiqh* (the *Maʿālim al-dīn*) which was separated off and formed an independent treatise, often given the title *Maʿālim al-uṣūl*.

Ḥasan mentions, "declare both [rulings] void, and return instead to *al-barāʾa al-aṣliyya*" (al-Shahīd al-Thānī 1995, 250). The implication here is that, for these scholars, the presence of contradictory rulings with equally strong indications is equivalent to there being no indication at all, and hence they believe one should return to the original state (that is, that of there being no legal duty placed upon the subject in relation to the action). This, one should add, is not Ḥasan's position; he merely mentions *al-barāʾa al-aṣliyya* in relation to the position of these other (unnamed) scholars. To him, and to subsequent Uṣūlīs (in the sense of non-Akhbārīs), was attributed the doctrine that in the case of conflicting indicators *al-barāʾa al-aṣliyya* means that one should determine which assessment would require the lighter burden on the believer. Because this lighter burden is closer to a "permitted" assessment, this becomes, for such scholars, the preferred assessment, and the indicator which supports it overrules the indicators pointing towards a more burdensome assessment. Whilst this is an important hermeneutic device in later jurisprudence, it constitutes a mechanism of strengthening one indicator over another, and is not directly my concern here. This chapter is focussed on those instances when there is judged to be no indicator, since that is the prime location for the operation of *al-barāʾa al-aṣliyya.*

3 *Al-barāʾa al-aṣliyya* and the Akhbārī-Uṣūlī Conflict

The Akhbārī school was a rejection of the juristic system which found its developed expression in the *uṣūl* of al-ʿAllāmā al-Ḥillī. Most overtly critical of the practice and operation of *ijtihād,* the Akhbārī school also rejected various other hermeneutic techniques. Muḥammad Amīn al-Astarābādī (d. 1033/1626–1627), the supposed founder of the Akhbārī school, was critical of the way in which *al-barāʾa al-aṣliyya* had been developed by al-ʿAllāma and his followers. In his famous Akhbārī tract *al-Fawāʾid al-Madaniyya*, he characterises *al-barāʾa al-aṣliyya* as a Sunnī Ashʿarī doctrine (al-Astarābādī 2003, 278):

> we say that adhering *to al-barāʾa al-aṣliyya* can only be proven for the Ashʿarīs. They deny that good and evil are essential [moral properties of things]. Similarly, it is only proven for one who says [good and evil] are [essential moral properties of things] but does not say that obligation and prohibition are essential moral properties... in accordance with the opinion of those Sunnis who permit there to be instances where God made no ruling.

Al-Astarābādī's argument here is that the assumption that actions are legally speaking unassessed in the absence of a legal indicator sits most comfortably within an Ashʿarī framework. This is not a compliment, but an insult within a Shīʿī context, since all Shīʿīs (Akhbārīs included) refute the so-called "Divine Subjectivism" of the Ashʿarīs. Al-Astarābādī, like many Akhbārīs after him, did not deny the role of reason in the discovery of an action's external moral properties; they ceded no ground to the Ashʿarī position. Their positions, like those of their opponents, were based, broadly speaking, on Muʿtazilī rationalism. So Al-Astarābādī here describing *al-barāʾa al-aṣliyya* as an essentially Ashʿarī position is an attempt to condemn it.

He justifies his linking Ashʿarism and the doctrine of *al-barāʾa al-aṣliyya* in the following way. If, as the Ashʿarīs argue, actions ("things") do not have intrinsic moral qualities of good or evil, or, as some others (non-Ashʿarīs) supposedly argue, of obligation or prohibition, then until God declares them so, such actions are "unassessed." Therefore, their performance cannot be judged to be illegal, immoral, or deserving of punishment. If their performance attracts no praise or blame, and no reward or punishment, then they are simply permitted. *Al-barāʾa al-aṣliyya* is, then, an essentially Ashʿarī doctrine.

Here we can see how the established Ashʿarī position of "suspension" (*waqf* – namely that one cannot determine an assessment for unregulated actions) can be easily conflated with the view that such actions are to be treated as if they are permitted. This is the case even though they are not explicitly permitted, since the categorization of permission (*ibāḥa*) requires the Lawgiver to explicitly state that the actions are permitted.

The polemic against al-Astarābādī's positions generally was widespread amongst Uṣūlīs, and, as we shall see, even some Akhbārīs felt he went too far. Specifically on *al-barāʾa al-aṣliyya*, there was a direct rebuttal of al-Astarābādī's statement cited in the *al-Shawāhid al-Makkiyya* of al-Astarābādī's near contemporary Nūr al-Dīn al-ʿĀmilī (d. 1062/1645)[7]:

> there is no doubt that adherence to *al-barāʾa al-aṣliyya* is more appropriate for one who believes in good and evil [as rationally deducible, external moral properties] than one who does not believe that. This is because the possibility of God requiring something from the individual legal subject, but not giving him the means to know it, is something

7 Al-ʿĀmilī was related to some of the major Uṣūlī scholars of his day; his brothers (through father and mother, respectively) included Shaykh Ḥasan b. al-Shahīd al-Thānī, the author of the *Maʿālīm* referenced above, and al-Sayyid Muḥāmmad al-ʿĀmilī (d. 1009/1539), author of the important *fiqh* work *Madārik al-aḥkām*. His critique of al-Astarābādī takes the form of a commentary in which statements by al-Astarābādī are highlighted and then refuted; for this reason, it was printed on the margins of the lithograph edition, and, according to the modern editor, also to be found on the margins of manuscripts of *al-Fawāʾid al-madaniyya*. See Buzurg 1987, 14:244 (number 2391).

> recognised by reason to be morally repugnant. [And it would also be] prohibited [for God] if by this He actually wants [the individual] to act in a particular way.[8]

Al-ʿĀmilī tries to do the reverse of al-Astarābādī: he claims that the doctrine of *al-barāʾa al-aṣliyya* is opposed to Ashʿarism and in line with Muʿtazilism. The reasoning here relates to God's quality of justice and fairness (*ʿadl*), a fundamental Muʿtazilī-Imāmī concept. If God has not legislated on an action, or He has legislated but not made it known to the individual legal subject, then He cannot punish him for the performance of that action. Such a punishment would be unjust and unfair, and this injustice can be rationally identified and is an intrinsic (that is, unchangeable) element of the act of punishment. Such a thing could not be attributed to God, and hence if no legislation is known to the legal subject, then he or she is in no way to be blamed for treating the action as permitted. For the Ashʿarīs, al-ʿĀmilī argues, it is quite possible for God to legislate, not to make his legal assessment clear to his subjects, and then to punish them for disobedience to God's ruling. *Al-barāʾa al-aṣliyya* is, for him, a doctrine wholly incompatible with Ashʿarism, and entirely in tune with the Imāmī-Muʿtazilī principles of the rationally discoverable external moral properties of actions.

The argument between al-Astarābādī and al-ʿĀmilī is given an added momentum over the issue of "the completion of religion" (*ikmāl al-dīn*). The idea that Islam is "complete", with no additional ruling or regulations added, is one interpretation of the Quranic verse "Today, I [i.e. God] have completed your religion for you" (Q. 5:3; *al-yawma akmaltu lakum dīnakum*). For al-Astarabādī, the completion of religion means that *al-barāʾa al-aṣliyya*, in which an assessment of permission is awarded to those areas where there is no obvious indicator (revelatory or otherwise), is invalid. For him, *al-barāʾa al-aṣliyya*, as it is understood by his opponents, indicates that religion is incomplete, and therefore the doctrine contradicts a basic Qur'anic dictum. Al-ʿĀmilī's response involves the assertion that *al-barāʾa al-aṣliyya* is not simply a presumption on the part of the jurist, but a rationally and scripturally established principle. That is, both reason and revelation assert the principle of *al-barāʾa al-aṣliyya*, and therefore it forms part of religion's completion, not an indication of its incompleteness. "The completion of religion does not bring about the invalidity of *al-barāʾa al-aṣliyya* because God's rule concerning its establishment is clear", al-ʿĀmilī (2003, 276) explains.

The Uṣūlī discussions around *al-barāʾa al-aṣliyya* developed a distinctly philosophical element, to be discussed in the next section. The Akhbārī discus-

---

8 Al-ʿĀmilī 2003, 276 (printed with *al-Fawāʾid al-madaniyya* mentioned above).

sions focussed mainly on the idea, established by revelation, that God has a ruling for every situation (*li-kull wāqiʿa ḥukm*); and if this is so, *al-barāʾa al-aṣliyya* (understood as meaning a presumption that there is no ruling) is somehow heretical. So, Ḥusayn b. Shihāb al-Dīn al-Karakī (d. 1075/1665), the author of a better organised work of Akhbārī legal theory (which follows, roughly, the order of chapters in a standard work of *uṣūl*) has a dedicated chapter on *al-barāʾa al-aṣliyya* (al-Karakī 1977, 266–270). Like al-Astarabādī he attributes the doctrine to the Sunnīs – and states that "it does not agree with the fundamental basis of the Shīʿa" (*lā yuwāfiq uṣūl madhhab al-Shīʿa*). The Shīʿa, he claims, have as a fundamental belief the view that God has a ruling for every situation, and this complete set of rulings has been deposited with the Imāms themselves. So *al-barāʾa al-aṣliyya* is only possible when "religion has not been completed"; and since it has been completed (as evidenced by the Qur'an itself – Q. 5:3), the order now is not to presume that there is no ruling, but to seek the rulings for that circumstances from the Imāms themselves or those who relate their reports. If this results in no knowledge of what the ruling is, we must refrain from giving an opinion and act cautiously (*yajib ʿalaynā al-tawaqquf fīhi ʿan al-fatwā wa-naʿmal fīhi bi'l-iḥtiyāṭ*).

For al-Karakī, the real issue here is that *al-barāʾa al-aṣliyya*, when employed by the jurist in order to determine an assessment and to give a *fatwā*, is never going to be certain. Assessments emerging out of the assumption of *al-barāʾa al-aṣliyya* are just that: assumptions (*ẓunūn*). Here al-Karakī repeats the standard Akhbārī position: the reports (*akhbār*) of the Imāms provide us with certainty as to God's rulings, since they are of unquestionable provenance. Given that the Imāms have provided us with all the answers necessary, the task is to understand those answers rather than presume that the answers have been left out, somehow, from the corpus. Rather "everything which it is essential to know is found in the [reports]" (*kull mā taʿamm al-balwā mawjūd fīhā*). For al-Karakī, the Sunnī (and Uṣūlī Imāmī) promotion of *al-barāʾa al-aṣliyya* is due to the fact that they downgrade the probative force of the *akhbār*. For al-Karakī, the debate around *al-barāʾa al-aṣliyya* really dissolves into a debate around the ability of the *ḥadīth* corpus to provide guidance to the believing community. Advocacy of *al-barāʾa al-aṣliyya* is, for him, a slur against the *ḥadīth* corpus, and its ability to answer every circumstance.

Clearly the Akhbārī complaint against *al-barāʾa al-aṣliyya* is that it asserts an assessment of permission to be the assessment of the "textless" situation. The only way *al-barāʾa al-aṣliyya* can operate, for al-Karakī and other Akhbārīs, is not as an assertion of an assessment as such, but as an allowance (*rukhṣa*) for those who, for a justifiable reason, are unable to gain knowledge of the actual assessment. For al-Karakī, the person ignorant of the assessment from the Lawgiver (that is, God, the Prophet, and the Imāms) is only permitted to treat the action concerned as permitted after "investigation" (*tafaḥḥuṣ*). That is, if, after searching for an indicator (rational or textual), none is found, then the individual can perform (or not perform) the action without blame. What the individual cannot do, though, is give a *fatwā* that the action is permitted. A *fatwā* is a claim to the status of the action within the law; it is an assertion of the ontological status of the act. This, in cases where the individual has found no indicators, is not permitted. This is what the Akhbārī take to be their opponents' (the Uṣūlīs') conception of *al-barāʾa al-aṣliyya.*

4 *Al-barāʾa al-aṣliyya* and the Philosophical Discussions of Non-Existence

The difference between the Akhbārī and Uṣūlī positions on *al-barāʾa al-aṣliyya*, practically speaking, may not be so great. The difference lies not in whether the action without indication can be performed without any legal infringement – since both agree to this. Rather, the difference lies in the rather technical distinction between the claim that, in the case under discussion, there is an assessment of permission (the Uṣūlī-*mujtahid* position) or there is no assessment, and the reversion to a more general, procedural rule (the Akhbārī position on caution). For the early Uṣulīs, *al-barāʾa al-aṣliyya* establishes an actual assessment; for the Akhbārīs, it establishes a legitimate (or on occasions, permitted) course of action, but not an actual assessment. The debate is, in a sense, around whether the non-existence of an indicator of an assessment is, in itself, an indicator of an assessment. The Akhbārīs say it is not; the Uṣūlīs tend to view it as an indicator of something.

The discussion here has overlapped with a number of philosophical issues. Two, in particular, were the subject of discussion in theological and philosophical circles and are relevant to the issue of *al-barāʾa al-aṣliyya*. First, there is the developed discussion of whether or not a possible but non-existent entity is a "thing" (*shayʾiyyat al-maʿdūm*), which was a point of issue both between Muʿtazilīs, and between Muʿtazilīs and Ashʿarīs. Second, there is the so-called *argumentum ad ignorantiam* (the argument from ignorance), in which the case is made that the lack of evidence for something is, in itself, evidence for its non-existence.

On the first of these ("the thingness of a non-existent" – *shayʾiyyat al-maʿdūm*), the link with the legal discussions of *al-barāʾa al-aṣliyya* lie first in the ontological status of the non-existent indicator (*ʿadam al-dalīl*). For Akhbārīs the non-existence of an indicator is not, in itself, anything. It cannot be turned into an indicator of anything else, as the Uṣūlīs (allegedly) do. The Akhbārīs fear the Uṣūlī promotion of the doctrine of *al-barāʾa al-aṣliyya* is a conjuring trick – trying to make something out of nothing: a sort of denial of absolute absence when there is no *dalīl*. Later Uṣūlīs appear to have taken on board elements of this Akhbārī critique (though they would not admit this) and argue explicitly that the lack of an indicator means that one is *justified* in treating the action as permitted, and God will not hold one responsible for a transgression if the action is actually assessed otherwise. In the more developed Uṣūlī positions (in the post-Akhbārī period), *al-barāʾa al-aṣliyya* is not a definitive pronouncement of the (ontologically) real rule; it establishes a way of action which absolves the individual from blame (a *ḥukm ẓāhirī* as it came to be known). The real rule (*ḥukm wāqiʿī*) remains undiscovered, but this does not mean the legal subject is unable to act.

Here too the philosophical conclusion that the non-existent is not a thing could be said to contribute to the ontological underpinnings of the legal position – since the lack of an indication does not act as an indication of the real law. The later Uṣūlīs are not imagining that the non-existent indicator somehow has indicatory power (which would imply it can have predication and therefore be a "thing"). Instead, they are arguing quite the opposite: the lack of an indicator provides no knowledge of the law in its ontological reality. Instead, the indicator's absence in *al-barāʾa al-aṣliyya*, as the Uṣūlīs understand it, establishes a justified course of action, which is quite separate from the real law. The philosophical discussions, then, formed the underpinnings (even though they were not explicitly expressed) of the positions of both Akhbārīs and Uṣūlīs on *al-barāʾa al-aṣliyya*.

In order to fully unpack the implications of *shayʾiyyat al-maʿdūm* for the Imāmī debates around *al-barāʾa al-aṣliyya*, one requires an understanding of how it, along with numerous other Muʿtazilī doctrines, was incorporated into Imāmī theological and legal discussions. The debate amongst the early theological schools is quite well known, though not yet fully documented. The famous Baṣran Muʿtazilī Abū Hāshim al-Jubbāʾī (d. 321/933) is reported as holding that the non-existent (*al-maʿdūm*) is a thing (*shayʾ*) – not of course in the sense of existing (by definition, the *maʿdūm* does not exist) – but rather in the sense of being an essence (*dhāt*) which must be distinguishable from other essences. It was important to establish this category since it preserves God's knowledge of both what He causes to exist, and what He chooses not to bring into existence. If the non-existent is not a "thing" in some sense of the term, then it cannot be the subject of knowledge, and therefore God must be ignorant of the things He does not bring into existence. To avoid this accusation of divine weakness, the non-existent must be a thing. Whilst it is not an existent (*mawjūd*), it is nonetheless stable, established, and real (*thābit*) in its non-existence. The non-existent can, therefore, be something known (*ma'lūm* – in the sense of being a legitimate subject of knowledge) without having the attribute of existence (*laysat lahu ṣifat al-wujūd*). Not all Mu'tazilīs held this view – it seems to have been an early distinctive Baṣran Mu'tazilī view, a doctrine of Abū Hāshim al-Jubbā'ī and his followers (known as the Bahshamiyya). Richard M. Frank (1980) links the debate around the thingness of the non-existent to the discussion over "possible" entities which have not yet, and may never, come into existence: they can be said to "exist" in the sense of being the objects of knowledge. Possibles, which have not yet, and may never, come into existence, do not exist, and yet are still "things" because they have attributes that belong to them by their essences, despite being uninstantiated.[9]

Here is not the place to rehearse the rich theological and philosophical discussions around the non-existent thing, since my interest is the debate's life within Twelver Shī'ī philosophical theology, and how it might inform a discussion of *al-barā'a al-aṣliyya*. Many other groups (including the Ash'ariyya and the Māturīdiyya) refuted the Bahshamiyya's view that the "non-existent is a thing" (*al-ma'dūm shay'*). Some outside the tradition, notably Ibn Taymiyya, identified the Shī'a (more polemically *al-rawāfiḍ*) as followers of the Bahshamī view in this matter. The truth appears to be more complex (Ansari and Schmidtke 2016).[10] Early references in the Imāmī theological writings indicate a rejection of the Bahshamī, perhaps in favour of the Baghdādī Mu'tazilī tradition. In his *Awā'il al-Maqālāt*, al-Shaykh al-Mufīd (1993, 98) appears to reject the Baṣran Mu'tazilī notion saying that the non-existent in not a "thing" in a literal (*ḥāqīqa*) but in a non-literal (*majāz*) sense. The notion that whatever the non-existent may be, it is not really a thing in the sense we understand and use the term, certainly undermines the doctrine that the non-existent has "thingness", and though al-Shaykh al-Mufīd's comments are rather brief, they fit with his more general rejection of the positions of the Bahmashiyya.

In the writings of his famous pupils, al-Sayyid al-Murtaḍā and al-Shaykh al-Ṭūṣī, there is greater sympathy for the Bahshamiyya's positions generally, and hence in the writings of both one finds agreement with the notion that the non-existent is, in fact, a thing. At one point al-Murtaḍā states "we only say

9 The extensive secondary literature on the question of the *shay'iyyat al-ma'dūm* includes Klein-Franke 1994; Adamson 2003, 57–9; Schmidtke 2009; Benevich 2018. On the linked issue of whether knowledge prevents assessment or evaluation, see Lameer 2014.

10 The rejection of the doctrine is identified regularly as an indication of the abandonment of Bahshamī views.

that an atom must be an atom whilst it is non-existent because, when it is in a state of non-existence, it must be in a state, on account of which, it can be distinguished [from other things] when it does come into existence" (al-Sharīf al-Murtaḍā 1984, 3:151; 1984, 4:23 (fifth *mas'ala*); al-Ṭūṣī n.d., 81). That is, the essence of, say, "atom" has the predicate of "taking such-and-such a form when it comes into existence." The actualised characteristics of the existent atom can be predicated of the non-existent atom in a formula like "When this atom comes into existence, it will have such-and-such characteristics." If predication is possible of the non-existent, then it must be a "thing", since predication must have a subject. Elsewhere al-Murtaḍā (2002, 41; Abdulsatir 2017, 62–63) states:

> Don't you see that "black" is black through itself [and not through something else], and it does not stop being black, neither in the state of non-existence, or in the state of existence, even if it is not actually existent. It achieves being black through itself, but it doesn't achieve being existent through itself. However, the Eternal One achieves His existence in the same way that blackness achieves being black.

The point here is, then, that the attribute of "existing" is something which happens to essences such as blackness when they come into existence; the attribute of "being black" though is something the essence "black" has through itself (*li-nafsihi*). "Being black" comes prior to "being existent", and is the thing that makes the essence what it is. Al-Murtaḍā's indebtedness to the Bahshamiyya tradition is clear in these passages, and one can see this more broadly in his theory of attributes, his approach to the attributes of God, and numerous other doctrines. Only in the areas which might be called "doctrinally Imāmi" (such as prophecy and the Imāmate) do we see a significant divergence from the Bahshamiyya.

The adoption of the Bahshamiyya's views did not establish itself permanently amongst the Imāmiyya, and the doctrine that the non-existent is a thing, championed by al-Murtaḍā and al-Ṭūsī, gradually lost its popularity amongst Imāmī theologians in the subsequent centuries. In its place, the views of the later Muʿtazilī Abū al-Ḥusayn al-Baṣrī (d. 436/1044), and his rejection of the extreme view of the Bahshamiyya, predominate amongst the Imāmiyya. On the matter of whether the non-existent is a thing, one sees a rejection of the doctrine in various treatises in the time after al-Murtaḍā and al-Ṭūsī, and this is continued to the present day. For example, al-ʿAllāma al-Ḥillī, in a detailed work of theology, adopts many of Abū 'l-Ḥusayn's opinions, often expressed with categories inherited from Ibn Sīna (d. 428/1037). On the issue of *shay'iyyat al-maʿdūm*, he is similarly dismissive of the Bahshamī position in a lengthy exposition of why the non-existent is not a thing. He does not, however, support the notion that holding the opinion that the non-existent is a thing is unbelief (*kufr*); that is, the Bahshamī/early Imāmī position is wrong and needs to be identified as such, but not so wrong as to make its proponent an unbeliever (an understandable position given the fact that al-Murtaḍā and al-Ṭūṣī had held this position) (al-ʿAllāma al-Ḥillī 1998, 1:53–76).[11] After al-ʿAllāma, Imāmī theologians generally asserted that the non-existent is not a thing and this generally translated into the standard Imāmī theological position in the subsequent tradition. The rejection of *shayʾiyyat al-maʿdūm* is carried over into the theological and philosophical writings of the Safavid period as the standard position.[12] Safavid philosophical discussions reflected a radical modification of Ibn Sīna's essence/existence distinction (and hence the primacy of the former) developed first by al-Suhrawardī and subsequently in the Iluminationist tradition which followed his lead. Philosophers influenced by al-Suhrawārdī (including the famous Shīrāz-based Dawwānī and the Dashtakīs mentioned above) considered neither existence nor essence as primary. Instead the ultimate reality is the divine, conceived of as the source of light, and that individual items are distinguishable in ultimate reality by the varying intensities of light which they derive from (or share with) the ultimate source. Whether a thing exists and what its essence might be are secondary questions, since the thing in itself does not exist except as an illumination emanating from the light source. In such a metaphysics, the notion that something which does not exist might have some form of stability is problematic since it relies on the Avicennan (and originally Aristotelian) strong notion of an essence/existence distinction. Later Safavid philosophical reaction against Illuminationist philosophical excesses can be viewed as a resurgence of the Avicennan framework, though with extensive modification. In the works of Mīr Dāmād and Mullā Ṣadrā, for example, the *shayʾiyyat al-maʿdūm* is rejected, as it was for the earlier Shīrāz school. For Mullā Ṣadrā (building on the work of Mīr Dāmād), famously, it is not essence which is primary (as it was for Avi-

11 He summarises the positions saying: "the non-existent is either something that cannot be established, and there is no dispute that this is pure negation; or it is something that could exist, and this is our view [...]. Others hold the view that [the non-existent] is a thing, based on the fact that existence is something in addition to essence, and one could empty this essence of all existences, and it would remain established/stable in concrete reality (*aʿyān*). They make existence other than stability [...]."

12 With respect to Mullā Ṣadra, see Rizvi 2009, 72–76. Also, the *shayʾiyyat al-maʿdūm* position could be said to be a natural outgrowth of Ibn Sīnā's view that essence is primary, and existence is secondary: if essence is primary, individual essences can be said to have "thingness" (that is, have stability – *thābit*) irrespective of their existence. The modification of the essence/existence distinction in the works of Mullā Ṣadrā (as we shall see below) means that holding *shayʾiyyat al-maʿdūm* is no longer tenable.

cenna), but existence (or "being"). His doctrine of the ontological primacy of existence/being (*aṣālat al-wujūd*) is perhaps the defining doctrine of Ṣadrian philosophy. Ṣadrā's most influential work is probably his *al-Asfār al-arbaʿa* and it is here we find an extended discussion, and categorical rejection, of the *shayʾiyyat al-maʿdūm* doctrine. This is perhaps predictable since the doctrine relies on the primacy of essence, rather than existence – it is possible-but-non-existent essences that need to be distinguished, and the Bahshamiyya expressed this distinction through making them a thing which is real (*thābit*) in its non-existence. If, as Mullā Ṣadrā asserts, existence is primary, the primary need to distinguish essences dissolves, and with it the stable nature of the non-existent. The belief that an essence is stable in both an existent or a non-existent state is nonsense for Mullā Ṣadrā (*ghāyat al-sakhāfa wa'l-wahn*) – if an essence is postulated as being something which does not exist, there is no meaning of calling it an essence. Non-existence, as a concept, is something purely verbal (*al-maʿdūm lā yakhbir ʿanhu ilā bi-ḥasab al-lafẓ*). The result here is similar to the conclusion of al-Shaykh al-Mufīd, mentioned above: the non-existent is a thing purely in a *majāz*, and not a *ḥaqīqa* manner) (Mullā Ṣadra 1981, 1:75).

The other element of Mullā Ṣadrā's doctrine is what Sajjad Rizvi has termed "the modulation of being" (*tashkīk al-wujūd*) (Rizvi 2009, 38–53), which rejects the idea of existence as a non-binary state, and instead postulates a spectrum whereby being or existence is more or less intensely present; variety is thereby discernable on a superficial level, but with an underlying unity of existence (drawing, if not explicitly, on the long history of the *waḥdat al-wujūd* doctrine in Ṣūfī philosophical circles). As with the primacy of being, Mullā Ṣadrā's "modulation of being" doctrine also has little room for the notion of *shayʾiyyat al-maʿdūm*, as "thingness" is a quality linked to existence (*wujūd*), and can be said to modulate in intensity in concert with existence (*musāwaqat al-wujūd li'l-shayʾiyya*). Mullā Ṣadrā (1981, 1:78) expresses amazement that people who peddle the Aristotelian doctrine of the primacy of essence are considered learned or insightful at all.[13]

The almost universal rejection in later Shīʿī philosophical theology of the *shayʾiyyat al-maʿdūm* doctrine makes the predication of a non-existent impossible, and this passes into the debate around *al-barāʾa al-aṣliyya* providing the presumptions underlying the various positions. As I have discussed elsewhere, the founder of Akhbarism Muḥammad Amīn al-Astarābādī was consistently critical of al-Dawwānī and the Dashtakīs (particularly Ṣadr al-Dīn) in his philosoph-

13 Ṣadrā goes on to quote (approvingly) al-Suhrawārdī condemning those who are besotted with Greek philosophical thinking.

ical and theological writings, arguing for a return to Avicennan philosophical structures (moderated, for al-Astarabādī, through Nasīr al-Dīn al-Ṭūsī, d. 672/1274) (Gleave 2007a, 102–139). For al-Astarābādī, God knows both existents and non-existents (or possibles – *mumkināt*) – a doctrine he fiercely defends. God knows the form (*ṣūra*) of each possible, but this form is not a thing (*shay'*), because things are only the actuals which have some form of external existence (*fī l-khārij*). Whilst he does not, to my knowledge, discuss the *shay'iyyat al-ma'dūm* doctrine directly, his acceptance of the purely mental existence for possible non-existents would seem to preclude the possibles being stable (*thābit*). Muḥsin Fayḍ al-Kāshānī (d. 1091/1680), another major Akhbārī thinker and a pupil of Mullā Ṣadrā, similarly does not give ground on the doctrine of the *shay'iyyat al-ma'dūm:* "the pure unsullied real existence is God, may He be praised. Non-existence has no essence, and no effect, and no distinction – in fact, it has no 'thing-ness' at all."[14]

It is interesting that later Akhbārīs, as far as we can tell, did not see fit to incorporate *shay'iyyat al-ma'dūm* into their theological visions, even though the doctrine was held by one of the Akhbārīs own traditionalist heroes (namely, Muḥammad b. Ḥasan al-Ṭūsī). The rejection of *shay'iyyat al-ma'dūm* forms one possible underpinning to the Akhbārī approach to *al-barā'a al-aṣliyya.* As outlined above, broadly speaking, the Akhbārī doctrine was that God has an assessment for every situation – and this assessment (*ḥukm*) has real ontological status. This doctrine, it should be said, is really a theological dogma rather than the conclusion of any philosophical reasoning. But this doctrine does not, necessarily, mean that there is a specific indicator for each specific ruling – there are cases where the sources (including reason) do not contain any indication of the assessment. However, Akhbārīs clearly held (as demonstrated above) that the lack of an indication is not itself an indication of anything. The lack of indication is, for them, pure absence: there is no hint of *shay'iyya* in the non-existent *dalīl.* If there were to be *shay'iyya* then it might open the door to the argument that the non-existence of an indicator is a "something" (and that something is an indication of no *ḥukm*). The Akhbārī position is, then, that the lack of an indication is a radical absence with no element of stability or "thingness"; and this

---

14 *Al-'adam al-baḥt lā dhāt lahu wa-lā athar, wa-lā tamayyuz bal huwa lā shay' maḥḍ*, in the basic exposition of belief of al-Kashānī 2007, 61 (repeated word for word in his 2005, 12). See also his more extended passage (2007, 80–81) where he states that nonexistence has no independent status, being entirely derivative from existence; and only those who cannot see the truth and have limited insight (*quṣūr al-naẓar*) are seduced into the whimsical belief (*wahm*) that "non-existence occurs to a thing (*al-'adam yaṭra'u 'alā shay'*) raising up the nonexistent's specific existence to the level of reality."

radical absence is entirely unable to tell us about the law in reality. That there is "something" in the absence of an indicator to indicate the real law is the logical mistake made by the Uṣūlīs; for the Akhbārīs the lack of thingness in the absent indicator facilitates the assertion that absence has no indicatory power.

The Uṣūlī response to this, typified by Ḥasan b. al-Shahīd al-Thānī referenced above, but developed into a full-blown theory of legal ontology in the nineteenth century, is that this is a gross mischaracterisation of their position. For them, the rejection of *shay'iyyat al-maʿdūm* forms a philosophical underpinning for the promotion (not rejection) of *al-barā'a al-aṣliyya*. When a scholar finds the sources to be silent on an issue (that is, finds an absence of any indicator), then there is an assertion that the sources have left us bereft of any indication. For Uṣūlīs too, the absence must be absolute with no hint of possible indication. If there was a hint of some form of thingness on which to base an indication (even if that was to be found in the absence of an indication), then that would mean this was no longer a case of *al-barā'a al-aṣliyya*. The sources must not only be silent, but the silence must not, in itself, have any indicatory power for the Uṣūlīs; only then can one treat this as a case of *al-barā'a al-aṣliyya*.[15] Once the absence of any indicatory power in the sources is established, the procedural remedy is activated – and that is the presumption that the performance or non-performance of the act will not attract divine punishment even if they are transgression of the law in its ontological reality.

As outlined above, the standard Imāmī rejection of *shay'iyyat al-maʿdūm* could act as a philosophical underpinning of both Akhbārī and Uṣūlī trends in Imāmī *uṣūl al-fiqh*[16] – and it is important to remember that theology and phi-

15 This is, I think, behind doctrines in post-Akhbārī *uṣūl* such as Mīrzā Qummī's assertion that the lack of an indication of an action's legal validity (of, for example, an act of worship) is an indication that the action is invalid (*ʿadam dalīl l-ṣihha dalīl ʿalā al-fasād*). Validity in relation to legal matters is an assertion of the existence of something (that is, a legal quality or ruling). The fundamental nature of things (*al-aṣl*) is to be free of such assessments. If that freedom is anything less than absolute (that is, if there is a *dalīl* that validity is possible), then the situation can be flipped. See for example, Qummī 2008, 1:355. Mīrzā Qummī, it should be added, is unusual in his view that *al-aṣl fī l-ʿibādāt wa'l-muʿāmalāt huwa al-fasād*.

16 The lack of any explicit referencing between the *shay'iyyat al-maʿdūm* and *al-barā'a al-aṣliyya* in *uṣūl* works composed between the sixteenth and late eighteenth centuries CE of *uṣūl* could indicate that the former (a metaphysical issue) was not considered as influencing the latter (a strictly legal question). However, the metaphysical nature of non-existence is linked to value ontology in post-Akhbārī works (that is, nineteenth century CE) – whether this linkage is merely authors enforcing a philosophical connection, or making explicit a link which was assumed previously is not clear. Muḥammad Taqī al-Iṣfahānī (d. 1148/1832–3), for example, composed a commentary on the classical work *Maʿālim al-uṣūl* of al-Ḥasan b. al-Shahīd al-

losophy do not always determine *uṣūl* doctrine, but instead forms the intellectual context in which particular *uṣūl* doctrines can be imagined. The situation with the *argumentum ad ignorantiam* (the argument from ignorance) is more divisive. In philosophical writings, the logical step from an absence of evidence for a thing to an absence of the thing itself formed part of a larger discussions, and opinion was predictably split. There were those who considered the absence of evidence for a thing to be irrelevant to whether the thing actually exists – the thing remains possibly existent irrespective of evidence. On the other hand, there were those who held that absence of evidence was, in fact, evidence of absence. Underlying this position was a concern that if one does not work on this basis, the whole structure of deducing conclusions from indicators would be undermined. The split does not always accord perfectly with the various schools of theology, indicating that this was not a fundamental matter (in terms of distinguishing between schools), though it could nevertheless remain an important theological and philosophical debate. The argument from ignorance was considered valid by many Muʿtazilīs and some Ashʿarīs. Among the Muʿtazilīs, the discussion was primarily confined to the Baṣran school; furthermore, both of the main branches of Baṣran Muʿtazilism – the followers of Abū Hāshim al-Jubbāʾī and the followers of Abū ʾl-Ḥusayn al-Baṣrī – used and affirmed the validity of the argument that from an absence of evidence for a thing can be deduced an absence of the thing itself. Amongst the early Ashʿarīs al-Bāqillānī (d. 403/1013) appears to have supported the argument, whilst later Ashʿarīs, al-Juwaynī (d. 478/1085) and Fakhr al-Dīn al-Rāzī, appear to have critiqued it rather harshly. The early discussion of the validity of the "argument

Thānī (d. 1030/1621) mentioned above. In the section discussing *al-barāʾa al-aṣliyya* his focus is not so much on the existence of the rule (*ḥukm*) itself – for the "real" law is accepted as ultimately unknowable in the strict sense of the word. Rather, the focus is on the existence or non-existence of the "evidence for the rule" (*dalīl al-ḥukm*). Al-Iṣfahānī proclaims the axiomatic notion that non-existence takes rational precedence over existence (*al-rājiḥ fī naẓar al-ʿaql min al-wujūd waʾl-ʿadam huwa al-ʿadam*). The proposal that the lack of evidence for a rule itself becomes evidence for a rule is to make absence into a thing which can have an effect (that is, the absence itself causes a rule of permission to come into being). This would violate the axiom that non-existence takes rational precedence over existence. Instead, there is here a case of absolute nothingness, and hence fundamentally there can be no required response from the individual legal agent. In this way the real qualities of non-existence feed into the justification of the assumption of no assessment. See al-Iṣfahānī 1420–1421/2000–2001, 3:543–544. The issues are also linked in Sunnī discussions of theology and jurisprudence. See Shihadeh 2013, 201, where Shihadeh notes that al-Juwaynī's use of *amr* for "thing" rather than the more common *shayʾ* is intentional in order "to avoid implying that a thing could be non-existent, a notion that the Ashʿarīs reject."

from ignorance" has been explained thoroughly by Ayman Shihadeh (2013, 171–220).

What we do see emerging in the earlier theological discussions around the so-called "argument from ignorance" is that there is a sharp distinction between the evidence one might have for a thing, and the thing itself, that is, between the epistemological element of the question (how knowledge about a thing is produced) and the actual thing. Evidence is seen as purely indicatory – and it might produce an opinion (*ẓann*) that the item exists, but it does not necessarily cause knowledge of its existence, since knowledge requires an opinion to "accord" (*muṭābiq*) with external reality. The connection between the evidence/indicator (*dalīl*) and the evidenced/indicated item (*madlūl*) is weakened in the more mature theological discussions. To say that God provided an indicator in His word (that is, the Qur'an), and that this indicator creates an assessment for an action, is to stray into the notion of a law created in time (and the concomitant problems of God's word being non-eternal and the potential for change in God's decisions – the doctrine of *badāʾ*). Whatever indicators indicate, for the Ashʿarīs they do not have the power to create reality. The connection between the indication and the thing indicated (in our case between the indicator and the *ḥukm*) was seen by some as essentially mythical. Shihadeh (2013, 205) quotes al-Juwaynī saying, "There is, hence, no real and intrinsic connection between the evidence and what is evidenced" (*taʿalluq al-dalīl al-ʿaqlī bi-madlūlihi lā ḥaqīqa lahu*). The discussion draws, of course, on the critique of Aristotelian notions of causality and the promotion of Ashʿarī occasionalism. That there is a causal connection between the *dalīl* and the *madlūl* underpins the system of indication (*dalāla*) in legal theory, where indicators produce internal states in the investigator which accord with suspicion, opinion and knowledge depending on the strength of the indicator. Breaking this connection would, for some legal theorists, undermine the whole legal system.

One popular solution was to argue that it is wrong to think of the indicator as the evidence, and the indicated thing as the ruling or assessment; rather, the indicator is the textual evidence and the thing indicated is the *knowledge* of the ruling (and not the ruling itself). The ontological existence of the assessment then is not caused by the existence of the indicator, though the knowledge of the assessment is so caused.[17] If the indicator cannot be said to cause the existence of the assessment, then, *mutatis mutandis* – and perhaps with greater force – the lack of an indicator would also be unable to do so. Alternatively, if an indicator can cause knowledge to come into being, could not, equally, lack of an

17 A detailed discussion of the causality of *dalāla* can be found in Ahmad 2018, 175–179.

indicator? Or to put it another way: the lack of an indicator might be said to cause the knowledge of the lack of an assessment, thereby providing the epistemological foundations of the legal doctrine of *al-barāʾa al-aṣliyya.*

As contributors to the same intellectual discussions, the Shīʿī authors of works of theology and legal theory explored the coherence of the argument from ignorance. The issue was a matter of discussion over valid and invalid types of argumentation in both disciplines. Al-Sharīf al-Murtaḍā, whose own Bahshamī Muʿtazilī tendencies were mentioned above, dedicates a short piece to this type of argument, entitled "the negation of the assessment on account of there being no indication for it" (al-Sharīf al-Murtaḍā 1984, 2:101–105). He argues that non-existence can be an indication on certain occasions (*fī baʿḍ al-mawāḍiʿ*). For example, the non-existence of a miracle is an indication that an individual is not a prophet. The lack of an indicator for another obligatory fast other than that of the month of Ramadan is an indication that there is no other obligatory fast. The form of argumentation is, he argues, a valid one. It is valid in these instances because the indications for the positive assertion (that is, that an individual is a prophet, and that Ramadan is the month of fasting) are the items which, due to their nature, require an indication; therefore, the lack of any indication make non-existence a valid conclusion. Propositions such as "Zayd is in the house" are different: one cannot be certain that Zayd is not in the house from the lack of evidence that he is there: Zayd's being in the house is not the sort of thing which must be evidenced (*laysa min al-bāb alladhī idhā waqaʿ fa-lā budda min naṣb dalīl ʿalayhi*) (al-Sharīf al-Murtaḍā 1984, 2:102). The argument then is valid conditionally – it depends on the sort of thing being proven here.

Developing from such early Imāmī discussions of valid argumentation technique (and the conditions under which the argument from ignorance might be employed), later elaborations emerged. The argument from ignorance emerges in later Imāmī theology through discussions of Ibn Sīnā's notion that the lack of an awareness of something's existence is not evidence of its non-existence (this is normally expressed in the slogan: *ʿadam al-wijdān lā yudullu ʿalā ʿadam al-wujūd*, though this precise formulation is not Ibn Sīnā's), which becomes a sort of fundamental principle (*qāʿida*) of legal and theological argumentation and which, in effect, states that the *argumentum ad ignorantiam* is invalid. In late classical, often philosophically informed, works one finds this principle cited at various points as a clinching argument in works of both theology and legal theory. For example, the Safavid scholar (normally categorised as an Akhbārī) Mullā Khalīl al-Qazwīnī (d. 1089/1678–1679) cites Ibn Sīnā's dictum on occasions when commenting on al-Ṭūsī's work of legal theory, *al-ʿUdda fī uṣūl al-fiqh*. He argues against al-Ṭūsī's assertion that he has searched through the rational proofs and found none that demonstrate the obligatory nature of acting on isolated traditions (*al-khabar al-wāḥid*). Al-Qazwīnī clearly feels this is not a strong argument, and cites the maxim *ʿadam al-wijdān lā yudillu ʿalā ʿadam al-wujūd*, adding "We do not accept that the non-existence of evidence (*ʿadam al-dalīl*) is an indication of non-existence (*dalīl al-ʿadam*). What is necessitated here is that it is not *known* to be obligatory, not that it is not obligatory, even though the first is implied by the second" (al-Qazwīnī n.d., 304; emphasis added). The point here being that a lack of evidence brings about a lack of knowledge, rather than a lack of existence – a distinction we see already exploited in al-Taftazānī's work referenced above. Since knowledge must be in accordance with reality, it is quite possible for the evidence for a thing's existence to be distinct and separable from the thing itself. In this case, al-Ṭūsī's inability to find arguments for the obligation to follow *khabar al-wāḥid* is not an argument for there being no obligations here.

It would seem inevitable that the philosophical framework of Mullā Ṣadrā, which came to dominate the philosophical curriculum in the Shīʿī seminaries of the eighteenth and nineteenth centuries, is also not conducive to the argument from ignorance. Having said this, Ṣadrā does not, to my knowledge, address the validity of the argument from ignorance directly. In the Ṣadrian context, the "primacy of being/existence" over essences is established, and this undercuts fundamental elements of the argument. First, as we have seen above, the argument from ignorance is built on the primacy of essence (not existence). The argument that a thing's existence cannot occur without evidence (*adilla*) of that existence entails the general proposition that "if there is no evidence, then there is no existence." Since evidence is always evidence of *something*, the conceptualisation of that thing (that is, its essence) has logical priority over the external actualisation of its existence. In order to decide that there is no evidence for a thing, there must be a notion of what that "thing" could be, and that places essence in priority over existence within the framework of the argument. Furthermore, the argument assumes that existence is a binary state, without any gradation and modulation – it is because of this assumption that, through the argument, one can assume a lack of evidence (an absolute state) indicates a lack of existence (another absolute state). All these premises would appear to be undermined in Mullā Ṣadrā's promotion of mental existence as an element of his ontology of graded being – not an inferior mode, but merely one of the three modes of being he envisages (the others being external and linguistic).[18] More fundamentally, though, in the Ṣadrian framework existence is primary, and essence

18 For an examination of Ṣadrā's concept of mental existence, see Marcotte 2011, 153–182.

becomes investigable only in a non-primary (let us call it "secondary") manner. The principal feature whereby existing things are distinguished from one another is, for Ṣadrā, the intensity of their modulated or gradated existence (that is, the doctrine of *tashkīk*), not that they contain radically distinct characteristics which characterise their essences. Predicating a thing as "existing" does not entail other attributes of that thing (which, under other formulations, might be considered essential). However, positing evidence for a thing necessarily entails a description of the thing's attributes. *Adilla* indicate a thing's quiddity (not simply its existence). Even non-existence can be considered as encompassed by Ṣadrā's modulated being/existence:[19] while such things exhibit an existence intensity value of zero, they are not categorically different from those that exhibit very low intensity values.

On the one hand, the popularity of Ṣadrā's philosophical framework could be said to be consistent with the Akhbārī argument against *al-barā'a al-aṣliyya*, namely that the lack of evidence for a ruling does not establish the ruling's non-existence, since the evidence and the ruling have quite distinct ontological realities, and one is not caused by the other. This could explain why Muḥsin Fayḍ al-Kāshānī, Ṣadrā's pupil, felt no need to modify his philosophical commitment with his Akhbārism (Gleave 2007b). Feeding into this is Mullā Ṣadrā's general dissatisfaction with the traditional causal mechanism of Aristotelian/Avicennan metaphysics (Rizvi 2005): the non-existence of a *dalīl* cannot bring about (that is, cause) the non-existence of a *ḥukm* since causation generally for Mullā Ṣadrā cannot be considered straightforwardly effective within a graded ontology of being. It cannot even (following al-Taftazānī's scheme mentioned above) be said to cause the non-existence of *knowledge* of the *ḥukm*, since even an imagined *ḥukm* is the subject of knowledge in one sense. For Akhbārīs (from al-Astarābādī onwards), whatever the relationship between evidence (*dalīl*) and ruling (*ḥukm*) might be (and I am yet to find an explicit Akhbārī statement on this point), it is not one of necessary causality. For them, the relationship is, in philosophical terms, accidental. Rulings exist without evidence of them being necessarily existent (hence the rejection of *al-barā'a al-aṣliyya*); the existence of evidence does not necessarily create the existence of a ruling (the prime example of this relationship breaking down is the prevalence of dissimulation, *taqiyya*); and even though at times, evidence exists and the rulings also exist, this does not mean the relationship is causal from the former to the latter.

19 Haq (1967, 267), in one of the first studies of Ṣadrā concept of being, states that "Mullā Ṣadrā asserts that even the concept 'nothingness' is contained within the bosom of Being because it is understandable only when considered in terms of Being, i.e. it cannot escape mental existence."

In many ways the power of these Akhbārī objections (philosophical and otherwise) to the "non-evidence = non-existence" argument created the solution developed in post-Akhbārī Shīʿī *uṣūl* – namely that later Shīʿī *uṣūlīs* ceased asserting that *al-barāʾa al-aṣliyya* is evidence of the existence of an actual ruling; instead it becomes a procedural principle on the basis of which the individual can act (or, more precisely, the *mujtahid* can proceed to rule), but the rulings thereby created had no ontological status. The law can be fulfilled without any knowledge as to its actual contents, and *al-barāʾa al-aṣliyya* becomes one method of its fulfilment. The question as to whether a procedural rule – which the individual is justified in following but is not the law "in reality" (*al-ḥukm al-wāqiʿī* as against *al-ḥukm al-ẓāhirī* in later Shīʿī *uṣūlī* terminology) – has existence (*wujūd*) in some secondary sense (or, perhaps with less intensity under the scheme of *tashkīk*) is not explored directly, but is left as a possible means of marrying jurisprudence and philosophy.

5 Conclusion

In the above exposition, two elements of the relationship between late classical Shīʿī *uṣūl* and contemporaneous Shīʿī philosophical trends can be discerned. First, there is the manner in which philosophical modes of thinking (not only terminology, but forms of argumentation) are directly taken up and explored in the works of *uṣūl al-fiqh*. This started hesitantly at first, but is fully exploited in the post-Akhbārī works of the late eighteenth/early nineteenth century – the example explored above is the *argumentum ad ignorantiam*. The second element is how certain doctrines (such as *shayʾiyyat al-maʿdūm*), though not referenced directly, create a philosophical background against which the development of legal theory can be placed. Here, the influence is not explicit, but philosophical positions make certain *uṣūl* arguments more convenient, or comfortable, within the framework of a wider theory. The manner in which a philosophical advance facilitates particular *uṣūl* arguments is clear, even though one could read the *uṣūl* without requiring a full-blooded commitment to the philosophy. The philosophers are often portrayed as uninterested in matters of law, but this presumes that philosophers and jurisprudents made up two distinct and conflicting groups of scholars. A seminary education in the late classical period rarely exhibited such a hardline separation. The doctrine of *al-barāʾa al-aṣliyya* is but one example of cross-fertilisation. The above analysis hopefully demonstrates that this was not confined to the supposedly more "rationally-orientated" Uṣūlī scholars; Akhbārīs too, despite the explicit rhetoric of some of their number against the *ḥukamāʾ*, often leaned heavily on notions emerging from contemporary philosophical discussions.

Amir Mohammad Emami and Mirza Mohammad Kazem Askari

Tajarrī as Religious Luck

1 Introduction

Suppose you are in a situation where you are morally obligated to tell the truth, but choose to say something that is opposed to your beliefs. Later on, it turns out that what you said was true, unbeknownst to you. We might say that you attempted to lie, but failed. Morally speaking, is your situation like that of someone who expressed a true belief with the intention to be honest? Or like someone who intentionally and successfully uttered a falsehood? Such cases illustrate the relation between knowledge, morality, and luck. The problem is a familiar one. Linda Zagzebski (1994) has sought to show that there are certain aspects of Christian theology, namely the traditional doctrines of grace and eternal reward or punishment in the afterlife, that magnify the problem of moral luck. She calls this revised version of the problem "religious luck." Taking inspiration from this idea, in the following we will explore how religious luck figured in a debate within Islamic jurisprudence concerning the concept of *tajarrī*. After reviewing contemporary discussions of moral and religious luck, we will introduce the notion of *tajarrī* in the jurisprudential context, and finally show how moral luck was dealt with in the Islamic legal tradition.

2 Zagzebski on Religious Luck

Philosophers have recently been interested in luck as a philosophical notion in a wide range of areas, including epistemology as well as ethics and philosophy of religion. Zagzebski's formulation of a concept of "religious luck" itself responds to literature on the general phenomenon of moral luck. This literature recognises that luck may play a role in both morality and law, though these roles need not coincide. In a paper entitled "Responsibility in Law and Morals", Joel Feinberg (1962) examines similarities and differences between moral and legal responsibility. Whereas he allows that luck may enter into questions of legal culpability, "moral responsibility must be regular and predictable; nothing can be left to chance or to unforeseeable contingencies. Above all, it cannot be a matter of luck" (Feinberg 1962, 346). He argues that, as the events and state of affairs in the external world are not solely caused by the agent's action, she cannot be morally responsible for them. Rather, she is responsible only for the inner

https://doi.org/10.1515/9783110552386-012

world of her mind. But for Feinberg even inner intentions are not entirely immune to luck since characteristics and circumstances of the person affect her inner intention, without being under her control. He therefore concludes that "the precise determinability of moral responsibility is an illusion; there are problematic cases even for the inner court, and these are undecidable in principle; and moral responsibility, so conceived, is less, not more, rational than that of the courts" (Feinberg 1962, 351).

Though Feinberg drew attention to the problem of moral luck, he did not yet use the term. It was first used and explained by Bernard Williams in his paper "Moral Luck" (1976) and in a paper with the same title by Thomas Nagel (1976).[1] Whereas Williams was particularly concerned with the effect of luck upon rational and moral justification, Nagel took up the problem of moral luck in what has become its familiar form. We speak of moral luck when an agent is morally responsible for things that are in part beyond her control.[2] This clashes with the intuition that moral value is distinctive in presupposing agent control, and that a person should not be judged for something out of her control, which is part of what we mean by speaking of "luck."[3]

As Nagel claims, there are different kinds of moral luck in our daily moral assessments, which fall into four categories: resultant, constitutive, circumstantial, and causal. Luck concerning the consequences of an action or "resultant" luck, as Nagel (1976, 140) defines it, is "luck, good and bad, in the way things turn out." This type of luck poses a problem for consequentialist moral theories, and is the one mostly explored by Williams. Secondly, and in contrast to resultant luck, "constitutive" luck is not related to one's actions. It rather concerns a person's characteristics, her virtues and vices: someone might be fortunate enough to be born with a tendency towards self-control or bravery, for example. Acknowledgment of this kind of luck poses a potential difficulty for virtue ethics. Thirdly, "circumstantial" has to do with the situations one faces: only people who have the misfortune to be involved in a war have the opportunity to display martial cowardice. Even Kantian deontological ethics, which looks only to intentions and gives no room to individual character or the results of actions, is not immune to this sort of luck. For certain intentions will or will not be formed

1 The two papers were first published in *The Aristotelian Society Supplementary* 1 (1976) and revised later by the authors. The revised versions are included in an anthology edited by Daniel Statman (1993).

2 Dana K. Nelkin (2013) proposes a slightly different definition of moral luck, presupposing that it occurs only when it is *correct* to judge an agent based on factors beyond her control.

3 Some have challenged this conception of luck and consequently dismissed the whole debate as dealing with a pseudo-problem (Pritchard 2006).

depending on the circumstances that arise. (Note, therefore, that all the main ethical theories – consequentialism, virtue ethics, and deontological ethics – have to confront some version of the problem of moral luck.) Finally, there is "causal" luck which, in contrast to resultant luck, is about the causes and determination of an action, rather than the outcome of an action. Some have, however, argued that it is character and situation that cause actions, so that causal luck is nothing more than circumstantial and constitutive luck (Latus 2001).

Following the publication of Williams and Nagel's papers on moral luck, philosophers have paid extensive attention to the topic. Nelkin (2013) divides approaches to the problem into three categories, each having further subcategories. First, one may simply deny the reality of moral luck, on the grounds that control is essential for morality. Second, one may accept moral luck by rejecting the essentiality of control for judging someone morally blameworthy; within this option one may argue that some revision of moral practices is therefore required, or not. Third, one may argue that both the denial and acceptance of moral luck lead to incoherence. Complicating matters further, each of these three options can be applied to a specific kind of moral luck to the exclusion of others. Recent scholarship on the subject has focused mostly on solving Nagel's version of the problem. In what follows, by contrast, we want to introduce a new formulation of the problem by calling attention to a specific version of religious luck arising out of the notion of *tajarrī* as discussed in the historical literature on the principles of Islamic jurisprudence.

3 *Tajarrī* in the Principles of Islamic Jurisprudence

The purpose of Islamic law, and the focus on studying the principles of Islamic jurisprudence (*uṣūl al-fiqh*) in particular, is to provide reasons (*ḥujaj*, sg. *ḥujja*)[4] for acting in agreement with divine commands and divine consent (al-Ṣadr 2015, 45). If not for reason, the believer would not be justified in acting, because she knows that God may punish her if she disobeys divine commands. Knowledge of the divine commands serves as such a reason. Suppose – to take a standard example from jurisprudential literature – that John knows based on valid sources of Islamic law that it is forbidden (*ḥarām*) to drink wine; then he must not

4 Although the precise translation of *ḥujja* is not "reason" (a more common translation is "proof"), this seems to capture its role in the current context; we take it to be roughly equivalent to "justification."

drink it and if he does, he will deserve divine punishment. Likewise, if someone knows that it is obligatory (*wājib*) to fast in Ramaḍān, she must behave in accordance with that, and if she follows the divine command sincerely, she will deserve divine reward.

Cases like these, where the believer has actual knowledge of what is required of her, are straightforward. But it is not always possible to gain knowledge of divine commands. Where knowledge is lacking, the responsible believer cannot neglect other probable duties; she must try her best to get near to them, so that she will have reason for acting. For she knows generally that she has *some* obligations toward God, and if she restricts her duties to the ones she knows particularly, she will be responsible for the ones she has omitted (al-Ṣadr 2015, 46). For example, if someone does not know the divine will as concerns eating caviar – a controversial question among scholars – she ought not to ignore the possibility that it is forbidden, simply because the case is unclear.

Reasons that fall short of certain knowledge are also discussed in principles of Islamic jurisprudence and used in Islamic law. When it is impossible to gain certain knowledge, the *ḥujja* assumed for one's action may be true or false, just like justified belief as discussed in modern-day epistemology. Obviously, one would not have any problem if one acts in accordance with a true *ḥujja*. If one's *ḥujja* is false, one would be excused (*maʿdhūr*) and God will not impose punishment. Nevertheless, if one acts in conflict with a true *ḥujja*, then one will be sinful and blameworthy. Jurists have consensus about these two features of *ḥujja* which are called *muʿadhdhariyya* ("exculpation") and *munajjaziyya* ("inculpation").[5] Thus, if John drinks a beverage which he does not know, but correctly believes, to be white wine, he will deserve divine punishment. If, however, he drinks wine, but holds the justified false belief that it is water, he will be excused and avoid punishment.

But what happens if an agent acts in defiance of a justified belief that turns out to be false? John may for example actually drink water, falsely believing it to be white wine, and thus accepting that he is disregarding a divine command (not realizing, of course, that he is not in reality). This sort of action is called *tajarrī* and the agent in question is called *mutajarrī* (al-Nāʾīnī 2016, 53; al-Ṣadr 2015, 190). Thus, *tajarrī* in the jurisprudential context could be defined as "opposing an actually false *ḥujja*." There is a long-running debate in *uṣūl al-fiqh* as to whether *tajarrī* is sin, and the *mutajarrī* deserves divine punishment.

This subject was first discussed with respect to particular issues in Islamic law. The different prayers (*ṣalāt*) said during the day are to be performed at spe-

---

5 Thus translated by Roy Parviz Mottahede (al-Ṣadr 2005, 70–71).

cific periods, for example the midday prayer between noon and sunset. The question arises whether it is a sin if someone postpones her prayer thinking she will miss the right time, but in fact being wrong about this. Jurists had different views about this question. The majority declared it a sin, according to al-Ḥillī's (d. 726/1325) report (al-ʿAllāmah al-Ḥillī 1991, 107; 2004, 111), while others rejected this view (al-ʿAllāmah al-Ḥillī 1993, 391; 2004, 111). Another example concerned dangerous paths. As it is forbidden to travel dangerous ways (al-Ṭūsī 1980, 369–370; al-Muḥaqqiq al-Ḥillī 1992, 312–313), the problem raised is whether it is a sin if someone travels along a path which is erroneously thought to be dangerous.

The question was raised to a more general level by ʿAbd al-ʿAzīz b. ʿAbd al-Salām (d. 660/1262), who collected cases of this kind while presupposing that the agent is certainly sinful (Ibn ʿAbd al-Salām 2000, 33).[6] In the end, without offering rational or scriptural arguments, he claims that the agent's punishment would be less than for a major (*kabīr*) sin, but more than a minor (*ṣaghīr*) sin (Ibn ʿAbd al-Salām 2000, 34). Muḥammad b. Makkī al-ʿĀmilī al-Shahīd al-Awwal (d. 786/1384) takes up this debate, though without using the term *tajarrī*. He considers it as one of several questions about the relation between intention and action. First, based on certain *ḥadīth*s, he explains that the mere intention to commit a sin, without actually committing it, would be forgiven by God and lead to no punishment. Then he frames the problem (al-ʿĀmilī n.d., 107–108):[7]

> If one intends a sin and commits what is thought to be a sin, but it afterwards appears that this was not the case, the outcome of the intention is unclear. On the one hand, as no sin was actually committed and there was mere intention, the agent will not be punished for that; on the other hand, there is an implication of a forbidden infraction and daring to commit sin.

He here grasps the core of the problem by setting out the two opposite intuitions that make for ambiguity in categorising these kinds of actions. Though al-Shahīd al-Awwal criticises the view of Ibn ʿAbd al-Salām, he himself suspends judgement about the problem. Subsequently jurists offer different opinions about it. For example, one of al-Shahīd al-Awwal's commentators, Miqdād b. ʿAbd Allāh al-Suyūrī (d. 826/1423), known as al-Fāḍil al-Miqdād and al-Fāḍil al-Suyūrī, prefers the view that such an agent does not deserve punishment (al-Suyūrī 1983,

6 In general, we focus on Shīʿī jurists, but Ibn ʿAbd al-Salām is mentioned here, despite being Sunnī, as background for al-Shahīd al-Awwal's response.

7 و لو نوى المعصية و تلبس بما يراه معصية، فظهر بخلافها، ففي تأثير هذه النية نظر، من أنها لما لم تصادف المعصي فيه صارت كنية مجردة، وهو غير مؤاخذ بها، ومن دلالتها على انتهاكه الحرمة وجرأته على المعاصي.

408). By contrast, Zayn al-Dīn b. ʿAlī (d. 966/1558), known as al-Shahīd al-Thānī, declares the contrary view when discussing a related problem in Islamic law (Ibn ʿAlī 1992, 202).

Another important jurist who touches on the issue is Muḥammad Bāqir Muḥaqqiq Sabzevārī (d. 1090/1679). Though his discussion is restricted to a particular subject mentioned above, namely the required time of prayer, his argument is generalisable. With reference to the jurisprudential law that the Muslim must pray when she knows certainly that her prayer is on time, he imagines a situation in which two persons delay their prayers in ignorance of the time of day. Afterwards, one of them says her prayers after the necessary period has ended, while the other does so at the right time by mere chance. He then notes that there are different possible answers to the question as to which of them deserves punishment: both, neither, or only one agent – either the first or the second. He declares that all options but the first are obviously implausible. In arguing for the implausibility of punishing only one of the two agents, he says that "they are equal in their free actions which are subject to praise and blame, and [differ only in] saying the prayers at the necessary time or not, which happened by mere chance" (Sabzevārī 1832, 209–210).[8] Therefore, in his opinion the right answer is that both of them deserve punishment. His argument is effectively the same as that given by philosophers who reject moral luck on the basis of the control principle.

Muḥammad Ḥusayn (d. 1254/1839) and Muḥammad Taqī al-Ḥāʾirī al-Isfahānī (d. 1248/1833) were brothers, and both important jurists. They were the first to apply the word *tajarrī* to our problem, though only as a more general term that includes this specific case. Muḥammad Taqī asserts that we must come to know that we have tried our best to fulfil our necessary duties. So if someone fails to gain this knowledge, which is not knowledge of divine rule, she will be *mutajarrī* according to his usage. This usage is obviously broader than the case we are interested in, where the agent does nothing wrong in reality. Muḥammad Taqī continues by arguing that in either case, the person is sinful and deserves divine punishment – whether it is because she has not fulfilled her primary duty, or because of her *tajarrī*[9] (al-Ḥāʾirī al-Isfahānī 2008, 359–360). He does not clearly state whether the sinfulness is the same in either case, or whether one is more sinful than the other, but this topic was taken up by his brother.

8 على الثالث يلزم خلاف العدل لاستوائهما في الحركات الاختيارية الموجبة للمدح أو الذم وإنما حصل مصادفة الوقت وعدمه بضرب من الاتفاق.

9 The use of this word here is different from the later common usage and closer to the literal meaning.

Muḥammad Ḥusayn al-Ḥā'irī al-Isfahānī is mostly known for his famous work on the principles of Islamic jurisprudence, *al-Fuṣūl al-gharawiyya fī 'l-uṣūl al-fiqhiyya*. He believes that it is not plausible to treat all instances of *tajarrī* similarly. However, by considering that one may deserve more punishment than another person, he declares that the real status of the action is also relevant. Rather, he asserts that if an instance of *tajarrī* is in fact obligatory its agent may not deserve any punishment from God, but if it is discouraged without being forbidden (*makrūh*), or permissible (*mubāh*), the amount of punishment she deserves will be different. For the sake of clarification, he appeals to a common sense example. Suppose that a master commands his slave to kill his enemy, and the slave thinks by mistake that one of the master's sons is that enemy. Fortunately, he disobeys his master's command and does not kill him. In such a case the master would not punish his slave (al-Ḥā'irī al-Isfahānī 1984, 431–432). Although he has adopted a slightly different position from other jurists, his view did not become influential because of the criticism of al-Shaykh al-Murtaḍā al-Anṣārī (d. 1281/1864) (al-Anṣārī 2011, 43–45).

Al-Anṣārī's two works on Islamic law and its principles, *al-Makāsib* and *Farā'id al-uṣūl*, are still used as textbooks in Shī'ī seminaries. He addresses our topic, and the approaches of other jurists, in his *Farā'id al-uṣūl* under a separate heading. By differentiating between intention and action, he discusses three aspects of the *action* of *tajarrī:* the wrongness of the action, the agent's blameworthiness, and the deserving of punishment. These aspects may be dealt with on the basis of rational or religious arguments; given the purpose of this chapter, we will only review briefly his rational arguments. He restates the argument given by Muḥaqqiq Sabzevārī in favour of the similarity of the sinner and the *mutajarrī* in deserving punishment. In response, al-Anṣārī distinguishes between two kinds of wrongness: the wrongness of an action itself, and the wrongness of a vice manifested in an action. While the latter is acceptable in *tajarrī*, the former is not. Thus, if one uses a substance which is wrongly thought to be a poison in order to kill an innocent person, and this has no effect on the intended victim, then no murder has been committed, yet the would-be killer is still blameworthy for what she attempted to do. Based on this distinction, even though the *mutajarrī* is blameworthy for her *tajarrī* as it shows her vice (that is, her state of aiming to commit a murder and thereby to disobey a divine command), she does not deserve divine punishment as this does not result from one's vice (that is shown by her action), but results only from wrong actions that were actually performed, not just attempted. It should be noticed that in al-Anṣārī's view, mere blameworthiness does not make one deserving of punishment; the action itself must also be in fact wrong. In support of this, he appeals to the intuition that, whereas punishing someone for something out of her control is unjust, it may not be unjust to *refrain* from punishing someone for her action, because of something that was out of her control, namely, in the case of *tajarrī*, the falsehood of her *ḥujja* (al-Anṣārī 2011, 38–41). For example, if someone drinks a glass of white wine believing it to be water, she will not deserve punishment, whereas if she drinks it with awareness she will deserve punishment. If, on the other hand, she drinks water falsely believing it to be white wine, she will not deserve divine punishment, even though what caused the difference between her and the former case is something beyond her control, namely the falsehood of her belief. Therefore, he concludes that there is no rational reason according to which we could deduce that the *mutajarrī* deserves divine punishment. Finally, in agreement with al-Shahīd al-Awwal's position he asserts: "there is no difference in the wrongness of different instances of *tajarrī* and there is no doubt that the *mutajarrī* is blameworthy, having revealed her internal wickedness and evil in her heart; still there is indeed doubt as to whether she is blameworthy within as concerns the action which has brought about *tajarrī*" (al-Anṣārī 2011, 45).[10]

After al-Anṣārī other jurists discussed this subject independently in works on the principles of Islamic jurisprudence, now putting the topic under the title of *tajarrī*. Mullā Muḥammad Kāẓim Ākhūnd al-Khurāsānī (d. 1329/1911) is a significant jurist after al-Anṣārī, who opposed him on various *uṣūlī* issues. Unsurprisingly, on our topic he adopts the opposite view from al-Anṣārī. Although he accepts the latter's criticism of Muḥaqqiq Sabzevārī's argument, his viewpoint is ultimately not unlike that of Sabzevārī. He agrees with al-Anṣārī that blameworthiness could apply to one's character, yet insists, contrary to al-Anṣārī, that deserving reward and punishment is solely based on one's will. Therefore, as there is no difference between the sinner's will and the *mutajarrī*'s, there is no difference in what they deserve. Nevertheless, he still holds that the actual rightness and wrongness of the action is independent of what one deserves (al-Khurāsānī 1989, 259–260). Muḥammad Ḥusayn al-Qarawī al-Isfahānī (d. 1361/1942) in his commentary on *Kifāyat al-uṣūl* develops al-Khurāsānī's view in detail (al-Qarawī al-Isfahānī 2008, 28–46).

Meanwhile, other jurists discussed this subject in further detail, among them Mīrzā Muḥammad Ḥusayn al-Nā'īnī (d. 1355/1936) (1973, 22–31) and his apprentice, Mīrzā Mahdī al-Isfahānī (d. 1365/1946) (2017, 623–627), and even contemporary jurists like Sayyid Abū al-Qāsim al-Khuyī (d. 1413/1992) (2001, 21–36), Sayyid Muḥammad Bāqir al-Ṣadr (d. 1400/1980) (2015, 190–191), and Sayyid Muḥam-

10 أنّه لا فرق في قبح التجرّي بين موارده، و أنّ المتجرّي لا إشكال في استحقاقه الذمّ من جهة انكشاف خبث باطنه و سوء سريرته بذلك و أمّا استحقاقه للذمّ من حيث الفعل المتجرّى في ضمنه، ففيه إشكال.

mad al-Ruḥānī (d. 1418/1997) (1993, 36–67). *Tajarrī* has thus become a frequent topic in *uṣūlī* books and classes.

4 *Tajarrī* as Religious Luck

It should be clear that there are remarkable similarities between what Zagzebski presents as religious luck and the notion of *tajarrī* in principles of Islamic jurisprudence. In both cases we have an agent who may be blameworthy, and deserving of divine punishment, for something that is somehow a matter of luck as it is out of the agent's control. In addition, in neither case are we dealing with a situation that is, however, *entirely* out of the agent's control: it is unanimously agreed both in Christian theology and Islamic law that an agent has no responsibility for things that are wholly out of her control, so that she will deserve no blame and no punishment. The case at issue is best illuminated through comparison between two imagined agents, both of whom act deliberately on the same belief, but only one of whom commits no sinful action (again, consider the contrast between two people who attempt to drink forbidden wine, where one does drink wine, the other water).

Yet, there is also a considerable difference between *tajarrī* and religious luck as we described it above. Typically, moral luck involves chance in the causes of one's actions: the characteristics of the agent, the circumstances and results of the action. The epistemic value of the agent's beliefs about moral and divine norms is not considered; by contrast, this is the whole point in the problem of *tajarrī*. Here the luck affects the correspondence of one's justification to what has truly been commanded by God.

Still, the notion of *tajarrī* can be generalised to articulate a specific kind of moral luck. If we take this sort of case and replace its religious elements with moral ones, replacing "divine command" with "moral judgement" and "*ḥujja*" with "justified belief", we can isolate an interesting sub-case: *acting against a justified moral belief, which by luck happens to be false.* The problem then is whether such an action is morally wrong, and whether its agent is blameworthy. Does the moral (or religious) value of an action change in accordance with the truth and falsehood of the justified belief that it would be wrong to perform the action? This is a distinct kind of moral luck which would need its own philosophical exploration.

Walter Edward Young

Concomitance to Causation: Arguing *Dawarān* in the Proto-*Ādāb al-baḥth*

1 Introduction

In what follows we will examine a snapshot taken from an enduring debate in Islamic legal theory and dialectic.[1] The point of contention is the epistemic capability of *dawarān*, a test for causation via concomitance, defined in our focal grundtext as: "the following of the effect from something which has rightness of causation, time after time."[2] The snapshot texts consist of a short section on *dawarān* from an influential treatise on juristic dialectic (*jadal*), the *Fuṣūl* of Burhān al-Dīn al-Nasafī (d. 687/1288) – our grundtext – along with (1) his self-commentary on that section, (2) the commentary of one of his most important students, Shams al-Dīn al-Samarqandī (d. 722/1322), and (3) the refutation commentary of an as-yet-unidentified contemporary (fl. before 759/1357), whom we will call al-Muntaqid, "the Critic," and who may or may not have been Ibn Taymiyya (d. 728/1328). Al-Nasafī and al-Samarqandī (and certainly al-Muntaqid,

1 Much of this research was conducted as a visiting fellow at the Käte Hamburger Kolleg: Dynamics in the History of Religions Between Asia and Europe, 2015–2016, Ruhr-Universität Bochum, Volkhard Krech, PI (that year's theme being "Religion and the Senses"). Critical editions and translations of al-Samarqandī (*Risāla*, *'Ayn al-Naẓar*) and al-Kīlānī (*Sharḥ*) were completed as a research officer with the ERC funded IMPAcT Project, 2014–2015, University of Oxford, Judith Pfeiffer, PI. Images of all Süleymaniye manuscripts cited were kindly acquired for me by Judith Pfeiffer, via IMPAcT funds. Thanks are owed to the following libraries for providing images or assisting in consultation: the Staatsbibliothek zu Berlin; the Süleymaniye Kütüphanesi; the British Library; and the Bodleian Library. And special thanks are due to Robert Wisnovsky for his generous support and numerous suggestions improving this research, as well as to the kindly shared thoughts and pointers of Jon Hoover, Khaled El-Rouayheb, Tony Street, Asad Ahmed, Nora Kalbarczyk, Riccardo Strobino – and of course to Peter Adamson for his kind invitation, and subsequent guidance (and patience). Finally, eternal gratitude to my wife, Saïs Mandjee, for her unflagging support throughout the interminable latter stages of writing.

2 Following Mario Bunge, I will use the term "causation" in connection to "the causal connection in general, as well as any particular causal nexus," and "causality" in connection to any principles or doctrines asserting laws of causation (Bunge 1959, 3–4). General discussions on *dawarān*, with its components of co-presence (*ṭard*) and co-absence (*'aks*), may be found in Hasan 1986a, 315–330; Weiss 1992, 623–624; Zysow 2013, 217–222; Miller 1984, 157–159; Hallaq 1997, 90–93; Hallaq 1993, 10, 46 and n. 4, 88, 123, 124, 125, 161; al-Nashshār 1984, 123–128. On *ṭard* alone as a test of causation, see: Hasan 1986a, 307–314.

https://doi.org/10.1515/9783110552386-013

if he is Ibn Taymiyya) were important in their own day, and had lasting impact long after; and their time was a critical one. Their societal and scholarly contexts and negotiations were inevitably affected by "The Mongol Moment" – the rapid eruption westward, and the establishment of the Īlkhānate (656/1258–756/1355).[3] Most importantly, the broader discipline in which they discussed *dawarān* was soon to undergo – due to the success of al-Samarqandī's method, and despite resistance by such as al-Muntaqid – a sweeping transformation. Starting with al-Samarqandī, a new set of streamlined and universalised theories, evolving in succeeding centuries under the rubric *ādāb al-baḥth wa'l-munāẓara*, "the protocol for dialectical inquiry and disputation," expanded into a discipline of some two hundred treatises and commentaries. Due to the substantive contribution of al-Nasafī and his immediate intellectual predecessors in juristic dialectic, I will sometimes refer to their works and those of their commentators as belonging to the "proto-*ādāb al-baḥth*," with those of al-Samarqandī and early commentators belonging to the "early *ādāb al-baḥth*."

The objectives of this study are first to publish this snapshot of *dawarān* discourse which, by virtue of its insights, eminent authors, and critical moment, is worthy of greater attention in its own right; second, to begin exploring certain of its implications, as I currently perceive them, for both Islamicate and World inquiries into causality. Al-Nasafī's section on *dawarān* from the *Fuṣūl*, divided into fourteen lemmata, will first be presented in parallel translation, with little comment. The commentators – al-Nasafī himself, al-Samarqandī, and al-Muntaqid – will follow in summary and paraphrase, along with my own interpretations.[4] Certain implications will then be further explored, with special attention paid to: (1) connected concepts such as "experience" (*tajriba*), and *dawarān*-relevant discussions in texts by Ibn Sīnā (d. 428/1037), Fakhr al-Dīn al-Rāzī (d. 606/1210), and others; (2) the longstanding distinction between the intellective cause (*'illa 'aqliyya*) and the legal cause (*'illa shar'iyya*); (3) the transition of *dawarān* discourse into the early *ādāb al-baḥth*; and (4) certain modern parallels in terms of regularity theories of causation and falsification schemes.

As for broader contexts, the teaching and practice of dialectic among Muslim jurists hearkens back at least to the first half of the second/eighth century, with theories and methods first systematically compiled in special treatises at the start of the fourth/tenth century, and developing steadily thereafter as a distinct

---

3 Our focus in this study will remain entirely on intellectual output, with little consideration for socio-cultural and political contexts. For an intimation of these, see Pfeiffer 2014; and the "intellectual-historical contexts" section of the introduction to Young Forthcoming b.

4 In a planned monograph covering a broader history of *dawarān*, I will allow the commentators to speak for themselves in parallel translation. The present article is much condensed.

discipline (*jadal* / *khilāf*).[5] In sixth-/twelfth-century Transoxiana there arose, through the teachings of Raḍī 'l-Dīn al-Nīsābūrī (d. 544/1149), and, especially, his student Rukn al-Dīn al-ʿAmīdī (d. 615/1218), a much streamlined and syllogistic dialectical method, at whose heart stood a trio of logical-dialectical concepts; viz. *talāzum* / *mulāzama* (implication), *tanāfin* / *munāfā* (negation), and *dawarān* (concomitance).[6] This method was taken up and further developed by the Ḥanafī theologian, philosopher, and logician Burhān al-Dīn al-Nasafī, and promulgated in such works as his *Fuṣūl* (also known as the *Muqaddima*) – whose section on *dawarān* is our grundtext.[7]

The *Fuṣūl* was likely a curricular text; it gained interest in its day and after, with a handful of commentaries besides al-Nasafī's own,[8] and including those of such polymath luminaries as Shams al-Dīn al-Iṣfahānī (d. 688/1289),[9] Shams al-Dīn al-Samarqandī,[10] our unknown critic, al-Muntaqid,[11] and others.[12] Al-Samar-

5 On juristic dialectic in general, see: Young Forthcoming a; Hallaq 1987a; Weiss 1992, 45–49; Miller 1984, 87–195; Young 2017, 19–43, 85–214, and sources cited therein; Fallūsī 2003.

6 Miller notes the appearance of these concepts in the *Irshād* of Rukn al-Dīn al-ʿAmīdī (Miller 1984, 148–149 and n. 158). On this logicised tradition of juristic dialectic from al-Nīsābūrī to al-Samarqandī, see Dadkhah's Persian Intro. in al-Samarqandī 2014, 42–45); Young Forthcoming b, Intro.

7 Ḥājjī Khalīfa records this work under three different titles (noting al-Samarqandī's *Sharḥ* under each, as well): the *Fuṣūl al-Nasafī fī ʿIlm al-Jadal*; the *Muqaddima al-Burhāniyya*; and the *Muqaddima fī 'l-Jadal wa'l-Khilāf wa'l-Naẓar* (Ḥājjī Khalīfa n.d., 2:1273, 1798, 1803). It is also recorded by, among others, Ibn Quṭlūbughā 1992, 247; Kaḥḥāla 1980, 11:297; al-Ziriklī 2002, 7:31; al-Laknawī 1324 [1906], 194–195; Dadkhah and Goodarznia's English intro. in al-Nasafī 2015, 6–7 (they consider *Muqaddima* and *Fuṣūl* the same and combine them into a single entry). See Miller's dissertation for an analytical overview of al-Nasafī's *Muqaddima* – marked "the key work" of Miller's "Final Period of Juristic Dialectics" (Miller 1984, 180–195). Miller also looks closely at our section on *dawarān* (157–159). The current study employs my collation from two editions of the text: the first by Pehlivan, the second by al-ʿImrān and Shams. For more on al-Nasafī, see also Young Forthcoming b, Intro.

8 See Ḥājjī Khalīfa n.d., 2:1803. The self-commentary has been edited by Sharīfa bint ʿAlī al-Ḥūshānī (see al-Nasafī 2012 in the bibliography), but at the time of writing I have not been able to acquire a copy. We will depend instead on a pair of manuscript witnesses: Amcazade Hüseyin 403 and Landberg 72. For more on al-Nasafī's self-commentary, see Young Forthcoming b, Intro.

9 See al-Ḥibshī 2004, 2:1321; al-Iṣfahānī 2012, (Editor's Intro.), 106; al-Iṣfahānī 1410/1989, (Editor's Intro.), 20; al-Iṣfahānī 1986, (Editor's Intro.), 22. That Shams al-Dīn al-Iṣfahānī has a commentary on al-Nasafī's *Fuṣūl* is further born out by citation glosses (signed with an overlined "Iṣfahānī") in the margins of Amcazade Hüseyin 403.

10 Ḥājjī Khalīfa records al-Samarqandī's *Sharḥ* thrice with its grundtext (Ḥājjī Khalīfa n.d., 2:1273, 1798, 1803). In the last entry (2:1803), he records the circumstances of composition, with a reference to students in Mārdīn and a dedication to Qarah Arslān, its Artuqid ruler. For more on al-Samarqandī and his commentary, see Young Forthcoming b, Intro.

qandī further developed the trio of logical-dialectical concepts learned from his teacher, al-Nasafī, in a short treatise entitled the *ʿAyn al-Naẓar*, and in his commentary on the *Fuṣūl*, and elsewhere; and his discipline-founding *Risāla fī Ādāb al-baḥth* owes much to the tradition al-Nasafī carried forward.

But the *Risāla* was unique in its universal, trans-disciplinary application. Al-Nasafī's logicised juristic dialectic was extended to govern disputation in any field – which al-Samarqandī demonstrates himself with illustrations drawn from theology (*kalām*), philosophy (*ḥikma*), and juristic disagreement (*khilāf*). And from this point forward, Islamic dialectics entered the era of the *ādāb al-baḥth*.[13] The texts of this study thus stand at a pivotal moment in the history of Islamicate dialectical theories. The commentaries of al-Nasafī and al-Samarqandī expand on and further refine the grundtext in ways which anticipate a new universalism. But despite the later success of the *ādāb al-baḥth*, this predecessor style of syllogistical, "Eastern" *jadal* was not universally well-received, as our more critical commentator al-Muntaqid will prove.

To be certain, our *dawarān* discourse unfolded in a legal-theoretical tradition fully immersed in, and engaged with, post-Avicennan, post-Rāzīan logical-philosophical concepts. This is obvious in much of the technical vocabulary, definitions, and illustrations encountered in the texts. It is a truly rich, "post-classical" legal-theoretical tradition, in this sense, and was to have lasting impact throughout much of the Islamic world. But it was also – from certain perspectives – "innovative," emerging from Transoxanian traditions driven or carried westwards with the Mongol expansion, along with other changes against

---

11 For the Rampur manuscript, see our discussion below. For Ibn Taymiyya's *Tanbīh*, see Ḥājjī Khalīfa n.d., 1:487. Note this entry has *Ghāfil* instead of *ʿĀqil*, which may be explained as an instance of *taḥrīf*. Ḥājjī Khalīfa also gives the incipit, and notes: [وهو كتاب كبير في الجدل].

12 I might have included Nuʿmān al-Khwārizmī (death date unknown; see Ahlwardt 1980–1981, 4:468–469, no. 5167) in this study, but time and space did not allow. A witness of his commentary (Ms. or. quart. 55) is available online via the Staatsbibliothek zu Berlin: <http://orient-digital.staatsbibliothek-berlin.de/receive/SBBMSBook_islamhs_00004370>. Another commentary, entitled *Maʿārik al-Fuḥūl fī Sharḥ al-Fuṣūl*, is attributed to Burhān al-Dīn al-Bulghārī (death date unknown; Ḥājjī Khalīfa n.d., 2:1273; also mentioned in 2:1798, sans author). Importantly, al-Bulghārī also authored a commentary on al-Samarqandī's *Risāla* (Ḥājjī Khalīfa n.d., 1:40; Ahlwardt 1980–1981, 4:527, no. 5292; al-Ḥibshī 2004, 1:56).

13 The *Risāla* alone attracted over fifty commentaries and glosses; and ʿAḍud al-Dīn al-Ījī's (d. 756/1355) single-folio précis generated some forty-five. On the *ādāb al-baḥth* in general, see: Miller 1984, 196–238; El-Rouayheb 2015, 60–96; Belhaj 2015, 2016a, 2016b; Karabela 2010; Young Forthcoming a and Forthcoming b, Intro.

which certain, more westerly critics militated. Ibn Taymiyya, of course is most famous among these.[14]

The editors of a Rampur Library manuscript, which they believe to contain Ibn Taymiyya's refutation of al-Nasafī,[15] quote something typical of his attitude.[16] Ibn Taymiyya said: "and in that time, that is, 615 H, the empire of the Mongol Jingis Khān appeared in the lands of the East (...) and innovations (*bidaʿ*) appeared among the *ʿulamāʾ* and layfolk, like the researches (*buḥūth*) of Ibn al-Khaṭīb, and the *just* [a Persian dialectical method] of al-ʿAmīdī, and the Sufism of Ibn al-ʿArabī" (Ibn Taymiyya [?] 2004 [editors' intro.], 20).

Later they cite a long diatribe by Ibn Taymiyya against a certain style of dialectic of his day.[17] The focus of critique is the *ṭarīqa* (method) of al-ʿAmīdī, or perhaps a derivation thereof.

> Then indeed seekers of knowledge of the sons of Fāris and Rūm grew fond of a type of dialectic of the pretenders (*jadal al-mumawwihīn*), invented by a group of Easterners, and they inflicted it on The Religion's legal science (*uṣūl al-fiqh*), dodging in it with the wiliness of foxes, turning away in it from the open path. And they embellished it with expressions found in the discourse of the *ʿulamāʾ* – saying them, but not putting them in their right places – and they joined authoritative indicants in incorrect combinations, and diverged from productive to futile composition.

He goes on (Ibn Taymiyya [?] 2004 [editors' intro.], 20–21) to accuse them of prolixity, using equivocal and tropical meanings in their premises, putting mere probabilities in the place of certainties, misusing indicants (*adilla*) to the extent they combine contradictories – in short, of immersing themselves in full-on sophistry of the sort forbidden by the Prophet.

The editors of the Rampur witness claim it was the threat of this counterfeit *jadal*, along with his students' requests to make sense of it, that prompted Ibn Taymiyya's refutation. And they believe that he was successful, that it was eventually abandoned and simply faded away (Ibn Taymiyya [?] 2004 [editors' intro.],

---

14 On Ibn Taymiyya's critical agenda, see Hallaq 1993, xi-xiv (note especially his stance against Fakhr al-Dīn al-Rāzī [d. 606/1210], al-Āmidī [d. 631/1233], and al-Urmawī [d. 682/1283]), xxxix, and lii and n. 176).

15 See the discussion on attribution, below.

16 Note that the editors themselves show considerable disdain for al-Nasafī's style of juristic dialectic and the tradition from which it developed (Ibn Taymiyya [?] 2004 [editors' intro.], 6–7).

17 Such is recorded by his student Ibn ʿAbd al-Hādī (d. 744/1343), from the preface of Ibn Taymiyya's *Tanbīh*. Firmly believing the Rampur manuscript – their single witness, whose first folia are missing – to be the *Tanbīh* itself, they have appended this preface recorded by Ibn ʿAbd al-Hādī to the start of their edition.

23). The truth, of course, is that it survived – transformed, streamlined, and universalised by al-Samarqandī – as the *ādāb al-baḥth wa'l-munāẓara*. And from there it exploded into a major discipline, as many hundreds of catalogued manuscripts attest.

As for the contents of the Rampur manuscript, I would make a few points. First, whether or not Ibn Taymiyya is the author of that work, there is no doubt that he is indeed the author of a work entitled *Tanbīh al-rajul al-ʿāqil ʿalā tamwīh al-jadal al-bāṭil*, the preface of which was recorded by Ibn ʿAbd al-Hādī (d. 744/1343), and the incipit and other details by Ḥājjī Khalīfa (d. 1067/1657) and others. So the above diatribe is undoubtedly Ibn Taymiyya, and, as we will see, its sentiments are echoed by al-Muntaqid in the Rampur witness's critiques. Second, whoever al-Muntaqid was, he commanded significant skills in argumentation, and his work in the Rampur manuscript was copied in 759/1357–8, at a time when al-Nasafī's *Fuṣūl* continued to influence and al-Samarqandī's *ādāb al-baḥth* had begun to pick up steam.

As for the attribution question, the Rampur manuscript presents several challenges,[18] and there are compelling arguments either way.[19] George Makdisi (1972, 286, 291–294) had no doubt it was the *Tanbīh*. Nor, of course, did the editors of the Rampur manuscript, ʿAlī b. Muḥammad al-ʿImrān and Muḥammad ʿUzayr Shams.[20] But Daghash b. Shabīb al-ʿAjmī (2006, 523–527) is adamant that it is not Ibn Taymiyya's *Tanbīh*, and to his refutation article the editors have published a response.[21] As for myself, I am unable to give preponderance to one side or the other, even though I have noted certain clues which seem to point to Ibn Taymiyya or someone much like him. For whoever al-Muntaqid is, he is certainly very much like Ibn Taymiyya in certain practices and views – perhaps, if not him, he was associated with his circle.[22]

Before proceeding to our study, a few words on the methodological context of *dawarān* are in order. I would begin by suggesting that what is most intriguing about the following texts is their potential as a site of inquiry. They form a locus

18 The sole surviving copy is in the Rampur Library, Patna, India (Riḍā Collection, Ms. no. 1746). See Makdisi 1972, 285–287, 289.

19 I am indebted to Jon Hoover for alerting me to the debate between al-ʿAjmī and the editors of the Rampur manuscript.

20 See their initial arguments in Ibn Taymiyya (?) 2004 [editors' intro.], 26–29.

21 This was to be published in the same journal as al-ʿAjmī's refutation. I am not certain it ever came to print, but both al-ʿAjmī's critique and the editors' response (al-ʿImrān and Shams 1428 [2007]) currently appear in the following thread of the al-Alūka website: <http://majles.alukah.net/t1512/>.

22 Certainly in terms of *dawarān*, Ibn Taymiyya's conception and practice was in full consonance with al-Muntaqid's. See section 4.1, below.

for investigation wherein we might find legal theory informing philosophical logic, rather than the other way round, and certainly informing a broader – indeed universal – dialectical theory. At the very least, they form a locus for cross-germination, with indeterminate ultimate sources: philosophical notions of causality influencing legal notions of causality, and vice versa, without evident priority.

Concomitance, whether under the rubric of *dawarān*, or "co-presence and co-absence" (*al-ṭard wa'l-ʿaks*), or "applying the cause to [the full gamut of] its effects" (*jarayān al-ʿilla fī maʿlūlātihā*), has a long and complex history in Sunnī *uṣūlī* discourse. Its functional domain is that broader method for discovering rulings for problematic or novel cases, in consonance with what is more firmly known of God's Law, called *qiyās*, or "correlational inference"[23] – or, more specifically, *qiyās al-ʿilla*, or "correlational inference of the cause / occasioning factor."[24] In this species of *qiyās*, a jurist determines the ruling (*ḥukm*) for an unresolved branch-case (*farʿ*) by conveying it from an authoritatively resolved root-case (*aṣl*), due to their sharing a property (*waṣf*) deemed to be the "occasioning factor" or "cause" (*ʿilla*) of that ruling.[25] In a standard example, drinking date-wine (the *farʿ*) is declared forbidden because it shares that property of intoxication (the *ʿilla*) which, it is conceded, "causes" the drinking of grape-wine (the *aṣl*) to be forbidden (the *ḥukm*).

The whole operation thus hinges on knowing what constitutes the "cause" (*ʿilla*) for the ruling (*ḥukm*) in the root-case (*aṣl*). What property of grape-wine occasions its ruling of proscription? Knowing that, and assuming the consistency of God's Law, we can assume the same proscription for other substances in which that property is found. And how do we come to know the cause? Sometimes we know it from unambiguous declarations in Qur'an and Sunna (*naṣṣ*), and sometimes from sanctioned consensus (*ijmāʿ*); but more often we must rely on rational inference (*istinbāṭ*).

For this critical operation, Sunnī theorists devised and debated series of tests for determining and validating proposed causes (*ʿilal*).[26] *Dawarān*, though con-

23 More often, though problematically, translated as "analogy." For a corrective, see Hallaq 1989.

24 For introductions to juristic *qiyās*, see, among others: Hasan 1980a, 1986a; Hallaq 1997, 83–107; Zysow 2013, 159–258; Young 2017, 108–128; al-Nashshār 1984, 111–129. For Ibn Taymiyya and juristic *qiyās*, see Hallaq 1993, xxxv–xxxix (section 8; wherein he holds juristic *qiyās* equal to the syllogism).

25 For comprehensive overviews of the *ʿilla*, see Hasan 1980b and 1986a, 167–368.

26 General discussions on the methods of *ʿilla*-validation may be found in Hasan 1986a, 232–352; Hasan 1986b; Weiss 1992, 585–624 (on "Ascertaining the Occasioning Factor"); Zysow 2013,

tested, was among the most important. One indication that the property of intoxication occasions the ruling of proscription in the established case of grape-wine, is that this property is concomitant with that ruling in existence (*wujūdan*), that is, they demonstrate co-presence (*ṭard*), and in non-existence (*ʿadaman*), that is, they demonstrate co-absence (*ʿaks*). When grape juice is pressed, neither the property of intoxication nor the ruling of proscription exist in it; when that juice ferments and becomes wine, both the property of intoxication and the ruling of proscription come to exist in it; and when that wine becomes vinegar, both the property of intoxication and the ruling of proscription cease to exist in it once more. This concomitance, in existence and in non-existence, is the fundamental ingredient of *dawarān*, though not the only one, as we will see.

2 Grundtext and Summary[27]

1	**Section on** *Dawarān*. Such being the following (*tarattub*) of the effect (*athar*) from something which has rightness of causation (*ṣulūḥ al-ʿilliyya*), time after time. And know that *dawarān* is not the concomitant presumed effect (*dāʾir*) and the concomitant presumed cause (*madār*), nor does its existence depend upon them.[28]	فصل في الدوران * وهو[29] ترتّب الأثر على الشيء الذي له صلوح[30] العلّيّة مرّة بعد أخرى * واعلم بأنّ الدوران غير الدائر والمدار ولا يتوقّف[31] وجوده عليهما *
2	Moreover, the *madār* might be a *madār* in existence and in non-existence, like illicit sexual activity (*zinā*) originating from the one who has had licit sexual access (*muḥṣan*) is	ثمّ المدار قد يكون مدارًا[32] وجودًا وعدمًا كالزنا الصادر من المحصن لوجوب الرجم عليه * فإنّه لو وُجِدَ يجب الرجم * ولولاه لمْ[33] يجب *

196–222 (processes of "eduction" [*istinbāṭ*] of the *ʿilla*, as opposed to *naṣṣ* and *ijmāʿ*); Hallaq 1997, 86–88 (validation via *naṣṣ* or *ijmāʿ*), and 88–94 (validation via *istinbāṭ*); al-Nashshār 1984, 119–129.

27 Burhān al-Dīn al-Nasafī, *al-Fuṣūl fī ʾl-Jadal : Faṣl fī ʾl-Dawarān* (al-Nasafī and Pehlivan 2015, 49–50; al-Nasafī 2004, 646–648).

28 Note here that the *madār* and *dāʾir* parallel in certain ways, grammatically and functionally, the *malzūm* (implicans) and *lāzim* (implicatum) of logical implication (*talāzum* / *mulāzama*).

29 al-Nasafī 2004 [هو] instead of [وهو].

30 NB: in the lemmata of the Rampur witness we find, here and elsewhere, consistently, [صلاح] rather than [صلوح].

31 al-Nasafī and Pehlivan 2015 [وهو لا يتوقّف].

32 [مدارًا] ommited from main text of al-Nasafī and Pehlivan 2015.

33 al-Nasafī 2004 [لا] instead of [لم].

	to the obligation of stoning (*rajm*) upon him. For when it exists, stoning is obliged. And if not for it, it would not be obliged.	
3	And it might be in existence but not in non-existence, like the contract of gift (*hiba*) is to confirmation of ownership (*milk*) [for the donee]. For indeed ownership exists upon the existence of donation, but by no means does it cease to exist upon its non-existence, due to the possibility that it be confirmed by way of inheritance (*irth*) or something else.	وقد يكون وجودًا لا عدمًا كالهبة لثبوت الملك * فإن الملك يوجد عند وجود الهبة[34] ولا يعدم عند عدمها قطعًا لاحتمال أن يكون ثابتًا بالإرث أو بغيره *
4	And it might be in non-existence, not in existence, like ritual purity (*ṭahāra*) is to allowance of prayer (*ṣalāt*). For indeed the allowance [of prayer] ceases to exist upon the non-existence of ritual purity, but it does not definitely exist upon its existence, due to the allowance that one of the [other] conditions (*sharṭ min al-sharāʾiṭ*) is not realised, like directing prayer towards the *qibla*, or something else.	وقد يكون عدمًا لا وجودًا كالطهارة لجواز الصلاة * فإن الجواز يعدم عند عدم الطهارة[35] ولا يوجد عند وجودها جزمًا لجواز أن لا يتحقّق شرط من الشرائط كاستقبال القبلة وغيره *
5	And it might be said that the *madār*, when it is not something specified (*lam yakun*	وقد يقال[38] بأنّ المدار إذا لم يكن معيّنًا لا يتمّ * كما إذا قال في مسئلة[39] الأكل والشرب شيء هو متحقّق ههنا[40]

34 al-Nasafī and Pehlivan 2015 [عند وجودها].

35 al-Nasafī and Pehlivan 2015 [عند عدمها].

36 General rulings and justifications regarding ritual expiation (*kaffāra*) and the various modes of invalidating the Ramaḍān fast may be found in *al-Mawsūʿa al-Fiqhiyya* 1983 – 2006, s.v. [كفارة], 35:37 – 106; and s.v. [صوم], 28:7 – 86; al-Miṣrī 1994, i1.18 – 20, 283 – 287; Ibn Rushd 1994 – 1996, 1:353 – 361; and Christian Lange, "Expiation," in EI3. The Sunnaic indicant (*dalīl*) obliging expiation for breaking the Ramaḍān fast via sex is a tradition on Abū Hurayra. In brief, a man comes to the Prophet and confesses having had sex with his wife during the fast; the Prophet inquires as to whether he can perform a certain expiation, dropping to simpler forms at each of the man's denials – from freeing a slave, to two months' consecutive fasting, to feeding sixty of the poor (Ibn Rushd 1994 – 1996, 1:353). As Ibn Rushd (d. 595/1198) tells us: "they differed over this on several points, including: whether breaking a fast intentionally by eating or drinking carries the same *ḥukm* as that for breaking the fast through sexual intercourse involving *qaḍāʾ* [doing it over] and expiation? [Etc.]" Those who held that both *qaḍāʾ* (doing it over) and expiation were obligatory for intentionally breaking the fast by eating and drinking include: Mālik and his companions, Abū Ḥanīfa and his companions, al-Thawrī, and "a group of jurists." Those who held that expiation is obligatory only for sex included: al-Shāfiʿī, Aḥmad, and the Ẓāhirīs (Ibn Rushd 1994 – 1996, 1:354, translation Nyazee's).

37 Note that, unlike other schools, Ḥanafīs don't believe that the cause for the obligation of expiation can be known (Lange 2018). Ibn Rushd reports the reasoning of those who obliged

	mu'ayyan), is not complete (*lā yatimmu*). Like when he says, regarding the problem-case of eating and drinking [during the Ramaḍān fast]: something here realised is a necessitator (*mūjib*) for the obligation of ritual expiation (*kaffāra*).[36] For indeed the obligation is concomitant with it in existence and in non-existence. As for in existence, in the breaking-factor of sex (*faṣl al-wiqā'*) a first time [in a single day]. And as for in non-existence, in breaking the fast with pebbles and date-pits and other things.[37]	مُوجِب لوجوب الكفّارة * فإنّ الوجوب دار معه وجودًا وعدمًا * أمّا وجودًا ففي فصل الوقاع أوّل مرّة * وأما عدمًا ففي الإفطار بالحصاة والنواة وغيرهما *
6	Because the opponent says: something here realised is a necessitator (*mūjib*) for the non-existence [of obligation of expiation]. For indeed the non-existence [of obligation] is concomitant with it in existence and in non-existence. As for in existence, in the breaking-act of eating and drinking (*faṣl al-akl wa'l-shurb*) a second time [in a single day]. And as for in non-existence, in the breaking-act of sex (*faṣl al-wiqā'*) a first time.	لأنّ الخصم يقول شيء هو[41] متحقّق هنا موجب للعدم * فإن العدم دار معه وجودًا وعدمًا * أمّا وجودًا ففي فصل الأكل والشرب مرّة ثانية * وأمّا عدمًا ففي فصل الوقاع أوّل مرّة *
7	As for when the *madār* is something specified (*mu'ayyan*), then it is complete. Like when he says for this problem-question (*mas'ala*)[42] that the violation (*hatk*) – such being the invalidation of the fast of Ramaḍān by one of the three acts, on purpose (*'an*	أمّا إذا كان المدار معيّناً فإنّه يتمّ * كما إذا قال في هذه المسئلة[43] بأنّ الهتْك وهو إفساد صوم رمضان بأحد الأفعال الثلثة[44] عن[45] تعمُّد أوّل مرّة موجب لوجوب الكفّارة لأنّ[46] الوجوب دار معه وجودًا وعدمًا * أمّا وجودًا ففي فصل الوقاع أوّل مرّة * وأمّا عدمًا فظاهر *

expiation: "the reason for their disagreement arises from their dispute over drawing an analogy between the person breaking the fast through sexual intercourse and one breaking it by eating and drinking. Those who maintained that they have a common basis, which is the violation of the sanctity of the fast, determined that the *ḥukm* should be the same for them both" (Ibn Rushd 1994–1996, 1:354, translation Nyazee's).

38 al-Nasafī 2004 [ويقال].

39 al-Nasafī 2004 [مسألة].

40 al-Nasafī 2004 [هنا].

41 al-Nasafī 2004 [وهو].

42 I.e., the contended *mas'ala* of whether or not eating and drinking a first time obliges expiation.

43 al-Nasafī 2004 [مسألة].

44 al-Nasafī 2004 [الثلاثة].

45 al-Nasafī 2004 [عند] instead of [عن].

46 al-Nasafī 2004 [فإن] instead of [لأن].

	taʿammud), a first time [in a single day] – is a necessitator (*mūjib*) for the obligation of ritual expiation (*kaffāra*), because the obligation is concomitant with it in existence and in non-existence. As for in existence, in the breaking-act of sex (*faṣl al-wiqāʿ*) a first time. And as for in non-existence, such is obvious (*fa-ẓāhir*).	
8	And the *dawarān* of the effect (*athar*) with something in existence and in non-existence is a sign (*āya*) of the *madār*'s being the cause (*ʿilla*) of the *dāʾir* – as in the parallel-solutions cases (*naẓāʾir*).	ودوران الأثر مع الشيء وجودًا وعدمًا آية كون المدار علّةً للدائر كما في النظائر *
9	And should one say: just as obligation of ritual expiation (*wujūb al-kaffāra*) is concomitant with the violation (*hatk*), so too is it concomitant with the sex (*wiqāʿ*), in existence and in non-existence. And when the sex is a *madār*, it is not possible that the violation be a *madār* in existence and in non-existence. Otherwise, there necessarily follows a convergence of two contradictories (*ijtimāʿ al-naqīḍayn*) – such being the obligation simultaneously with the non-existence [of obligation], in the case (*ṣūra*) which you've mentioned.	ولئن قال وجوب الكفّارة كما دار مع الهتك فكذلك دار مع الوقاع وجودًا وعدمًا * ومتى كان الوقاع مدارًا لا يمكن أن يكون الهتك مدارًا وجودًا وعدمًا * وإلّا يلزم اجتماع النقيضين وهو الوجوب مع العدم فيما ذكرتم من الصورة *
10	Then we say: we ourselves do not claim the concomitant causation (*madāriyya*) in existence in the breaking-factor of sex (*faṣl al-wiqāʿ*) with specific designation (*ʿalā ʾl-taʿyīn*). Rather, we claim [it] in every one of the cases of obligation a first [time]. And the *dawarān* according to this explanation (*tafsīr*) provides indication for nothing but the concomitant causation (*madāriyya*) of the violation (*hatk*) in existence and in non-existence.	فنقول نحن لا ندّعي المداريّة وجودًا في فصل الوقاع على التعيين * بل ندّعي في كلّ صورة من صور الوجوب أوّلًا [47] * والدوران على هذا التفسير لا يدلّ إلّا على مداريّة الهتك وجودًا وعدمًا *
11	And should one say: it is concomitant with what is specific (*mukhtaṣṣ*) to that case (*ṣūra*). Then we say: it is concomitant with	ولئن قال دار مع ما يكون مختصًّا بتلك الصورة * فنقول دار مع ما يكون مشتركًا بينها وبين صورة النزاع *

47 Al-Samarqandī, reiterating the grundtext, employs [أوّل مرّة]. So [أوّلًا] here and in similar contexts can be understood to mean [أوّل مرّة].

	what is shared (*mushtarak*) between [that case] and the contended case (*ṣūrat al-nizāʿ*).	
12	And should one say: it is concomitant with what is specific (*mukhtaṣṣ*) [to that case] – otherwise, it would not be obliged therein. Then we would say: it is concomitant with what is shared (*mushtarak*) – otherwise it would not be obliged therein.	ولئن قال دار مع المختصّ وإلّا لا يجب ثمّة * فنقول دار مع المشترك وإلّا لا يجب ثمّة *
13	And should one say: we concede that the *dawarān* is realised (*mutaḥaqqaq*), but why did you say that it conveys (*yufīdu*) the causation (*ʿilliyya*) of the *madār*? Rather, it does not convey. Otherwise, it would be something which conveys in matters of chance (*umūr ittifāqiyya*). For indeed the effects (*āthār*) are things generated (*ḥāditha*) in places and times, but the *madār* is not a cause (*ʿilla*) for the *dāʾir*.	ولئن قال سلّمنا بأنّ الدوران متحقّق ولكن لِمَ قلتم بأنّه يفيد[48] علّيّة المدار * بل لا يفيد * وإلّا لكان مفيدًا في الأمور الاتّفاقيّة * فإن الآثار حادثة في الأمكنة والأزمنة ولا يكون المدار علّةً للدائر[49] *
14	Then we say: the discourse (*kalām*) is about when the *madār* is right for causation (*ṣāliḥan li'l-ʿilliyya*). So if the *madār* in what you've stated is right (*ṣāliḥ*), then we don't concede that it is not a cause (*ʿilla*). But even if [the *madār*] is not a cause (*ʿilla*), it points to no inconsistency (*naqḍ*).	فنقول الكلام فيما إذا كان المدار[50] صالحًا للعلّيّة فلو كان المدار فيما ذكرتم صالحًا فلا نسلّم بأنّه لا يكون علّة * وإن لم يكن علّة فلا يتّجه نقضًا *

Summary Outline

§1. Defines *dawarān* as "the following of the effect from something which has rightness of causation, time after time;" and asserts that *dawarān* is neither the concomitant presumed effect (*dāʾir*) nor the concomitant presumed cause (*madār*).

§2. Introduces a first type of *dawarān*, in which the *madār* is concomitant with its *dāʾir* in both existence and non-existence (**E&N**); example: the *madār* of adultery by one who has licit sexual access, with the *dāʾir* of stoning.

48 al-Nasafī 2004 [بأنّه لا يفيد].
49 [للدائر] ommited from al-Nasafī and Pehlivan 2015.
50 al-Nasafī and Pehlivan 2015 [الدار] instead of [المدار].

§3. Introduces a second type of *dawarān*, in which the *madār* is concomitant with its *dā'ir* in existence but not in non-existence (**E-not-N**); example: the *madār* of a donor's contracting a gift to a donee, with the *dā'ir* of confirmation of (the latter's) ownership.

§4. Introduces a third type of *dawarān*, in which the *madār* is concomitant with its *dā'ir* in non-existence but not in existence (**N-not-E**); example: the *madār* of ritual purity, with the *dā'ir* of allowance of prayer.

§5. Asserts that the unspecified *madār* is not complete; example: indication that ritual expiation is obliged for eating and drinking during the Ramaḍān fast, because some efficient *madār* X is co-existent with the *dā'ir* of obligation of ritual expiation in the case of sex a first time during a day of Ramaḍān, and co-absent with it in the case of swallowing pebbles and date-pits during a day of Ramaḍān.

§6. Explains why the unspecified *madār* is not complete: because the opponent simply brings a counter-indication of the same form (*muʿāraḍa bi'l-mithl*); example: indication that ritual expiation is *not* obliged for eating and drinking during the Ramaḍān fast, because some efficient *madār* X is co-existent with the *dā'ir* of *non-existence* of obligation of ritual expiation in the case of eating and drinking a second time during a day of Ramaḍān, and co-absent with it in the case of sex a first time during a day of Ramaḍān.

§7. Asserts that the specified *madār* is complete; example: indication that ritual expiation is obliged for eating and drinking during the Ramaḍān fast, because the efficient *madār* of violation (that is, wilful invalidation of the fast) is co-existent with the *dā'ir* of obligation of ritual expiation in the case of sex a first time during a day of Ramaḍān, and co-absent with it in an "obvious" case (that is, eating and drinking a second time during a day of Ramaḍān).

§8. Asserts that E&N *dawarān* is a sign (*āya*) that the *madār* is the cause (*ʿilla*) of the *dā'ir*.

§9. First critique: a questioner (**Q**) asserts that besides violation, there is also E&N *dawarān* between the obligation of ritual expiation and sex. But if sex is an E&N *madār*, then violation cannot be an E&N *madār*, due to the contradiction entailed should one *madār* exist without the other: simultaneous existence and non-existence of the *dā'ir*.

§10. Response to first critique: the respondent (**R**) points out his *madār* claim is for all cases of first-time obligation of expiation, not just the case of sex, and so only violation can be the *madār*.

§11. Second critique and response: Q asserts that the obligation of expiation is concomitant with what is case-specific (*mukhtaṣṣ*); R counters that it is concomitant with what is shared between cases (*mushtarak*).

§12. Third critique and response: Q argues that were obligation of expiation *not* concomitant with what is case-specific, then expiation would not be obliged in that very case itself; R counters that were it not concomitant with what is shared between cases, then expiation would not be obliged in that very case itself.

§13. Fourth critique: Q concedes the realisation of *dawarān*, but argues against its conveying the *madār*'s causation: if it did convey causation, then it would do so in matters of chance, wherein effects are concomitant with their *madār*s of place and time; but it does not, for the *madār*s of place and time are not causes of such effects.

§14. Response to fourth critique: R reminds Q that by definition a *madār* must be "right for causation;" nor would R ever concede that such "right" *madār*s are not causes. Moreover, there is no inconsistency (*naqḍ*) on R's part, even should the *madār* not be the cause.

3 Commentary[51]

§§1–4

Al-Muntaqid (Ibn Taymiyya [?] 2004, 79–80) prefaces his treatment of al-Nasafī's grundtext with a lexical explication, a summary of opinions on *dawarān*'s power, and analyses of its mechanics. As for whether or not *dawarān* indicates that a property (*waṣf*) is a cause (*ʿilla*),[52] the majority of jurists and theorists say yes, but some say no. The naysayers argue: (1) when we do know causation (*ʿilliyya*), it is not from *dawarān* but other *ʿilla*-validation methods – like "suita-

51 Burhān al-Dīn al-Nasafī, *Sharḥ al-Fuṣūl fī 'l-Jadal : Faṣl fī 'l-Dawarān* (Amcazade Hüseyin 403, foll. 19b–25a; Landberg 72, fol. 54a–58a); Shams al-Dīn al-Samarqandī, *Sharḥ Fuṣūl al-Nasafī fī 'l-Jadal : Faṣl fī 'l-Dawarān* (Esad Efendi 3034, foll. 16a–19b; Or. 11183, foll. 15b–19b); al-Muntaqid, the Rampur Library witness, edited as the *Tanbīh al-Rajul al-ʿĀqil ʿalā Tamwīh al-Jadal al-Bāṭil : Faṣl fī 'l-Dawarān* (Ibn Taymiyya [?] 2004, 79–103).

52 In varying contexts, I would ordinarily translate *ʿilla* differently: either as "occasioning factor" in the legal domain (following Bernard Weiss), or as "cause" in philosophical or theological domains, due to the distinction drawn by many Muslim scholars between the *ʿilla sharʿiyya* and *ʿilla ʿaqliyya*. As there is no hint of such a distinction in the proto- or early *ādāb al-baḥth*, however, and a firm attachment of the term *ʿilla* to its philosophical notions, I will translate *ʿilla* as "cause," *ʿilliyya* as "causation," and *taʿlīl* as "causal justification" throughout this study. On Weiss's preference for "occasioning factor" (capturing the sense of *bāʿith*, which al-Āmidī attaches to the *ʿilla sharʿiyya*), see Weiss 1992, 546–547, 562.

bility" (*munāsaba*) and "analytical division" (*al-sabr wa'l-taqsīm*);[53] (2) since co-presence (*ṭard*) alone does not convey causation, and co-absence (*ʿaks*) is not a necessary condition (*sharṭ*) for legal causes (*ʿilal sharʿiyya*), then both together – which is *dawarān* (called *al-ṭard wa'l-ʿaks* by the Iraqis) – do not convey causation;[54] and (3) there are many known instances where *dawarān* simply does not convey causation, for instance, when there is concomitance between the judgment (*ḥukm*) and parts (*ajzāʾ*) of the cause (*ʿilla*), or between two effects with each other, or two correlatives (*mutaḍāyifayn*), or between definiens and definiendum, or name and named. The majority view, however, is that *dawarān* conveys causation (*ʿilliyya*) overall (*fī 'l-jumla*), with disagreement only over whether it does so with certainty (*qaṭʿan*) or probability (*ẓannan*).

He proceeds (Ibn Taymiyya [?] 2004, 80) to a general definition of *dawarān* as "existence (*wujūd*) of the judgment (*ḥukm*) upon existence of a property (*waṣf*), and its non-existence (*ʿadam*) upon its non-existence; or the existence of a thing upon [the existence of] something which could possibly be a cause (*ʿilla*) for it, and its non-existence upon its non-existence." Importantly, he underscores certain conditions: (1) that concomitance be in *both* existence and non-existence (E&N), (2) that no other *madār* "compete" with the presumed cause (*lam yuzāḥimhu*),[55] and (3) that, as some say, it not be known from elsewhere that the *madār* does *not* convey causation. We learn, moreover, that the *madār* is so named because it is the locus (*mawḍiʿ*) of the *dawarān*, and the receptacle (*maḥall*) for the judgment (*ḥukm*) – as the property of intoxication becomes a receptacle for proscription midway through the life-cycle of grape

53 On *munāsaba* see: Hasan 1986a, 250–294; Weiss 1992, 599–620, *passim* ("suitability test"); Hallaq 1997, 88–90; Zysow 2013, 196–204; Hallaq 1993, 46 n. 3. On *al-sabr wa'l-taqsīm* see: Hasan 1986a, 330–342; Hallaq 1997, 92–94; Weiss 1992, 596–597; Hallaq 1993, 45, 119–120, 123; al-Nashshār 1984, 120–123.

54 On co-absence (*ʿaks*) not being a condition (*sharṭ*) for the legal causes, Zysow notes: "although for most jurists, consistency [*ṭard*] was a necessary condition (*sharṭ*) for the validity of a cause, it was not a sufficient one (*dalāla*). The converse is true of convertibility [*ʿaks*]. Because a plurality of causes was regarded as possible, failure of convertibility did not invalidate a cause. Convertibility was not a necessary condition of validity." (Zysow 2013, 222, n. 385). On the epistemic value of combining *ṭard* and *ʿaks* being superior to the sum of their individual values, see al-Rāzī 1992, 215–216.

55 See al-Muntaqid's discourse on the problematics of competing *madārs* in his commentary on §7, below.

juice from freshly pressed, to wine, to vinegar; and this single-receptacle type is more potent than multiple-receptacle *dawarān*.[56]

As for the first part of lemma §1 (the definition), al-Nasafī, in his self-commentary, merely opens with a pair of truncated variant definitions, whereby *dawarān* is either "the following of the effect from something which has rightness of causation (*ṣulūḥ al-ʿilliyya*)" or "the following of the effect from something in existence (*fī 'l-wujūd*), time after time (*marratan baʿda ukhrā*)."[57]

Al-Samarqandī, however, explains key terms and phrases of the definition: the "something" is the *madār*, the "effect" is the *dāʾir*, and "'rightness of causation' (*ṣulūḥ al-ʿilliyya*) is the validity of causal justification (*ṣiḥḥat al-taʿlīl*) of that effect by way of that something, like the causal justification of purgation via the drinking of scammony."[58] Al-Samarqandī thus illustrates a key juristic operation with an *empirical* example drawn from medicine.[59] If, for example, the *madār* "intoxication" is to be considered as having "rightness of causation," then we must prove sound the causal justification (*taʿlīl*), by way of it, for the *dāʾir* "forbidden" (*ḥarām*). And this, we understand, is the same as: if the *madār* of drinking scammony is to be considered as having "rightness of causation," then we must prove sound the causal justification, by way of it, for the *dāʾir* of purgation.

Al-Muntaqid (Ibn Taymiyya [?] 2004, 81), on the other hand, having faithfully rendered al-Nasafī's definition of *dawarān*,[60] proceeds directly to three critiques. The first is a charge of circularity, in that "the following (*tarattub*) of the effect from something" already entails – without *dawarān* – that we know the causation (*ʿilliyya*) of that something for that effect. The second critique involves

56 For example, the E concomitance (in existence) between the minimal amount for alms-tax consideration and the obligation of paying the alms tax (*zakāt*) in one receptacle, and N concomitance (in non-existence) between them in another.

57 Amcazade Hüseyin 403, fol. 19b; Landberg 72, fol. 54a.

58 He also implies the precision of al-Nasafī's definiens as a proper "includer-excluder" (*jāmiʿ mānīʿ*) by explaining how (1) "rightness of causation" (*ṣulūḥ al-ʿilliyya*) excludes concomitance between the effect and a part (*juzʾ*) of the cause (*ʿilla*), or its condition (*sharṭ*), or its implicatum (*lāzim*), or between two effects (light and smoke) of the same cause (fire); and (2) "time after time" (*marratan baʿda ukhrā*) excludes a singular following by chance (*tarattub ittifāqī*). Esad Efendi 3034, foll. 16a–b; Or. 11183, fol. 15b.

59 An example going back, ultimately, at least as far as Ibn Sīnā. See section 4.1, below. Miller takes note of al-Samarqandī's interpretation of *ṣulūḥ al-ʿilliyya*, along with his scammony example (Miller 1984, 233–234).

60 Note that in the lemmata of the Rampur witness we find, here and elsewhere, consistently, *ṣalāḥ al-ʿilliyya* rather than *ṣulūḥ al-ʿilliyya*. Both terms, however, denote "goodness, incorruptness, rightness or rectitude, justness, righteousness, virtue, honesty," and so on (Lane 1968, 2: 1715). Moreover, manuscript witnesses of the *Fuṣūl* sometimes themselves have *ṣalāḥ* rather than *ṣulūḥ*, as do copies of the commentaries. On *ṣalāḥ* and the *ʿilla*, see: Hasan 1986a, 255, 326–327.

a set of problematising interpretations for "rightness of causation" (*ṣalāḥ al-ʿilliyya*), in that it means either (1) "the *madār* is suitable (*munāsib*) to the effect," or (2) nothing is known to be wrong about attaching that effect to that thing. The problem with the first is that the method of *ʿilla*-justification (*taʿlīl*) known as *munāsaba* (suitability) is alone insufficient for indicating causation; making it a part of *dawarān* is merely adding insufficiency to insufficiency. And the problem with the second interpretation is that it reduces the intention of *ṣalāḥ al-ʿilliyya* to mere possibility (*imkān*), opening the door to less stringent practices – like pure co-presence-based correlational inferences (*al-aqyisa al-ṭardiyya al-maḥḍa*), "especially for those who treat the causes (*ʿilal*) as signs (*ʿalāmāt*) and indications (*dalālāt*), never stipulating for them necessitation (*iqtiḍāʾ*) and efficiency (*taʾthīr*)."[61] And as for the third definitional critique, al-Muntaqid objects that "following from it time after time" seems only to denote E-not-N concomitance. Moreover, he observes that al-Nasafī does not stipulate E&N for *dawarān*, which is "the contrary/contradictory (*khilāf*) of what most legal theorists and dialecticians hold"; still, however, he admits: "perhaps some of them used to say: '[*dawarān*] is the following of the effect from something, in existence (*fī ʾl-wujūd*), time after time.'"[62]

And as for the second part of lemma §1, al-Samarqandī explains why *dawarān* neither is, nor depends upon the existence of, the *dāʾir* and *madār*. In short, "the following (*tarattub*) of something from something else is [itself] something besides those two [things], by way of immediate necessity (*biʾl-ḍarūra*)." Which is to say, exactly as in the case of necessary implication (*talāzum*), "the relation (*nisba*) between two things might be in terms of their essential conceptions (*ḥaqāʾiq*), so there is no need for their existence – like possibility (*imkān*) and impossibility (*imtināʿ*)."[63] He is careful, however, to forestall any mistaken claim of identity. A key quality, born of their different natures, distinguishes *talāzum* from *dawarān*, in that "the separation (*infikāk*) of the *lāzim* from the *malzūm* is not possible, but the separation of the *dāʾir* from the

61 On causes (*ʿilal*) as signs: "for al-Baṣrī, the status of legal causes as signs precluded their treatment by rational methods. For others it was precisely their quality as signs that legitimated the method of consistency [*ṭard*]" (Zysow 2013, 221); see also Hasan 1986a, 397–402.

62 Note that this in-existence-only definition is the same, verbatim, as the second of the two truncated variants al-Nasafī mentions at the opening of his self-commentary.

63 Esad Efendi 3034, foll. 5b–6a; Or. 11183, foll. 6b–7a. Al-Samarqandī makes reference to his earlier treatment of al-Nasafī's chapter on necessary implication (*faṣl fī ʾl-talāzum*). For the grundtext, see: al-Nasafī and Pehlivan 2015, 44; al-Nasafī 2004, 642; and for his commentary, see: Esad Efendi 3034, foll. 4b–6a; Or. 11183, foll. 6a–7a.

madār is possible, by way of some impeding factor (*māniʿ*) – like purgation from drinking scammony."[64]

This distinction is essential; it plays a critical role in *dawarān* argumentation. And as for the impeding factor (*māniʿ*), it is in fact a basal element of causal reasoning, along with "cause" itself (*ʿilla*, *sabab*) and "condition" (*sharṭ*), and plays a special role in that controversial practice of "specialising the cause" (*takhṣīṣ al-ʿilla*).[65] Al-Zarkashī (d. 794/1392) explains (1992, 3:329) the complementary differences between these three causal fundaments:[66]

> The cause (*sabab*) is such as from whose existence is entailed existence, and from whose non-existence is entailed non-existence, due to its essence (*dhāt*). And the impeding factor (*māniʿ*) is such as from whose existence is entailed non-existence but from whose non-existence is entailed neither an existence nor a non-existence, due to its essence. And such being the case, what is considered with respect to the impeding factor is its existence, and with respect to the condition (*sharṭ*) its non-existence, and with respect to the cause its existence and its non-existence. This is exemplified by the alms tax (*zakāt*). For the cause [of having to pay it] is [possessing] the minimal amount liable to tax (*niṣāb*), while the one-year period (*ḥawl*) is a condition, and debt (*dayn*) is an impeding factor – according to those [jurists] who opine it to be an impeding factor.

Al-Muntaqid's exposition continues its critical edge (Ibn Taymiyya [?] 2004, 82). The second part of lemma §1 "is but obvious talk (*kalām ẓāhir*);" he reviews it nonetheless, noting, among other things, that *dawarān* depends upon the existence of neither *madār* nor *dāʾir* "due to the allowance of their being two things qualified by non-existence," as with necessary implication (*talāzum*).

Both al-Nasafī and al-Muntaqid here introduce a set of higher-order categories of *dawarān*, each a pairing of existential statuses for *madār* and *dāʾir*, illustrated with standard examples.[67] In sum:

64 Esad Efendi 3034, fol. 16b; Or. 11183, fol. 15b. On the role a preponderant "impeding factor" (*māniʿ*) might play in suppressing the causation of the *madār*, see the closing discussion on lemma §14, below. On the *māniʿ* in general, see Hasan 1986a, 403–408.

65 Zysow gives primary place to the *māniʿ* in *takhṣīṣ al-ʿilla:* "perhaps the fundamental notion at the heart of specialization is that of the specializing 'impediment' (*al-māniʿ*) (...)" (Zysow 2013, 251; see 252 for Abū Zayd al-Dabūsī's scheme for the *māniʿ*). See also Hallaq 1997, 110.

66 See also his technical definition (citing al-Qarāfī) of the condition (*sharṭ*): "such as from whose non-existence is entailed non-existence, but from whose existence is entailed neither an existence nor a non-existence, due to its essence (*dhāt*)" (al-Zarkashī 1992, 3:327). For more on cause (*sabab*) and condition (*sharṭ*), see Hasan 1986a, 369–396; Hasan 1982.

67 Al-Nasafī: Amcazade Hüseyin 403, fol. 19b; Landberg 72, fol. 54a; al-Muntaqid: Ibn Taymiyya (?) 2004, 82. Neither commentator gives examples for Type IV; I have supplied them in brackets according to the obvious pattern.

I.		II.	
madār **existent**	***dā'ir*** **existent**	***madār*** **non-existent**	***dā'ir*** **non-existent**
rising of sun	daytime	rising of sun	daytime
intoxication	proscription	intoxication	proscription
III.		**IV.**	
madār **existent**	***dā'ir*** **non-existent**	***madār*** **non-existent**	***dā'ir*** **existent**
daytime	nighttime	[daytime]	[nighttime]
impeding factor (*māniʿ*)	causally justified rulings (*aḥkām muʿallala*)[68]	[impeding factor]	[causally justified rulings]

Note that these are not implications, but simply sets of possible pairings of existentially qualified concomitants. Note also that neither al-Nasafī nor al-Muntaqid (nor al-Samarqandī, as we see elsewhere) makes any apparent distinction between "intellective causes" (*ʿilal ʿaqliyya*) and "causes in God's Law" (*ʿilal sharʿiyya*).

Beginning in lemma §2 and over the next two lemmata, al-Nasafī completes a typology of *dawarān* whereby the *madār*'s modes of concomitance with the *dā'ir* (E&N, E-not-N, or N-not-E) constitute subdivisions of each existential pairing. In sum:

Existential Pairing	**I.** Both qualified by existence (*wujūdī*)	**II.** Both qualified by non-existence (*ʿadamī*)	**III.** *Madār* is *wujūdī* and *Dā'ir* is *ʿadamī*	**IV.** *Madār* is *ʿadamī* and *Dā'ir* is *wujūdī*
Mode of Concomitance	E&N E-not-N N-not-E	E&N E-not-N N-not-E	E&N E-not-N N-not-E	E&N E-not-N N-not-E

As for al-Samarqandī on lemma §2, he first illustrates the E&N mode with an example from the natural world – it is "like the rising of the sun with the existence of the daytime" – before reiterating a version of al-Nasafī's juristic example of stoning and adultery (*zinā*).[69] He does the same in the following examples,

68 That is, such rulings as would be occasioned or caused were it not for the impeding factor (*māniʿ*).

69 Esad Efendi 3034, fol. 16b; Or. 11183, fol. 15b.

betraying a certain agenda: he is actively and intentionally universalising *dawarān* (as he does later for dialectic as a whole), promoting a parity of method between the normative, speculative, and empirical.

Al-Muntaqid (Ibn Taymiyya [?] 2004, 83), on the other hand, after critiquing al-Nasafī's Arabic, connects this first mode of E&N *dawarān* directly to co-equal implication, equating the *dāʾir* in this case to the "co-equal implicatum" (*al-lāzim al-musāwī*), and providing a series of juristic examples (for instance, the *madār* of intoxication with the *dāʾir* of proscription, or the *madār* of valid marriage or concubinage with the *dāʾir* of permitted sexual intercourse). Neither *madār* nor *dāʾir* can exist, or not exist, independent of the other.

Again for lemma §3, al-Samarqandī inserts an empirical illustration of the E-not-N mode, before a version of al-Nasafī's juristic example: when drinking scammony exists, so does purgation; but non-existence of drinking scammony does not necessarily entail non-existence of purgation, since it can be "actualised by some other medicine."[70] Likewise, as we see with al-Nasafī, when donation exists, so does the donee's ownership; but non-existence of donation does not necessarily entail non-existence of ownership, since it can be "confirmed by way of inheritance (*irth*), or something else – like giving for the sake of God (*taṣadduq*)."[71] And likewise, among several of al-Muntaqid's examples (Ibn Taymiyya [?] 2004, 83), when necessitating causes (*asbāb mūjiba*) like apostasy, premeditated murder, and so on, exist, so does lawful execution (*dam*); but non-existence of one of these causes does not necessarily entail non-existence of lawful execution, since it might be actualised by one of the other causes.

And again for lemma §4, al-Samarqandī inserts a natural world example of the N-not-E mode, before a reiteration of al-Nasafī's juristic example: when life does not exist, neither does knowledge; but existence of life certainly need not entail existence of knowledge.[72] And a more precise version of the juristic example, with further reference to conditions, is supplied by al-Nasafī. Ritual purity is a condition (*sharṭ*) for allowance of prayer, so: when ritual purity does not exist, neither does allowance of prayer, "since the conditionally contingent thing (*mashrūṭ*) does not exist without the condition"; but existence of ritual purity need not entail existence of allowance of prayer, "since one of the other conditions of allowance might not exist, like directing one's prayer towards the *qibla*,

70 Esad Efendi 3034, fol. 16b; Or. 11183, fol. 15b.

71 Amcazade Hüseyin 403, fol. 20a; Landberg 72, fol. 54b. To this list al-Samarqandī adds commutation (*bayʿ*), and al-Muntaqid adds bequest, taking booty, hunting, collecting dry herbage, and gathering firewood.

72 Esad Efendi 3034, fol. 16b; Or. 11183, fol. 15b.

and covering the private parts, and so on."[73] Al-Muntaqid (Ibn Taymiyya [?] 2004, 83–84) expands on this, citing, among other examples,[74] the collective of ritual rulings for prayer, pilgrimage, and fasting, along with their conditions.

In sum, then, the three modes of concomitance with examples are as follows:

E&N		**E-not-N**		**N-not-E**	
madār	***dā'ir***	***madār***	***dā'ir***	***madār* (*sharṭ*)**	***dā'ir* (*mashrūṭ*)**
adultery	stoning penalty	donation	ownership	ritual purity	allowance of prayer
intoxication	proscription	apostasy, etc.	lawful execution	having licit sexual access	the penalty for adultery
valid marriage or concubinage	permitted sex	defecation, etc.	invalid ablution	the one-year period	obligation to pay alms-tax
rising of sun	existence of daytime	drinking scammony	purgation	life	knowledge

At this point, al-Muntaqid (Ibn Taymiyya [?] 2004, 84) makes clear his disapproval of the latter two modes of *dawarān* (E-not-N and N-not-E). Such is the method (*ṭarīqa*) of certain Shāfiʿī, Ḥanafī, and Ḥanbalī proponents of co-presence (*ṭard*) "who make mere association (*iqtirān*) of the judgment with the property and its being safe from inconsistency (*naqḍ*) an indicant for causation (*ʿilliyya*)."[75] It is important to note, however, his acknowledgment that such proponents of non-E&N *dawarān* are not satisfied with mere co-presence (*ṭard*), but observe the further and vital condition of immunity to *naqḍ*, or inconsistency (that is, the existence of the cause [*ʿilla*] without the judgment [*ḥukm*] in another case).[76]

73 Amcazade Hüseyin 403, foll. 20a–b; Landberg 72, fol. 54b.

74 Namely: the (singular) *madār*-condition of having had licit sexual access (*iḥṣān*) with the *dā'ir* of the penalty for adultery (*zinā*), and the *madār*-condition of the one-year period (*ḥawl*) with the obligation to pay alms tax (*zakāt*).

75 See Zysow 2013, 218–219, on the generally negative attitude towards proponents of *ṭard*-only *qiyās*.

76 In earlier juridical dialectic, Abū 'l-Walīd al-Bājī (d. 474/1081) defined *naqḍ* as: "existence of the occasioning factor with non-existence of the judgment (*wujūd al-ʿilla maʿa ʿadam al-ḥukm*)" (al-Bājī 1978, 14, §18; 185, §412). Al-Samarqandī, in his *Risāla fī Ādāb al-baḥth*, defines *naqḍ* as: "the absence of the judgment (*ḥukm*) from the indicant (*dalīl*)" (Young Forthcoming b §15; al-

Nor is this no-*naqḍ* condition restricted to proponents of co-presence-only *qiyās*; it was understood as a general requirement for valid *qiyās* by all but those who subscribe to the theory of "specialisation of the occasioning factor" (*takhṣīṣ al-ʿilla*).[77] In fact, as al-Muntaqid himself appears to show us in his closing comments on the final lemma, the no-*naqḍ* condition is at least a component of al-Nasafī's test of "rightness of causation" (*ṣulūḥ al-ʿilliyya*). The logical power of an opponent's charge of *naqḍ*, and the requirement that valid *qiyās* be free of *naqḍ*, secured a place for this objection at the core of dialectic's formative dynamic. Moreover, one might consider the no-inconsistency (*naqḍ*) requirement as part of a larger falsification scheme (along with, as we will see below, a no-counter-indication [*muʿāraḍa*] requirement). Which is to say, valid justification of the cause demanded the absence or negation of particular objections which might be brought against the claim, as much as it demanded the presence and confirmation of evidence for the claim. This not only places *naqḍ* and *muʿāraḍa* at the very heart of dialectic, but confirms the absolutely vital role of dialectic as the chief engine of falsification, and, consequently, of pushing causal justification towards greater explanatory power.[78]

Returning to the commentary, al-Muntaqid (Ibn Taymiyya [?] 2004, 84) is quick to point out that mere co-presence and immunity from inconsistency (*naqḍ*) is still not enough: the condition of "rightness" for causal justification (*taʿlīl*) must be met as well, or patently absurd correlational inferences can be made via "weak co-presence" (*ṭard rakīk*).[79] He chides Eastern jurists for accept-

Samarqandī 1353 [1934], 126). Elsewhere, he distinguishes this mode as "collective inconsistency" (*naqḍ ijmālī*), with a more particular "distinguishing inconsistency" (*naqḍ tafṣīlī*) equated to the move of "contradicting" (*munāqaḍa*) (Young Forthcoming b §23; al-Samarqandī 1353 [1934], 126). In his commentary on the *Risāla*, Quṭb al-Dīn al-Kīlānī (fl. ca. 830/1427) offers an expanded definition, whereby *naqḍ* is: "absence of the judgment (*ḥukm*) whose confirmation or denial is claimed, from the indicant (*dalīl*) of the respondent (*muʿallil*) who is providing indication for it, in one of the cases" (Young Forthcoming b §15.1; Damad İbrahim 1043 fol. 18a; Laud Or. 192 fol. 34b). For more on the dialectical move of *naqḍ* in juristic dialectic and the *ādāb al-baḥth*, see: Miller 1984, 127–129; Belhaj 2010, 134–136; El-Rouayheb 2015, 72, 73; Young 2017, 169–173.

77 See, for example, al-Shīrāzī 1987, 104. For an extended history and explanation of this "doctrine of specialization," see Zysow 2013, 243–254. See also Young 2017, 172–173; and Hallaq 1997, 110–111 ("limitation of the ratio legis"). Hallaq offers a handy formula: "limitation occurs when the reasoner argues that the ratio of a case is X and the rule generated by X is Y, but due to an impediment (*māniʿ*) existing in the case, X is restricted in its scope; the resultant being a rule that is not Y but Z" (Hallaq 1997, 110).

78 Further on this, see the end of section 4.4, below.

79 He provides two examples which, though confirmed of *ṭard* and free from *naqḍ*, are patently absurd.

ing mere co-presence (*ṭard*) alone, when their Khurāsānian predecessors were not even satisfied with the full combination of co-presence and co-absence (*al-ṭard wa'l-ʿaks*) as indicative of causation (*ʿilliyya*).[80] Nevertheless, he presents – without direct rebuttal – the argument of those who hold to mere co-presence as an indicant, in that they have seen it "convey probability (*ẓann*) of the causation (*ʿilliyya*)," while "preponderant probability (*al-ẓann al-rājiḥ*), when nothing stronger opposes it, must be followed." Such a principle safeguards against "following the outweighed (*marjūḥ*), or conjunction of opposites/contraries (*ḍiddayn*), or obstructing the novel case (*ḥāditha*) from getting a judgment."

Nonetheless, for al-Muntaqid (Ibn Taymiyya [?] 2004, 85) only the E&N mode is the true, majority conception of *dawarān*; nothing else deserves the title, though he insists that E&N association does not, independently, indicate causation – it can only do so in conjunction with another indicant (*dalīl*)[81] from among such usual methods (*masālik*) of validating the cause as suitability (*munāsaba*), efficiency (*ta'thīr*), or witness of the authoritative cases (*shahādat al-uṣūl*). And, in fact, the mere co-presence proponents never called such *dawarān*; only certain "latter-day scholars" (presumably al-Nasafī and predecessors) do so.

Setting this aside as technical semantics, al-Muntaqid (Ibn Taymiyya [?] 2004, 85) cuts straight to the epistemic heart of the issue: mere co-presence is a problem, "for such as from which the scent of necessitation (*iqtiḍā'*) and efficiency (*ta'thīr*) are not smelled, there is speculation (*naẓar*) with regard to making the judgment in God's Law (*ḥukm sharʿī*) dependent upon it, and binding such to it." Despite this, and despite its rejection by the great majority of "verifiers" (*muḥaqqiqūn*), the practice of non-E&N *dawarān* is "more than can be counted" in the writings of latter-day jurists.[82] In his final assessment, although possibly of some minor benefit, mere co-presence (*ṭard*) should be considered only as a last resort, and is basically non-productive.[83]

---

80 This can be marked as yet another sign of the author's critical agenda against the perceived tide of innovations from the East. On the near universal disapproval of mere-*ṭard qiyās*, see Zysow 2013, 218–219. In n. 361, he provides evidence that Ibn Taymiyya despised mere-*ṭard qiyās* in terms similar to what we find in the Rampur witness: "not only the Ḥanafīs, but the mainstream of Muslim jurists of all allegiances, were united in their contempt for the practice of consistency, and the very term became synonymous with mere unfounded assertions," citing al-Shahrastānī: *Nihāyat al-Iqdām*, and Ibn Taymiyya: *Bughyat al-Murtād al-Manʿūt.*

81 On the juristic *dalīl*, see: Hallaq 1997, 187–189; Weiss 1992, 41–45.

82 On the status of "verifier" (*muḥaqqiq*) and the practice of "verification" (*taḥqīq*), see El-Rouayheb 2006; Ahmed 2013; Wisnovsky 2013 and 2014.

83 On *ṭard* as a last resort of minimal use: "this view of consistency as the minimal fulfilment of the obligation of analogy is preserved by al-Qarāfī (d. 684/1285), for whom consistency is legitimate as a last resort 'to exclude arbitrariness (in the law) insofar as possible'" (Zysow 2013, 221).

Importantly, the commentators at this point build upon the grundtext by appending additional features and considerations critical to a fuller picture of *dawarān*. Al-Nasafī embarks on a supplementary discussion on the question of multiple *madār*s in the various modes of *dawarān*, working out a number of practical implications of interest to the historian of logic. First, he deduces the impossibility that E&N *madār*s for a given case be multiple (*muta'addid*), should they also be separable. The absurd consequence, assuming the possible existence of one of the *madār*s without the other, is the simultaneous existence and non-existence of the *dā'ir*. In such cases, one *madār* is said to "compete" (*yuzāḥimu*) with the other.[84]

I would highlight at this point a fact which should now be quite clear: the three modes of *dawarān* discussed here (and elsewhere in *uṣūl* and *ādāb al-baḥth* treatises and commentaries) are functionally equivalent to the notions of necessary and sufficient conditions familiar from modern logic. In brief:

- an E&N *madār* is both a sufficient and necessary condition for the *dā'ir*
- an E-not-N *madār* is a sufficient, but not necessary, condition for the *dā'ir*
- an N-not-E *madār* is a necessary, but not sufficient, condition for the *dā'ir*

An interesting question, therefore, and assuming the (separable) E&N *madār* can only be one, is whether any effect with a necessary and sufficient condition can only have the one. Presuming this is tackled in other traditions, it would be worthwhile to compare them with relevant formulations and arguments in the Arabic sources.[85]

Whatever the case, al-Nasafī reports that the *madār* seen in such a light is said to be an intellective cause (*'illa 'aqliyya*).[86] This, too, is of considerable import. The E&N *madār*, functionally "necessary and sufficient" – and necessarily single – is now identified by al-Nasafī with the intellective rather than legal cause, despite the fact that his own illustrative example is juristic.[87] Here is another site wherein a convergence is apparent – and from the teacher of al-Samarqandī, whose universalising agenda is manifest. Moreover, and considering al-Muntaqid's assertion that the only true *dawarān* is E&N *dawarān*, it may also have been that the only true *dawarān* was such as produced the intellective cause, or its equal, or that the two were one and the same, being the strongest inferred (as opposed to revealed) cause in God's Law.

---

84 Amcazade Hüseyin 403, fol. 20b; Landberg 72, fol. 54b. See al-Muntaqid's more intensive discussion on competition (*muzāḥama*) of *madār*s in the commentary for lemma §7, below.
85 See section 4.4, below.
86 Amcazade Hüseyin 403, fol. 20b; Landberg 72, fol. 54b.
87 We will return to the *'aqliyya* vs. *shar'iyya* distinction in section 4.2, below.

From here, al-Nasafī pronounces on multiple *madārs* in the other modes. The E-not-N – or "sufficient but not necessary" – *madār* can in fact be unproblematically plural, as we saw with donation, inheritance, and so on, for the confirmation of ownership.[88] And the N-not-E – or "necessary but not sufficient" – *madār* can also be plural, as we saw with ritual purity, covering the private parts, and so on, for the allowance of prayer.[89]

Al-Samarqandī, however, explores the implications of multiple *madārs* differently, and even more thoroughly.[90] As for E&N *madārs*, his first approach is positive, since they can indeed be multiple if also inseparable, as with (1) the sun's rising, and (2) the sun's light, for the existence of daytime.[91] With the *madārs* of rising and light being inseparable, no untenable "convergence of two contradictories" (*ijtimāʿ al-naqīḍayn*) – that is, both existence and non-existence of daytime – can ever result. The same, of course, does not hold for separable, multiple E&N *madārs*, which may entail such an absurdity.[92]

Al-Samarqandī now expands significantly on al-Nasafī's commentary. In the course of treating further cases of E&N and mixed E&N and non-E&N *madārs*, he introduces new categories for analysis, depending on whether the concomitant causation (*madāriyya*) is implicative (*luzūmiyya*) or occurring by chance (*ittifāqiyya*), or the separation (*infikāk*), when possible, is essential (*dhātī*) or occurrent (*wuqūʿī*).[93] In general, the disallowance of a certain combination is due to its possibly entailing a contradiction: the simultaneous existence and non-existence of the *dāʾir*. The surprising allowance of separable multiple E&N *madārs*, when separation (*infikāk*) is possible with essential possibility (*imkān dhātī*), is, on the other hand, due to the fact that what is possible (*mumkin*) via essential possibility is allowed to necessarily entail an absurdity (*muḥāl*).

Al-Samarqandī's analyses, in outline summation, would read as follows:

I. When the concomitant causation (*madāriyya*) is implicative (*luzūmiyya*) in existence and in non-existence, and separation (*infikāk*), when possible, is with occurrent possibility (*imkān wuqūʿī*):
   - multiple E&N *madārs*

88 Amcazade Hüseyin 403, fol. 20b; Landberg 72, fol. 54b–55a.

89 Amcazade Hüseyin 403, foll. 20b–21a; Landberg 72, fol. 55a.

90 Although al-Nasafī and al-Samarqandī found it such rich ground for elaboration, al-Muntaqid treats the proposition of multiple *madārs* only briefly, saying: "and what is a *madār* in existence and non-existence does not multiply; as for what is a *madār* in existence only, or in non-existence only, its multiplicity (*taʿaddud*) is allowed" (Ibn Taymiyya [?] 2004, 85–86).

91 Esad Efendi 3034, fol. 16b; Or. 11183, fol. 15b.

92 Esad Efendi 3034, fol. 16b; Or. 11183, fol. 17a.

93 Esad Efendi 3034, foll. 16b–17a; Or. 11183, fol. 17a.

    - inseparable are allowed
    - separable are not allowed
  - mixed E&N and non-E&N *madārs*
    - unrealised E&N with realised E-not-N is not allowed
    - realised E&N with unrealised N-not-E is not allowed
    - realised E-not-N with unrealised N-not-E is not allowed

II. When the concomitant causation is implicative in existence, but occurring by chance (*ittifāqiyya*) in non-existence:
  - multiple E&N *madārs*
    - separable, with the realised being fully implicative, and the unrealised occurring by chance in non-existence, is allowed

III. When the concomitant causation is implicative in existence and in non-existence, and separation, when possible, is with essential possibility (*imkān dhātī*):
  - multiple E&N *madārs* are allowed
  - mixed E&N and non-E&N *madārs*
    - unrealised E&N with realised E-not-N is allowed
    - realised E&N with unrealised N-not-E is allowed
    - realised E-not-N with unrealised N-not-E is allowed

Finally, al-Samarqandī closes his discourse on lemma §4 by raising and answering an innovative critique. In short, with regard to al-Samarqandī's explanation for the allowance of the separables whose separation is with essential possibility (in set III), the questioner spies a loophole which would also allow for separable E&N *madārs* of the sort al-Samarqandī claimed were not allowed (in set I). Why not simply consider both the multiplicity of the *madārs* and the separation between them to be possible things, the convergence of which (in the realisation of multiple, separable *madārs*) is allowed to entail an absurdity (that is, the simultaneous existence and non-existence of the *dā'ir*)? Al-Samarqandī rejects this out of hand: if it produces an absurdity, the union itself is absurd. Thus, the realisation of multiple, separable *madārs* is never possible in the first place.[94]

94 Esad Efendi 3034, fol. 17a; Or. 11183, fol. 17a.

§§5–6

Al-Nasafī, having situated the example in lemma §5 among disputed cases (*khilāfiyyāt*), first explains that "being not complete" (*lā yatimmu*) means that the unspecified *madār* neither completes the argument nor vindicates the claim. Why not? Because "it is counter-indicated by its like (*muʿāraḍ bi-mithlihi*)."[95] In other words, no *dawarān* with an unspecified *madār* can ever be safely and completely executed, since one's opponent – drawing from the same ambiguity – can always assemble a mirror argument of equal strength: a counter-indication by like (*muʿāraḍa bi'l-mithl*).[96] As will become clear, this constitutes a no-counter-indication ("no-*muʿāraḍa*") stipulation, in the way of the no-inconsistency ("no-*naqḍ*") requirement we encountered above; and the two might be considered components of a general falsification scheme.

Drawing on al-Nasafī's commentary, we might represent the respondent's *dawarān* in lemma §5 (with "X" representing the unspecified *madār*), as follows:

95 Amcazade Hüseyin 403, fol. 21a; Landberg 72, fol. 55a.

96 In earlier juridical dialectic, theorists such as Abū 'l-Walīd al-Bājī (d. 474/1081) defined *muʿāraḍa* as: "the questioner (*sā'il*) opposing the respondent [lit. 'the one drawing indication'] (*mustadill*) with the like of his indicant (*dalīl*) or what is stronger than it" (al-Bājī 1978, 14, §18). Al-Samarqandī, in his *Risāla fī Ādāb al-baḥth*, defines *muʿāraḍa* as: "setting up an indicant (*dalīl*) in opposition to that for which the opponent set up his indicant" (Young Forthcoming b §14; al-Samarqandī 1353 [1934], 126). In his commentary on the *Risāla*, Quṭb al-Dīn al-Kīlānī (fl. ca. 830/1427) provides a revised definition, whereby *muʿāraḍa* is: "concession (*taslīm*) to [R's] indicant (*dalīl*), but denial (*manʿ*) of what is indicated (*madlūl*), and setting up an indicant (*dalīl*) for the negation of what was indicated [by R's indicant]" (Young Forthcoming b §14.11; Damad İbrahim 1043 fol. 17b; Laud Or. 192 fol. 34b). Elsewhere, he also provides the following important distinction: "if the indicant (*dalīl*) brought by the counter-indicator (*muʿāriḍ*) is the self-same indicant brought by the respondent [lit. 'causal-justifier'] (*muʿallil*), then it is called 'reversal' (*qalb*); otherwise, if its form (*ṣūra*) is like its form, then such is called 'counter-indication by like' (*muʿāraḍa bi'l-mithl*); otherwise, it is 'counter-indication by unlike' (*muʿāraḍa bi'l-ghayr*)" (Young Forthcoming b §22.3; Damad İbrahim 1043 fol. 22b; Laud Or. 192 fol. 39a). For more on the dialectical move of *muʿāraḍa* in juristic dialectic and the *ādāb al-baḥth*, see: Miller 1984, 111–113, 133–134, 215–216, 234 – and 185–187 for al-Nasafī on *muʿāraḍa* and *ghaṣb* (the illegal move of *muʿāraḍa* before R completes his *dalīl*); Belhaj 2010, 136–7; El-Rouayheb 2015, 72, 73–4; Young 2017, 176–182.

E Case	N Case	THUS →	Contended Case
breaking fast with sex first time	breaking fast with pebbles and pits	"X" is a *madār* E&N (it is necessary and sufficient; it can only be one; it must be a necessitator [*mūjib*] for expiation).	breaking fast with eating and drinking
"X" exists	"X" does not exist		"X" exists
obligation of expiation exists	obligation of expiation does not exist	THUS →	[obligation of expiation exists]

Al-Nasafī further explains that even if an opponent denies (*manaʿa*) "X" in the E demonstration-case (sex), one can appeal to such properties as exist in both that case and the contended case – for example, "deliberate intention of invalidation" (*al-taʿammud fī ʾl-ifsād*),[97] or "invalidation in intending one of the three acts" (*al-ifsād fī ʾl-taʿammud bi-aḥad al-afʿāl al-thalātha*)[98] – then claim that "X" is either one or some combination of these.[99] He also explains how to deflect a denial (presumably by a Mālikī opponent) of "X" in the N demonstration-case (pebbles and pits) by selecting another N case from among its parallels, for example, breaking the fast via eating and drinking a second time.[100] Al-Samarqandī suggests the respondent (*muʿallil*)[101] should specify a case sanctioned by consensus (*ijmāʿ*), citing the same example.[102]

Al-Muntaqid (Ibn Taymiyya [?] 2004, 86), on the other hand, finds the problematics inherent to Stet ambiguous approach in lemma §5 far too obvious: a claim of *dawarān* for a judgment (*ḥukm*) attached to an ambiguous property (*waṣf mubham*) should never be conceded in the first place. Why not? Because *dawarān* requires a survey of a *madār*'s existence and non-existence in all cases of existence and non-existence of the judgment; and how can all such cases be investigated when the *madār* itself is not first specifically identified? We must first be able to conceive of a thing before we can discover the judgments attached to it. And it is only after this general critique that al-Muntaqid notes:

97 A gloss in Amcazade Hüseyin 403 (fol. 21a): "meaning that he aimed at invalidating the fast; that is, he carefully considered it (*naẓaruhu*) for invalidation" (signed: جلی [NB: it is tempting to read this attribution as "Ḥillī," but the glossator consistently points the *jīm* throughout]).

98 A gloss in Amcazade Hüseyin 403 (fol. 21a): "that is, sex (*wiqāʿ*), eating (*akl*), and drinking (*shurb*)" (signed: Iṣfahānī).

99 Amcazade Hüseyin 403, fol. 21a; Landberg 72, fol. 55a.

100 Amcazade Hüseyin 403, foll. 21a–b; Landberg 72, fol. 55a–b.

101 Literally, "the one doing *taʿlīl* (causal justification)."

102 Esad Efendi 3034, foll. 17b; Or. 11183, fol. 17a.

"also: its counter-indication by its like (*muʿāraḍatuhu bi-mithlihi*) is indeed possible."

And so indeed al-Nasafī first identifies the questioner's move in lemma §6 as *muʿāraḍa* (counter-indication).[103] Again drawing on al-Nasafī's commentary, we might represent the questioner's counter-*dawarān* (with "Y" representing the unspecified *madār*), as follows:

E Case	**N Case**		**Contended Case**
breaking fast with eating and drinking a second time	breaking fast with sex a first time	**THUS →** "Y" is a *madār* E&N (it is necessary and sufficient; it can only be one; it must be a necessitator [*mūjib*] for expiation). **THUS →**	breaking fast with eating and drinking
"Y" exists	"Y" does not exist		"Y" exists
non-existence of obligation of expiation exists	non-existence of obligation of expiation does not exist		[non-existence of obligation of expiation exists]

And as before, al-Nasafī explains that even if the respondent denies "Y" in the questioner's E demonstration-case (eating and drinking a second time), he can appeal to what exists in both that and the contended case – for example, the non-existence of "deliberate intention of invalidation via sex" (*ʿadam al-taʿammud fī ʾl-ifsād biʾl-wiqāʿ*), or the non-existence of "invalidation with deliberate intention by way of sex" (*ʿadam al-ifsād fī taʿammud biʾl-wiqāʿ*) – then claim that "Y" is either one or some combination of these.[104] And should the respondent deny "Y" in the questioner's N demonstration-case, then Q should do just as R himself was instructed to do in lemma §5.[105]

At this point, al-Nasafī makes a further distinction for arguing from an unspecified *madār*. What precedes, he says, "is for when the *madār* is an indeterminate-general thing (*munakkaran ʿāmman*)." But one can also claim *dawarān* – with possible success – for "an indeterminate-specific thing (*munakkaran khāṣṣan*)." He proceeds to illustrate this with a dialectical

103 Amcazade Hüseyin 403, fol. 21b; Landberg 72, fol. 55b.

104 Amcazade Hüseyin 403, fol. 21b; Landberg 72, fol. 55b.

105 Amcazade Hüseyin 403, fol. 21b; Landberg 72, fol. 55b. Al-Muntaqid's suggestions are along the same line (Ibn Taymiyya [?] 2004, 87).

sequence.[106] The first is one in which R's *dawarān* is "completed when the judgment (*ḥukm*) is something which disaccompanies (*mutakhallifan*) what is said in opposition to it (*fī muqābalatihi*)."[107]

Now, in summarising this sequence, let:

(A) = existence of the property "invalidation of the fast enjoined for him from the start" (*ifsād al-ṣawm al-wājib ʿalayhi ibtidāʾan*)
(B) = existence of the property "beginning of invalidation of the fast enjoined for him" (*ibtidāʾ ifsād al-ṣawm al-wājib ʿalayhi*)
(C) = existence of the obligation of expiation
(¬A) = non-existence of (A)
(¬B) = non-existence of (B)
(¬C) = non-existence of (C)

R's *dawarān* would then appear as follows:

E Case	**N Case**		**Contended Case**
sex, first time	eating and drinking, second time	**THUS →** "(A) or (B)" is a *madār* in both existence and non-existence	eating and drinking, first time
either (A) or (B)	either (¬A) or (¬B)		either (A) or (B)
(C)	(¬C)	**THUS →**	[(C)]

And Q's potential counter-indication, as posited by al-Nasafī – in which the judgment (C) disaccompanies either (A) or (B), via sex (*bi'l-wiqāʿ*), in the case of *ẓihār*-repudiation[108] – may be presented as follows:

106 Amcazade Hüseyin 403, foll. 21b–22a; Landberg 72, fol. 55b–56a.
107 A gloss in Amcazade Hüseyin 403 (fol. 22a), reads: "that is, when the judgment which the counter-indicator (*muʿāriḍ*) affirms in the counter-indication (*muʿāraḍa*) – such being non-existence of the obligation of expiation in our contended case – is disaccompanying what the respondent (*muʿallil*) makes a *madār* for it" (signed: Iṣfahānī), reading [معلل] instead of [معارض].
108 Amcazade Hüseyin 403, fol. 22a; Landberg 72, foll. 55b–56a. NB: most Mālikīs, Abū Ḥanīfa, and Aḥmad say that "he resolves to have intercourse with her" constitutes the retraction of the *ẓihār* oath which obliges the expiation. It is not intercourse itself. And with al-Shāfiʿī it is the act of retaining her for a considerable time without divorcing her. Ẓāhirīs say it is repeating the formula a second time (in the retraction) (Ibn Rushd 1994–1996, 2:129). Thus in none of these opinions is the actual sex act (*wiqāʿ*) itself concomitant with the obligation of expiation.

***muʿāraḍa* case**		**Contended Case**
ẓihār-oath		eating and drinking, first time
	THUS →	
either (¬A) or (¬B)		either (A) or (B)
(C)		[(¬C)]

Thus, al-Nasafī shows us that when R's *madārs* with judgment (C) are two disjuncts, either (A) or (B), in both existence and non-existence, then whether Q asserts the concomitant causation (*madāriyya*) of (¬A) or of (¬B) in his counter-indication, the result will be to complete R's *dawarān* by confirming the other disjunct. If Q asserts (¬A) with (C), then R's *madār* is confirmed as (B) with (C) in existence and non-existence; and if Q asserts (¬B) with (C), then R's *madār* is confirmed as (A) with (C) in existence and non-existence. Either way, R's *dawarān* is completed. Moreover, as al-Muntaqid notes (Ibn Taymiyya [?] 2004, 87): "the objector (*muʿtariḍ*) cannot possibly counter-indicate it by its like (...) because the judgment is different from what is said in opposition to it; so the *dawarān*[109] of the objector is not completed."[110]

But as for when the judgment is *not* "something which disaccompanies what is said in opposition to it," then the *dawarān* "is not completed except by way of what gives [one of the two] preponderance over [the other] (*yurajjiḥuhu ʿalayhi*)."[111] In other words, if there is no *muʿāraḍa*-case wherein (A) disaccompanies judgment (C) – thus confirming (B) as the sole *madār* of (C) – or wherein (B) disaccompanies judgment (C) – thus confirming (A) as the sole *madār* of (C) – then the only way to complete R's *dawarān* is by giving preponderance (*tarjīḥ*) to either (A) or (B) via some other indicant (*dalīl*).

§§7–8

At the start of lemma §7, al-Samarqandī clarifies that the specified *madār*'s being "complete" means that it is "completed safe from the like (*mithl*)" – that is, safe from Q's counter-indication by like (*muʿāraḍa bi'l-mithl*) – another expression of the "no-*muʿāraḍa*" stipulation. He also fills in the blank left by al-Nasafī's "such is obvious (*fa-ẓāhir*)," citing the N concomitance case of eating and drinking a

109 Reading [دوران] instead of [دون].

110 Similarly to al-Nasafī, he calls this type of unspecified *madār* "*munakkar makhṣūṣ*."

111 Amcazade Hüseyin 403, fol. 22a; Landberg 72, fol. 56a.

second time.[112] And al-Muntaqid (Ibn Taymiyya [?] 2004, 88) approves that drawing indication (*istidlāl*) by way of the specified, known *madār* is allowed overall (*fī 'l-jumla*), noting that the *madār* of lemma §7 has indeed been specified, despite the diverse forms of potential invalidation (*ifsād*), since violation (*hatk*) is a measure shared by the collective.

Al-Nasafī himself expands on the grundtext by introducing and responding to a potential critique. In brief, Q objects that R has not truly specified a single, distinct *madār*, since the locus of the violation (*hatk*) "among the acts" (eating, drinking, sex) is not specified. The response is: "what we mean by one of the acts is what is shared (*mushtarak*) between the three acts, and such is among specified (*muʿayyan*), known (*maʿlūm*) things."[113] Al-Samarqandī's response to the same critique clarifies further: "we mean by 'invalidation via one of the acts' (*ifsād bi-aḥad al-afʿāl*) what is shared (*mushtarak*) between the three acts – such being invalidation of the Ramaḍān fast deliberately, a first time – and it is something existing in each of the three acts, rationally understood (*mafhūm*), known (*maʿlūm*), and specified by measure of the intellect (*muʿayyan bi-ḥasab al-ʿaql*)."[114]

Here al-Muntaqid (Ibn Taymiyya [?] 2004, 88), though sanctioning *dawarān*'s conveyance of the *madār*'s causation, enriches the conversation with new conditions, warning of the consequences of their neglect. In brief, there must be either (1) no competition (*muzāḥama*) between the presumed causal *madār* and another *madār*, or (2) a distinguishing indicant (*dalīl*) in the case of multiple *madār*s. Selecting among multiple *madār*s without an authoritative indicant would be imposing God's Law via mere opinion (*ra'y*). Moreover, when there are multiple *madār*s which are all "right" for connecting with the judgment, there can be no selecting one of them without a clarification of its efficiency (*ta'thīr*). Note that this is akin to saying: *dawarān* is not enough on its own, it must be twinned with another of the methods (*masālik*) of causal justification (*taʿlīl*).

On this basis, al-Muntaqid (Ibn Taymiyya [?] 2004, 89) finds fault with al-Nasafī's example case. The problem is: although there is juristic consensus

---

112 Esad Efendi 3034, fol. 17b; Or. 11183, fol. 17a. A "useful note" gloss (*fā'ida*) in one of our manuscript witnesses of al-Nasafī's self-commentary (Amcazade Hüseyin 403) also suggests the conclusion "such is obvious" (*fa-ẓāhir*) refers to the breaking-act (*faṣl*) of eating and drinking a second time.

113 Amcazade Hüseyin 403, fol. 22a; Landberg 72, fol. 56a. A *fā'ida* gloss in Amcazade Hüseyin 403 confirms that that shared thing is what "is understood of the three acts (*mafhūm al-afʿāl al-thalātha*), being the violation of the sacrosanct (*hatk al-ḥurma*)."

114 Esad Efendi 3034, foll. 17b–18a; Or. 11183, foll. 17a–b.

(*ijmāʿ*) regarding its particular judgment – that is, that “sex by which the fast of Ramaḍān is invalidated with intent, a first time, obliges the greater expiation” – there is disagreement (*khilāf*) as to the universal rule (*ḍābiṭ*) which subsumes it and assures that obligation. Providing a succinct account of the disagreement (*khilāf*) between Mālik (d. 179/795), Abū Ḥanīfa (d. 150/767), al-Shāfiʿī (d. 204/820), and Aḥmad ibn Ḥanbal (d. 241/855) as to what constitutes the “necessitator” (*mūjib*) for the judgment,[115] he initiates a long series of arguments, followed by a partial set of responses, to be made against the respondent (*mustadill*)[116] who claims the *madār* of violation (*hatk*).

The first objection (Ibn Taymiyya [?] 2004, 90) is that he has failed to prove *dawarān*; he has brought only a single case of concomitant causation (*madāriyya*) in existence (that is, the case of sex), not a proper collective. Worse yet, there is disagreement as to what constitutes the cause (*ʿilla*) for that single case. Thus, using it as a proof of E concomitance for violation (*hatk*) is circular, as indeed it would be even if he brought several demonstration cases, so long as they were all under contention: “the confirmation of each [case] would be dependent upon confirmation of the other – and such is an invalid circularity (*dawr bāṭil*).” In fact, those who ignore this, and argue from a single case of E concomitance without the others, are not engaged in real *dawarān* at all.

The second objection (Ibn Taymiyya [?] 2004, 90–91) denies R’s claim to N concomitance for his violation-*madār*, while taking him to task over his casual use of “such is obvious” (*fa-ẓāhir*). In fact, N concomitance is anything but obvious; beyond this sex-case, the negation of expiation is confirmed by neither unambiguous source-text (*naṣṣ*) nor consensus (*ijmāʿ*). In the face of manifest juristic disagreement (*khilāf*), R might at least have provided a *qiyās* indicant, but failed to do even that.

The final objection (Ibn Taymiyya [?] 2004, 91) is a charge of unacknowledged “competition” (*muzāḥama*). It is a prequel to (and expansion upon) Q’s argument in §9 of al-Nasafī’s grundtext. In short, there are other cause-candidate *madār*s for obligation of expiation – for instance, “the sex violating (*hātik*) the sanctity of Ramaḍān,” or “the violating fast-breaking,” or “sex violating the

115 For Mālik: unrestricted fast-breaking, on purpose (even with pebbles and date-stones); for Abū Ḥanīfa: fast-breaking, on purpose, with what is sold by its genus, or by way of one of the three acts; for al-Shāfiʿī: sex preventing obligatory fasting during the day in Ramaḍān, on purpose; and for Aḥmad b. Ḥanbal: (1) sex in the daytime of Ramaḍān by one for whom abstinence (*imsāk*) is obliged, or (2) the skin-to-skin contact (*mubāshara*) necessitating greater ablution (*ghusl*), or... (he continues at some length).

116 That is, the one doing *istidlāl*, or drawing indication.

fast" – but R has provided no argument for choosing violation (*hatk*) from among them.

The commentary on lemma §8 brings us one of the most fascinating bridges between normative, speculative, and empirical sciences to be found in *dawarān* discourse. Al-Nasafī himself brings a compelling justification for *dawarān*, drawn from the practices of certain empirical arts and sciences:[117]

> For indeed when the physicians, astronomers [or astrologers], and Folk of Custom (*ahl al-ṭibb wa'l-tanjīm wa'l-ʿurf*) observe (*shāhadū*) certain effects following from certain nourishments, medicines, conjunctions of heavenly bodies, and name-calling with bad nicknames, there obtains in them the probable supposition (*ẓann*) of the causation (*ʿilliyya*) of the *madār*s for the *dā'irs*.

Thus, a plain statement of juristic *dawarān* theory (lemma §8) is reinforced by parallels in the practice or custom of empirical arts and sciences – with empirical verbs and phenomena, and, in fact, an empirical observation of the fruits of their practice (the obtainment of *ẓann*); and it seems we are as close as one might come to answering what became of intellective vs. legal causes: there is simply no longer a distinction. Notably, the argument form is itself analogical: as it is in these empirical sciences, so should it be in the science of jurisprudence. When jurists *observe* legal effects (*aḥkām*) following from things (properties), then probable supposition (*ẓann*) should also obtain in them with regard to the causation (*ʿilliyya*) of the *madār*s for the *dā'irs*.

But al-Nasafī anticipates and answers an objection to the example's epistemology. In short, should Q claim their knowing (*ʿirfān*) is not by way of *dawarān*, but by way of transmission from prophets and sages who are themselves enlightened via "pure inspiration and true dreams," R is simply to reply that such may hold for non-conventional evidences (*ghayr al-ʿurfiyya min al-shawāhid*), but not for the conventional.[118] And the epistemic strength of convention (*ʿurf*) is considerable, being such as is resolved in the intellects, and wholeheartedly received by sound natures.[119] But most importantly, this empiric analogy is sanctioned by consensus, for:[120]

> the rationally minded (*ʿuqalā'*) in their entirety believe in the causation of the *madār*, and scholars (*ʿulamā'*) justify causes with it (*yuʿallilūna bihi*) in numerous places; and were it not that it is a cause, their beliefs would have been in error, and their causal justification

---

117 Amcazade Hüseyin 403, fol. 22b; Landberg 72, fol. 56a.
118 Amcazade Hüseyin 403, fol. 22b; Landberg 72, fol. 56a.
119 Amcazade Hüseyin 403, fol. 22b; Landberg 72, foll. 56a–b.
120 Amcazade Hüseyin 403, foll. 22b–23a; Landberg 72, foll. 56a–b.

> (*taʿlīl*) with it likewise. But it is not so. For indeed their consensus (*ijmāʿ*) on error time and time again goes against [both] intellect (*ʿaql*)[121] and indicant (*dalīl*)[122].

Al-Samarqandī raises the same empirical parallel,[123] with elucidating variation: the physicians and astronomers are the Folk of Experience (*ahl al-tajriba*), and the belief in causation of the *madārs* which obtains in them after their observations is the same that obtains in the Folk of Custom (*ahl al-ʿurf*) after theirs.[124] Then, anticipating the same critique of transmission from prophets and sages, he responds:[125]

> [whether] by transmission (*naql*) from them, or by experience (*tajriba*), we know their causation. And even if we concede [that it is by transmission], that does us no harm; since there suffices for us the judgment of the intellect (*ḥukm al-ʿaql*) from the Folk of Custom (*ahl al-ʿurf*) for the causation of *madārs* in all the experiential concomitances (*dawarānāt tajribiyya*). And such are more than can be counted.

So even if first knowledge of causation in the arts and sciences is transmitted from prophets and sages who did not gain it from *dawarān*, we nevertheless have after them the collective experience of the Folk of Custom (*ahl al-ʿurf*), unanimous on the causation of *madārs* for uncountable experiential concomitances. Perhaps what is most important here is al-Samarqandī's linking of *dawarān* to *tajriba*.[126]

But he builds further on the empirical parallel by answering another potential critique – one problematising the parallel's analogical and inductive qualities. In short, Q asks: "how is the universal principle (*qāʿida kulliyya*) confirmed via examples (*amthila*)?" R's answer is that examples constitute an appeal to the self-evident (*tanbīh*); *dawarān* by al-Nasafī's definition is understood by "every sound mind (*ʿāqil*)" to bestow belief in the *madār*'s efficiency (*taʾthīr*) vis-à-vis the *dāʾir*, "and for this reason, the philosophers (*ḥukamāʾ*) judged that experien-

---

121 Perhaps this *ʿaql* reference points to Aristotle's theory of *endoxa* premises. But note that *ʿaql* arguments for the authoritativeness of *ijmāʿ* can be found in the *uṣūl* works of such as al-Juwaynī, al-Ghazālī, and al-Āmidī (Hallaq 1986, 439–440, 443, 445–446).

122 This "*dalīl*" almost certainly points to *uṣūlī* indicants for the authoritativeness of *ijmāʿ*, drawn from such primary material as Q. 4:115 and the Prophet's saying: "my community will never agree on an error" (see Hallaq 1986; and Hallaq 1997, 75–76).

123 In the Rampur witness, on the other hand, we find only an echo of the empirical parallel (see the response to critique 4.A, below). But still it is there, meaning either that al-Muntaqid accessed other commentaries, or that such arguments were current in his own circles.

124 Esad Efendi 3034, fol. 18a; Or. 11183, fol. 17b.

125 Esad Efendi 3034, fol. 18a; Or. 11183, fol. 17b.

126 See section 4.1, below.

tial propositions (*tajribiyyāt*) were immediately necessary propositions (*ḍarūriyyāt*)."[127] Reminding ourselves this is a commentary on *juristic* dialectic, the implications are plain: for al-Samarqandī the mechanics and epistemic potency of *dawarān* are established in the realm of legal reasoning by their paralleling the *tajriba* of empirical philosophy, a method so grounded in the self-evident that philosophers group its results (the *tajribiyyāt*) under the rubric of immediately necessary propositions (*ḍarūriyyāt*).

Still, al-Samarqandī closes this section as a true, truth-seeking "verifier" (*muḥaqqiq*) would, raising a problem for inquiry (*baḥth*) into his own presumptions, and without forwarding a resolution.[128]

> We ourselves have conceded that the *madārs* are causes (*ʿilal*) for the *dāʾirs*, but that they need not necessarily be "complete causes" (*ʿilal tāmma*). And the disaccompaniment (*takhalluf*) of the effect (*maʿlūl*) from the non-complete cause is permitted, due to some impeding factor (*māniʿ*), or unfulfilled condition (*fiqdān sharṭ*). So why is it not permitted that it be likewise, here, in this case? For it is allowed that the violation (*hatk*) be a cause for the obligation of expiation, though with a condition (*sharṭ*) regarding sex (*wiqāʿ*),[129] or that there be an impeding factor (*māniʿ*) for [the violation's] efficiency (*taʾthīr*) with regard to eating and drinking – like the fact that, even if drinking scammony is a cause (*ʿilla*) for purgation, [purgation] might nevertheless disaccompany it – as it would in cold countries, and in strong humours.

Note that, though problematising his own assumptions, al-Samarqandī still links the normative and empirical realms via the stock example of scammony. Expiation might disaccompany the violation cause (*ʿilla*), even though it is an *ʿilla*, due to some impeding factor (*māniʿ*) or unfulfilled condition (*sharṭ*), *in the same way* that purgation might disaccompany the drinking scammony cause, even though it is an *ʿilla*, due to some *māniʿ* (like its being consumed in the wrong clime, or counteracted by strong humours).[130]

Turning now to al-Muntaqid (Ibn Taymiyya [?] 2004, 91), we find that his critiques for §7 continue for the lemma of §8. His fourth critique, then, is directed against the "*dawarān* is a sign (*āya*)" statement, and in fact consists of three sub-

---

127 Esad Efendi 3034, fol. 18a; Or. 11183, fol. 17b.

128 Esad Efendi 3034, fol. 18a; Or. 11183, fol. 17b. This is reminiscent of his *Risāla fī Ādāb al-baḥth*, where it is difficult to pin his adherence to any particular doctrine.

129 A gloss in Esad Efendi 3034 reads: "it [the *sharṭ*] is its [sexual intercourse's] being the more heinous of the breaches (*afḥash al-kharaq*) with regard to invalidation (*ifsād*) [of the Ramaḍān fast]."

130 Cf. Hasan 1986a, 319. See also the *Qānūn fī ʾl-Ṭibb*, where Ibn Sīnā makes similar observations re. scammony (Ibn Sīnā 1999, 1:35, 594, respectively; for the second passage, Ibn Sīnā 1993–1998, vol. 2 [Book II], 264).

critiques, each of which receives its response only later.[131] In short: (4.A) R mentioned no indicant (*dalīl*) that *dawarān* does what he says in lemma §8, so it is not conceded; (4.B) nor did R provide confirmation for the referenced parallel cases (*naẓā'ir*); (4.C) nor is there reason to believe that the cause-to-judgment relationship in a given case is the result of *dawarān*, without an indicant (*dalīl*) to that effect, so *dawarān* alone is not conclusive – this being the well-known doctrine of those who deny *dawarān*'s conveyance of causation.

The fifth and final critique (Ibn Taymiyya [?] 2004, 91–92), though conceding *dawarān*'s conveyance of causation, denies that it does so when there are competing *madārs* – as indeed there are in al-Nasafī's example – and demands that there be a further indicant (*dalīl*). And anticipating a response that the problem of competing *madārs* can be solved via the "right for causation" (*ṣulūḥ al-ʿilliyya*) test, al-Muntaqid says: "all of these *madārs* are right for causation. So why did you specifically designate one of them without the other?"

Looking back at these five critiques, al-Muntaqid (Ibn Taymiyya [?] 2004, 92–93) claims them unanswerable, and damning for the misusers of *dawarān*, "exposing the secret of these deceptions (*talbīsāt*)." Still, he forwards a strong response to the first two critiques, attacking their assumption that *dawarān* requires a complete survey of E and N cases, with all that such would entail. In short: *dawarān* aims at indicating the cause (*ʿilla*) in a known case so as to make its judgment (*ḥukm*) dependent upon it in another. But if, before we did this, we first had to know all the cases of shared existence and non-existence for both the claimed cause and the judgment, then *dawarān* would become superfluous. Against this, he launches three counter-responses. First, *dawarān* need not be sought after as a self-contained, comprehensive method for establishing judgments, but can be appreciated in its simpler role of linking judgment to shared property (*mushtarak*) in the E cases. Second, it is only right we should assume *dawarān* across the cause-bearing root-cases (*uṣūl*), or those established via unambiguous source-text (*naṣṣ*) or consensus (*ijmāʿ*), as it is the means for doing *qiyās* to cases enjoying neither *naṣṣ* nor *ijmāʿ*. And third, confirmation of E *dawarān* in fact requires an indicant (*dalīl*) for E&N *dawarān* – so if there is no indicant confirming *both* co-presence and co-absence, then there can be no confirmation of *dawarān* in the first place.

Turning to his fourth critique (Ibn Taymiyya [?] 2004, 93), which we will recall is actually three sub-critiques (4.A-C), al-Muntaqid launches a set of

---

131 See the responses to critiques 4.A–C, below.

replies.[132] The first (matching critique 4.A) is an echo of the empirical parallel earlier brought by al-Nasafī and al-Samarqandī. Whatever prophets and sages may have transmitted of causation without relying on *dawarān*, the fact is that causal arrangement with its accompanying *dawarān* has subsequently been testified to time and time again by ordinary, non-inspired folk to the extent that the whole complex of repeated observations is itself evidenced by custom (*ʿurf*). Moreover, *dawarān*, with its potential to meet the standard of "overwhelming probability" (*ghalabat al-ẓann*), has attained the minimum requirement for all authoritative indicants (*adilla*) – and, having done so, *it must be followed* unless it is counter-indicated by its like.[133]

Again, note the power of this last "no-*muʿāraḍa*" condition. Here is a principle of adherence based on the *absence* of valid counter-indication, thus securing a place for *muʿāraḍa* – along with inconsistency (*naqḍ*) – at the very core of dialectic's formative dynamic, and as vital components of a larger falsification scheme. As chief falsifier, the dialectical questioner compels the contended *ʿilla*-justification towards either extinction or greater explanatory power. Moreover, the absence of further critique following this response indicates that al-Muntaqid was of the same mind as al-Nasafī and al-Samarqandī as regards the empirical parallel: what gives potency to *dawarān* in the natural world is what gives it potency in the normative; there is no (practical) distinction between intellective vs. legal causes.

Al-Muntaqid's second response (Ibn Taymiyya [?] 2004, 93–94) should match critique 4.B, but appears not to. If I understand correctly, he merely points to the following: the very fact that every judgment (*ḥukm*) must have a cause (*sabab*) itself guarantees that such a cause must be a *madār* with that judgment – how could it be otherwise? For cause and judgment (as is confirmed in the next response) are inseparable; when one exists so must the other, and when one does not, neither must the other. The *sabab* can only be a *madār*; and, for this reason, *madār*s must be the specific focus when validating causes.[134]

And the third response (Ibn Taymiyya [?] 2004, 94), matching critique 4.C, is an argument against the notion of *dawarān* occurring by chance (*ittifāqiyyan*), as what occurs by chance "neither multiplies nor persists." Thus *dawarān* can only be implicative (*luzūmī*) for property and judgment, and only a cause (*ʿilla*) or fellow effect (*maʿlūl*) of a single cause can be an implicans. Once we have narrowed

---

132 The first appears to match [A], and the third matches [C], but I am uncertain as to how (or whether) the second matches [B].

133 On *ghalabat al-ẓann* see Hallaq 1997, 39, 91.

134 The text of the edition reads: [الثاني أن ذلك الحكم لا بدَّ له من سبب والأصل عدم ما سوى المدار فتعيَّن المدار].

potential causation to the *madār* and what it entails, we can eliminate the entailment(s) from the *madār* via the principle of "rightness of causation" (*ṣulūḥ al-ʿilliyya*), so that only the *madār* remains to be identified as the cause.

§§9–10

Lemma §9 begins the first grundtext cycle of critique and response, and Q (likely a Shāfiʿī) is tying expiation to something specific to the case of sex (*wiqāʿ*) – i.e., the sex act itself – partly in order to prevent R (likely a Ḥanafī) from extending this obligation to the contended case.[135] Moreover, as al-Nasafī explains in both grundtext and commentary, it can't be that both sex and violation be E&N *madārs* without entailing "convergence of two contradictories" (*ijtimāʿ al-naqīḍayn*): the simultaneous existence and non-existence of expiation in the contended case of eating and drinking a first time.[136] Note this is in perfect consonance with al-Nasafī's earlier observation: "such as is a *madār* in existence and in non-existence cannot possibly be multiple (*mutaʿaddid*)."

Al-Samarqandī, having paralleled al-Nasafī's commentary, closes by underscoring the power of this critique, which: "even if thrown back [by R] against the concomitant causation (*madāriyya*) of the sex,[137] still (...) bestows doubt (*shakk*) on the concomitant causation of the violation, so that its confirmation does not follow of necessity."[138] Al-Muntaqid (Ibn Taymiyya [?] 2004, 94) in fact finds this first grundtext critique valid and unanswerable. This should not surprise us; it is an instance of the multiple *madār* "competition" problem already highlighted in his commentary on lemma §7.

But R counters in lemma §10, denying specific designation of E concomitant causation in the case of sex, and affirming it for all cases of obligation a first

---

135 A particular genius of al-Nasafī's problem-question (*mas'ala*) is thus plain: it not only illustrates concerns intrinsic to debating *ʿilla*-validation, but further narrows focus to the historical tension between transitivity and intransitivity, between restricted specialization (*takhṣīṣ*) and general extendibility (*taʿdiya*) of juristic causes. See Zysow 2013, 224–225, 243–254; Hallaq 1997, 110–111.

136 Amcazade Hüseyin 403, fol. 23a; Landberg 72, fol. 56b. He further notes the same problem would arise in breaking the fast by way of sex a second time, since the existence of sex and non-existence of violation would again entail the simultaneous existence and non-existence of expiation (Amcazade Hüseyin 403, foll. 23a–b; Landberg 72, foll. 56b–57a).

137 That is, the argument holds just as true against the concomitant causation (*madāriyya*) of the sex as it does against the concomitant causation of the violation, so R could in fact throw it straight back to Q.

138 Esad Efendi 3034, fol. 18b; Or. 11183, fol. 17b.

time. Al-Nasafī reformulates that affirmation: "in that we say: the obligation of expiation is concomitant with the violation in existence and in non-existence; as for in existence, then in every one of the cases of obligation a first time (...) and as for in non-existence, then in every one of the cases of eating and drinking a second time."[139] Having thus re-articulated R's E&N *dawarān* so that the violation-*madār* more clearly exists where it should and not where it shouldn't, he responds to the objection of an obstinate Q who denies the realization of violation in every case of obligation a first time. In fact, he retorts, the *only* causes of obligation of expiation a first time (at least among cases relevant to the Ramaḍān fast, not, for instance, oath-breaking) are sex, eating, and drinking (i.e., the "three acts"). So as long as R means only these cases, Q cannot deny (*manaʿa*) the realization of violation in them.[140]

Then, having reproduced lemma §10's closing assertion, al-Nasafī demonstrates the impossibility that Q could come back with a parallel argument. He simply cannot say "expiation is concomitant with sex in existence and in non-existence; as for in existence, in every one of the cases of the obligation a first time."[141] In this fashion, al-Nasafī presumably considers the first critique thoroughly refuted. Al-Samarqandī goes further, however, first explaining why Q's objection does no harm to R. In brief, the concomitant causation (*madāriyya*) of the violation is universal (*kulliyya*), while that of sex is particular (*juzʾiyya*); so in the case of eating and drinking, the latter neither competes with nor counter-indicates the former.[142]

That said, he again provides an escape for Q, or a means for him to maintain his critique – showing, at the very least, the typical consciousness of broader counter-argument we see in his *Risāla*.[143] Q concedes the violation-property as consequent to his sex-*madār*, but this concession is not to be taken universally – it is restricted to Q's conception of "all cases of obligation," which are only cases of sex. Extending it further than that is to include as proof what is in fact the very point being argued: whether it can be extended further. One cannot

139 Amcazade Hüseyin 403, fol. 23b; Landberg 72, fol. 57a.

140 Amcazade Hüseyin 403, fol. 23b; Landberg 72, fol. 57a. For more on the dialectical move of *manʿ* in juristic dialectic and the *ādāb al-baḥth*, see: Miller 1984, 113–118, 207–209; Belhaj 2010, 124–125, 133–134; Young 2017, 152–154.

141 Amcazade Hüseyin 403, foll. 23b–24a; Landberg 72, fol. 57a.

142 Esad Efendi 3034, fol. 19a; Or. 11183, fol. 17b.

143 See Young Forthcoming b, Intro. Al-Samarqandī's reserve in openly championing a particular legal solution might stem from his own undecidedness on matters still contested in his day. Alternately, he may himself have been a Shāfiʿī, for which there are other potential indicants. For example, the Shāfiʿī respondent appears to have the final word in the third practice *mas'ala* of the *Risāla* (see Young 2018).

assume a universal violation-*madār* without assuming "the very thing under contention (*ʿayn al-nizāʿ*)."[144] Thus, as we will soon see of al-Muntaqid, Q is pointing to a circularity in R's claim.

In fact, al-Muntaqid engages extensively with lemma §10 (Ibn Taymiyya [?] 2004, 95–97). First he objectively explains R's response and points to how it generates a problem for Q, in that he cannot rightly claim the concomitant causation of his property (*waṣf*) "in the cases of obligation" as R can; sex-*madār* E demonstration is limited to cases of sex, whereas R's violation-*madār* E demonstration cases include cases of sex and all "cases of obligation." Then, however, al-Muntaqid declares R's response wrong, and launches a series of five counter-arguments against it. The first is that both R and Q are wrong to claim their *madār*s in "[all] the cases of obligation." In fact, there are other acknowledged cases of fast-breaking wherein expiation is obliged besides sex, eating, and drinking with intent – among them: Mālik's "unrestricted fast-breaking" (*muṭlaq al-ifṭār*), or most jurists' "impeding sex" (*al-jimāʿ al-māniʿ*), or Aḥmad b. Ḥanbal's "second sex" (*al-jimāʿ al-thānī*) and "absent-minded sex" (*al-jimāʿ al-nāsī*) – and R and Q need not necessarily find their claimed *madār*s in these.

The second counter-argument (Ibn Taymiyya [?] 2004, 96) presents R with a dilemma. It begins with our taking a step back and hypothetically deleting R's current evidence (*bayyina*) for his claim of the violation's concomitant causation (*madāriyya*) "in every case of obligation." Without evidence, of course, this would simply constitute a bald assertion of doctrine, and thus be inadmissible according to the norms of juristic dialectic. In order to make it right, however, al-Muntaqid presents R with only two equally unappetizing options. He can either (1) retract his universal "in every case of obligation" claim, and step back to claiming his violation-*madār* for the case of sex, specifically – at which point Q will counter-indicate with like; or (2) he can continue to assert his claim for "every case of obligation," at which point Q will demand the indicant (*dalīl*) for that. The problem now – as al-Muntaqid has cleverly made more apparent via his initial, hypothetical deletion of R's *bayyina* – is that such an indicant, in order to work for R, would have to include the very cases of E&N concomitance he is supposed to be proving via indicant now – cases which are currently mere *madhhab* opinion (not enjoying consensus), and still contested. The horns of the dilemma close, for R must commit either retraction, prolongation, or a circular fallacy of indicants each drawing from the other.

The third counter-argument builds on this dilemma with another, one path again leading to retraction and the other to circularity. Assuming R does not

144 Esad Efendi 3034, fol. 19a; Or. 11183, foll. 17b–18a.

mean cases resolved by unambiguous source-text (*naṣṣ*) or consensus (*ijmāʿ*), since these include only sex cases, then "cases of obligation" can only mean cases he claims to be such. However, whether or not they are in truth cases wherein expiation is obliged depends upon his ability to prove as much, and his ability to prove as much depends upon his current *dawarān* argument, but his current *dawarān* argument depends on the very "cases of obligation" he needs first to prove, for which he'll need the current *dawarān*, and so on – a tight, inescapable circle. Thus, in order for R's claim to hold, he is dependent upon an indicant incorporating his solution to the very case under contention, and "circularity (*dawr*) follows of necessity."

The fourth counter-argument is that R simply cannot claim *dawarān* for "all cases of obligation," as he understands them, without untenable consequences; whereas Q can in fact claim as much, with his more limited set of "cases of obligation." The objector (*muʿtariḍ*) Q can, in fact – against what the "indicator" (*mustadill*) R says – claim concomitance of his sex-*madār* in "the cases of obligation" (*ṣuwar al-wujūb*) because this means only "the cases in which the obligation is confirmed" (*al-ṣuwar allatī thabata fīhā 'l-wujūb*) – confirmed, that is, via *naṣṣ* and *ijmāʿ* – and these (as we saw earlier) are only cases in which sex exists. R, on the other hand, need not – and cannot – verify his claim of concomitance of his violation-*madār* in "the cases of obligation" via *ijmāʿ*, because there is no *ijmāʿ* on all the cases he would be claiming it for. *Dawarān* of the violation with the obligation of expiation in all "the cases of obligation" is merely his *madhhab*-doctrine; and, as we have seen, this is inadmissible as an argument.

Moreover, such a claim should never be allowed in the first place. If R is allowed to claim "all the cases of obligation" even though some are merely his *madhhab*, then Q can never claim his own *madār* for "all the cases of obligation" until either he concedes R's *madhhab* opinion(s) – including R's opinion on the contended case (!) – or himself claims a broader set of cases than his opponent (including, like R's set, such as are his *madhhab*-doctrine, not *ijmāʿ* or *naṣṣ*). Either way, "it is known that this is invalid via immediate necessity (*bi'l-ḍarūra*)," since it entails either (1) yet another circularity (*dawr*), confirming unproven *madhhab* via unproven *madhhab* (with no grounding in *naṣṣ* or *ijmāʿ*); or (2) the disputant's adherence (*ilzām*) to the very *madhhab* he seeks to contradict.[145]

Finally, al-Muntaqid's fifth counter-argument (Ibn Taymiyya [?] 2004, 97) suggests another way out for Q. The fact that R confirms obligation both where Q confirms it (in the case of sex a first time) and elsewhere, is, as we

145 On immediately necessary knowledge (*ʿilm ḍarūrī*), see Weiss 1992, 36–40.

saw earlier, a problem for Q. He simply can't make a counter-claim with as many cases as R. If, however, Q were able to confirm obligation in another case in which R has not also confirmed it (for instance, in "absent-minded sex"), then Q's counter-claim against R would be lifted to the same potency as R's claim against Q. That is, Q might equally be able to claim his *madār* "in the cases of obligation," and, in doing so, block R's pursuit of the argument in §10 via another counter-indication by like (*muʿāraḍa bi'l-mithl*).

§§11–12

Al-Nasafī first clarifies Q's objection in lemma §11, the second grundtext critique: expiation is concomitant with what is specific (*mukhtaṣṣ*) to the case of sex a first time: for instance, the sex act itself;[146] and specificity (*ikhtiṣāṣ*) is defined in contradistinction to "sharing" (*sharika*).[147] Thus, Q is again employing a restrictive strategy, limiting the range of concomitant causation (*madāriyya*) to a concomitance between expiation and something, like his sex-*madār* itself, specific to the known case and not shared (like R's violation-*madār*) with others. But R's response, now amplified by al-Nasafī, is that the same concomitance holds with what is shared (*mushtarak*), "since the shared thing is also realised in [that case] while the expiation is obliged."[148]

R's strategy, the mirror image of Q's, is again a counter-indication by like (*muʿāraḍa bi'l-mithl*). Alternately, we might read Q and R as bringing their case-specific (*mukhtaṣṣ*) and shared (*mushtarak*) *madār*s to "compete" with each other, for, as al-Samarqandī notes of Q's claim: "when the obligation [of expiation] is a *dā'ir* with the specific thing (*mukhtaṣṣ*) it is not [a *dā'ir*] with the shared thing (*mushtarak*); otherwise a conjunction of two contradictories (*ijtimāʿ al-naqīḍayn*) follows of necessity in [the case of] eating and drinking, as we have discussed."[149] Of course, having presented R's mirror response, he also notes: "when [obligation of expiation] is concomitant with the shared thing (*mushtarak*) it is not a *dā'ir* with the specific thing (*mukhtaṣṣ*); otherwise there necessarily follows the mentioned conjunction."[150] Note how neatly R's

146 Along with this possible property, al-Samarqandī mentions: "deliberate invalidation via sex" (*al-ifsād bi'l-wiqāʿ ʿamdan*).

147 Amcazade Hüseyin 403, fol. 24a; Landberg 72, foll. 57a–b.

148 Amcazade Hüseyin 403, fol. 24a; Landberg 72, fol. 57b.

149 Esad Efendi 3034, fol. 19a; Or. 11183, fol. 18a.

150 Esad Efendi 3034, fol. 19a; Or. 11183, fol. 18a.

muʿāraḍa (in fact a counter-counter-indication) blocks Q's counter-indicant, via "competing" *madār*, and with equal form and weight.

Uniquely, al-Muntaqid (Ibn Taymiyya [?] 2004, 97–98) brings two interpretations for Q's objection: either (1) the true *madār* in the authoritative case of sex is the one that is specific to that case (for example, the sex itself), and is not found in the contended case, or (2) every one of the "cases of obligation" has its own peculiar *madār*, outcompeting (or supplanting) the shared violation-*madār*.

As for R's response, al-Muntaqid finds it superior – that is, should Q have intended (2), above – filling in supporting details to prove it so. First he posits a rule: linking the judgment to what is common among relevant cases is of higher epistemic value than linking it to what is peculiar to each case by itself. This he further supports with two assertions: (1) the default condition (*aṣl*) is that the cause (*ʿilla*) for a particular judgment be one, not many; and (2) just as R's shared violation-*madār* allows co-presence simultaneously for a slew of cases, so does it allow co-absence simultaneously for a slew of cases, whereas Q's multiple, case-specific *madār*s do not. Thus concomitant causation (*madāriyya*) of the shared thing (*mushtarak*) is superior (*awlā*) to concomitant causation of the case-specific thing (*mukhtaṣṣ*). All this holds true, however, only if Q intended the second interpretation above. R's response is inadequate if Q's claim of case-specific-concomitant causation holds true only for cases settled by unambiguous source-text (*naṣṣ*) or consensus (*ijmāʿ*) (like sex a first time). If this was Q's aim, then Q's objection holds firm.

Al-Muntaqid (Ibn Taymiyya [?] 2004, 98) now shows where all this is heading, presuming a great deal of al-Nasafī's agenda along the way. In short, an initial counter-indication (*muʿāraḍa*) clash of *madār*s, or case-specific (*mukhtaṣṣ*) vs. shared (*mushtarak*) conflict, degenerates into a contest whose outcome is determined via preponderance of counter-indicating *madār*s. Whichever side gains the additional *madār* becomes free from the other side's counter-indication, thus winning. Alternately, though to the same effect, one could take the view that linking the judgment to a *madār* safe from counter-indication is obligatory in the first place (consequent to the no-*muʿāraḍa* requirement earlier expressed by al-Nasafī).

Having thus interpreted the lemma, al-Muntaqid launches his critique. This preponderance contest, he tells us, "is also among the invalid general principles (*qawāʿid*) upon which they construct many of their arguments." Ultimately, *madār*s in and of themselves are not the same as full-on instances of E&N *dawarān*; only the latter constitutes a full indicant (*dalīl*), and only full indicants accumulate in such a manner as achieves vindication through preponderance. So al-Nasafī's method in §11 (or what al-Muntaqid has presumed of it) is simply wrong by any rational standard.

From here al-Muntaqid (Ibn Taymiyya [?] 2004, 98–99) expands his critique, pressing his view that multiple *madārs* are a real cause for difficulty – unless, that is, there exists a confirming indicant which establishes causation (*ʿilliyya*) for one of them, or for some collective portion of them. Without such an indicant, there is simply no reason to believe in one, or some, over another, or some others. One cannot simply note that the branch-case (*farʿ*) shares numerous properties with the root-case (*aṣl*), and then assume that most of them have causation in conveying the judgment from the root-case to the branch-case. Again, properties (*ṣifāt*) are not indicants (*adilla*), and their accumulation does not deliver vindication via preponderance.

This being said, he becomes more constructive, laying down the law for confirming causation of a *madār*. In brief: every competitor (*muzāḥim*) of the *madār*-which-is-to-be-cause must be eliminated before it can be declared the cause; at the same time, it is preferable to link the judgment to a collective of properties (*ṣifāt*) enjoying rightness for causal justification (*ṣāliḥ li'l-taʿlīl*), over linking it to just one (Ibn Taymiyya [?] 2004, 99).

Notably, all of our commentators build on lemma §11 with an additional critique and response.[151] In al-Samarqandī's version, Q says: "we don't concede that this is other than the first, for indeed the violation and the shared thing (*mushtarak*) are a single thing;" and R replies: "'the violation' is more particular (*akhaṣṣ*) than 'the shared thing,' so it is distinct from it (*mughāyiran lahu*)." Thus Q in effect accuses R of a clever redundancy – of just saying "shared thing" instead of "violation;" and R's response is to point out a validating distinction between them. Al-Muntaqid (Ibn Taymiyya [?] 2004, 99) does not find this adequate, however. Just because R has claimed a technical distinction does not mean he has demonstrated it sufficiently for the case at hand, nor to the extent that his *madār* claim be considered valid. Moreover, by pointing out that the shared-*madār* is not itself the violation-*madār*, but something necessarily entailing the violation-*madār* (for nothing else but the violation is shared by "all the cases of obligation"), R has contributed more to Q's current objection than to his own defense. That is, R's saying: "it's the shared thing" is still more or less the same as his saying: "it's the violation," and thus redundant.

As for unpacking the terse objection and response of lemma §12, we are helped somewhat from the commentaries and marginal glosses. Al-Nasafī's Q asserts that without his case-specific *madār*'s concomitance, "expiation would not be obliged in [the sex case], by way of the negator safe from the decisive

---

151 Al-Nasafī's version: Amcazade Hüseyin 403, fol. 24a; Landberg 72, fol. 57b; al-Samarqandī's: Esad Efendi 3034, fol. 19a; Or. 11183, fol. 18a; al-Muntaqid's: Ibn Taymiyya (?) 2004, 99.

counter-indicant (*al-nāfī al-sālim ʿan al-muʿāriḍ al-qaṭʿī*), such [counter-indicant] being the concomitant causation (*madāriyya*) of the case-specific thing (*mukhtaṣṣ*) for the obligation in [that sex case]." While R responds in kind for his shared *madār*, without which "expiation would not be obliged in [the sex case] by way of the negator safe from the decisive counter-indicant, such being the causal concomitance of the shared thing (*mushtarak*) for [that sex case]."[152]

Fortunately, a "useful note" gloss (*fāʾida*) in the margins of Amcazade Hüseyin 403, fol. 24a, comes to our aid in untangling this still terse critique and response. When the author says "by way of the negator (*al-nāfī*)" it means: "[1] by way of the negating texts (*al-nuṣūṣ al-nāfiya*), due to [the Prophet's] saying, God bless and save him: 'there shall be neither harming in the first instance nor harming in requital in Islam' (*lā ḍarara wa-lā ḍirāra fī 'l-Islām*), and [2] by way of negating instances of *qiyās* (*al-aqyisa al-nāfiya*)."[153]

Q's critique – a reductio in the modus tollens ($p \rightarrow q$; $\neg q \therefore \neg p$)[154] – may thus be interpreted as follows. First, the obligation of expiation must be fully concomitant with what is specific (*mukhtaṣṣ*) to the sex case. Why? Because if it isn't, then expiation could not be obliged there in the first place. Why not? Because there is a general negator (*al-nāfī*) to the obligation of expiation – for example, the principle: *lā ḍarar wa lā ḍirār* – which would simply go into effect here as it does elsewhere. The only reason it does not, in fact, is because of the "decisive counter-indicant" (*muʿāriḍ qaṭʿī*), i.e., the concomitant causation (*madāriyya*) of the case-specific thing (*mukhtaṣṣ*). Thus, in taking that away (by assuming the non-concomitance of the case-specific thing), the negator becomes "safe from decisive counter-indicant" (*sālim ʿan muʿāriḍ qaṭʿī*), and goes into effect, negating the obligation of expiation. However, we of course know that the expiation is obliged (*wājiba*) in this sex case – the case, after all, is an authoritative root-case (*aṣl*) – so it must be that there is concomitance between obligation of expiation and the case-specific thing. As al-Samarqandī puts it, evincing the modus tollens

152 Amcazade Hüseyin 403, foll. 24a–b; Landberg 72, fol. 57b. Cf. al-Samarqandī: Esad Efendi 3034, fol. 19b; Or. 11183, fol. 18a; al-Muntaqid: Ibn Taymiyya (?) 2004, 100.

153 NB: this is supported by al-Muntaqid's reference to the negator as an "*aṣl*" (Ibn Taymiyya [?] 2004, 100).

154 In this case: if obligation of expiation were not concomitant with what is specific to that case, then expiation would not be obliged in that case; but expiation is obliged in that case; so obligation of expiation is concomitant with what is specific to that case [$\neg p \rightarrow \neg q$; $\neg(\neg q) \therefore \neg(\neg p)$]. On Muslim jurists' use of reductios, Weiss notes: "(...) the favourite stratagem of the Muslim dialectician in seeking to refute his adversary was the reductio ad absurdum, the demonstration that the adversary's position led to impossible conclusions" (Weiss 1992, 40). See also Young 2016.

form of the critique: "but the implicatum (*lāzim*)[155] is negated, and likewise the implicans (*malzūm*)[156]" (¬q ∴ ¬p).

Put differently: if R assumes non-concomitance between expiation and the case-specific thing, then he has removed the decisive counter-indicant (*muʿāriḍ qaṭʿī*) which prevents that negator (for example, *lā ḍarar wa lā ḍirār*) from negating the expiation. But expiation remains obliged in the sex-case, so it must be tied to the case-specific thing. R's response – again a counter-indication by like (*muʿāraḍa bi'l-mithl*) – is a perfectly-mirrored reductio in the modus tollens, simply substituting shared thing (*mushtarak*) for case-specific thing (*mukhtaṣṣ*).

Al-Muntaqid's treatment of lemma §12 (Ibn Taymiyya [?] 2004, 100) roughly parallels the others. As we have come to expect, however, he is not satisfied with R's response. In short, it is merely destructive, not constructive: it serves only to block Q's critique, not to bolster R's case through further indication of the concomitant causation of the shared thing (*mushtarak*). Worse yet, R has in effect declared the shared thing to be of the same genus as the case-specific thing in terms of what the two indicate: presumably, obligation of expiation; and this implies, or amounts to, a concession of "causation (*ʿilliyya*) of the *madār* in the case of obligation." That is, by replying to Q with an immediate counter-indication by like, rather than giving preponderance to his shared *madār* over Q's case-specific *madār*, R has in effect conceded Q's case-specific *madār* as present in the same case as his shared-thing *madār*. It thus remains a "competing" *madār*; and R's *dawarān* cannot be validated.

§§13–14

In lemma §13, Q argues – again a reductio in the modus tollens – that although we must concede that *dawarān* takes place – there is no reason to concede that *dawarān* conveys causation of the *madār*. Why not? Because if we concede that it conveys causation of the *madār* overall, then we would have to concede its conveyance of causation in matters of chance (*umūr ittifāqiyya*). Why? Because effects (*āthār*) are things generated (*ḥāditha*) in places and times – like, as al-Nasafī illustrates, "finding treasure upon heading out to some place or other

155 A gloss in Esad Efendi 3034 reads: "that is, the non-existence of the obligation of the expiation in the case of sex."

156 A gloss in Esad Efendi 3034: "that is, the non-existence of the concomitant causation (*madāriyya*) of the case-specific thing (*mukhtaṣṣ*)." Esad Efendi 3034, foll. 19a–b; Or. 11183, fol. 18a.

(...) and likewise losing it at some time or another; and so, too, with the motions and cessations (*ḥarakāt wa sakanāt*) originating from animals, and the rest of the changes (*taghayyurāt*) occurring in the world."[157] And being generated in places and times, such effects are concomitant with them. But (we are left to assume) the causation of "at such a time" and "in such a place" for the effects which are generated at them and in them is absurd – and that absurdity (as al-Nasafī's commentary shows us) would extend to "the rest of the changes occurring in the world." He does not repeat the final phrase of Q's argument from the grundtext; it nevertheless makes plain that times and places are not causes for effects that are generated in them: "but the *madār* [i.e., some place or time] is not a cause for the *dā'ir* [i.e., some effect]."[158]

In our final lemma §14, al-Nasafī's R reminds Q that the *madār* must, in the first place, be demonstrably "right for causation" in order to be a candidate for the cause (*'illa*). Thus, if any of the mentioned "by chance" *madār*s are "right" to be causes for the mentioned effects, then R simply does not concede their non-causation. On the other hand, if none are "right," then R cares nothing for them to begin with. He has already disowned non-right *madār*s, so it would be useless for Q to wield non-right *madār*s as inconsistency cases (*masā'il al-naqḍ*) in an attempt to trap him with inconsistency (*naqḍ*).[159]

Al-Samarqandī, on the other hand, provides three separate responses to Q's fourth and final critique, the first being a more detailed reformulation of the lemma, and the second and third additions of his own devising. The first adds little to the grundtext; and in the second, R merely points out that matters of chance (*umūr ittifāqiyya*) do not fulfil the E&N requirement of *dawarān* – *madār*s must be in existence and in non-existence in order to qualify as potential causes. The third response, however, hearkens back to the empirical parallel we encountered in lemma §8.[160]

> The third: it suffices us that the *madār* is a cause (*'illa*) for our knowledge or overwhelmingly probable supposition (*li-'ilminā aw ẓanninā 'l-ghālib*) of the realization of the *dā'ir*, since this [epistemic] extent (*qadr*) suffices for the indicant (*dalīl*). So we ourselves claim

157 Amcazade Hüseyin 403, fol. 24b; Landberg 72, fol. 57b. Cf. al-Samarqandī: Esad Efendi 3034, fol. 19b; Or. 11183, fol. 18a.

158 In his *Maḥṣūl*, Fakhr al-Dīn al-Rāzī presents two arguments of those who deny that *dawarān* conveys probability (*ẓann*) of causation. A component of the first argument consists of fourteen proofs, the seventh of which is "that the place, the situated thing, the motion, the time – not one of these things is separated from the other, despite the non-existence of causation" (al-Rāzī 1992, 5:212).

159 Amcazade Hüseyin 403, fol. 24b; Landberg 72, fol. 57b.

160 Esad Efendi 3034, fol. 19b; Or. 11183, fol. 18a.

> [only] this extent, and there is no doubt that *dawarān* – in existence and in non-existence, taken along with rightness of the *madār* for the causation of the *dā'ir* – conveys as much.

We recall, in lemma §8, that al-Nasafī claimed, subsequent to the observations of the experts, "there obtains in them the probable supposition (*ẓann*) of the causation (*'illiyya*) of the *madārs* for the *dā'irs*"; and that al-Muntaqid took the implications further, claiming our obligation to follow such *dawarān* as conveys overwhelming probability (*ghalabat al-ẓann*) and is not counter-indicated by its like or by something stronger, "because this is what is necessitated of all the authoritative indicants (*adilla*)." That *dawarān* meets the minimum requirement for all authoritative indicants (*adilla*) is precisely what al-Samarqandī means by "this extent (*qadr*) suffices for the indicant (*dalīl*)"; no less is demanded of *dawarān*, and proper E&N *dawarān* with the *madār*'s rightness of causation provides the requisite "overwhelmingly probable supposition." *Dawarān* satisfies the epistemic requirements of a juristic indicant; the "matters of chance" critique is therefore irrelevant.

Al-Nasafī himself builds on the grundtext by supplying Q with a fifth objection – in fact an extension on that in lemma §13 – along with a set of responses for R. In the first part of his critique, Q claims *dawarān* cannot be assumed to be an indicant for causation of the *madār*, since there are so many instances of *dawarān* in which the *madār* is not the cause. By way of example he brings the conditions (*shurūṭ*) of conditional oaths (*ta'līqāt*); the sworn consequences (*ajziya*)[161] are concomitant with the conditions, but it is not the case that a causation (*'illiyya*) of the conditions is realised – and of course it can't be, with cause (whether *'illa* or *sabab*) and condition (*sharṭ*) usually defined in contradistinction to each other. Conditions do not "cause" their consequences, although they are concomitant with them.[162] To this Q brings further instantiation of non-conveying *dawarān:* the very relationship of cause (*'illa*) and effect (*ma'lūl*) itself suggests that *dawarān* cannot be assumed to indicate the causation – they are concomitant, but the notion that an effect might cause its own cause is of course absurd; so too the notion that fellow effects of a single cause might cause each other, despite their concomitance.[163]

---

161 The singular is *jazā'*. Among other things, it is the "final clause in a conditional sentence," which matches well with the idea of the consequent of an oath: "if [event X] happens, then I will [action Y]." Such promised actions are *ajziya*.

162 Amcazade Hüseyin 403, foll. 24b–25a; Landberg 72, foll. 57b–58a.

163 Amcazade Hüseyin 403, fol. 25a; Landberg 72, fol. 58a.

R's first response is similar to that in lemma §14: the *madār* has to be right for causation but in what you've mentioned it is not[164] – and with good reason: a condition (*sharṭ*) in a *taʿlīqa*-oath does not have "rightness" to be a cause for its *jazāʾ*-consequence; nor does an effect (*maʿlūl*) have rightness to be a cause for its own cause (*ʿilla*), nor a cause for its fellow effects.

An alternate response brought by al-Nasafī draws on a different principle. In effect, R asserts his innocence of *naqḍ*-inconsistency, since his *dawarān* claims have been only for cases in which nothing else competes with the *madār* for the causation of the *dāʾir*. In the case of the *taʿlīqāt*-oaths, however, Q specified the conditions (*shurūṭ*), and in the following instance he specified the effects (*maʿlūlāt*). These cannot be wielded as inconsistency-proving cases (*masāʾil al-naqḍ*) against R, as they engender nothing inconsistent with his conception of *dawarān*.[165]

Al-Nasafī's third and final point is important.[166]

> What is claimed is the indicative power (*dalāla*) of *dawarān* and its conveyance (*ifāda*) of the causation of the *madār*,[167] and it is not to be doubted that the non-existence of causation does not negate that conveyance. For indeed it is possible that [*dawarān*] be something which conveys (*mufīd*), but its conveyance is not evident due to an impeding factor (*māniʿ*) brought to preponderate against it (*al-rājiḥ ʿalayhi*).

Thus, even in the absence of causation of the *madār*, we should not mistakenly think that either the indicative power (*dalāla*) or conveyance (*ifāda*) of *dawarān* has been cancelled. It is, rather, still there, but overpowered by a preponderant impeding factor (*māniʿ*).

Al-Muntaqid, who treats lemmas §§13–14 together (Ibn Taymiyya [?] 2004, 101), picks up his critique by faulting the author's grammar.[168] He then explains the closing argument of lemma §14 as al-Nasafī's "response (*jawāb*) to the charge of inconsistency (*naqḍ*) via disaccompaniment (*takhalluf*) of the causation of the

---

164 Amcazade Hüseyin 403, fol. 25a; Landberg 72, fol. 58a.
165 Amcazade Hüseyin 403, fol. 25a; Landberg 72, fol. 58a.
166 Amcazade Hüseyin 403, fol. 25a; Landberg 72, fol. 58a.
167 A gloss in Amcazade Hüseyin 403 (fol. 25a): "indicative power (*dalāla*) and conveyance (*ifāda*), for there does not necessarily follow, from the non-existence of causation (*ʿilliyya*) of the *madār* for the *dāʾir*, the non-existence of the indicative power of the *dawarān* and its conveyance for the causation. For it is allowed that the *dawarān* be an indicator (*dāll*) for the causation of the *madār* for the *dāʾir* and a conveyor (*mufīd*) for it, despite the non-existence of causation, by way of the impeding factor (*māniʿ*) preponderant over it (*al-rājiḥ ʿalayhi*), so that its conveyance is not evident" (signed: Iṣfahānī).
168 Among other things, the author completes a "*law*" conditional with "*fa-lā nusallimu*" rather than "*lam nusallim*."

madār from some of the *dāʾirs*." This response is then opened to critique. First, al-Muntaqid once more highlights the ambiguity of the expression "rightness of causation" (*ṣalāḥ al-ʿilliyya*), raising possible interpretations (in fact, a return to the first three objections he raised at the start of his commentary on lemma §1). Does it mean the *madār* must be suitable (*munāsib*) to the judgment (*ḥukm*), or that there be the possibility (*imkān*) of the judgment's following from it – "such being that [the *madār*] is in a condition (*ḥāl*) whereby it is not known that it is *not* a cause (*ʿilla*)" – or does it mean something else?

If "rightness of causation" simply means "suitability" (*munāsaba*), then *dawarān* becomes superfluous. *Munāsaba* is described as something like a sufficient but not necessary condition for *ʿilla*-validation. First, "it is not a condition (*sharṭ*) for *madārs*, but another method (*ṭarīq*)[169] [of *ʿilla*-validation]." And, though al-Muntaqid does not mention this, it is always prior to *dawarān* in the hierarchies of methods found in *uṣūl* works.[170] Second, "when the suitability is complete, it suffices (*al-munāsaba idhā tammat kafat*)." So if the conveyance of causation via *dawarān* cannot be completed without first establishing the *munāsaba*-suitability of the *madār*, then what need do we have for *dawarān* at all? But if, on the other hand, "rightness of causation" simply means "unrestricted possibility" (*muṭlaq al-imkān*), then the stipulation itself becomes practically meaningless in the face of so many potentially causal – but non-actualised – *madārs*. And that multitude of "possible" causes is compounded by al-Nasafī's apparent acceptance of both E-not-N and N-not-E, in addition to E&N, *dawarān*.

Al-Muntaqid's second critique (Ibn Taymiyya [?] 2004, 102) is especially enlightening, with two excellent illustrations of how multiple *madārs* can cause problems in the absence of a further indicant (*dalīl*):

> We say: he whom we have seen giving, time after time, to a person who is scholarly, poor, and related to him – the giving (*iʿṭāʾ*) has been concomitant with these *madārs* right for causation. So if you attach the giving to the aggregate [of *madārs*], or to one specifically, before the indicant (*dalīl*), you are in error. Because you might ask the man giving, and he might say: "I gave to him only due to his being related to me" – or "due to his poverty," or "due to his knowledge" – "and I paid no heed to the other property (*waṣf*), and was not aware of it." And likewise the one who spies on or insults the Sultan and violates his sanctity (*intahaka ḥurmatahu*) multiple times; so he punishes him. It could be he would say: "I punished him only due to such-and-such, and not such-and-such." And similar [cases] are many.

169 More often *maslak* (pl. *masālik*) in *uṣūl* texts.

170 In Fakhr al-Dīn al-Rāzī's hierarchy of nine *masālik* for *ʿilla*-validation, *munāsaba* ranks #3 and *dawarān* #6; in al-Zarkashī's hierarchy of ten *masālik*, *munāsaba* ranks #5 and *dawarān* #8.

Note how a proponent of stand-alone *dawarān* might attribute causation to one, or some, of these *madār*s deemed to have "rightness of causation" (*ṣalāḥ al-ʿilliyya*), only to be confounded by the donor or Sultan himself who – in certain knowledge of his motive – identifies the cause differently.

Al-Muntaqid now turns to another problem inherent to al-Nasafī's *ṣalāḥ*-centric notion of *dawarān*. In short, his denial that any "right" *madār* not be a cause "is a denial of reality known by immediate necessity (*bi'l-ḍarūra*). This is clear should we consider R claiming the cause to be X, while the donor or Sultan confirms it to be Y; if the confessions of donor and Sultan count as immediately necessary conveyors of reality, then R's choice of cause would constitute its denial.

In his third critique, al-Muntaqid returns focus to the multitude of cases – compounded by al-Nasafī's acceptance of non-E&N *dawarān* – in which there is *dawarān* without causation (Ibn Taymiyya [?] 2004, 102). In fact, not only does he claim that there are more cases in which al-Nasafī's *dawarān* exists without causation than otherwise, he again qualifies such a claim as immediately necessary knowledge (*ʿilm ḍarūrī*).

And at the last al-Muntaqid's critique turns constructive, with a set of alternate and more accurate formulations to replace al-Nasafī's (Ibn Taymiyya [?] 2004, 102–103). One can either say: "*dawarān* conveys the causation, but falls short (*takhallafa*) in many cases due to some impeding factor (*māniʿ*)," or "it does not convey [causation], and knowledge of the causation in some cases occurs only due to something else besides *dawarān*."[171]

Al-Muntaqid now broadens the discussion to include what others have offered in terms of solutions for al-Nasafī's *dawarān* (Ibn Taymiyya [?] 2004, 103). The first is that "*dawarān* conveys causation so long as no other *madār* competes with it"; the second, that "*dawarān* conveys causation unless an indicant (*dalīl*) provides indication for *non-existence* of its causation – so an aggregate of the two things: *dawarān* and absence of knowledge of an impeding factor (*māniʿ*), conveys causation"; and the third, that "*dawarān* conveys causation of the *madār* wherever it is not specifically designated for causation."[172]

A fourth solution echoes al-Nasafī himself, in that "*dawarān* provides indication for (*yadullu ʿalā*) the causation of the *madār*, and conveys as much," and "the disaccompaniment (*takhalluf*) from [the indicant] of what is indicated (*madlūl*) by that indicant (*dalīl*), combined with an impeding factor (*māniʿ*),

171 He deems the second formula superior.

172 That is, *dawarān* is applicable only in such cases in which the *madār*-property has not been specifically designated by some other means or method – for instance, by unambiguous source-text (*naṣṣ*), or consensus (*ijmāʿ*), or a superior method of *ʿilla*-validation.

does not nullify [that indicant's] indication (*dalāla*)." And thus: "the non-existence of causation does not negate [*dawarān*'s] being a conveyor of causation, for something might be a conveyor while its conveyance is not manifest, due to the existence of the preponderant impeding factor (*al-māniʿ al-rājiḥ*)."

A fifth and final solution is in fact al-Muntaqid's reformulation of al-Nasafī's *dawarān:*

> *Dawarān* conveys the causation of the *madār* when it is right for causal justification (*ṣāliḥan li'l-taʿlīl*); so if the *madār* is right (*ṣāliḥ*), its destruction-by-inconsistency (*intiqāḍ*) is not conceded, and if it is destroyed by inconsistency (*intaqaḍa*), its rightness of causation is not conceded. And this is the response (*jawāb*) of the author.

Although we may not have heard al-Nasafī articulate this reciprocity between *madār*s and inconsistency (*naqḍ*) in al-Nasafī's own texts, it is difficult to imagine how else one could judge a *madār* thus proven inconsistent. In fact, what al-Muntaqid has done here is first to equate al-Nasafī's "rightness of causation" (*ṣulūḥ al-ʿilliyya*) to rightness, or validity, for causal-justification (*taʿlīl*), as did al-Samarqandī in his commentary on §1, and as al-Muntaqid confirms in his closing remark, below. He then equates (and not without reason) rightness / validity for causal-justification with freedom from inconsistency (*naqḍ*), which, as we have seen, was a critical stipulation of those who are satisfied with mere co-prensence (*ṭard*). So, in his final estimation, al-Nasafī's *dawarān* demands only concomitance and that the *madār* be safe from inconsistency (*naqḍ*).

And having attributed as much to the author, al-Muntaqid of course critiques it (Ibn Taymiyya [?] 2004, 103). In short, if the real meaning of "*madār* X's rightness for causal-justification (*taʿlīl*)" is "validity (*ṣiḥḥa*) and possibility (*imkān*) of causal-justification by way of *madār* X,"[173] then it should never be the case that "right" *madār*s exhibit non-causation. However – and note this itself is a broader charge of inconsistency (*naqḍ*) – we know with the epistemic strength of "immediate necessity" (*iḍṭirār*) that there exist "right" *madār*s divorced of causation. Ultimately, we must go further than the "no-*naqḍ*" requirement, for we know without doubt there are inconsistency-free *madār*s which are nevertheless not causes.

173 Cf. al-Samarqandī's explanation of the lemma *ṣulūḥ al-ʿilliyya* in his commentary on §1.

4 Implications

What we have witnessed in this complex of arguments, though only a small cutting from a larger tapestry of Islamic juristic debate on concomitance, is sophisticated enough on its own merits to count as a worthy addition to the intellectual-historical inquiry into causality. The nature of *dawarān* has been vigorously analysed and expanded upon with variant definitions, typologies, new rules and principles, and exhaustive treatments of logical implications. At the same time, all of our authors (not only al-Muntaqid) problematised and dismantled certain conceptions of *dawarān*, whether in terms of its definition, precise nature, epistemic power, or method. The grundtext's illustrative example was likewise critiqued, whether in terms of its overall conception, its players' arguments, or its betrayal of some condition proper to *dawarān* (or to dialectic). Importantly, our authors reported and responded to further critiques, exposing areas of ongoing contention – a dialectic on *dawarān*. All of this of course unfolded in a context of juristic dialectic, our authors putting forward observations, rules, strategies, and strategy-critiques of use to the disputant, especially when reviewing the illustrative example of fast-breaking and expiation. And in the end, a number of positions and pronouncements on *dawarān*'s potential for conveying causation were introduced, altered, and corrected.

Again, this vibrant commentators' web is worthy of study in its own regard. But, as we have also seen, it teases with implications: not only for the development of argumentative sciences in Islam, but for the World intellectual-historical inquiry into causality. Before concluding this study, I would like to touch briefly on certain themes, with the hope they might draw further attention to the topic of *dawarān*; mainly, (1) links to prior and contemporaneous notions, such as Ibn Sīnā's "experience" (*tajriba*), (2) the apparent merging of "intellective" (*ʿaqliyya*) and "juristic" (*sharʿiyya*) causation, (3) the smooth transition of *dawarān* from al-Nasafī's juristic *jadal* to al-Samarqandī's universal *ādāb al-baḥth*, and (4) parallels in modern theories relevant to causal inquiry. What follows is a very preliminary look at some intriguing areas I hope might eventually be pursued more fully.

4.1 Connected Texts

Many characteristics of proto- and early *ādāb al-baḥth* might be labelled "post-Rāzian Avicennan"; we would thus be justified in inaugurating a search through preceding intellectual currents in select works of Ibn Sīnā (d. 428/1037) and

Fakhr al-Dīn al-Rāzī (d. 606/1210). Of course, debating *dawarān* in the *uṣūl* literature (as *ṭard* and *ʿaks*, for instance) far predates Ibn Sīnā. Nonetheless, we are compelled by evident parallels to examine Ibn Sīnā's notion of experience (*tajriba*). Note, however, that the term *dawarān* appears nowhere in the *Manṭiq* of the *Shifāʾ* in its technical sense, nor even in the *Qānūn fī ʾl-Ṭibb* (despite its many scammony examples). Nor do *madār* and *dāʾir* appear anywhere in these texts with anything like their technical meanings.

There is, however, an interesting parallel in Avicenna's thought to the shadowy interplay between the "intellective" (*ʿaqliyya*) and "legal" (*sharʿiyya*) causes. In discussing Avicenna's notion of "causal reciprocity," Robert Wisnovsky observes (1994, 35 and n. 130): "what really seems to interest Avicenna is the notion that the middle term both behaves as a cause within the syllogism but also causes the thing in the real world, so that the middle term thereby serves as a link between language and reality."[174] This becomes especially interesting when we consider the categorical rendering of cause-judgment pairs as we find them, for instance, serving as classic examples of demonstration (*burhān*) in Ibn Qudāma's (d. 620/1223) *Rawḍat al-Nāẓir* (2002, 1:80): "every date-wine (*nabīdh*) is an intoxicant (*muskir*), and every intoxicant is forbidden (*ḥarām*), therefore every date-wine is forbidden."[175] We are in the normative realm, but as with Ibn Sīnā, the cause (being an intoxicant) is the middle term. One might ask whether the middle term qua "legal cause" thus links the overall legal pronouncement to the normative "reality" of God's *Sharīʿa* in a manner parallel to the way in which the "intellective cause" links, for instance, empirical propositions to the "reality" of God's cosmos.

And as for Ibn Sīnā's notion of *tajriba*, or "experience,"[176] ʿAlī Sāmī al-Nashshār (1984, 126) observes that legal theoreticians were cognizant of the connection, or even identity, between *dawarān* and *tajriba*, saying: "*dawarān* is based on *tajriba* – indeed, the *uṣūlī*s considered them to be one and the

---

174 Citing the *Burhān* (ʿAfīfī ed., 71), and transliterating the relevant passage. Returned to Arabic type, it reads: [وكثيرا ما يتفق أن يكون الحد الأوسط في القياس وهو علة القياس علة أيضا للأمر في نفسه فيكون قد اجتمع المطلبان معا في بيان واحد].

175 The full passage reads: [كل نبيذ مسكر وكل مسكر حرام فيلزم منه أن كل نبيذ حرام ضرورة متى سلمت المقدمتان إذ كل عقل صدّق بالمقدمتين صدّق بالنتيجة مهما أحضرهما في الذهن].

176 The most pertinent discussion on *tajriba* – including two Q&A exchanges and the scammony example – is in the *Burhān* of the *Manṭiq* of the *Shifāʾ*, *maqāla* 1, *faṣl* 9 (*fī kayfiyyat taʿarruf mā laysa li-maḥmūlihi sabab fī mawḍūʿihi, wa fī ʾl-istiqrāʾ wa mūjibihi waʾl-tajriba wa mūjibihā*; ʿAfīfī ed., 93–98). Note that besides a thorough treatment in McGinnis 2003, the whole section of interest has been translated in McGinnis and Reisman 2007, 147–152.

same." He then quotes al-Qarāfī's (d. 684/1285) *Nafā'is al-Uṣūl fī Sharḥ al-Maḥṣūl:*

> The *dawarāns* are *tajriba* itself; and *tajriba* might recur with frequency and so convey certainty (*al-qaṭ'*), and it might not arrive at such. Decapitation is something which entails death with certainty; but we [merely] presume it with poison.

Then, from the same source, al-Nashshār cites none other than Raḍī 'l-Dīn al-Nīsābūrī (fl. 582/1186), teacher of Rukn al-Dīn al-'Amīdī (d. 615/1218) – intellectual predecessor to al-Nasafī:

> The *dawarāns* which indicate the causation (*'illiyya*) of the *madār* are very many, beyond enumeration; and that is because a great many precepts of medicine (*qawā'id 'ilm al-ṭibb*) are established only by way of *tajriba* – which is *dawarān* itself. Such being like purgation, and heat, and cold – for they are concomitant with the ingestion of certain medicines and nutriments, in existence and in non-existence (*wujūdan wa 'adaman*).

Ibn Sīnā himself makes a clear distinction between *tajriba* and induction;[177] and, as in *dawarān*, repetition of observations plays a central role.[178] Moreover, the purgative power of scammony is Ibn Sīnā's standard example for the *mujarrabāt*, described by Dimitri Gutas (2012, 396) as propositions based on "tested and proven data (...) things whose proof is acknowledged by testing repeated experience [*tajriba*], through the formation of a syllogism, that proves the stated proposition." And, of course, Ibn Sīnā instantiates *tajriba* with drinking scammony. In McGinnis's translation (2003, 317) from the *Burhān:* "[it] is like our judgement that the scammony plant is a purgative for bile; for since this [phenomenon] is repeated many times, one abandons that it is among the things which occur by chance, so the mind judged that it belongs to the character of scammony to purge bile and [the mind] gave into it, that is, purging bile is an intrinsic characteristic (*'araḍ lâzim*) belonging to scammony."[179]

With *tajriba*, repeated observations of scammony purging bile allow us to rule out coincidence;[180] this is fully consonant with our understanding of E-not-N *dawarān* ruling out "chance occurrences" (*umūr ittifāqiyya*). And, against an interpretation that "the sheer volume of positive cases" alone points

---

177 Gutas 2012, 428–430; McGinnis 2003, 317; Richardson 2015, §4.1. See also McGinnis 2008, 146, wherein the relevant text from Ibn Sīnā is translated (and includes a scammony example).
178 Gutas 2012, 399; Richardson 2015, §4.1.
179 Not surprisingly, scammony features prominently in Ibn Sīnā's *Qānūn fī 'l-Ṭibb*. See especially its description and applications in the encyclopaedic listing of *materia medica* (Ibn Sīnā 1999, 1:593–594; Ibn Sīnā 1993–1998, vol. 2 [Book II], 262–264).
180 McGinnis 2003, 317–318.

to causation, McGinnis posits: "one could emphasize the absence of 'falsifying instances'; or in Ibn Sīnā's words, the fact that 'it does not turn out that there is anything arbitrary [*ikhtiyār*],'" with the advantage being that "the number of positive cases does not convince one of the necessary relation; rather, the lack of any negative cases or falsifying instances indicates a non-accidental power belongs to scammony to purge." This, of course, is a clear parallel to what we have suggested of *dawarān*'s "no-*naqḍ*, no-*muʿāraḍa*" falsification scheme. Moreover, McGinnis (2003, 318) supports his interpretation with two further claims by Ibn Sīnā, both of which parallel notions we have encountered in *dawarān:* (1) *tajriba* does not perform an exhaustive survey of cases (such is the job of induction); and (2) "multiple observations alone are not sufficient to produce necessary knowledge."[181]

Ibn Sīnā's *tajriba* also parallels *dawarān*'s need for an additional indicant (*dalīl*) for the causation of the *madār*.[182] As Gutas (2012, 399) explains:

> At an initial stage (...) experiences are something repeatedly perceived. But to express an epistemologically proven and true proposition they need to be associated with a syllogism which attributes the observed repeated occurrence to some intrinsic cause, like the essential nature of something. In the example of the scammony, the experience of the repeatedly observed fact, that it causes purging, is taken as the conclusion of a syllogism whose middle term, which provides the cause, is the nature of scammony, and that is that it has the power to purge.

And, moreover, the procedure by which the middle term is arrived at parallels the legal theoreticians' procedure of analytical division (*al-sabr wa'l-taqsīm*).[183]

Yet another parallel arises in Ibn Sīnā's response to a counter-example wherein an instance of supposed *tajriba* is shown to lead to a false conclusion. In brief, the knowledge gained through *tajriba* is universal, but conditional, in that "this thing which is repeated to the senses adheres to its nature as an ongoing thing with respect to the domain in which it is repeated to the senses, *unless there is an obstacle*."[184] The word for "obstacle" employed by Ibn Sīnā (1956, 96, end of line 6) is *māniʿ*, and both word and notion match what we have seen in our *dawarān* commentary. Likewise, in concluding his response, Ibn Sīnā says (in McGinnis's translation [2003, 325]):[185]

181 See also McGinnis 2008, 146.
182 Gutas 2012, 399–400.
183 See, for example, McGinnis 2003, 319–320.
184 McGinnis 2003, 323; translation is McGinnis's, italics are mine.
185 See also McGinnis 2008, 147.

> Thus, we also do not disallow that in some country a disposition (*mizāj*) and proprium (*khāṣṣīya*) is associated with scammony not to purge (or there is absent in it a disposition and proprium [to purge]); however, it is necessary that the experimental judgement we possess is that the scammony commonplace to us and perceived [before us], either from its essence or from the nature (*ṭab*ʿ) in it purges bile, unless it is opposed by an obstacle.

The word McGinnis translates "obstacle," again, is *mānī*ʿ;[186] and in similar fashion we have seen al-Samarqandī problematise *dawarān* due to the presence of a *mānī*ʿ like climate and humour.

A final parallel arises when McGinnis (2003, 325) describes a major problem for *tajriba:* the linking of judgments to accidental rather than essential properties, and the three ways it occurs. Importantly, from the vantage of *dawarān* discourse, none of the properties discussed exhibit "rightness for causation" (*ṣulūḥ al-ʿilliyya*); they are *madār*s but not causes.

Turning to Fakhr al-Dīn al-Rāzī, we find, in his *Maḥṣūl* (1992, 5:207), a relatively standard *uṣūlī* account of *dawarān*. It is "that the judgment (*ḥukm*) be confirmed upon confirmation of a property (*waṣf*), and negated upon its negation;" it occurs within single or between multiple cases, and conveys probability (*ẓann*) of causation (*ʿilliyya*), although others claim certainty (*yaqīn*) of causation, or neither certainty nor probability.[187]

His first of two arguments supporting probability is as follows: the cause (*ʿilla*) is either the [concomitant] property (*waṣf*; he never uses the term *madār*) or something else [X]; and if the property then the proof is finished. If the something else [X], however, then [X] is either existent before the judgment (*ḥukm*) or not existent before the judgment. If before, then there is an untenable disaccompaniment (*takhalluf*) of the judgment from the cause; if not before, then the default condition (*aṣl*) is that things remain as they are – so there is probability (*ẓann*) that [X] remains *not* a cause. And, therefore, there is probability that the property (not [X]) is the cause.

Against this he introduces a critique we would recognize as the problem of multiple *madār*s: the judgment is concomitant with other things – viz. specification (*taʿayyun*) of that property (*waṣf*), and occurrence of the actualization (*ḥuṣūl*) of that property in that locus – so these must also be considered for causation; and, thus, general extendibility (*taʿdiya*) of the property is denied. His response, in brief, is first to demonstrate that both this specification and this actualization are things qualified by non-existence (*ʿadamī*), and so can be nei-

186 See Ibn Sīnā 1956, 97, end of line 14.

187 On al-Rāzī's account of *dawarān* in the *Maḥṣūl*, see also Hasan 1986a, 318, 321–323.

ther causes (*ʿilal*) nor parts of causes, and then to demonstrate why not (al-Rāzī 1992, 5:208–210).

His second of two arguments supporting probability (1992, 5:210) is simply that: (1) some *dawarān*s convey probability of the causation, so (2) it is necessary that all *dawarān*s do the same. His explanation of (1) is via the familiar example of name-calling making someone angry: repeated observation of *dawarān* between name-calling and anger actualises probability in the observer. Importantly, he adds:

> That probability (*ẓann*) is actualised only from that *dawarān*, because if it is said to people: why do you believe that? They would say: due to the fact that we saw the anger with that name-calling time after time (*marratan baʿda ukhrā*). So they justified the cause (*ʿilla*) with probability via the *dawarān*.

We recognize this "time after time" stipulation as a critical component of al-Nasafī's *dawarān*, and of *tajriba*, and key to the exclusion of chance occurrences. As for his explanation of (2), it is via Q. 16:90: "verily God commands justice (*ʿadl*) and doing good (*iḥṣān*)." Al-Rāzī explains (1992, 5:210–211) that justice (*ʿadl*) means equalization (*taswiya*), "and equalization does not occur among *dawarān*s except after their sharing in the conveyance of probability (*ẓann*)."

Shifting to the opposition (1992, 5:211–216), al-Rāzī reports the first of two arguments denying *dawarān*'s conveyance of probability: (A) some *dawarān*s don't convey probability of the causation, so (B) it is necessary that no *dawarān*s convey probability of the causation. This we might recognize as the opponent's "counter-indication by like" (*muʿāraḍa bi'l-mithl*). And al-Rāzī's explanation of (A) contains no less than fourteen proofs, most of which point to non-causative E&N concomitants, for instance: substance and accident; place, situated thing, motion, and time; definiens and definiendum; the smell of wine and its proscription; and so on. In brief, the assumption that some other *dawarān* necessarily entails causation would mean either (1) this entailment depends on the joining of something else to it, or (2) it does not. If the first, then *dawarān* alone does not entail causation. The second option, however, calls for an absurd giving of causal preponderance to one of the two concomitants due to something other than a properly preponderance-giving factor (*lā li-murajjiḥ*).

The response to this first opposing argument is a more general version of what we have called the "no-*naqḍ*, no-*muʿāraḍa*" requirement. Whoever argues so, al-Rāzī says, only rejects causation of *dawarān by itself*, "but we don't say that (...), we claim that *dawarān* conveys the probability of causation with the condition (*bi-sharṭ*) that no indicant (*dalīl*) rejecting its being a cause is established against it." Again, we might see in this something like a precursor to the stipulation of falsifiability in proper scientific method.[188]

And as for the second argument opposing *dawarān*'s conveyance of probability, it is an ancient argument related in many *uṣūl* texts, and we have also seen it in al-Muntaqid's preliminaries. In brief, co-presence (*iṭṭirād*) alone does not prove causation, and co-absence (*inʿikās*) is not considered relevant for legal causes (*al-ʿilal al-sharʿiyya*); and if neither indicates causation individually, then it cannot be that their aggregate does. Al-Rāzī's response conforms to what is reported elsewhere:

> Why did you say that when each one of them doesn't convey probability of causation, it is necessary that the aggregate (*majmūʿ*) be likewise? For indeed we know that the state (*ḥāl*) of the aggregate might be opposed to the state of each one of its parts.

Beyond Ibn Sīnā and al-Rāzī, intriguing parallels are to be found in key logic manuals of al-Nasafī's time and after. In fact, al-Nashshār (1984, 72) proposes that latter-day logicians, in their research into analogy (*tamthīl*), laboured under the influence of *uṣūlī* studies to the extent that they differed entirely from Aristotle. The extent to which this is true or not might be gleaned from the popular logic treatises of al-Kātibī al-Qazwīnī (d. 657/1276) and Saʿd al-Dīn al-Taftāzānī (d. 793/1390).

Dawarān is indeed mentioned, as a means of establishing analogy (*tamthīl*), in al-Kātibī's *Shamsiyya* (1854, 36–37, §94); it is judged, however, along with a kind of disjunctive analytical division (*taqsīm*), to be a weak method for confirming causation.[189] As for *dawarān*, we are only told it is weak because: "the last part of the cause (*ʿilla*) and the rest of the conditions (*shurūṭ*) are a *madār* despite the fact that they are not a cause," a familiar enough argument. And the explanation as to why *taqsīm* is in fact denied (*mamnūʿ*) contains yet further parallels. *Taqsīm* is denied because of: (1) the "allowance of the causation (*ʿilliyya*) of something besides what was mentioned;" and (2) "assuming concession of causation of the shared thing (*mushtarak*) in the root-analogue (*al-maqīs ʿalayhi*) does not necessarily entail a causation in the branch-analogue (*al-maqīs*), due to the allowance that the specificity (*khuṣūṣiyya*) of the root-analogue be a condition (*sharṭ*) for the causation, or the specificity of the branch-analogue be an impeding factor (*māniʿa*) for it."[190] We are reminded by this "specificity" critique

188 See our discussion in 4.4, below.
189 I am indebted to Khaled El-Rouayheb for directing my attention to treatments of *dawarān* in both al-Kātibī's *Shamsiyya* and al-Taftāzānī's *Tahdhīb*.
190 Cf. Sprenger's translation, 33, §96.

of the case-specific (*mukhtaṣṣ*) *madār* argument in al-Nasafī's illustration (lemmas §§11–12), and of the cause-suppressing potentials of condition (*sharṭ*) and impeding factor (*māniʿ*).

Despite this, *dawarān* discourse in al-Kātibī does not much resemble what we see in al-Nasafī and commentators. In his commentary on the *Shamsiyya*, even al-Taftāzānī (2011, 366), though recognizing that theologians call analogy (*tamthīl*) "drawing indication via the perceptible for the imperceptible" (*istidlāl bi'l-shāhid ʿalā 'l-ghā'ib*), and jurists call it *qiyās*, nevertheless maintains a distinction and describes each separately. His attempt to improve on al-Kātibī's definition of analogy, for example, certainly brings it no closer to juristic definitions. But his treatment of "specific" *dawarān* (*al-dawarān al-khāṣṣ*)[191] is quite familiar. *Dawarān* is "the following (*tarattub*) of the judgment (*ḥukm*) from the thing that has a rightness of causation (*ṣulūḥ al-ʿilliyya*) for that judgment, in existence or [sic][192] in non-existence." The "judgment" is the *dā'ir*, the "thing" is a *madār*, and "*dawarān* is a sign (*ʿalāma*) of the *madār*'s being a cause (*ʿilla*) for the *dā'ir*, but it does not convey certainty."

Al-Taftāzānī (2011, 366) proceeds to two critiques; the second we would recognize as the existence of known, non-causal *madār*s. The first is more unique.

> Following (*tartīb*) in existence and in non-existence in [only] some cases does not convey causation (*ʿilliyya*); and in all [cases] is only by way of total induction (*istiqrā' tāmm*), and such is impossible or impractical. And if it is testified to in some other way, it reverts to the form of syllogism whose middle term is the uniting thing (*jāmiʿ*), for instance, "The heavens are composite, and all composite things are incipient things," so it can do without the root-analogue (*aṣl*) of the analogy and the remainder of the *dawarān*'s premises.

Thus *dawarān*, in the end, is either unproductive, impossible, or superfluous.

Of course, here al-Taftāzānī attributes this critiqued conception of *dawarān* only to the jurists.[193] In his own *Tahdhīb al-Manṭiq*, *dawarān* – though only briefly mentioned – appears a method (*ṭarīq*) for analogy (*tamthīl*), generally.[194] The commentaries on the *Tahdhīb* make plain, however, that this *dawarān* is that of the proto- and early *ādāb al-baḥth*. In fact, early twentieth-century glossators on al-Dasūqī's (d. 1230/1815) *Ḥāshiya* directly cite from the *Masʿūdī*, perhaps the

---

191 Cf. the "particular" *dawarān* of Quṭb al-Dīn al-Kīlānī and Masʿūd al-Shirwānī al-Rūmī, below in 4.3.

192 This "or" is probably a scribal or editorial error, and should be "and."

193 al-Taftazānī 2011, 366, ln. 1, *wa-lahum* refers back to *al-fuqahā'*.

194 al-Maḥallī, al-Taftazānī, and al-Kurdī 1913, 202; al-Yazdī 1405 [1984], 108.

most famous commentary on al-Samarqandī's *Risāla fī Ādāb al-baḥth.*[195] And al-Yazdī (d. 981/1573) directs us to "the multiple methods detailed in the books of *uṣūl al-fiqh*" for *ʿilla*-validation (al-Yazdī 1405 [1984], 108). His definition of *dawarān*, however, with its example of the life-cycle of wine, is very familiar; *dawarān* is the "following (*tarattub*) of the judgment (*ḥukm*) from the property (*waṣf*) which has 'rightness for causation' (*ṣalāḥiyyat al-ʿilliyya),* in existence and in non-existence."[196]

Al-ʿAllāma al-Ḥillī (d. 726/1325) – who, like al-Samarqandī, was a student of al-Nasafī – did not share his teacher's confidence in *dawarān*. Then again this should not surprise us, considering the general rejection of juristic *qiyās* in Imāmī Shīʿī circles.[197] In his commentary on the *Shamsiyya* (1412 [1992], 389), he first translates al-Kātibī's logical elements into the familiar terms of legal theory, then reports, among other things, that it is said: "*dawarān* of something with something else provides overwhelming probability (*yaghlibu ʿalā 'l-ẓann*) for the causation of the *madār* for the *dāʾir*." His final assessment (390), however, is in conformity with al-Kātibī's: *dawarān* is weak. Al-Quṭb al-Rāzī al-Taḥtānī (d. 766/1364), following more or less the same approach as al-Ḥillī, also asserts that *dawarān* is weak.[198]

As for al-Ḥillī's commentary on the *Tajrīd* of Naṣīr al-Dīn al-Ṭūsī (d. 672/1274), there is no mention of *dawarān* in the section on analogy (*tamthīl*) (1990, 297–298). Here, however, his explanation of the incapacity of analogy to produce certainty more or less matches the *dawarān* critiques of al-Kātibī and al-Taftāzānī. Even the strongest type of analogy/*qiyās* does not convey certainty, due to the possibility that the cause be specific only to the root-case (*aṣl*), or that there be a suppressing condition in the root-case, or impeding factor in the branch-case (*farʿ*). And if ever free of all this, it becomes superfluous anyway – the root-case mere "stuffing" (*ḥashw*), as the analogy becomes a demonstrative syllogism (*qiyās burhānī*). Al-Ḥillī concludes (298): "and know that analogy (*tamthīl*) resembles *qiyās* were it not for the root-case, insofar as the uniting thing (*jāmiʿ*) occurs as a middle term between the minor and major [premises]."

Upon reflection, there is a warning we might take away from these treatments of *dawarān* in logic manuals and commentaries: they are not representa-

---

195 al-Dasūqī, al-Khabīṣī, and al-Taftāzānī 1328 [1910], 240, top right margin. We will review part of Masʿūd's commentary, below, in section 4.3.

196 See also al-Maḥallī, al-Taftazānī, and al-Kurdī 1913, 202.

197 See Gleave 2002, especially 288–289, for al-Ḥillī's arguments, including his rejection of *dawarān.*

198 See al-Rāzī al-Taḥtānī, al-Kātibī al-Qazwīnī, and al-Jurjānī 2003, 455.

tive of the complexity of contemporaneous juristic discourse – even when the authors were intimately connected to it. Whatever the reason, should one only have read these brief, negative assessments of *dawarān*, one would never even suspect the sophisticated analyses and vibrant debates we have witnessed between al-Nasafī, al-Samarqandī, and al-Muntaqid.

For our final connected texts, we will turn to Ibn Taymiyya, who – whether or not he was the author of the critical work in the Rampur manuscript – was clearly conversant with the *dawarān* discourse of his day. Moreover, his assessment of *dawarān*, in conjunction with other modes of *ʿilla*-validation, is consonant with that in the Rampur manuscript. Whatever its attribution, Ibn Taymiyya himself demonstrates, in other works unquestionably his, the impact of *dawarān* debate in his own thought – and thus himself becomes a conduit for this discourse in wider circles. In his *Kitāb al-Radd ʿalā ʾl-Manṭiqiyyīn* (1976, 93; 2005, 134–135),[199] in a longer discussion on the nature of experience-based propositions (*mujarrabāt*; *tajribiyyāt*), Ibn Taymiyya marks *dawarān* and *munāsaba* as the two foundations of experience (*tajriba*); he also plays up the role of analytical division (*al-sabr waʾl-taqsīm*) in determining the cause.[200]

> Experience (*tajriba*) occurs by way of one's examination (*naẓar*) and consideration (*iʿtibār*) and contemplation (*tadabbur*), like the actualization of the specified effect (*athar muʿayyan*) as a *dāʾir* with the specified effector (*muʾaththir muʿayyan*), perpetually. For one sees this habitually and constantly (*ʿādatan mustamirratan*), especially if one perceives the suitable cause (*sabab munāsib*). So one joins "suitability" (*munāsaba*) to "concomitance" (*dawarān*), along with "analytical division" (*al-sabr waʾl-taqsīm*) – for indeed, in all of this there has to be analytical division, which negates the competing [property] (*al-muzāḥim*). Otherwise, when the effect occurs as associated (*maqrūn*) with two things, its attachment to one and not the other won't be more appropriate than the other way round, nor its attachment to both of them. And that by which the jurists draw proof, in confirming the property's being the cause (*ʿilla*) of the judgment (*ḥukm*), of *dawarān* and suitability (*munāsaba*) and other things, conveys the aimed-at conclusion (*maqṣūd*) only with the negation of the competing [property] (*nafī ʾl-muzāḥim*). And this is known via analytical division. And if the negation of the competing [property] is probable (*ẓannī*), then the belief in the causation (*ʿilliyya*) is probable; and if it is certain (*qaṭʿī*), then the belief is certain – when it is decisive (*qāṭiʿ*) that the judgment (*ḥukm*) must have a cause, and decisive that

199 On Ibn Taymiyya's *Radd*, see Hallaq 1993. Note that, as Hallaq explains in his introduction, the work translated is not Ibn Taymiyya's *Radd* (= *Naṣīḥat Ahl al-Īmān fī ʾl-Radd ʿalā Manṭiq al-Yunān*), but Jalāl al-Dīn al-Suyūṭī's (d. 911/1505) faithful abridgment of the same: the *Jahd al-Qarīḥa fī Tajrīd al-Naṣīḥa*. For a detailed survey of Ibn Taymiyya's critique of peripatetic logic see also al-Nashshār 1984, 187–282.

200 Importantly, in *Majmūʿ al-Fatāwā*, Ibn Taymiyya also discusses the necessity of analytical division (*al-sabr waʾl-taqsīm*), in conjunction with *dawarān*, i.e., with *dawarān* as a mode of confirmation during the procedure of analytical division (Ibn Taymiyya 1995, 25:244).

> nothing is right (*yaṣluḥu*) for the cause except for such-and-such a property (*waṣf*). And likewise of this kind are the customary propositions (*al-qaḍāyā al-ʿādiyya*) among those of medicine (*al-ṭibb*), and other [sciences]; and likewise of this kind are the propositions of syntax (*al-naḥw*) and inflection (*al-taṣrīf*), and Arabic linguistics (*al-lugha*).

And in his *al-Jawāb al-Ṣaḥīḥ li-man Baddala Dīn al-Masīḥ* (1999, 6:415–416), Ibn Taymiyya argues a proof for Muḥammad's prophethood – E&N concomitance between obeying Muḥammad and victory – employing the more circumscribed *dawarān* supported by al-Muntaqid.[201]

> And the *madār* for victory and mastery is the following of the Prophet, in existence and in non-existence, without a cause (*sabab*) competing with that; and *dawarān* of the judgment (*ḥukm*) with the property (*waṣf*), in existence and in non-existence, without the competition (*muzāḥama*) of another property, is a necessitator (*mūjib*) of the knowledge that the *madār* is a cause (*ʿilla*) of the *dāʾir*. And our saying: "without the competition (*muzāḥama*) of another property" eliminates contravening inconsistencies (*nuqūḍ*); so this inductive and successive investigation (*al-istiqrāʾ wa'l-tatabbuʿ*) clarifies that the victory of God and His giving mastery are because of (*bi-sabab*) the following of the Prophet.

4.2 What Happened to the Distinction Between Intellective and Legal Causes?

Accounts of the distinction between intellective causes (*ʿilal ʿaqliyya*) and legal causes (*ʿilal sharʿiyya*) may be found in a variety of sources. Here, we will draw upon: (1) the fourth-/tenth-century historian Muṭahhar b. Ṭāhir al-Maqdisī, in the opening chapter – devoted entirely to dialectical theory – of his *Kitāb al-Bad' wa'l-Taʾrīkh* (1899–1919, 1:31 [Fr. trans. 28]);[202] (2) the renowned *uṣūlī* and dialectical theorist Abū Isḥāq al-Shīrāzī (d. 476/1083), in his *Kitāb al-Lumaʿ* (2013, 262–263); and (3) the famed *uṣūlī* Badr al-Dīn al-Zarkashī (d. 794/1392), in his encyclopaedic *Baḥr al-Muḥīṭ* (1992, 5:114).[203] In collating these accounts, we arrive at the following summary of distinctions.

---

201 Other examples may be found. In one *fatwā* Ibn Taymiyya employs a consonant mode of *dawarān* in the course of argument over a problem-case of purity – viz. the status of human sperm and that of pure beasts (Ibn Taymiyya 1987, 1:372, and 21:540), and he does so again in another *fatwā*, in the course of argument over a problem-case of dry ablution (*tayammum*) – viz. its precise effect on minor ritual impurity (*ḥadath*) (Ibn Taymiyya 1995, 21:352).

202 Miller includes al-Maqdisī among his theologian dialecticians and (1984, 17–21) takes note of this discussion, citing Huart's ed. of the *Bad' wa'l-Tārīkh*, and van Ess's treatment of this passage in his "Logical Structure of Islamic Theology," 36.

203 See also Hasan 1986a, 172, 174, 184–185.

intellective cause (*ʿilla ʿaqliyya*)	legal cause (*ʿilla sharʿiyya*)
– a necessitator (*mūjib*) by way of its essence (*dhāt*) – cannot exist in a state (*ḥāl*) without necessitating – necessitates judgment (*ḥukm*) by itself	– a probable sign (*amāra*) and indication (*dalāla*) for the judgment; (some say necessitator [*mūjib*] after being appointed) – can exist in a state (*ḥāl*) without necessitating – itself an effect of a preceding cause
– a cause in itself, not via the appointing of an appointer (*bi-jaʿl jāʿil*)	– becomes a cause via the appointing of an appointer; comes to something and changes its judgment (*ḥukm*)
– not temporally prior to its effects – not changing in different times	– peculiar to one time not another, but not one individual and not another – existent before God's Law (but not occasioning the ruling then)
– cause in literal sense (*ḥaqīqa*)	– cause in tropical sense (*majāz*), or by extension (*ittisāʿan*)
– like the motion of the thing in motion (*ḥarakat al-mutaḥarrik*), and the stasis of the unmoving (*sukūn al-sākin*)	– like intoxication with regard to wine

And to these we might add an important derivative distinction, for, as we have seen, *ʿaks* (co-absence) is not a necessary condition (*sharṭ*) for the legal cause. Indeed, this distinction is incorporated by Ibn Qudāma (d. 620/1223) into his explanation of what distinguishes the legal cause from a condition itself (2002, 2:100): "the cause (*ʿilla*) is such as from whose existence is entailed the existence of the effect (*maʿlūl*), but from whose non-existence is not entailed its non-existence, in the cases of God's Law (*sharʿiyyāt*)." And in his *Kāfiya fī 'l-Jadal* (1979, 68, §163), Imām al-Ḥaramayn al-Juwaynī (d. 478/1085) notes: "the required condition for efficiency (*sharṭ al-taʾthīr*) is not the loss of the ruling due to the loss of the cause (*ʿilla*) – this is the condition of co-absence (*sharṭ al-ʿaks*), and such is obliged only for intellective causes (*ʿilal al-ʿaql*); loss of efficiency for legal causes (*ʿilal al-Sharʿ*) might be for all the properties of the cause and for some of them."[204]

204 See also Young 2017, 161. The introduction (*muqaddima*) of the early theoretician al-Khaffāf's (fl. early fourth/tenth century) *al-Aqsām wa'l-Khiṣāl* has a section on the intellective and legal cause, as noted by its editor Ahmed El Shamsy (in El Shamsy 2017, 512; the relevant passage is no. 28 on 531). Further on the distinction between intellective and legal causes in the context of dialectical theory, see: Ibn Fūrak 2005, 321.

To be certain, interpretational divisions are evident, but the key contention was pragmatic. Aron Zysow (2013, 220) best captures the focus of debate as "the assimilation of legal to rational causes." As for the "for" camp, he recognizes that the earlier, predominantly Shāfiʿī "formalist methods" of *dawarān* "rest on the assumption that the methods of the rational sciences are suitable for law." And despite variant justifications, it was understood that "the causes of the natural world are consistent and convertible, and this standard is applicable to the causes of the law." Particularly impacted was the method of *ṭard* (co-presence), but the justification of full E&N *dawarān* through this parallelism was inevitable.

As for the "against" camp, however, "this assimilation of legal to rational causes was repudiated by the Muʿtazilī master Abū ʿAbd Allāh al-Baṣrī [d.436/1044], who explained that the two fields differed in subject matter and that the one cause could not be treated like the other 'because the former really necessitates while the latter is like a sign and a motive'" (Zysow 2013, 220–221). And Sayf al-Dīn al-Āmidī (d. 631/1233) cites (2003, 4:12–13) the great Baṣran Muʿtazilī al-Naẓẓām (d. between 220–230/835–845) arguing against the method of *qiyās* due to the distinction between intellective and legal causes:

> Al-Naẓẓām said: the intellect (*ʿaql*) requires equalization (*taswiya*) between similar things (*mutamāthilāt*) with respect to their judgments (*aḥkām*), and dissimilarity (*ikhtilāf*) between dissimilar things (*mukhtalifāt*) with respect to their judgments. But we have seen the Law Giver (*al-Shāriʿ*) making distinction between similar things while uniting dissimilar things – such being in opposition to the judging of the intellect (*qaḍiyyat al-ʿaql*). And that indicates that correlational inference in God's Law (*al-qiyās al-sharʿī*) is not something "occurring to the taste of the intellect" (*ghayr wārid ʿalā madhāq al-ʿaql*), so the intellect is not permitted to engage in it.

In a section on al-Āmidī's defense of *qiyās*, Weiss (1992, 631) relates eight of his counter-arguments against detractors. In the seventh, after the interlocutor objects that "things that are taken to be the *ʿilla*s of rules of divine law are not truly their causes, since God is not subject to causation," al-Āmidī replies: "it has already been pointed out[205] that *ʿilla* has the sense, not of 'cause,' but of 'occasioning factor' [*bāʿith*] (or, in the view of a minority of jurisprudents, of 'sign' [*amāra*])." However, as Zysow notes (2013, 246), any consideration of the legal causes as signs was opposed by those who "assimilated" them to the truly efficient intellective causes. He identifies this, in the context of debate over "specializing the cause" (*takhṣīṣ al-ʿilla*), as a clear instance of "the role of theology as the paradigm of rationality," with such as al-Baṣrī known "for

205 He refers back to the second problem-question (*mas'ala*). See al-Āmidī 2003, 3:254.

his insistence on the necessity of distinguishing between legal and rational causes."

Clearly, there is a significant history of distinction and debate, and a great deal of subtle argument both within and between the camps for and against "assimilation of legal to rational causes." And yet, for all that, we perceive in al-Nasafī, al-Samarqandī, and al-Muntaqid an apparent indifference to any distinction at all. Moreover, our commentators frequently employ empirical examples in illustrating juristic lemmata, with scammony in particular of great service. But the strongest sign of assimilation is found in the parallel drawn by the commentators to the empirical arts and sciences. Objections problematizing induction and counter-claiming the transmission of inspired knowledge from prophets and sages were rendered moot by the epistemic quality of experience (*tajriba*), arguments to consensus (*ijmāʿ*), and the overwhelming, collective evidence of the Folk of Custom (*ahl al-ʿurf*).

Importantly, Zysow notes (2013, 246): "the possibility of regarding legal causes in the light of rational ones depended on their acquiring such a validity within the Islamic legal order as to mark a break with their former ineffectiveness." And to this he adds: "the assimilation of legal causes to rational ones was carried furthest by early theologian jurists." Considering this, I would posit that what we see in our proto-*ādāb al-baḥth* commentary, from the pens of post-Avicennan, post-Rāzian *philosophical*-theologian jurists, is more than a continuation of this trend. It is its completion. The confirmation of *dawarān* as an epistemically authoritative indicant (*dalīl*) had been achieved, overall, through the rigorous analyses and arguments of its proponents, and, to an evident degree, the parallelism of Avicennan experience (*tajriba*). Perhaps the non-conventional knowledge and induction-problematizing critiques represent, for our commentators, the dying sigh of the opposition.

4.3 From al-Nasafī's *Jadal* to al-Samarqandī's *Ādāb al-baḥth*

In the context of juridical dialectic (*jadal*), our commentators' *dawarān* discourse makes a significant study in its own right. But this significance, potentially, expands far beyond the juristic domain into all domains of intellectual inquiry – especially considering the resounding success of al-Samarqandī's universal method: the *ādāb al-baḥth wa'l-munāẓara*, or "protocol for dialectical inquiry and disputation." Here we will get a sense of the transition from al-Nasafī's *jadal* to the *ādāb al-baḥth*, by presenting al-Samarqandī's understanding of *dawarān* along with that of some early commentators.

In his *Kitāb ʿAyn al-Naẓar*, a short outline of three core logical notions for dialectic which seems to prefigure the universalist project (not all examples are juristic), al-Samarqandī's definition of *dawarān* is the same as al-Nasafī's, and he presents the same modes of E&N, E-not-N, and N-not-E concomitance.[206] In subsequent exposition, however, he adds further to what we have seen in our commentaries. Among other things: (1) he provides a name for E&N concomitant causation (*madāriyya*), such being called: "generating" (*ījād*),[207] thus considering it truly productive of the judgment (*ḥukm*), the way intellective causes are for their effects; (2) he provides a name for N-not-E concomitant causation, such being called "conditional" (*sharṭiyya*), with its *madār* and *dāʾir* called "condition" (*sharṭ*) and "conditioned" (*mashrūṭ*),[208] thus drawing a solid link between these relations, and showing that the *sharṭ* is truly the necessary but not sufficient condition; (3) he confirms the implicative nature of *dawarān* (and thus its subjugation to many of the rules of implication [*talāzum*]), "since the *madār* in [E&N] concomitant causation is an implicans (*malzūm*) and an implicatum (*lāzim*), and in the [E-not-N]: an implicans, and in the [N-not-E]: an implicatum";[209] (4) he reformulates certain aspects of the multiple-*madār*s problem, confirming multiple-*madār*s are impossible for E&N concomitant causation (when the *madār*s are separable), "unless one of the two *madār*s is a *madār* for the other, in [both] existence and non-existence,"[210] and that the *madār* can be multiplied in non-E&N modes;[211] and (5) he provides derivative rules for non-E&N *madār*s.[212]

Turning to his *Risāla*, however, al-Samarqandī's definition of *dawarān* is truncated, and enjoys no further elaboration. He merely says:[213]

> *Dawarān* is the following (*tarattub*) of something from something [else] which has a rightness of causation (*lahu ṣulūḥ al-ʿilliyya*), either in existence, or in non-existence, or in both together; and the first is the *dāʾir*, while the second is the *madār*.

206 Young 2019, §§43–47; Or. 3730, fol. 75a–b; Or. 3908, foll. 4b–5a.
207 Young 2019, §45; Or. 3730, fol. 75a; Or. 3908, fol. 4b.
208 Young 2019, §47; Or. 3730, fol. 75b; Or. 3908, fol. 5a.
209 Young 2019, §48; Or. 3730, fol. 75b; Or. 3908, fol. 5a.
210 That is, not only must the *madār*s be inseparable, but one in fact must be the E&N *madār* of the other. In following sections, he confirms the reasoning behind this: separation (*iftirāq*) between them leads to a "meeting of two contradictories" (*ijtimāʿ al-naqīḍayn*).
211 Young 2019, §49; Or. 3730, fol. 75b; Or. 3908, fol. 5a.
212 Young 2019, §54–56; Or. 3730, foll. 75b–76a; Or. 3908, fol. 5a.
213 Young Forthcoming b, §§11–12; al-Samarqandī 1353 [1934], 126.

Note he neglects the “time after time” (*marratan baʿda ukhrā*) component, which in fact rewards us with further speculation in the commentaries. But other than this, we hear nothing more of *dawarān* in the *Risāla* except in the form of *madār*-based arguments in his third illustrative problem-case (*mas'ala*).[214]

The early commentator Quṭb al-Dīn al-Kīlānī (fl. ca. 830/1427) builds considerably on this scant lemma, with customary linguistic usages, scammony illustrations, term explanations for *tarattub* and *ṣulūḥ al-ʿilliyya*, and a definitional analysis (whereby “*tarattub*... etc.” is the genus, and “*alladhī lahu ṣulūḥ*... etc.” is the differentia). At the start he presents two definitions: (1) that of his grundtext, which lacks the “time after time” component; and (2) the “in existence” (*fī ʾl-wujūd*) definition we saw reported by al-Muntaqid after his “time after time” critique.[215] Against the second definition is levelled an unanswered critique of inclusional inadequacy, due to the obvious exclusion of “concomitance qualified by non-existence” (*dawarān ʿadamī*);[216] and the first definition is critiqued for exclusional inadequacy, in that it doesn't exclude “chance occurrences” (with the finding treasure example). In the end, al-Kīlānī's solution is simply to tack on the “time after time” component (bringing the grundtext definition almost all the way back to matching al-Nasafī's).[217] Two critiques of this solution – that it is unnecessary since (1) *tarattub* embodies a kind of perpetuity or frequency, and (2) the *ṣulūḥ* clause cancels out coincidence – are then countered by al-Kīlānī: perpetuity or frequency have never been attributes of *tarattub* in technical usage, and the chance occurrence is a possible thing (*mumkin*), thus requiring a cause (the *madār*).[218]

Then al-Kīlānī proffers a remarkable argument:[219]

> But even if we concede that [chance occurrences] are excluded without our stated qualification [of “time after time”], nevertheless, the specification of that qualification in this definition is obligatory. Because absolute certainty (*jazm*) or probable supposition (*ẓann*) of the causation (*ʿilliyya*) of the *madār* does not come about except after the *dāʾir*'s following from it, time after time (*marratan baʿda ukhrā*) – as in the case of drinking scammony. For indeed, absolute certainty of its causation for the purgation of yellow bile occurs only through experience (*tajriba*), and experience only comes about through the medium (*wāsiṭa*) of repeated observations (*mushāhadāt mutakarrira*). And the correct solution is

214 On this, see Young 2018.

215 Young Forthcoming b, §§11.1–2; Damad İbrahim 1043 fol. 14b; Laud Or. 192 fol. 31b.

216 Young Forthcoming b, §§11.8; Damad İbrahim 1043 fol. 15a; Laud Or. 192 fol. 32a.

217 The only difference at this point being al-Samarqandī's “*tarattub al-shay' ʿalā ʾl-shay*'” as opposed to al-Nasafī's “*tarattub al-athar ʿalā ʾl-shay'*.”

218 Young Forthcoming b, §§11.3–5; Damad İbrahim 1043 foll. 14b–15a; Laud Or. 192 foll. 31b–32a.

219 Young Forthcoming b, §§11.6–7; Damad İbrahim 1043 fol. 15a; Laud Or. 192 fol. 32a.

to say: "[*dawarān*] is the following (*tarattub*) of the effect (*athar*) from something which has rightness of causation (*ṣulūḥ al-ʿilliyya*), time after time."

I think we would be hard pressed to find a more forthright "assimilation" of jurisprudential to scientific method than this; and it is also noteworthy that al-Kīlānī's final definition is a perfect match for al-Nasafī's.

After this, al-Kīlānī illustrates the E-not-N *madār* with scammony and purgation, the N-not-E *madār* with life and knowledge, and the E&N *madār* with stoning and adultery; and he explains that *dawarān* is neither *madār* nor *dāʾir*, in similar terms as we have seen for al-Nasafī's *Fuṣūl*.[220] Importantly, however, he also brings us an additional "*dawarān* is not X" observation:[221]

And [know] also that *dawarān* is not necessary implication (*mulāzama*) – because separation (*infikāk*) of the implicatum (*lāzim*) from the implicans (*malzūm*) is not possible, but separation of the *dāʾir* from the *madār* is possible, as with purgation from drinking scammony. And [*dawarān* is] more general (*aʿamm*) than necessary implication from a certain perspective, due to: [1] their holding true, together, for that matter wherein the implicans is a cause (*ʿilla*) for the implicatum; [2] necessary implication's holding true, without *dawarān*, in that matter wherein the implicans is an effect (*maʿlūl*) of the implicatum; and [3] *dawarān*'s holding true, without necessary implication, in that matter wherein the *dāʾir* is "possible-of-separation" (*mumkin al-infikāk*) from the *madār.*

Thus, while the implicative nature of *dawarān* is confirmed, al-Kīlānī clearly and systematically lays out the differences between necessary implication (*mulāzama*) and *dawarān* – a useful set of argumentative pragmatics for both combining and dividing the labour of these two logical staples of dialectic.

Finally, he closes by introducing another useful analytical category for *dawarān*. In short, *dawarān* is either: (1) universal (*kullī*), with "the *dāʾir*'s following from the *madār* the whole time for which the *madār* is established, and in all cases"; or (2) particular (*juzʾī*), with "the *dāʾir*'s following from the *madār* some of the time for which the *madār* is established, and in some cases."[222]

Masʿūd al-Shirwānī al-Rūmī (fl. ca. 840/1436), perhaps the most famous commentator on al-Samarqandī's *Risāla* (and definitely the greatest stimulator of super-commentaries and glosses), also contributed observations on the relationship between *dawarān* and necessary implication. His initial treatment of the lemma on *dawarān* (2010, 157) brings little we have not already seen, but he closes with an interesting variant on al-Kīlānī:

---

220 Young Forthcoming b, §§12.1–2; Damad İbrahim 1043 fol. 15a–b; Laud Or. 192 fol. 32a–b.
221 Young Forthcoming b, §12.3; Damad İbrahim 1043 fol. 15b; Laud Or. 192 fol. 32b.
222 Young Forthcoming b, §12.4; Damad İbrahim 1043 fol. 15b; Laud Or. 192 fol. 32b.

> And it is said: indeed, from a certain perspective, there lies between necessary implication (*talāzum*) and concomitance (*dawarān*) a general (*ʿumūm*) and a particular (*khuṣūṣ*), based on [1] their coming together in a certain case wherein the *dāʾir* and the *madār* are mutually implicating propositions (*qaḍiyyatayn mutalāzimatayn*), with one of the two being right to be the cause (*ʿilla*) of the other.[223] But [2] *dawarān* holds true without necessary implication (*talāzum*) in a certain case wherein the *dāʾir* and *madār* are unique individuals (*mufridayn*).[224] And [3] necessary implication (*mulāzama*) holds true without [*dawarān*] regarding the necessary entailment (*istilzām*) of the existence of the effect (*maʿlūl*) for the existence of its cause (*ʿilla*).[225] And this explanation conveys the relationship (*nisba*) between *dawarān* and the normative implication (*al-mulāzama al-ḥukmiyya*) which the author, may God have mercy on him, defined in the preceding [section].

As we see in al-Kīlānī and Masʿūd, it is quite possible that focus had shifted in their time from an interdisciplinary distinction between intellective and legal causes to an intra-logical distinction between necessary implication (*mulāzama*/*talāzum*) and *dawarān*, coloured somewhat by the variant historical developments of these methods in logic and law.

Finally, Masʿūd provides (2010, 157–158) somewhat more than al-Kīlānī's set of universal vs. particular categories for analysis, with a further measure of the absolute, or unqualified (*muṭlaq*).

> And if you desire explanation of the relation (*nisba*) between *dawarān* and "absolute implication" (*muṭlaq al-luzūm*), then consider such a case wherein the *dāʾir*'s following (*tarattub*) from the *madār* is "most of the time" (*aktharīyyan*), not "necessarily universally" (*kulliyyan ḍarūriyyan*), like purgation in relation to the drinking of scammony. And this also pertains to "absolute, universal necessary implication" (*muṭlaq al-mulāzama al-kulliyya*). As for "absolute necessary implication" (*muṭlaq al-mulāzama*), under which [both] the universal (*kulliyya*) and the particular (*juzʾiyya*) are subsumed, it is therein inconceivable that *dawarān* be separated from [*mulāzama*], because between every two things, even two contradictories (*naqīḍayn*), there is, definitively, a "particular necessary implication" (*mulāzama juzʾiyya*).

Interestingly, while both al-Kīlānī and Masʿūd account – via this universal vs. particular distinction – for instances of *dawarān* in which causation is *not* conveyed to the *madār*, neither raises the role which a condition (*sharṭ*) or impeding factor (*māniʿ*) might play in suppressing that causation in "particular *dawarān*."

To be sure, neither in al-Samarqandī's *Risāla*, nor in either of these two early and important commentaries, is there any acknowledgment whatever of a dis-

223 This corresponding to al-Kīlānī's case #1: *mulāzama*-with-*dawarān*.

224 This constituting a very different interpretation than we see in al-Kīlānī's case #3: *dawarān*-without-*mulāzama*.

225 This corresponding to al-Kīlānī's case #2: *mulāzama*-without-*dawarān*.

tinction between intellective vs. legal causes. It would seem that the assimilation apparent in al-Nasafī's *jadal* theory, bolstered with yet further analyses, transferred without rough passage into al-Samarqandī's *ādāb al-baḥth* – and from there, potentially, with its cargo of jurist-manufactured typologies, principles, and dialectical strategies, into the broader realms wherein the universal *ādāb al-baḥth* was brought to govern disputation.

4.4 Modern Parallels

In modern parlance, *dawarān* might be labelled a "regularity theory of causation";[226] and in his modern classic on causality, Mario Bunge (1959, 42) briefly traces what he labels the "constant-conjunction formula of causation," from antiquity to Hume. In a summary of the formula's elements (1959, 40), he notes "three notions that are usually associated with causality: the conditionalness peculiar to lawfulness, the existential priority of the cause over the effect, and lack of exception," questioning whether these are sufficient "to describe causation unambiguously."[227] We may recognize in the "lack of exception" notion our commentators' "no-inconsistency" (*naqḍ*) requirement, and in the question as to whether these three notions are sufficient: the many critiques of al-Muntaqid. In the end, Bunge critiques and rejects the Humean "reduction of causation to regular association" as "mistaking causation for one of its tests" (1959, 46). Regardless of his conclusions, I believe Bunge's twentieth-century critique of eighteenth-century causality theory, held in comparison to our commentators' thirteenth- and fourteenth-century justifications and critiques, serves only to highlight the relative sophistication of Islamic legal-theoretical discourse on causation.

Modern parlance also makes regular use of the notion of necessary and sufficient conditions. Peter White (1990, 5) notes: "although many philosophers have attempted to distinguish between causes and conditions, some have analysed the causal relation in terms of conditionals."[228] On the other hand, as we have seen, Muslim scholars defined "cause" (*ʿilla* or *sabab*) in contradistinc-

226 On regularity theory see, for example, Hitchcock 2018 (§1.1 "Problems for Regularity Theory"); White 1990, 3, 4, *passim*.

227 Hume's conditions, besides "constant conjunction between the cause and the effect," were "contiguity in time and place," and "priority in time" (Khoo, Chan, and Niu 2002, 52).

228 The most prominent modern theorizer in terms of conditions is J.L. Mackie, most famous for introducing the *INUS* condition, whereby a cause is, minimally, "an *insufficient* but *non-redundant* part of an *unnecessary* but *sufficient* condition" (Mackie 1974, 62 and n. 5).

tion to "condition" (*sharṭ*), accompanying these causal fundaments with a distinct "impeding factor" (*māniʿ*) as well. Still, I have found it useful to analyse our commentators' E, N, and E&N modes of concomitance as parallels to "sufficient," "necessary," and "necessary and sufficient" conditions. Bunge (1959, 33–34) does something similar with Galileo, claiming: "one of the clearest [definitions of the efficient cause] was given by Galileo (...) as the *necessary and sufficient condition for the appearance of something:* 'that and no other is to be called cause, at the presence of which the effect always follows, and at whose removal the effect disappears.'"[229]

We might recognize this as a statement that the one, truly causation-conveying *dawarān* is E&N *dawarān*, that the true cause must be an E&N *madār*, and that such a *madār* is the "intellective cause" (*ʿilla ʿaqliyya*). But we should also remember that, like Bunge – who notes a lack of "efficacy," among other things (1959, 34–35, 40–46)[230] – none of our commentators found such concomitance-only formulae adequate for conveying causation without the *madār*'s "rightness for causation" or another *dalīl* indicating its causation for the *dāʾir*. As Bunge was to prescribe some six hundred years later, our commentators had already moved considerably beyond the "constant-conjunction formula of causation."

Perhaps the closest parallels to *dawarān* in modern philosophy may be found among J.S. Mill's "Four Methods of Experimental Inquiry" – in particular, for E&N *dawarān*, with his "Joint Method of Agreement and Difference."[231] Mill encapsulates his methods in a set of five "canons," the first three of which are most relevant for comparison with our Nasafian formulae. The *First Canon* is meant to embody the "Method of Agreement," and, as Zysow holds, corresponds best with co-absence (*ʿaks*).[232] Mill states (1963–1991, 7:390, §1): "if two or more

229 Italics are his; citing "Galileo (1623), *Il Saggiatore*, in *Opere*, vol. 6, 265."

230 Cf. al-Muntaqid on the absence of necessitation (*iqtiḍāʾ*) and efficiency (*taʾthīr*) in pure co-presence (*ṭard*) *qiyās*.

231 ʿAlī Sāmī al-Nashshār recognizes the parallel between *dawarān* and Mill's "Joint Method of Agreement and Difference" (al-Nashshār 1984, 128); earlier (118–119) he links the condition of *ṭard* (co-presence) with Mill's "Method of Agreement," and *ʿaks* (co-absence) with Mill's "Method of Difference." Zysow corrects him on both counts, linking *ṭard* to Difference and *ʿaks* to Agreement (Zysow 2013, 219 and nn. 362, 364). Miller, with a nod towards J.S. Mill, translates *dawarān* as "method of agreement and disagreement" (Miller 1984, 149, 157–159, 233; citing Mill's *System of Logic* and al-Nashshār's *Manāhij al-Baḥth* in 149, n. 158).

232 "Convertibility (*ʿaks*) tests for necessary conditions. In the absence of the cause, the qualification, too, should be absent (-c → -q). It corresponds to Mill's *Method of Agreement*" (Zysow 2013, 219 and n. 364). Note that Mill himself does not speak in terms of necessary or sufficient

instances of the phenomenon under investigation have only one circumstance in common, the circumstance in which alone all the instances agree, is the cause (or effect) of the given phenomenon."

The *Second Canon* is meant to embody the "Method of Difference," and, as Zysow holds, corresponds best with co-presence (*ṭard*).[233] Mill states (1963–1991, 7:391, §2): "if an instance in which the phenomenon under investigation occurs, and an instance in which it does not occur, have every circumstance in common save one, that one occurring only in the former; the circumstance in which alone the two instances differ, is the effect, or the cause, or an indispensable part of the cause, of the phenomenon."

And the *Third Canon*, most pertinent to E&N *dawarān* theory, is meant to embody the "Joint Method of Agreement and Difference."[234] Mill states (1963–1991, 7:396, §4): "if two or more instances in which the phenomenon occurs have only one circumstance in common, while two or more instances in which it does not occur have nothing in common save the absence of that circumstance; the circumstance in which alone the two sets of instances differ, is the effect, or the cause, or an indispensable part of the cause, of the phenomenon."

Thus, with Mill, E&N concomitance conveys that the *madār* is either the cause of the judgment, "an indispensable part" of the cause of the judgment, or an effect of the judgment. And, presumably, with our commentators, either the test of rightness of causation (*ṣulūḥ al-ʿilliyya*) or an additional indicant (*dalīl*) would weed out the effect and the part, leaving only the cause, with an overwhelming probability.

There is at least one other, and important, parallel in Mill's "Four Methods of Experimental Inquiry." In a section entitled "Of Plurality of Causes; and of the Intermixture of Effects," Mill states (1963–1991, 7:435, §2): "one of the principal consequences of this fact of Plurality of Causes is, to render the first of the inductive methods, that of Agreement, uncertain." The same does not hold, however, for the "Joint Method of Agreement and Difference" (7:437–438, §2).

> For, in the joint method, it is supposed not only that the instances in which *a* is, agree only in containing A, but also that the instances in which *a* is not, agree only in not containing

---

conditions / causes in his "Four Methods of Experimental Inquiry," although his methods are often described in such terms (see, for example, Khoo, Chan, and Niu 2002, 52).

233 "The method of consistency (*ṭard*) is a test for sufficient conditions and is so expounded by the legal theorists. If the cause exists, so does the qualification (c → q). It thus corresponds to Mill's *Method of Difference*" (Zysow 2013, 219 and n. 362).

234 "The requirement that a cause be both consistent and convertible corresponds to Mill's *Joint Method of Agreement and Difference*. The technical term for this is *dawarān*, 'concomitance,' literally, 'revolution'" (Zysow 2013, 219 and nn. 366–367).

> A. Now, if this be so, A must be not only the cause of *a*, but the only possible cause: for if there were another, as for example B, then in the instances in which *a* is not, B must have been absent as well as A, and it would not be true that these instances agree *only* in not containing A. This, therefore, constitutes an immense advantage of the joint method over the simple Method of Agreement.

Mill, in so many words, has not only recognized the problematics of multiple *madār*s, but, like al-Nasafī and commentators, concluded that the true E&N *madār* can only be one.

Finally, in terms of modern parallels,[235] we will recall such requirements as we have encountered that *dawarān* be "safe from inconsistency," and "not counter-indicated by its like or by stronger than it," and my suggestion that such "no-*naqḍ*" and "no-*muʿāraḍa*" clauses be considered part of a larger falsification scheme. Clearly, causal justification required a negative proof: the absence or negation of potential objections to the claim, just as it required a positive proof: the presence and confirmation of evidence for the claim.

This, I argued, places the objections of inconsistency (*naqḍ*) and counter-indication (*muʿāraḍa*) at dialectic's core, and confirms its vital role as a vehicle for falsification, pushing causal justification towards greater explanatory power. For if no-*naqḍ*, no-*muʿāraḍa* is a *requirement* of causal validity, then the only means of fulfilling that requirement is to *seek out* – whether privately or in disputation – potential objections of inconsistency and counter-indication. Only upon seeking to falsify one's thesis, and failing to do so, can one properly claim its validity – and in seeking one is confirming that one's thesis is at least potentially falsifiable in the first place, and thus the product of a properly "scientific" methodology. I am of course drawing upon Karl Popper; and among his famous conclusions (1962, 36–37) are:

> "Every genuine test of a theory is an attempt to falsify it, or to refute it. Testability is falsifiability."
>
> "A theory which is not refutable by any conceivable event is non-scientific. Irrefutability is not a virtue of a theory (as people often think) but a vice."
>
> "Confirming evidence should not count except when it is the result of a genuine test of the theory; and this means that it can be presented as a serious but unsuccessful attempt to falsify the theory."
>
> And, finally:

---

235 As for commonalities between Ibn Taymiyya and certain modern philosophers, see Hallaq 1993, xlviii–l.

> "The criterion of the scientific status of a theory is its falsifiability, or refutability, or testability."

With inconsistency (*naqḍ*) and counter-indication (*muʿāraḍa*) being the two chief means of "falsifying" *dawarān*, Muslim jurists' conscious and frequent engagement in disputation powered a great falsifying engine – in matters of causation as elsewhere in the jurisprudential endeavour. And the fact that this juristic enterprise was absorbed into the universalist *ādāb al-baḥth* points to its potential application to the causal concerns of the speculative and natural sciences as well, experimental and theoretical alike.

5 Closing

Pondering the comparative contribution of our commentaries' juristic *dawarān*, I would first note that Ibn Sīnā seems not to have developed refined typologies for experience (*tajriba*), nor to have exhausted the multiple *madār* problem, nor to have engaged in some of the deeper causal analyses of our commentaries. We must of course consider Ibn Sīnā an influence in our *dawarān* discourse, but the development of *dawarān* in legal circles was far more complicated than his exposition on *tajriba*, even before his time. Perhaps we might better see Ibn Sīnā as a bridge between the normative, speculative, and empirical sciences, a corridor through which such as al-Samarqandī, with plentiful references to scammony, could draw together disparate disciplines with a single thread of causal theory – most finely spun on the jurist's wheel, but fruitfully woven into the fabric of *all* causal inquiries. That is to say, converting Zysow's phrase: an "assimilation of rational cause to legal cause" – or, perhaps, "of rational *tajriba* to legal *dawarān*."

But even if true, the question would still remain as to whether this was also proven in practice. Did the prominent place of *dawarān* in Samarqandian *ādāb al-baḥth* bring new vistas for applying the refined juristic model? Did *dawarān* have a new impact, was it used in new ways, are the marks of this *dawarān* to be found outside the juristic domain? The answers can only follow a great deal more study and analysis of causal arguments in pre- and post-Samarqandian theology and philosophy. Nor are these the only questions raised by our study.

Have we seen, for example, the final fusion of rational and legal causes? Only further research can reveal whether it was hereafter a given that both are subject to the same method of *dawarān*, or whether distinctions continued.

And how might the answer interact with the debate on specializing the cause (*takhṣīṣ al-ʿilla*)? The question remains as to whether that topic was still hot, or whether it had cooled off, as we might consider Zysow to have suggested.[236] More generally, we might also ask what the *dawarān* arguments of proto- and early *ādāb al-baḥth* brought to *uṣūlī* discussions. Whether and to what extent purely juristic discourse was altered has yet to be measured.[237]

And broadening the scope to World intellectual history, what further contributions might be found in this *dawarān* discourse? We have seen parallels to Mill's "Four Methods of Experimental Inquiry" and Popper's stipulation of falsifiability. But are there other parallels – or even advances beyond what has been developed, for instance, in modern logics? Mill seems to have grasped the problem of multiple, separable *madārs*, and that the true E&N *madār* can only be one. But what of the further configurations and analytical categories we have seen with our commentators, such as mixed E&N and non-E&N *madārs*, or essential vs. occurrent separation? Have the implications of these been worked out in scientific approaches, or can they be applied, for instance, to the contemporary justification of norms in ethics and law?

Dawarān discourse, even in the short snapshot examined in this study, is marked by rigorous analysis, grounded justification, and penetrating critique. It is sophisticated, and points towards promising comparative studies and applications. Most importantly, and considering the virtually unplumbed ocean of later *uṣūl* and *ādāb al-baḥth* commentaries and glosses, there is a great deal of exciting material yet to explore, and no telling what fresh insights future inquiries might bring.

---

236 "Later writers on *uṣūl al-fiqh* offer a highly compressed and unsympathetic account of what had come to be regarded as a dispute without substance. The controversy surrounding the specialization of the cause is labelled as merely verbal (*lafẓī*)" (Zysow 2013, 243).

237 Perhaps a key improvement wrought after al-Nasafī and al-Samarqandī was to "complete" *dawarān* by folding suitability (*munāsaba*) into it – as the ultimate expression of "rightness of causation" (*ṣulūḥ al-ʿilliyya*) – or to consider a refined version of *dawarān* alongside *munāsaba* and analytical division (*al-sabr wa'l-taqsīm*), as a streamlined trio of complementary and mutually supportive methods. We have witnessed as much in Ibn Taymiyya; and such as Najm al-Dīn al-Ṭūfī (d. 716/1316, a fellow Ḥanbalī) treats, in his *Mukhtaṣar al-Rawḍa* and self-commentary, only three modes of inferential *ʿilla*-validation: *munāsaba*, *al-sabr wa'l-taqsīm*, and *dawarān*.

Bibliography

Abdulsatir, Hussein Ali. *Shīʿī doctrine, Muʿtazilī theology: al-Sharīf al-Murtaḍā and Imamī Discourse*. Edinburgh: Edinburgh University Press, 2017.

Abrahamov, Binyamin. "Necessary Knowledge in Islamic Theology." *British Journal of Middle Eastern Studies* 20 (1993): 20–32.

Abrahamov, Binyamin. "Al-Ghazālī and the Rationalization of Sufism." In *Islam and Rationality: the Impact of al-Ghazālī. Papers collected on his 900th anniversary*, ed. Georges Tamer, vol. 1, 35–48. Leiden: Brill, 2015.

Adamson, Peter. "Al-Kindī and the Muʿtazila: Divine attributes, Creation and Freedom." *Arabic Sciences and Philosophy* 13.1 (2003): 45–77.

Adamson, Peter. "The Last Philosophers of Late Antiquity in the Arabic Tradition." In *Entre Orient et Occident: la philosophie et la science gréco-romaines*, ed. Ulrich Rudolph and Richard Goulet, 1–43. Vandoeuvres: Fondation Hardt, 2011.

Adamson, Peter. "Arabic Philosophy and Theology Before Avicenna." In *The Oxford Handbook of Medieval Philosophy*, ed. J. Marenbon, 58–82. Oxford: Oxford University Press, 2012.

Adamson, Peter. "State of Nature: Human and Cosmic Rulership in Ancient Philosophy." In *Menschennatur und politische Ordnung*, ed. B. Kellner and A. Höfele, 79–94. Paderborn: Wilhelm Fink, 2015.

Adamson, Peter and Peter E. Pormann, eds. *Philosophy and Medicine in the Formative Period of Islam*. London: Warburg Institute, 2017.

Adang, Camilla (et al.), eds. *Ibn Ḥazm of Cordoba: the Life and Works of a Controversial Thinker*. Leiden, Boston: Brill, 2013.

Ahlwardt, Wilhelm. *Verzeichnis der arabischen Handschriften*. 10 vols. Hildesheim: G. Olms, 1980–1981. [Reprint: originally published 1887–1899.]

Ahmad, Najah Nadi. *Theorising the Relationship Between Kalām and Uṣūl: the Theological-Legal Epistemology of Saʿd al-Dīn al-Taftazānī (d.792/1390)*. PhD diss., University of Oxford, 2018.

Ahmed, Asad. "Post-Classical Philosophical Commentaries/Glosses: Innovation in the Margins." *Oriens* 41.3–4 (2013): 317–348.

Ahmed, Asad and Robert Gleave. "Rationalist Disciplines and Postclassical Islamic Legal Theories: Introduction." *Oriens* 46 (2018): 1–5.

Al-ʿAjam, Rafīq. *Al-Manṭiq ʿinda al-Ghazālī fī abʿādihi al-arisṭawiyya wa-khuṣūṣiyyatihi al-islāmiyya: Dirāsa wa-taḥlīl*. Beirut: Dār al-Mashriq, 1989.

al-ʿAjmī, Daghash b. Shabīb. "Tanbīh al-Ghāfil ilā ʿadam Ṣiḥḥat Nisbat al-Kitāb al-Maṭbūʿ bi-Ism 'Tanbīh al-Rajul al-ʿĀqil ʿalā Tamwīh al-Jadal al-Bāṭil' li-Ibn Taymiyya." *ʿĀlam al-Kutub* 27.5–6 (2006): 523–532.

Al-Akiti, M. Afifi. "The Three Properties of Prophethood in Certain Works of Avicenna and al-Ġazālī." In *Interpreting Avicenna: Science and Philosophy in Medieval Islam, Proceedings of the Second Conference of the Avicenna Study Group*, ed. Jon McGinnis with the assistance of David C. Reisman, 189–212. Leiden, Boston: Brill, 2004.

Al-ʿAllāma al-Ḥillī, Jamāl al-Dīn Ḥasan. *Maʿārij al-uṣūl*. Qum: Muʾassasat Āl al-Bayt, 1983.

Al-ʿAllāma al-Ḥillī, Jamāl al-Dīn Ḥasan. *Al-Jawhar al-naḍīd fī Sharḥ Manṭiq al-tajrīd; wa-yalīhi Risālat al-Taṣwīr wa'l-taṣdīq li-Ṣadr al-Mutaʾallihīn Muḥammad b. Ibrāhīm al-Shīrāzī*, ed. Muḥsin Bīdārfar. Qum: Intishārāt Bīdār, 1990.

https://doi.org/10.1515/9783110552386-014

Al-ʿAllāma al-Ḥillī, Jamāl al-Dīn Ḥasan. *Al-Qawāʿid al-jaliyya fī Sharḥ al-Risāla al-shamsiyya*, ed. Fāris Ḥassūn Tabrīziyān. Qum: Muʾassasat al-Nashr al-Islāmī al-Tābiʿa bi-Jamāʿat al-Mudarrisīn, 1412 [1992].

Al-ʿAllāma al-Ḥillī, Jamāl al-Dīn Ḥasan. *Nihāyat al-marām fī ʿilm al-kalām*. Qum: Muʾassisat al-Imām al-Ṣādiq, 1998.

Alon, Ilai. "Al-Ghazālī on Causality." *Journal of the American Oriental Society* 100 (1980): 397 – 405.

Al-Āmidī, Sayf al-Dīn Abū ʾl-Ḥasan ʿAlī b. Muḥammad. *Al-Iḥkām fī uṣūl al-aḥkām*, ed. ʿAbd al-Razzāq al-ʿAfīfī, 4 vols. Riyadh: Dār al-Ṣumayʿī, 2003.

Al-ʿĀmilī, Nūr al-Dīn. *al-Shawāhid al-Makkiyya*. Qum: Muʾassasat al-Nashr al-Islāmī, 2003.

Ammonius. *Ammonius in Aristotelis de Interpretatione commentarius*, ed. Adolfus Busse, vol. 4, pars 5. Berlin: Reimer, 1897.

Anjum, Ovamir. *Politics, Law, and Community in Islamic Thought: the Taymiyyan Moment.* Cambridge, UK: Cambridge University Press, 2012.

Ansari, Hasan and Sabine Schmidtke. "The Shīʿī reception of Muʿtazilism (II): Twelver Shīʿīs." In *The Oxford Handbook of Islamic Theology*, ed. Sabine Schmidtke, 196 – 215. Oxford: Oxford University Press, 2016.

Anzenbacher, Arno. *Einführung in die Ethik.* Düsseldorf: Patmos Verlag, 1992.

Arberry, Arthur John. *The Seven Odes: the First Chapter in Arabic Literature.* London: Allen & Unwin, 1957.

Arfa-Mensia, Mokdad. "Al-Fārābī et la Science des Uṣūl al-Fiqh." *Arabic Sciences and Philosophy* 27 (2017): 139 – 163.

Aristotle. *Die Hermeneutik des Aristoteles in der arabischen Übersetzung des Isḥāq Ibn Ḥunayn*, ed. Isidor Pollak. Abhandlungen für die Kunde des Morgenlandes, vol. 13, no. 1. Leipzig: Brockhaus, 1913.

Aristotle. *Manṭiq Arisṭū*, ed. ʿAbd al-Raḥmān Badawī, 3 vols. Cairo: Maṭbaʿat Dār al-Kutub al-Miṣriyya, 1948 – 1952.

Aristotle. *Aristotle's Categories and De Interpretatione*, ed. John L. Ackrill. Oxford: Oxford University Press, 1963 (many reprints).

Aristotle. *Aristotelis Categoriae et Liber de Interpretatione*, ed. Lorenzo Minio Paluello. Oxford: Oxford University Press, 1974 (repr.).

Aristotle. *Mantiq Arisṭū*, ed. ʿAbd al-Raḥmān Badawi, 3 vols. Beirut: Dār al-Qalam, 1980.

Aristotle. *Aristotle's Ars Rhetorica: the Arabic Version*, ed. Malcolm C. Lyons, 2 vols. Cambridge: Pembroke Arabic Texts, 1982.

Aristote. *Topiques I* [Livres I–IV], edition and French trans. J. Brunschwig. Paris: Les Belles Lettres, 2009.

Arslan, Hakki. *Juridische Hermeneutik (uṣūl al-fiqh) der hanafitischen Rechtsschule am Beispiel des uṣūl al-fiqh-Werks* Mirqāt al-wuṣūl ilā ʿilm al-uṣūl *von Mulla Ḫusraw (gest. 885/1480).* Frankfurt: Peter Lang, 2016.

Al-Astarābādī, Muhammad Amīn. *Al-Fawāʾid al-madaniyya*. Qum: Muʾassasat al-Nashr al-Islāmī, 2003.

Auda, Jasser. *Maqasid al-Shariah as Philosophy of Islamic Law: a Systems Approach.* London, Washington: the International Institute of Islamic Thought, 1428/2007.

Al-Bābartī, Akmal al-Dīn Muḥammad b. Maḥmūd. *Al-Rudūd wa'l-nuqūd: Sharḥ Mukhtaṣar Ibn al-Ḥājib*, vol. 1. ed. Ṣāliḥ b. ʿAwn al-ʿUmarī; vol. 2 ed. Tarḥīb b. Rabīʿān al-Dawsrī. Riyadh: Maktabat al-Rushd Nāshirūn, 2005.

Al-Bājī, Abū 'l-Walīd Sulaymān. *Kitāb al-Minhāj fī tartīb al-ḥijāj* (*L'art de la Polémique: Édition Critique d'al-Minhāǧ de Bāǧī*), ed. 'Abd al-Majīd Turkī. Paris: Maisonneuve et Larose, 1978.

Al-Bāqillānī, al-Qāḍī Abū Bakr. *Al-Taqrīb wa'l-irshād*, ed. 'Abd al-Ḥamīd b. 'Alī Abū Zunayd. Beirut: Mu'assasat al-Risāla, 1998.

Al-Baṣrī, Abū 'l-Ḥusayn. *Kitāb al-Mu'tamad fī uṣūl al-fiqh*, ed. Muḥammad Ḥamīd Allāh. Damascus: al-Ma'had al-'ilmī al-faransī li'l-dirāsāt al-'arabiyya, 1964–1965.

Bauer, Thomas. *Die Kultur der Ambiguität: Eine andere Geschichte des Islams*. Berlin: Verlag der Weltreligionen, 2011.

Al-Bayḍāwī, 'Abdallāh b. 'Umar. *Minhāj al-wuṣūl ilā 'ilm al-uṣūl*, ed. Salīm Shab'āniyya. Damascus: Dār Dāniya, 1989.

Bdaiwi, Ahab. "Some Remarks on the Confessional Identity of the Philosophers of Shiraz: Sadr al-Dīn Dashtakī (d. 903/1498) and his Students Mullā Shams al-Dīn Khafrī (942/1535) and Najm al-Dīn Mahmūd Nayrīzī (948/1541)." *Ishraq* 5 (2014): 61–85.

Becheri, Larabi. *Raisonnement juridique par analogie (qiyās) chez Ġazālī: Étude et traduction de* Asās al-qiyās. Université d'Aix-Marseille: Thèse de doctorat (unpublished), 2009.

Becker, Carl Heinrich "Ubi sunt qui ante nos in mundo fuere?" In *Islamstudien*, ed. Carl Heinrich Becker, vol 1, 501–519. Leipzig: Quelle und Meyer, 1924.

Belhaj, Abdessamad. *Argumentation et Dialectique en Islam: Formes et Séquences de la Munāẓara*. Bruxelles: Presses Universitaires de Louvain, 2010.

Belhaj, Abdessamad. "Al-Samarqandi's *Adab al-Bahth:* the Art of Disputation in Medieval Islam." In *Il dialogo nella cultura araba: strutture, funzioni, significati (VIII-XIII secolo)*, ed. Mirella Cassarino and Antonella Ghersetti, 35–45. Soveria Mannelli: Rubbettino, 2015.

Belhaj, Abdessamad. "*Ādāb al-Baḥth wa-al-Munāẓara:* the Neglected Art of Disputation in Later Medieval Islam." *Arabic Sciences and Philosophy* 26.2 (2016a): 291–307.

Belhaj, Abdessamad. "Ṭāshköprüzāde's *Ādāb al-baḥth wa-l-munāẓara:* Intersection of Ethics, Logic, and Law." In *Arabic and Islamic Studies in Europe and Beyond*, ed. Maurus Reinkowski et al., 289–300. Leuven: Peeters, 2016b.

Bell, Joseph Norment. *Love Theory in Later Ḥanbalite Islam*. Albany, NY: State University of New York Press, 1979.

Benevich, Fedor. "The Reality of the Non-Existent Object of Thought." *Oxford Studies in Medieval Philosophy* (2018): 31–61.

Bernand, Marie. "Ḥanafī *Uṣūl al-Fiqh* through a Manuscript of al-Ǧaṣṣāṣ." *Journal of the American Oriental Society* 105 (1985): 623–635.

Bernand, Marie. "Controverses Médiévales sur le *Dalīl al-Khiṭāb*." *Arabica* 33.3 (1986): 269–294.

Bernand, Marie. "Al-Ghazālī, artisan de la fusion des systèmes de pensée." *Journal Asiatique* 278 (1991): 223–251.

Al-Bihārī, Muḥibb Allāh b. 'Abd al-Shakūr. *Musallam al-thubūt*. Ms. Maktabat Jāmi'at al-Malik Sa'ūd 8144.

Black, Deborah L. *Logic and Aristotle's Rhetoric and Poetics in Medieval Arabic Philosophy*. Leiden, New York: Brill, 1990.

Black, Deborah L. "Practical Wisdom, Moral Virtue, and Theoretical Knowledge: the Problem of the Autonomy of the Practical Realm in Arabic Philosophy." In *Les philosophies morales et politiques au Moyen Âge*, ed. B. Carlos Bazán, Eduardo Andújar, and Léonard G. Sbrocchi, vol. 1, 476–485. New York, Ottawa, and Toronto: Legas, 1995.

Black, Deborah L. "Knowledge (*ʿilm*) and Certitude (*yaqīn*) in al-Fārābī's Epistemology." *Arabic Sciences and Philosophy* 16 (2006): 11–46.

Black, Deborah L. "Certitude, Justification, and the Principles of Knowledge in Avicenna's Epistemology." In *Interpreting Avicenna: Critical Essays*, ed. Peter Adamson, 120–142. Cambridge: Cambridge University Press, 2013.

Bori, Caterina. "One or Two Versions of *Al-Siyāsa al-Sharʿiyya* of Ibn Taymiyya? And what do they tell us?" ASK Working Paper 26. Bonn: Annemarie Schimmel Kolleg, 2016: 1–27.

Bou Akl, Ziad. "Averroès à propos de la définition de l'acte légal: le miracle comme levier d'adhésion à la Loi." *Mélanges de l'Université Saint-Joseph* 64 (2012): 239–260.

Bou Akl, Ziad. "Averroes on juridical reasoning." In *Interpreting Averroes*, ed. Peter Adamson and Matteo Di Giovanni, 45–63. Cambridge: Cambridge University Press, 2018.

Bouhafa, Feriel. "Averroes' Corrective Philosophy of Law." in *Interpreting Averroes*, ed. Peter Adamson and Matteo Di Giovanni, 64–80. Cambridge: Cambridge University Press, 2018.

Bouyges, Maurice. *Essai de chronologie des œuvres de al-Ghazali (Algazel)*, ed. Michel Allard. Beirut: Imprimerie Catholique, 1959.

Brunschvig, Robert. "Logic and Law in Classical Islam." In *Logic in Classical Islamic Culture*, ed. G.E. von Grunebaum, 9–20. Wiesbaden: Otto Harrassowitz, 1970.

Brunschvig, Robert. "Pour ou contre la logique grecque chez les théologiens-juristes de l'islam: Ibn Ḥazm, al-Ghazālī, Ibn Taimiyya." In *Oriente e occidente nel medioevo: Filosofia e Scienze.* Atti dei convegni de l'Accademia Nazionale dei Lincei, vol. 13, 185–209. Rome: Accademia Nazionale dei Lincei, 1971.

Brunschvig, Robert. "Rationalité et tradition dans l'analogie juridico-religieuse chez le Muʿtazilite *ʿAbd al-Ǧabbār*." In *Études islamologie*, vol. 2, 395–403. Paris: Maisonneuvre et Larose, 1976.

Bunge, Mario. *Causality: the Place of the Causal Principle in Modern Science.* Cambridge: Harvard University Press, 1959.

Butterworth, Charles E. "Ethics in Medieval Islamic Philosophy." *The Journal of Religious Ethics* 11.2 (1983): 224–239.

Butterworth, Charles E. "The Political Teachings of Avicenna." *Topoi* 19 (2000): 35–44.

Butterworth, Charles E. "Alfarabi's Goal: Political Philosophy, Not Political Theology." In *Islam, the State, and Political Authority: Medieval Issues and Modern Concerns*, ed. Asma Afsaruddin, 53–74. New York: Palgrave Macmillan US, 2011.

Buzurg, Aghā. *Al-Dharīʿa ilā taṣānīf al-shīʿa*. Qum: Muʾassasat Ismāʿīliyyān, 1987.

Calder, Norman. "Doubt and Prerogative: the Emergence of an Imāmī Shīʿī Theory of *Ijtihād*." *Studia Islamica* 70 (1989): 57–78.

Campanini, Massimo. "Alfarabi and the Foundation of Political Theology in Islam." In *Islam, the State, and Political Authority: Medieval Issues and Modern Concerns*, ed. Asma Afsaruddin, 35–52. New York: Palgrave Macmillan US, 2011.

Carter, Michael G. "Analogical and Syllogistic Reasoning in Grammar and Law." In *Islam: Essays on Scripture, Thought and Society, A Festschrift in Honour of Anthony H. Johns*, ed. Peter G. Riddell and Tony Street, 104–112. Leiden: Brill, 1997.

Chehata, Chafik. "Études de philosophie musulmane du droit I: Logique juridique et droit musulman." *Studia Islamica* 23 (1965): 5–25.

Chejne, Anwar G. "Ibn Ḥazm of Cordova on Logic." *Journal of the American Oriental Society* 104 (1984): 57–72.

Cook, Michael. *Commanding Right and Forbidding Wrong in Islamic Thought.* Cambridge, UK: Cambridge University Press, 2000.

Crubellier, Michel. "Du *sullogismos* au syllogism." *Revue philosophique de la France et de l'étranger* 136 (2011): 17–36.

Al-Dasūqī, Muḥammad b. Aḥmad, Fakhr al-Dīn al-Khabīṣī, and Sa'd al-Dīn al-Taftāzānī. *Kitāb al-Tajrīd al-Shāfī 'alā Tadhhīb al-Manṭiq al-Kāfī wa hiya Ḥāshiyat al-'Allāma al-Muḥaqqiq al-Dasūqī 'alā Sharḥ al-Khabīṣī 'alā Tahdhīb al-Manṭiq li'l-Taftāzānī* [...]. Cairo: Maṭba'at Kurdistān al-'Ilmiyya, 1328 [1910].

Davidson, Herbert A. *Alfarabi, Avicenna, and Averroes on Intellect: Their Cosmologies, Theories of the Active Intellect, and Theories of Human Intellect.* New York: Oxford University Press, 1992.

Druart, Thérèse-Anne. "The Human Soul's Individuation and its Survival After the Body's Death: Avicenna on the Causal Relation Between Body and Soul." *Arabic Sciences and Philosophy* 10 (2000): 259–273.

Dutton, Blake. "Al-Ghazālī on Possibility and the Critique of Causality." *Medieval Philosophy and Theology* 10 (2001): 23–46.

EI2 = *Encyclopaedia of Islam*^{2}. Edited by H.A.R. Gibb et al. Leiden: Brill, 1960–2005.

EI3 = *Encyclopaedia of Islam*^{3}. Edited by G. Krämer, K. Fleet et al. Leiden: Brill, 2008-.

El-Rouayheb, Khaled. "Opening the Gate of Verification: the Forgotten Arab-Islamic Florescence of the 17th Century." *International Journal of Middle East Studies* 38.2 (2006): 263–281.

El-Rouayheb, Khaled. *Islamic Intellectual History in the Seventeenth Century: Scholarly Currents in the Ottoman Empire and the Maghreb.* New York: Cambridge University Press, 2015.

Emon, Anver M. *Islamic Natural Law Theories.* Oxford: Oxford University Press, 2010.

Endress, Gerhard. "Die dreifache Ancilla: Hermeneutik und Logik im Werk des Sayfaddīn al-Āmidī." In *Logik und Theologie: Das Organon im arabischen und im lateinischen Mittelalter*, ed. Dominik Perler and Ulrich Rudolph, 118–145. Leiden: Brill, 2005.

Endress, Gerhard. "Reading Avicenna in the *Madrasa:* Intellectual Genealogies and Chains of Transmission of Philosophy and the Sciences in the Islamic East." In *Arabic Theology, Arabic Philosophy: From the Many to the One: Essays in Celebration of Richard M. Frank*, ed. James E. Montgomery, 371–422. Leuven: Peeters, 2006.

Fakhry, Majid. "Ethics in Islamic philosophy," *Routledge Encyclopaedia of Philosophy Online.* London: Taylor and Francis, 1998.

Fallūsī, Mas'ūd. *Al-Jadal 'inda 'l-uṣūliyyīn: bayna 'l-naẓariyya wa'l-taṭbīq.* Riyadh: Maktabat al-Rushd Nāshirūn, 2003.

Al-Fārābī, Abū Naṣr. "Kitāb Īsāġūǧī ay al-Madḫal", ed. D.M. Dunlop. *The Islamic Quarterly* 3 (1956–1957): 117–138.

Al-Fārābī, Abū Naṣr. *Al-Fārābī's Commentary on Aristotle's* Peri Hermēneias (De Interpretatione), ed. William Kutsch and Stanley Marrow. Beirut: Imprimerie Catholique, 1960.

Al-Fārābī, Abū Naṣr. "Plato's *Laws*," trans. Muhsin Mahdi. In *Medieval Political Philosophy*, ed. Ralph Lerner and Muhsin Mahdi, 83–94. Ithaca: Cornell University Press, 1963a.

Al-Fārābī, Abū Naṣr. *Al-Fārābī's Short Commentary on Aristotle's* Prior Analytics, trans. into English by Nicholas Rescher. Pittsburgh: University of Pittsburgh Press, 1963b.

Al-Fārābī, Abū Naṣr. *Al-Fārābī's Commentary and Short Treatise on Aristotle's* de Interpretatione, trans. Fritz Zimmermann. London: Oxford University Press, 1981.

Al-Fārābī, Abū Naṣr. *Al-Manṭiq ʿinda al-Fārābī*, ed. Rafīq al-ʿAjam, vol. 1. Beirut: Dār al-Mashriq, 1985.

Al-Fārābī, Abū Naṣr. *Al-Manṭiq ʿinda al-Fārābī*, ed. Rafīq al-ʿAjam, 3 vols. Beirut: Dār al-Mashriq, 1985–1986.

Al-Fārābī, Abū Naṣr. *Al-Manṭiqiyyāt li'l-Fārābī*, ed. Muḥammad Taqī Dānishpazhūh, 3 vols. Qom: al-Marʿashī al-Najafī, 1408–1410/1987–1989.

Al-Fārābī, Abū Naṣr. *Alfarabi: the Political Writings: "Political Regime" and "Summary of Plato's Laws"*, trans. Charles Butterworth. Ithaca, NY: Cornell University Press, 2001.

Fontaine, Resianne. "'Happy is he whose children are boys': Abraham Ibn Daud and Avicenna on Evil." In *The Arabic, Hebrew and Latin Reception of Avicenna's Metaphysics*, ed. Dag Nikolaus Hasse and Amos Bertolacci, 159–76. Berlin, Boston: De Gruyter, 2012.

Frank, Richard M. "Al-Maʿdum wa-l-Mawjud: the Non-Existent, the Existent and the Possible, in the Teaching of Abu Hashim and his Followers." *Mélanges de l'Institut Dominicain des Études Orientales* 14 (1980): 185–210.

Frank, Richard M. *Creation and the Cosmic System: Al-Ghazâlî & Avicenna.* Heidelberg: Carl Winter, 1992.

Frank, Richard M. *Al-Ghazālī and the Ashʿarite School.* Durham: Duke University Press, 1994.

Garden, Kenneth. "Revisiting al-Ghazālī's Crisis through His *Scale for Action (Mīzān al-ʿAmal)*." In *Islam and Rationality: the Impact of al-Ghazālī. Papers Collected on his 900th Anniversary*, ed. Georges Tamer, vol. I, 207–218. Leiden: Brill, 2015.

Geoffroy, Marc. "L'almohadisme théologique d'Averroès." *Archives d'Histoire Doctrinale et Littéraire du Moyen-Âge* 66 (1999): 9–47.

Germann, Nadja. "Al-Fārābī's Philosophy of Society and Religion." *Stanford Encyclopedia of Philosophy* (online), ed. Edward N. Zalta. 2018.

Al-Ghazālī, Abū Ḥāmid. *Iḥyāʾ ʿulūm al-dīn*, 5 vols. Beirut: Dār al-Maʿrifa, 1403/1982.

Al-Ghazālī, Abū Ḥāmid. *Al-Qisṭās al-mustaqīm*, ed. Victor Chelhot. Beirut: Imprimerie Catholique, 1959.

Al-Ghazālī, Abū Ḥāmid. *Miʿyār al-ʿilm*, ed. Sulaymān Dunyā. Cairo: Dār al-Maʿārif, 1961.

Al-Ghazālī, Abū Ḥāmid. *Al-Iqtiṣād fī l-iʿtiqād*, ed. Ibrahim Agâh Çubkçu and Hüseyin Atay. Ankara: Nur Matbaası, 1962.

Al-Ghazālī, Abū Ḥāmid. *Faḍāʾiḥ al-Bāṭiniyya*, ed. ʿAbd al-Raḥmān Badawī. Cairo: Dār al-Qawmiyya li-Ṭibāʿa wa'l-Nashr, 1383/1964.

Al-Ghazālī, Abū Ḥāmid. *Mīzān al-ʿamal*, ed. Sulaymān Dunyā. Cairo: Dār al-Maʿārif, 1964.

Al-Ghazālī, Abū Ḥāmid. *Al-Munqidh min al-ḍalāl/Erreur et délivrance*, ed. and trans. Farid Jabre. Beirut: Commission libanaise pour la traduction des chefs-d'œuvre, 1969.

Al-Ghazālī, Abū Ḥāmid. *Al-Mustaṣfā min ʿilm al-uṣūl*, ed. M.M. Abū l-ʿUlā. Cairo: Maktabat al-Jundī, 1971.

Al-Ghazālī, Abū Ḥāmid. *Shifāʾ al-ghalīl fī bayān al-shabah wa'l-mukhīl wa-masālik al-taʿlīl*, ed. Ḥamd ʿUbayd al-Kubaysī. Baghdad: Maṭbaʿat al-Irshād, 1390/1971.

Al-Ghazālī, Abū Ḥāmid. *Al-Qisṭās al-mustaqīm*, ed. V. Chelhot. Beirut: Dār al-Mashriq, 1991.

Al-Ghazālī, Abū Ḥāmid. *Al-Mustaṣfā min ʿilm al-uṣūl*, ed. Ḥamza b. Zuhayr Ḥāfiẓ, 4 vols. Medina: Sharikat al-Madīna al-Munawwara li'l-Ṭibāʿa wa'l-Nashr, 1993.

Al-Ghazālī, Abū Ḥāmid. *Miḥakk al-naẓar*, ed. Rafīq al-ʿAjam. Beirut: Dār al-Fikr al-Lubnānī, 1994.
Al-Ghaẓālī, Abū Ḥāmid. *al-Musṭaṣfā fī uṣūl al-fiqh*. Beirut: Dār al-Kutub al-ʿIlmiyya, 1996.
Al-Ghazālī, Abū Ḥāmid. *Al-Mustaṣfā min ʿilm al-uṣūl*, ed. Muḥammad Sulaymān al-Ashqar, 2 vols. Beirut: Muʾassasat al-Risāla, 1997.
Al-Ghazālī, Abū Ḥāmid. *Al-Ghazali: Deliverance from Error. Five Key Texts Including His Spiritual Autobiography, al-Munqidh min al-Dalal*, trans. Richard J. McCarthy. Louisville: Fons Vitae, 2000.
Al-Ghazālī, Abū Ḥāmid. *Abū Ḥāmid al-Ghazālī. Das Kriterium des Handelns*, trans. ʿAbd-Elṣamad ʿAbd-Elḥamīd Elschazlī. Darmstadt: Wissenschaftliche Buchgesellschaft, 2006.
Al-Ghazālī, Abū Ḥāmid. *Le livre de la science*, trans. Jean Abd-al-Wadoud Gourand (Beirut: Dar Albouraq, 2009).
Gianotti, Timothy J. *Al-Ghazālī's Unspeakable Doctrine of the Soul: Unveiling the Esoteric Psychology of the* Iḥyāʾ. Leiden: Brill, 2001.
Glassen, Erika. *Der mittlere Weg: Studien zur Religionspolitik und Religiosität der späteren Abbasidenzeit.* Wiesbaden: Franz Steiner Verlag, 1981.
Gleave, Robert. "Imāmī Shīʿī Refutations of *Qiyās*." In *Studies in Islamic Legal Theory*, ed. Bernard Weiss, 267–293. Leiden; Boston: Brill, 2002.
Gleave, Robert. *Scripturalist Islam: the History and Doctrines of the Akhbārī School of Shiʿi Thought.* Leiden: Brill, 2007a.
Gleave, Robert. "Scripturalist Sufism and Scripturalist Anti-Sufism: Theology and Mysticism amongst the Shīʿī Akhbariyya." In *Sufism and Theology*, ed. Ayman Shihadeh, 158–176. Edinburgh: Edinburgh University Press, 2007b.
Gleave, Robert. *Islam and Literalism: Literal Meaning and Interpretation in Islamic Legal Theory.* Edinburgh: University Press, 2013.
Gleave, Robert. "Deriving Rules of Law." In *The Ashgate Research Companion to Islamic Law*, ed. Rudolph Peters and Peri Bearman, 57–72. Farnham: Ashgate, 2014.
Griffel, Frank. "The Harmony of Natural Law and Shari'a in Islamist Theology." In *Shari'a: Islamic Law in the Contemporary Context*, ed. Abbas Amanat and Frank Griffel, 38–61. Stanford, California: Stanford University Press, 2007.
Griffel, Frank. *Al-Ghazālī's Philosophical Theology.* Oxford: Oxford University Press. 2009.
Griffel, Frank. "Al-Ghazālī's Use of 'Original Human Disposition' (*fiṭra*) and its Background in the Teachings of al-Fārābī and Avicenna." *The Muslim World* 102 (2012): 1–32.
Griffel, Frank, ed. *Islam and Rationality: the Impact of al-Ghazālī. Papers Collected on his 900th Anniversary*, vol. 2. Leiden: Brill, 2016.
Gurāyā, Muḥammad Yūsuf. "Historical Background of the Compilation of the Muwaṭṭaʾ of Mālik b. Anas." In *Islamic Studies* 7.4 (1968): 379–392.
Gutas, Dimitri. *Greek Wisdom Literature in Arabic Translation.* New Haven: American Oriental Society, 1975.
Gutas, Dimitri. "Intuition and Thinking: the Evolving Structure of Avicenna's Epistemology." In *Aspects of Avicenna*, ed. Robert Wisnovsky, 1–38. Princeton: Marcus Wiener, 2000.
Gutas, Dimitri. "Certainty, Doubt, Error: Comments on the Epistemological Foundations of Medieval Arabic Science." *Early Science and Medicine* 7 (2002a): 276–288.

Gutas, Dimitri. "The Heritage of Avicenna: the Golden Age of Arabic Philosophy, 1000–ca 1350." In *Avicenna and his Heritage*, ed. Jules Janssens and Daniel De Smet, 81–97. Leuven: University Press, 2002b.

Gutas, Dimitri. "The Empiricism of Avicenna." *Oriens* 40 (2012): 391–436.

Gutas, Dimitri. "Avicenna's philosophical project." In *Interpreting Avicenna: Critical Essays*, ed. Peter Adamson, 28–47. Cambridge: University Press, 2013.

Gutas, Dimitri. *Avicenna and the Aristotelian Tradition: Introduction to Reading Avicenna's Philosophical Works. Second, Revised and Enlarged Edition, Including an Inventory of Avicenna's Authentic Works*. Leiden: Brill, 2014.

Gwynne, Rosalind Ward. *Logic, Rhetoric, and Legal Reasoning in the Qur'ān*. London: Routledge Curzon, 2004.

Gwynne, Rosalind Ward. "Reasoning in the Qur'ān" In *The Routledge Companion to Islamic Philosophy*, ed. Richard C. Taylor and Luis Xavier López-Farjeat, 20–30. London: Routledge, 2016.

Haarmann, Ulrich. "Religiöses Recht und Grammatik im klassischen Islam." *Zeitschrift der Deutschen Morgenländischen Gesellschaft*, Suppl. 2 (1974): 149–169.

Al-Ḥā'irī al-Isfahānī, Muḥammad Ḥusayn. *Al-Fuṣūl al-gharawiyya fī l-uṣūl al-fiqhiyya*. Qom: 1984.

Al-Ḥā'irī al-Isfahānī, Muḥammad Taqī. *Al-Hidāyah al-mustarshidīn*, 3 vols. Qom: 2008.

Ḥājjī Khalīfa (Kâtip Çelebi). *Kashf al-ẓunūn ʿan asāmī 'l-kutub wa'l-funūn*, ed. Muḥammad Sharaf al-Dīn Yāltaqāyā and Rifʿat Bīlgah al-Kilīsī, 2 vols. Beirut: Dār Iḥyā' al-Turāth al-ʿArabī, n.d. [Reprint of Istanbul: Wakālat al-Maʿārif, 1941–1943.]

Hallaq, Wael B. "Caliph, Jurists, and the Saljūqs in the Political Thought of Juwaynī." *Muslim World* 74 (1984a): 26–41.

Hallaq, Wael B. "Considerations on the Function and Character of Sunnī Legal Theory." *Journal of the American Oriental Society* 104 (1984b): 679–689.

Hallaq, Wael B. "Was the Gate of Ijtihad Closed?" *International Journal of Middle Eastern Studies* 16 (1984c): 3–41.

Hallaq, Wael B. "Legal Reasoning in Islamic Law and the Common Law: Logic and Method." *Cleveland State Law Review* 34 (1985–1986): 79–96.

Hallaq, Wael B. "On the Authoritativeness of Sunni Consensus." *International Journal of Middle East Studies* 18 (1986): 427–454.

Hallaq, Wael B. "A Tenth-Eleventh Century Treatise on Juridical Dialectic." *Muslim World* 77 (1987a): 197–228.

Hallaq, Wael B. "The Development of Logical Structure in Sunni Legal Theory." *Der Islam* 64 (1987b): 42–67.

Hallaq, Wael B. "Non-Analogical Arguments in Sunnī Juridical *Qiyās*." *Arabica* 36 (1989): 286–306.

Hallaq, Wael B. "Logic, Formal Arguments and Formalization of Arguments in Sunnī Jurisprudence." *Arabica* 37 (1990): 315–358.

Hallaq, Wael B. *Ibn Taymiyya Against the Greek Logicians*. Oxford: Clarendon, 1993.

Hallaq, Wael B. *A History of Islamic Legal Theories: an Introduction to Sunnī Uṣūl al-Fiqh*. Cambridge: Cambridge University Press, 1997.

Hallaq, Wael B. *Sharīʿa: Theory, Practice, Transformations*. Cambridge: Cambridge University Press, 2009.

Hana, Ghanem-Georges. "Zur Logik al-Ġazālīs." In *XVIII. Deutscher Orientalistentag (1972). Zeitschrift der Deutschen Morgenländischen Gesellschaft.* Supplement II, ed. W. Voigt, 178–185. Wiesbaden: Harrassowitz, 1974.

Haq, Muhammad Abdul. "Mullā Ṣadrā's Concept of Being." *Islamic Studies* 6.3 (1967): 267–276.

Hasan, Ahmad. "The Definition of *Qiyās* in Islamic Jurisprudence." *Islamic Studies* 19.1 (1980a): 1–28.

Hasan, Ahmad. "The Legal Cause in Islamic Jurisprudence: an Analysis of *ʿillat al-ḥukm.*" *Islamic Studies* 19.4 (1980b): 247–270.

Hasan, Ahmad. "Definition of *Sabab* and its Kinds in Islamic Jurisprudence." *Islamic Studies* 21.3 (1982): 48–60.

Hasan, Ahmad. *Analogical Reasoning in Islamic Jurisprudence: a Study of the Juridical Principle of Qiyās.* Islamabad: Islamic Research Institute, 1986a.

Hasan, Ahmad. "Methods of Finding the Cause of a Legal Injunction in Islamic Jurisprudence." *Islamic Studies* 25.1 (1986b): 11–44.

Hassan, Mona. "Modern Interpretations and Misinterpretations of a Medieval Scholar: Apprehending the Political Thought of Ibn Taymiyya." In *Ibn Taymiyya and His Times*, ed. Yossef Rapoport and Shahab Ahmed, 338–366. Karachi: Oxford University Press, 2010.

Hassan, Mona. *Longing for the Lost Caliphate: a Transregional History.* Princeton, NJ: Princeton University Press, 2016.

Al-Ḥibshī, ʿAbd Allāh Muḥammad. *Jāmiʿ al-shurūḥ wa'l-ḥawāshī: muʿjam shāmil li-asmāʾ al-kutub al-mashrūḥa fī l-turāth al-islāmī wa-bayān shurūḥihā*, 3 vols. Abū Dhabī: al-Majmaʿ al-Thaqāfī, 2004.

Hilpinen, Risto, ed. *New Studies in Deontic Logic: Norms, Actions, and the Foundations of Ethics.* Dordrecht: D. Reidel Publ. Co., 1981.

Hintikka, Jaakko. *Time and Necessity: Studies in Aristotle's Theory of Modality.* Oxford: Clarendon Press, 1973.

Hitchcock, Christopher. "Probabilistic Causation." *Stanford Encyclopedia of Philosophy* (online), ed. Edward N. Zalta. 2018.

Hodgson, John A. *Wordsworth's Philosophical Poetry: 1797–1814.* Lincoln: University of Nebraska Press. 1980.

Hoover, Jon. "Perpetual Creativity in the Perfection of God: Ibn Taymiyya's Hadith Commentary on God's Creation of this World." *Journal of Islamic Studies* 15.3 (2004): 287–329.

Hoover, Jon. *Ibn Taymiyya's Theodicy of Perpetual Optimism.* Leiden: Brill, 2007.

Hoover, Jon. "Islamic Universalism: Ibn Qayyim al-Jawziyya's Salafī Deliberations on the Duration of Hell-Fire." *The Muslim World* 99.1 (2009): 181–201.

Hoover, Jon. "God Acts by His Will and Power: Ibn Taymiyya's Theology of a Personal God in his Treatise on the Voluntary Attributes." In *Ibn Taymiyya and His Times*, ed. Yossef Rapoport and Shahab Ahmed, 55–77. Karachi: Oxford University Press, 2010a.

Hoover, Jon. "God's Wise Purposes in Creating Iblīs: Ibn Qayyim al-Ǧawziyyah's Theodicy of God's Names and Attributes." In *A Scholar in the Shadow: Essays in the Legal and Theological Thought of Ibn Qayyim Al-Ǧawziyyah*, ed. Caterina Bori and Livnat Holtzman, *Oriente Moderno* monograph series 90.1 (2010b): 113–134.

Hoover, Jon. "A Muslim Conflict over Universal Salvation." In *Alternative Salvations: Engaging the Sacred and the Secular*, ed. Hannah Bacon, Wendy Dossett, and Steve Knowles, 160–171. London: Bloomsbury, 2015.

Hoover, Jon. "Ibn Taymiyya between Moderation and Radicalism." In *Reclaiming Islamic Tradition: Modern Interpretations of the Classical Heritage*, ed. Elisabeth Kendall and Ahmad Khan, 177–203. Edinburgh, UK: Edinburgh University Press, 2016.

Hoover, Jon. "Reconciling Ibn Taymiyya's Legitimisation of Violence with His Vision of Universal Salvation." In *Violence in Islamic Thought from the Mongols to European Imperialism*, ed. Robert Gleave and István Kristó-Nagy, 107–116. Edinburgh: Edinburgh University Press, 2018.

Hourani, George F. *Reason and Tradition in Islamic Ethics*. Cambridge: Cambridge University Press, 1985.

Ibn Fūrak, Muḥammad. *Maqālāt al-Shaykh Abī 'l-Ḥasan al-Ash'arī, imām ahl al-Sunna*, ed. Aḥmad 'Abd al-Raḥīm al-Sāyiḥ. Cairo: Maktabat al-Thaqāfa al-Dīniyya, 2005.

Ibn al-Ḥājib, Jamāl al-Dīn. *Kitāb Muntahā al-wuṣūl wa'l-amal fī 'ilmay al-uṣūl wa'l-jadal*, editor unknown. Beirut: Dār al-Kutub al-'Ilmiyya, 1985.

Ibn al-Ḥājib, Jamāl al-Dīn. *Mukhtaṣar al-muntahā fī l-sū'l wa'l-amal fī 'ilmay al-uṣūl wa'l-jadal*, ed. Naẓīr Ḥamādū. 2 vols. Algiers: Dār Ibn Ḥazm, 2006.

Ibn Ḥazm. *Al-Iḥkām fī uṣūl al-aḥkām, li'l-ḥāfiẓ Abī Muḥammad 'Alī b. Ḥazm al-Andalusī al-Ẓāhiri*, ed. Aḥmad Muḥammad Shākir, 5 vols. Cairo: Maṭba'at al-Sa'āda [1345–1347].

Ibn Ḥazm. *Al-Nubadh fī uṣūl al-fiqh al-Ẓāhirī, ta'līf al-Imām Ibn Ḥazm*, edited Muḥammad Zāhid al-Kawtharī. Beirut: al-Shirka al-Dawliyya li'l-Ṭibā'a, 2010/1431. Reprint of the Cairo edition of 1940.

Ibn Ḥazm. *Rasā'il Ibn Ḥazm al-Andalusī*, ed. Iḥsān 'Abbās, 4 vols. Beirut: al-Mu'assasa al-'Arabiyya li'l-Dirāsāt wa'l-Nashr, 1980–1983.

Ibn Khaldūn. *Al-Muqaddima*, ed. Étienne M. Quatremère: *Prolégomènes d'Ebn Khaldoun*, 3 vols. Paris: Didot, 1958a.

Ibn Khaldūn. *Ibn Khaldûn. The Muqaddimah: an Introduction to History*, trans. into English by Franz Rosenthal, 3 vols. New York: Pantheon Books, 1958b.

Ibn Khallikān, Aḥmad b. Muḥammad. *Wafayāt al-a'yān wa-anbā' abnā' al-zamān*, ed. Iḥsān 'Abbās. Beirut: Dār al-thaqāfa, 1968–1972.

Ibn Manẓūr. *Lisān al-'Arab al-muḥīṭ*, 7 vols. Būlāq: al-maṭba'a al-amīriyya, 1883–1890.

Ibn Qudāma al-Maqdisī, Muwaffiq al-Dīn 'Abd Allāh. *Rawḍat al-nāẓir wa jannat al-munāẓir fī uṣūl al-fiqh 'alā madhhab al-imām Aḥmad b. Ḥanbal*. Beirut: Mu'assasat al-Rayyān li'l-Ṭibā'a wa'l-Nashr wa'l-Tawzī', 2002.

Ibn Quṭlūbughā, Zayn al-Dīn al-Qāsim b. 'Abd Allāh. *Tāj al-tarājim fī ṭabaqāt al-Ḥanafiyya*, ed. Muḥammad Khayr Ramaḍān Yūsuf. Damascus: Dār al-Qalam, 1992.

Ibn Rushd. *Bidāyat al-mujtahid wa-nihāyat al-muqtaṣid*, ed. 'A. M. Mu'awwaḍ et 'A. A. 'Abd al-Mawjūd, 2 vols. Beirut: Dār al-kutub al-'ilmiyya, 2003.

Ibn Rushd. *The Distinguished Jurist's Primer* [trans. of *Bidāyat al-mujtahid wa nihāyat al-muqtaṣid*]. 2 vols, trans. Imran Ahsan Khan Nyazee. Rev. Mohammad Abdul Rauf. Reading, UK: Centre for Muslim Contribution to Civilization: Garnet, 1994–1996.

Ibn Rushd, *On the Harmony of Religion and Philosophy*, trans. George F. Hourani. London: Gibb Memorial Trust, 2012.

Ibn Rushd. *Averroès: le philosophe et la loi. Édition, traduction et commentaire de l'Abrégé du Mustaṣfā*, ed. Ziad Bou Akl. Berlin: De Gruyter, 2015.

Ibn Ṣā'id al-Andalusī. *Kitāb Ṭabaqāt al-umam li'l-qāḍī... Ibn Ṣā'id al-Andalusī*, ed. Louis Cheikho. Beirut: al-Maṭba'a al-Kāthūlīkiyya li'l-Ābā' al-Yasū'iyyīn, 1912.

Ibn Sīnā. *Manṭiq al-Mashriqiyyīn*, no ed. Cairo: al-Maktaba al-Salafiyya, 1910.

Ibn Sīnā. *Avicenna's Psychology: an English Translation of* Kitāb al-Najāt, *Book II, Chapter VI with Historico-Philosophical Notes and Textual Improvements on the Cairo Edition by F. Rahman*. Westport, Connecticut: Hyperion Press, 1952a.

Ibn Sīnā. *Kitāb al-Shifā', al-Manṭiq, al-Madkhal*, ed. Ibrāhīm Madkūr, Jurj Qanawātī, et al. Cairo: al-Hay'a al-'Āmma li-Shu'ūn al-Maṭābi' al-Amīriyya, 1952b.

Ibn Sīnā. *Kitāb al-Shifā', al-Manṭiq, Kitāb al-Burhān*. Ed. Abū l-'Alā 'Afīfī. Cairo: al-Hay'a al-'Āmma li-Shu'ūn al-Maṭābi' al-Amīriyya, 1956.

Ibn Sīnā. *Kitāb al-Shifā', al-Ilāhiyyāt*, ed. Jurj Qanawātī and Sa'īd Zāyid, 2 vols. Cairo: al-Hay'a al-'Āmma li-Shu'ūn al-Maṭābi' al-Amīriyya, 1960.

Ibn Sīnā. "Logyca." In *Avicennae perhypatetici philosophi ac medicorum facili primi opera in lucem redacta ac nuper quantum ars niti potuit emendata*. Venedig: Scotus, 1508 (Reprint: Frankfurt a.M.: Minerva, 1961).

Ibn Sīnā. *Al-Aḍḥawiyya fī l-ma'ād*. Tehran: Shams Tabrīsī, 1962.

Ibn Sīnā. *Kitāb al-Shifā', al-Manṭiq, al-Qiyās*, ed. Sa'īd Zāyid. Cairo: al-Maṭba'a al-Amīriyya, 1964.

Ibn Sīnā. *Kitāb al-Shifā', al-Manṭiq, al-Jadal*, ed. Aḥmad Fu'ād al-Ahwānī. Cairo: al-Maṭba'a al-Amīriyya, 1965.

Ibn Sīnā. *Al-Ishārāt wa'l-tanbīhāt, al-Taṣawwuf*. Cairo: Dār al-Ma'ārif bi-Miṣr, 1968.

Ibn Sīnā. *'Uyūn al-ḥikma*. Kuweit, Beirut: Wakālat al-Maṭbū'āt, Dār al-Qalam, 1980.

Ibn Sīnā. "Ibn Sīnā's 'Essay on the Secret of Destiny' [*Risāla fī sirr al-qadar*]." In *Reason and Tradition in Islamic Ethics*, ed. George F. Hourani, 227–248. Cambridge: Cambridge University Press, 1985.

Ibn Sīnā. *Al-Shifā', al-Ṭabī'iyyat, Kitāb al-Nafs*. Paris, Beirut: n.p., 1988.

Ibn Sīnā. *Al-Qānūn fī l-ṭibb* [*English Translation*], 2 vols. New Delhi: Dept. of Islamic Studies, Jamia Hamdard, 1993–1998.

Ibn Sīnā. *Al-Qānūn fī l-ṭibb*, ed. Muḥammad Amīn al-Ḍinnāwī, 3 vols. Beirut: Manshūrāt Muḥammad 'Alī Bayḍūn, Dār al-Kutub al-'Ilmiyya, 1999.

Ibn Sīnā. *The Metaphysics of the Healing (al-Shifā': al-Ilāhiyyāt). A parallel English-Arabic text translated, introduced, and annotated by Michael E. Marmura*. Provo, Utah: Brigham Young University Press, 2005.

Ibn Sīnā. *Tis' rasā'il fī l-ḥikma wa'l-ṭabī'iyyāt*. Cairo: Dār al-'Arab, n.d.

Ibn Taymiyya. *Majmū'at al-rasā'il al-kubrā*, 2 parts. Cairo: Al-Maṭba'a al-'āmira al-sharafiyya, 1323/1905.

Ibn Taymiyya. *Majmū'at al-rasā'il wa'l-masā'il*, ed. Muḥammad Rashīd Riḍā, 5 parts. Cairo: Maṭba'at al-manār, 1341–1349/1922–1930.

Ibn Taymiyya. *Majmū' fatāwā Shaykh al-Islām Aḥmad Ibn Taymiyya*, ed. 'Abd al-Raḥmān b. Muḥammad b. Qāsim and Muḥammad b. 'Abd al-Raḥmān b. Muḥammad, 37 vols. Riyadh: Maṭābi' al-Riyāḍ, 1961–1967.

Ibn Taymiyya. *Kitāb al-Radd 'alā 'l-manṭiqiyyīn*. Lahore: Idārah-yi Tarjamān al-Sunnah, 1976.

Ibn Taymiyya. *Al-Amr bi'l-ma'rūf wa'l-nahy 'an al-munkar*, ed. Ṣalāh al-Dīn al-Munajjad. Beirut: Dār al-kitāb al-jadīd, 1984.

Ibn Taymiyya. *Public Duties in Islam: the Institution of Ḥisba*, trans. Muhtar Holland. Leicester, UK: the Islamic Foundation, 1985.

Ibn Taymiyya. *Minhāj al-sunna al-nabawiyya fī naqḍ kalām al-Shīʿa al-Qadariyya*, ed. Muḥammad Rashād Sālim, 9 vols. Riyadh: Jāmiʿat al-Imām Muḥammad b. Suʿūd al-Islāmiyya, 1406/1986.
Ibn Taymiyya. *Al-Fatāwā al-kubrā li-Ibn Taymiyya*, 6 vols. Beirut: Dār al-Kutub al-ʿIlmiyya, 1987.
Ibn Taymiyya. *Majmūʿ al-fatāwā*, ed. ʿAbd al-Raḥmān b. Muḥammad b. Qāsim. Medina: Majmaʿ al-Malik Fahd li-Ṭibāʿat al-Maṣḥaf al-Sharīf, 1995.
Ibn Taymiyya. *Al-Jawāb al-ṣaḥīḥ li-man baddala dīn al-masīḥ*, ed. ʿAlī b. Ḥasan et al., 6 vols. Riyadh: Dār al-ʿĀṣima al-Suʿūdiyya, 1999.
Ibn Taymiyya. *Al-Istiqāma*, ed. Muḥammad Rashād Sālim, 2 parts. Beirut: Dār Ibn Ḥazm, 1420/2000.
[Ibn Taymiyya (?)]. *Tanbīh al-rajul al-ʿāqil ʿalā tamwīh al-jadal al-bāṭil*, ed. ʿAlī b. Muḥammad al-ʿImrān and Muḥammad ʿUzayr Shams. Mecca: Dār ʿĀlam al-Fawāʾid li'l-Nashr wa'l-Tawzīʿ, 2004.
Ibn Taymiyya. *Kitāb al-Radd ʿalā 'l-manṭiqiyyīn, al-musammā ayḍan Naṣīḥat ahl al-īmān fī l-radd ʿalā manṭiq al-yunān*, ed. ʿAbd al-Ṣamad Sharaf al-Dīn al-Kutubī. Beirut: Muʾassasat al-Rayyān, 2005.
Ierodiakonou, Katerina. "Alexander of Aphrodisias on Medicine as a Stochastic Art." In *Ancient Medicine in its Socio-Cultural Context*, ed. P. van der Eijk, H.F.J. Horstmanshoff, and P.H. Schrijvers, vol. 2, 473–485. Amsterdam: Brill, 1995.
Al-Ījī, ʿAḍud al-Dīn. *Sharḥ Mukhtaṣar al-Muntahā* (with glosses by al-Taftazānī and al-Jurjānī), ed. Fādī Naṣīf and Ṭāriq Yaḥyā. Beirut: Dār al-Kutub al-ʿIlmiyya, 2000.
Al-ʿImrān, ʿAlī b. Muḥammad and Muḥammad ʿUzayr Shams. "Al-Adilla al-Qawiyya fī Ithbāt Nisbat *Kitāb Tanbīh al-Rajul al-ʿĀqil ʿalā Tamwīh al-Jadal al-Bāṭil* li-Muʾallifihi Shaykh al-Islām Ibn Taymiyya." Online at majles.alukah.net/t1512. 1428 [2007].
Inati, Shams C. *The Problem of Evil: Ibn Sīnā's Theodicy.* Albany, NY: State University of New York Press, 2000.
Al-Iṣfahānī, Abū l-Faraj. *Kitāb Adab al-ghurabāʾ*, ed. Ṣalāḥ al-Dīn al-Munajjid. Beirut: Dār al-Kitāb al-Jadīd, 1972.
Al-Iṣfahānī, Abū l-Faraj. *The Book of Strangers: Medieval Arabic Graffiti on the Theme of Nostalgia*, trans. Patricia Crone and Shmuel Moreh. Princeton: Wiener, 2000.
Al-Iṣfahānī, Muḥammad Taqī. *Hidāyat al-mustarshidīn fī sharḥ Maʿālim al-dīn.* Qum: Muʾassasat al-Nashr al-Islāmī, 1420–1421/2000–2001.
Al-Iṣfahānī, Shams al-Dīn. *Bayān al-Mukhtaṣar: Sharḥ Mukhtaṣar Ibn al-Ḥājib*, ed. Muḥammad Maẓhur Baqqā. Makka: Jāmiʿat Umm al-Qurā, 1986.
Al-Iṣfahānī, Shams al-Dīn. *Sharḥ al-Minhāj li'l-Bayḍāwī fī ʿilm al-uṣūl*, ed. ʿAbd al-Karīm b. ʿAlī b. Muḥammad al-Namla. Riyadh: Maktabat al-Rushd, 1999 [1420].
Al-Iṣfahānī, Shams al-Dīn. *Tasdīd al-qawāʿid fī sharḥ Tajrīd al-ʿaqāʾid*, ed. Khālid b. Ḥammād al-ʿAdwānī. Kuwait: Dār al-Ḍiyāʾ, 2012.
Al-Isnawī, Jamāl al-Dīn. *Nihāyat al-sūʾl fī sharḥ Minhāj al-wuṣūl ilā ʿilm al-uṣūl li'l-qāḍī Nāṣir al-Dīn al-Bayḍāwī*, editor unknown. Beirut: ʿĀlam al-Kutub, n.d.
Jabr, Farīd and Rafīq al-ʿAjam. *Mawsūʿat muṣṭalaḥāt ʿilm al-manṭiq ʿinda al-ʿarab.* Beirut: Maktabat Lubnān Nāshirūn, 1996.
Al-Jaṣṣāṣ, Abū Bakr. *al-Fuṣūl fī l-uṣūl.* Kuwait: Wizārat al-Awqāf wa-al-Shuʾūn al-Islāmiyyah, 1994.

Johansen, Baber. *Contingency in a Sacred Law: Legal and Ethical Norms in the Muslim Fiqh.* Leiden: Brill, 1999.

Al-Juwaynī, Imām al-Ḥaramayn. *Al-Kāfiya fī l-jadal*, ed. Fawqiya Ḥusayn Maḥmūd. Cairo: Maṭba'at 'Īsā al-Bābī al-Ḥalabī, 1979.

Al-Juwaynī, Imām al-Ḥaramayn. *Al-Talkhīṣ fī uṣūl al-fiqh*, ed. Muḥammad Ḥasan Ismā'īl. Beirut: Dār al-Kutub al-'Ilmiyya, 2003.

Johansen, Baber. "A Perfect Law in an Imperfect Society: Ibn Taymiyya's Concept of 'Governance in the Name of the Sacred Law'." In *The Law Applied: Contextualizing the Islamic Shari'a*, ed. Peri Bearman et al., 259–293. London: I.B. Tauris, 2008.

Al-Jurjānī, 'Abd al-Qāhir. *Dalā'il al-i'jāz*, ed. Muḥammad 'Abd al-Mun'im Khafājī. Cairo: Maktabat al-Qāhira, 1969.

Kaḥḥāla, 'Umar Riḍā. *Mu'jam al-mu'allifīn: tarājim muṣannifī l-kutub al-'arabiyya*, 15 vols in 8. Beirut: Dār Iḥyā' al-Turāth al-'Arabī, 1980.

Kalbarczyk, Nora. *Sprachphilosophie in der islamischen Rechtstheorie. Zur avicennischen Klassifikation der Bezeichnung bei Faḫr ad-dīn ar-Rāzī (gest. 606/1210).* Leiden: Brill, 2018a.

Kalbarczyk, Nora. "Explicitly Said or Only Implied? The Development of the *manṭūq/mafhūm* Dichotomy in Islamic Legal Hermeneutics." *Oriens* 46 (2018b): 186–221.

Kamali, Mohammad Hashim. *Principles of Islamic Jurisprudence.* Cambridge: Islamic Texts Society, 2003.

Karabela, Mehmet Kadri. "The Development of Dialectic and Argumentation Theory in Post-Classical Islamic Intellectual History." PhD diss., McGill University, 2010.

Al-Karakī, Ḥusayn b. Shihāb al-Dīn. *Hidāyat al-abrār ilā ṭarīq al-a'imma al-aṭhār.* Baghdad: 1977.

Karimullah, Kamran I. *Avicenna (d. 1037), Logical Theory, and the Aristotelian Tradition.* Montreal: McGill University, 2014.

Karimullah, Kamran I. "Unusual Syllogisms: Avicenna and Najm al-Dīn al-Kātibī on *per impossibile* Syllogisms and Implication (*luzūm*)." *Oriens* 43.1–2 (2015): 223–271.

Al-Kashānī, Muḥsin Fayḍ. *'Ayn al-yaqīn/al-Anwār wa'l-asrār.* Qum: Anwār al-Hudā, 2007.

Al-Kashānī, Muḥsin Fayḍ. *Anwār al-ḥikma.* Beirut: Dār al-Amīra, 2005.

Al-Kātibī al-Qazwīnī, 'Alī b. 'Umar. *Logic of the Arabians* [*al-Risāla al-Shamsiyya*], ed. and trans. Aloys Sprenger. Calcutta: F. Carbery, Bengal Military Orphan Press, 1854.

Kaya, M. Cüneyt. "Prophetic Legislation: Avicenna's View of Practical Philosophy Revisited." In *Philosophy and the Abrahamic Religions: Scriptural Hermeneutics and Epistemology*, ed. Torrance Kirby et al., 205–223. Cambridge: Cambridge Scholars Publishing, 2013.

Khoo, Christopher, Syin Chan, and Yun Niu. "The Many Facets of the Cause-Effect Relation." In *The Semantics of Relationships*, ed. Rebecca Green et al., 51–70. Dordrecht: Springer, 2002.

Al-Kīlānī, Quṭb al-Dīn. *Sharḥ 'alā Ādāb al-baḥth li'l-Samarqandī.* MS Istanbul, Süleymaniye Kütüphanesi, Damad İbrahim 1043 (826 H); foll. 1b–40b.

Al-Kīlānī, Quṭb al-Dīn. *Sharḥ al-Risāla al-Samarqandiyya fī ādāb al-baḥth.* MS Oxford, Bodleian Library, Laud Or. 192 (834 H); foll. 17b–55b.

Klein-Franke, Felix. "The Non-Existent is a Thing." *Le Muséon* 107 (1994): 375–390.

Kleinknecht, Angelika. "Al-Qisṭās al-mustaqīm: Eine Ableitung der Logik aus dem Koran." In *Islamic Philosophy and the Classical Tradition*, ed. S.M. Stern, A. Hourani, and V. Brown, 159–187. Oxford: Cassirer, 1972.

Kneale, William and Martha Kneale. *The Development of Logic*. Oxford: Clarendon Press, 1962 (reprint 2008).
Knuuttila, Simo. "The Emergence of Deontic Logic in the Fourteenth Century." In *New Studies in Deontic Logic: Norms, Actions, and the Foundations of Ethics*, ed. Risto Hilpinen, 225–248. Dordrecht: D. Reidel Publ. Co., 1981.
Krawietz, Birgit. "Zum Verhältnis von Sprache, Recht und Theologie in der islamischen Rechtstheorie von Sayf al-Dīn al-Āmidī." *Der Islam* 72 (1995): 137–147.
Krawietz, Birgit and Tamer, Georges, eds. *Islamic Theology, Philosophy and Law: Debating Ibn Taymiyya and Ibn Qayyim al-Jawziyya*. Berlin: de Gruyter, 2013.
Al-Laknawī, Niẓām al-Dīn al-Anṣārī. *Fawātiḥ al-raḥamūt bi-sharḥ Musallam al-thubūt*, ed. ʿAbdallāh Maḥmūd Muḥammad ʿUmar. Beirut: Dār al-Kutub al-ʿIlmiyya, 2002.
Al-Laknawī al-Hindī, Abū ʾl-Ḥasanāt Muḥammad ʿAbd al-Ḥayy. *Kitāb al-Fawāʾid al-bahiyya fī tarājim al-Ḥanafiyya*, ed. Muḥammad Badr al-Dīn Abū Firās al-Naʿsānī. Cairo: Maṭbaʿat al-Saʿāda, 1324 [1906].
Lameer, Joep. *Al-Fārābī and Aristotelian Syllogistics: Greek Theory and Islamic Practice*. Leiden: Brill, 1994.
Lameer, Joep. *Conception and Belief in Ṣadr al-Dīn Shīrāzī*. Teheran: Iranian Institute of Philosophy, 2006.
Lameer, Joep. "Ibn Ḥazm's Logical Pedigree." In *Ibn Ḥazm of Cordoba: the Life and Works of a Controversial Thinker*, ed. Camilla Adang et al., 417–428. Leiden: Brill, 2013.
Lameer, Joep. "*Ghayr al-Maʿlūm Yamtaniʿ al-Ḥukm ʿalayhi:* an Exploratory Anthology of a False Paradox in Medieval Islamic Philosophy." *Oriens* 42 (2014): 397–453.
Lane, Edward W. *An Arabic-English Lexicon*, 8 vols. Beirut: Librarie du Liban, 1968; New Delhi: Asian Educational Services, 2003 [reprints; first published in 1863–1893].
Lange, Christian. "Expiation." In *EI3*.
Laoust, Henri. *Essai sur les doctrines sociales et politiques de Taḳī-d-Dīn Aḥmad b. Taimīya*. Cairo: Imprimerie de l'institute français d'archéologie orientale, 1939.
Legenhausen, Hajj Muhammad. "Ibn Sīnā's Practical Philosophy." In *Religious Inquiries* 2 (2013): 5–27.
Mackie, John Leslie. *The Cement of the Universe: a Study of Causation*. Oxford: Clarendon Press, 1974.
Madelung, Wilferd. "Al-Ghazālī's Changing Attitude to Philosophy." In *Islam and Rationality: the Impact of al-Ghazālī. Papers Collected on his 900th Anniversary*, ed. Georges Tamer, vol. 1, 23–34. Leiden: Brill, 2015.
Al-Maḥallī, Aḥmad, Saʿd al-Dīn al-Taftazānī, and ʿAbd al-Qādir al-Kurdī. *Tanwīr al-mashriq sharḥ Tahdhīb al-manṭiq*. Cairo: Maṭbaʿat al-Saʿāda, 1913.
Mahdi, Muhsin. "Language and Logic." In *Logic in Classical Islamic Culture*, ed. G. E. von Grunebaum, 51–83. Wiesbaden: Otto Harrassowitz, 1970.
Makdisi, George. "The *Tanbīh* of Ibn Taimīya on Dialectic: the Pseudo-ʿAqīlian *Kitāb al-Farq*." In *Medieval and Middle Eastern Studies in Honour of Aziz Suryal Atiya*, ed. Sami A. Hanna, 285–294. Leiden: Brill, 1972.
Makdisi, George. "Ethics in Islamic Traditionalist Doctrine." In *Ethics in Islam*, ed. Richard Hovannisian, 47–63. Malibu, California: Undena Publications, 1985.
Al-Maqdisī, Muṭahhar b. Ṭāhir. *Kitāb al-Badʾ waʾl-Taʾrīkh*, ed. and French trans. Clément Huart, 6 vols. Paris: Ernest Leroux, 1899–1919.

Marcotte, Roxanne. "*Al-Masāʾil al-Qudsiyya* and Mullā Ṣadrā's Proofs for Mental Existence." *Journal of Islamic Studies* 22.2 (2011): 153–182.
Marlow, Louise. "Kings, Prophets and the ʿUlamāʾ in Mediaeval Islamic Advice Literature." *Studia Islamica* 81 (1995): 101–120.
March, Andrew F., "Falsafa and Law." In *The Oxford Handbook of Islamic Law*, ed. Anver M. Emon and Rumee Ahmed. New Haven: Yale Law School, 2015 online (printed 2018).
Marmura, Michael E. "Ghazali's Attitude to the Secular Sciences and Logic." In *Essays in Islamic Philosophy and Science*, ed. George Hourani, 100–111. Albany: State University of New York Press, 1975.
Al-Matroudi, Abdul Hakim. *The Ḥanbalī School of Law and Ibn Taymiyyah: Conflict or Conciliation.* London: Routledge, 2006.
Al-Matroudi, Abdul Hakim. "The Removal of Blame from the Great Imāms: an Annotated Translation of Ibn Taymiyyah's *Rafʿ al-malām ʿan al-aʾimmat* [sic] *al-aʿlām*." *Islamic Studies* 46.3 (2007): 317–380.
Matilla, Janne. "The Ethical Progression of the Philosopher in al-Rāzī and al-Fārābī." *Arabic Sciences and Philosophy* 27 (2017): 115–137.
Al-Mawsūʿa al-fiqhiyya, 45 vols. Kuwait: Wizārat al-Awqāf wa'l-Shuʾūn al-Islāmiyya, 1983–2006.
McGinnis, Jon. "Scientific Methodologies in Medieval Islam." *Journal of the History of Philosophy* 41.3 (2003): 307–327.
McGinnis, Jon. "Avicenna's Naturalized Epistemology and Scientific Method." In *The Unity of Science in the Arabic Tradition*, ed. Shahid Rahman et al., 129–152. Dordrecht: Springer, 2008.
McGinnis, Jon. *Avicenna.* Oxford: Oxford University Press, 2010.
McGinnis, Jon and David C. Reisman. *Classical Arabic Philosophy: an Anthology of Sources.* Indianapolis: Hackett, 2007.
McNamara, Paul. "Deontic Logic." *Stanford Encyclopedia of Philosophy* (online), ed. Edward N. Zalta. 2014.
Mehren, August F.M. *Die Rhetorik der Araber.* Copenhagen: Otto Schwartz, 1853.
Michot, Jean. *La destinée de l'homme selon Avicenne.* Leuven: Peeters, 1986.
Michot, Yahya. "Un célibataire endurci et sa maman: Ibn Taymiyya (m. 728/1328) et les femmes." *Acta Orientalia Belgica* 15 (2001): 165–190.
Michot, Yahya. *Muslims under Non-Muslim Rule.* Oxford, UK: Interface Publications, 2006.
Michot, Yahya. *Ibn Taymiyya Against Extremisms.* Beirut: Dar Albouraq, 2012a.
Michot, Yahya. "L'autorité, l'individu et la communauté face à la *sharīʿa:* quelques pensées d'Ibn Taymiyya." *Mélanges de l'Université Saint-Joseph* 54 (2012b): 261–286.
Michot, Yahya. "Ibn Taymiyya's Critique of Shīʿī Imāmology." *The Muslim World* 104.1–2 (2014): 109–149.
Mikhail, John. "Islamic Rationalism and the Foundation of Human Rights." In *Pluralism and Law: Proceedings of the 20th IVR Congress*, vol. 3: Global Problems, ed. Arend Soeteman, 61–70. Frankfurt: Steiner, 2004.
Mill, John Stuart. *A System of Logic: Ratiocinative and Inductive.* In *The Collected Works of John Stuart Mill*, ed. John M. Robson, vols. 7–8. Toronto: University of Toronto Press, 1963–1991.

Miller, Larry Benjamin. "Islamic Disputation Theory: a Study of the Development of Dialectic in Islam from the Tenth Through Fourteenth Centuries." PhD diss., Princeton University, 1984.

Mīrzā Qummī. *Qawānīn al-uṣūl (al-Qawānīn al-muḥkama fī l-uṣūl al-mutqana)*. Qum: Dār al-Mahajja al-Bayḍā', 2008.

Al-Miṣrī, Ibn al-Naqīb Aḥmad b. Lu'lu'. *Reliance of the Traveller: the Classic Manual of Islamic Sacred Law 'Umdat al-Sālik*, trans. Nuh Ha Mim Keller. Evanston: Sunna Books, 1994.

Mohamed, Yasien. 2015. "The Duties of the Teacher: Al-Iṣfahānī's *Dharī'a* as a Source of Inspiration for al-Ghazālī's *Mīzān al-'Amal*." In *Islam and Rationality: the Impact of al-Ghazālī. Papers Collected on his 900th Anniversary*, Vol. I, ed. Georges Tamer, 186–206. Leiden: Brill.

Morris, James W. "The Philosopher-Prophet in Avicenna's Political Philosophy." In *The Political Aspects of Islamic Philosophy: Essays in Honor of Muhsin S. Mahdi*, ed. Charles E. Butterworth, 152–198. Cambridge, Massachusetts: Harvard University Press, 1992.

Muehlethaler, Lukas. "Revising Avicenna's Ontology of the Soul: Ibn Kammūna on the Soul's Eternity *a Parte Ante*." *The Muslim World* 102.3–4 (2012): 597–616.

Mullā Khusraw. *Mir'āt al-uṣūl fī sharḥ Mirqāt al-wuṣūl fī uṣūl al-fiqh li'l-'allāma Manla Khusru*, 3 vols. Istanbul: Fazilat Neşriyat ve Ticaret A.Ş. [1307].

Mullā Khusraw. [On the margin of:] al-Izmīrī, Sulaymān b. 'Abdallāh. *Ḥāshiyat al-Izmīrī 'alā Mir'āt al-uṣūl fī sharḥ Mirqāt al-wuṣūl fī uṣūl al-fiqh li'l-'allāma Munlā Khusrū*, 3 vols. [Istanbul]: al-Sharīka al-Ṣaḥīfiyya al-'Uthmaniyya [1309].

Mullā Ṣadra. *Al-Ḥikma al-muta'aliyya fī l-asfār al-'aqliyya al-arba'a*. Beirut: Dār Iḥyā' al-Turāth al-'Arabī, 1981.

Al-Nasafī, Burhān al-Dīn. *Sharḥ al-Fuṣūl fī 'ilm al-jadal*. MS Istanbul, Süleymaniye Kütüphanesi, Amcazade Hüseyin 403, foll. 19b–25a.

Al-Nasafī, Burhān al-Dīn. *Sharḥ al-Fuṣūl fī 'ilm al-jadal*. MS Berlin, Staatsbibliothek zu Berlin, Landberg 72, fol. 54a–58a

Al-Nasafī, Burhān al-Dīn. *Al-Fuṣūl fī al-jadal*. In [Ibn Taymiyya (?)], *Tanbīh al-rajul al-'āqil 'alā tamwīh al-jadal al-bāṭil*, ed. 'Alī b. Muḥammad al-'Imrān and Muḥammad 'Uzayr Shams, 639–668. Mecca: Dār 'Ālam al-Fawā'id li'l-Nashr wa'l-Tawzī', 2004.

Al-Nasafī, Burhān al-Dīn. *Sharḥ al-Fuṣūl fī 'ilm al-jadal*, ed. Sharīfa bint 'Alī al-Ḥūshānī. Riyadh: Jāmi'at al-Malik Sa'ūd al-Nashr al-'Ilmī wa'l-Muṭābi', 2012.

Al-Nasafī, Burhān al-Dīn. *Commentary upon the Foundation of Intellectual Perspicacity: Concerning Logic, Natural Philosophy, Metaphysics and Mathematics; Sharḥ 'Asās al-Kiyāsa [Sharḥ Asās al-kiyāsa fī l-'ulūm al-arba'a al-manṭiq wa'l-ṭabī'ī wa'l-ilāhī wa'l-riyāḍī]*, ed. Gholamreza Dadkhah and Abbas Goodarznia. Costa Mesa, CA: Mazda Publishers, 2015.

al-Nasafī, Burhān al-Dīn. *Al-Fuṣūl*. In Necmettin Pehlivan and Hadi Ensar Ceylan, "Ādābu'l-Baḥs̱ Devrimine Doğru Son Evrim: Burhānuddīn en-Nesefī'nin el-*Fuṣūl*'ü." *Ankara Üniversitesi İlahiyat Fakültesi Dergisi* 56.2 (2015): 1–75 (at 41–75).

Al-Nashshār, 'Alī Sāmī. *Manāhij al-baḥth 'inda mufakkirī al-islām wa-iktishāf al-manhaj al-'ilmī fī al-'ālam al-Islāmī*. Beirut: Dār al-Nahḍa al-'Arabiyya, 1984.

Nasr, Seyyed Hossein. "The Meaning and Concept of Philosophy in Islam." In *History of Islamic Philosophy*, ed. Seyyed Hossein Nasr and Oliver Leaman, vol. 1, 21–26. London: Routledge, 1996.

Niẓām al-Mulk. *The Rules of Government or Rules for Kings: the Siyar al-Muluk or Siyasat-nama of Nizam al-Mulk*, trans. Hubert Darke. London: Routledge and Kegan Paul, 1960.

Nuseibeh, Sari. "*Al-ʿAql al-Qudsī:* Avicenna's Subjective Theory of Knowledge." *Studia Islamica* 69 (1989): 39–54.

Oertmann, Paul. *Interesse und Begriff in der Rechtswissenschaft.* Leipzig: A. Deichertsche Verlagsbuchhandlung, 1931.

Opwis, Felicitas. "*Maṣlaḥa* in Contemporary Islamic Legal Theory," *Islamic Law and Society* 12 (2005): 182–223.

Opwis, Felicitas. Maṣlaḥa *and the Purpose of the Law: Islamic Discourse on Legal Change from the 4th/10th to 8th/14th Century.* Leiden: Brill, 2010.

Opwis, Felicitas. "Shifting Legal Authority from the Ruler to the *ʿUlamāʾ:* Rationalizing the Punishment for Drinking Wine During the Saljūq Period." *Der Islam* 86 (2011): 65–92.

Opwis, Felicitas. "Attributing Causality to God's Law: the Solution of Fakhr ad-Dīn ar-Rāzī." In *Islamic Philosophy, Science, and Religion: Studies in Honor of Dimitri Gutas*, ed. Felicitas Opwis and David C. Reisman, 397–418. Leiden: Brill, 2012.

Ormsby, Eric. "Review of A. Kevin Reinhart: *Before Revelation.*" In *Islamic Law and Society* 5 (1998): 118–123.

Ormsby, Eric. "Response to A. Kevin Reinhart." *Islamic Law and Society* 6 (1999): 419–420.

Pfeiffer, Judith. "Introduction. From Baghdad to Marāgha, Tabriz, and Beyond: Tabriz and the Multi-Cephalous Cultural, Religious, and Intellectual Landscape of the 13th to 15th Century Nile-to-Oxus Region." In *Politics, Patronage, and the Transmission of Knowledge in 13th–15th Century Tabriz*, ed. Judith Pfeiffer, 1–11. Leiden: Brill, 2014.

Polansky, Roland. *The Cambridge Companion to Aristotle's Nicomachean Ethics.* Cambridge: Cambridge University Press, 2014.

Popper, Karl R. *Conjectures and Refutations: the Growth of Scientific Knowledge.* New York: Basic Books, 1962.

Al-Qarāfī, Shihāb al-Dīn. *Nafāʾis al-uṣūl fī sharḥ al-Maḥṣūl*, 4 vols. ed. Muḥammad ʿAbd al-Qādir ʿAṭā. Beirut: Dār al-kutub al-ʿilmiyya, 2000.

Al-Qarawī al-Isfahānī, Muḥammad Ḥusayn. *Nihāyat al-dirāya fī sharḥ al-Kifāyah*, 3 vols. Beirut: 2008.

Al-Qazwīnī, Mullā Khalīl. *Ḥāshiyat al-ʿUdda.* Qum: Muʾassasat Āl Bauy, n.d.

Rahman, Fazlur. "Law and Ethics in Islam." In *Ethics in Islam*, ed. Richard Hovannisian, 103–121. Malibu, California: Undena Publications, 1985.

Rahman, Shahid and Mohamed Iqbal. "Unfolding Parallel Reasoning in Islamic Jurisprudence: Epistemic and Dialectical Meaning in Abū Isḥāq al-Shīrāzī's System of Co-Relational Inferences of the Occasioning Factor." *Arabic Sciences and Philosophy* 28.1 (2018): 67–132.

Ramić, Shukrija H. *Language and the Interpretation of Islamic Law.* Cambridge: Islamic Texts Society, 2003.

Rapoport, Yossef. "Ibn Taymiyya's Radical Legal Thought: Rationalism, Pluralism and the Primacy of Intention." In *Ibn Taymiyya and His Times*, ed. Yossef Rapoport and Shahab Ahmed, 191–226. Karachi: Oxford University Press, 2010.

Al-Rāzī, Abū Ḥātim. *Aʿlām al-nubuwwa: al-radd ʿalā l-mulḥid Abī Bakr al-Rāzī.* [A new printing by Georges Tarabishi of the Tehran edition.] Beirut: Dār al-Sāqī, 2003.

Al-Rāzī, Fakhr al-Dīn. *Al-Maḥṣūl fī ʿilm uṣūl al-fiqh*, ed. Ṭaha Jābir Fayyāḍ al-ʿAlwānī. Riyadh: Jāmiʿat al-Imām Muḥammad b. Suʿūd al-Islāmiyya, 1979.

Al-Rāzī, Fakhr al-Dīn. *Nihāyat al-Ījāz fī dirāyat al-iʿjāz*, ed. Bakrī Shaykh Amīn. Beirut: Dār al-ʿilm li'l-malāyīn, 1985.

Al-Rāzī, Fakhr al-Dīn. *Al-Maḥṣūl fī ʿilm uṣūl al-fiqh*, ed. Ṭaha Jābir Fayyāḍ al-ʿAlwānī, 6 vols. Beirut: Mu'assasat al-risāla, 1991/2.

Al-Rāzī, Fakhr al-Dīn. *Al-Maʿālim fī uṣūl al-fiqh*, ed. Muḥammad Ḥasan Ismāʿīl. Beirut: Dār al-Kutub al-ʿIlmiyya, 2007.

Al-Rāzī, Fakhr al-Dīn. *Al-Tafsīr al-kabīr aw Mafātīḥ al-ghayb*, ed. Ibrāhīm Shams al-Dīn and Aḥmad Shams al-Din. Beirut: Dār al-Kutub al-ʿIlmiyya, 2013.

Al-Rāzī al-Taḥtānī, Quṭb al-Dīn, ʿAlī b. ʿUmar al-Kātibī al-Qazwīnī, and al-Sayyid al-Sharīf al-Jurjānī. *Taḥrīr al-qawāʿid al-manṭiqiyya fī sharḥ al-Risāla al-shamsiyya li-Najm al-Dīn ʿAlī al-Kātibī al-Qazwīnī*, ed. Muḥsin Bīdārfar. Qum: Intishārāt Bīdār, 2003.

Reinhart, A. Kevin. "Islamic Law as Islamic Ethics." *Journal of Religious Ethics* 11.2 (1983):186–203.

Reinhart, A. Kevin. *Before Revelation: the Boundaries of Muslim Moral Thought*. New York: State University of New York Press, 1995.

Reinhart, A. Kevin. "Response to Eric Ormsby's review of *Before Revelation*." In *Islamic Law and Society* 6 (1999): 417–419.

Reinhart, A. Kevin. "Mollā Ḫüsrev: Ottoman Jurist and *uṣūlī*". In *Studies in Islamic Law*, ed. Andreas Christmann and Robert Gleave, 245–281. Oxford: Oxford University Press, 2007.

Repp, Richard Cooper. *The Müfti of Istanbul: a Study in the Development of the Ottoman Learned Hierarchy*. London: Ithaca Press, 1986.

Rescher, Nicholas. *The Development of Arabic Logic*. Pittsburgh: University of Pittsburgh Press, 1964.

Richardson, Kara. "Causation in Arabic and Islamic Thought." In *Stanford Encyclopedia of Philosophy* (online), ed. Edward N. Zalta. 2015.

Rizvi, Sajjad H. "Mullā Ṣadrā and Causation: Rethinking a Problem in Later Islamic Philosophy." *Philosophy East and West* 55.4 (2005): 570–583.

Rizvi, Sajjad H. *Mullā Ṣadra and Metaphysics: Modulation of Being*. Routledge: London, 2009.

Rizvi, Sajjad H. "Mulla Sadra." In *Stanford Encyclopedia of Philosophy* (online), ed. Edward N. Zalta. 2018.

Robinson, Chase. "The Rise of Islam: 600–700." In *The New Cambridge History of Islam*, ed. Chase Robinson, 193–202. Cambridge: Cambridge University Press, 2010.

Rosenthal, Franz. *Das Fortleben der Antike im Islam*. Zürich: Artemis Verlag, 1965.

Rosenthal, Franz. "On Art and Aesthetics in Graeco-Arabic Wisdom Literature," in *Four Essays on Art and Literature in Islam*, 1–19. Leiden: Brill, 1971.

Rosenthal, Franz. *"Sweeter than Hope": Complaint and Hope in Medieval Islam*. Leiden: Brill, 1983.

Roth, Norman. "Forgery and Abrogation of the Torah: a Theme in Muslim and Christian Polemic in Spain." *Proceedings of the American Academy of Jewish Research* 54 (1987): 203–236.

El-Rouayheb, Khaled. "Theology and Logic." In *The Oxford Handbook of Islamic Theology*, ed. Sabine Schmidtke, 408–431. Oxford: Oxford University Press, 2016.

Rudolph, Ulrich. "Die Neubewertung der Logik durch al-Ġazālī." In *Logik und Theologie: Das Organon im arabischen und im lateinischen Mittelalter*, ed. Dominik Perler and Ulrich Rudolph, 73–97. Leiden: Brill, 2005.

Rudolph, Ulrich. "Abū Naṣr al-Fārābī." In *Philosophy in the Islamic World*, vol. 1: *8th–10th Centuries*, ed. Ulrich Rudolph, Rotraud Hansberger, and Peter Adamson, 527–654. Leiden: Brill, 2017.

Rudolph, Ulrich. "Auf der Suche nach Erkenntnis zwischen Asien und Europa: al-Ġazālī, Descartes und die moderne Forschungswissenschaft." *Asiatische Studien* 72 (2018): 1–29.

Rudolph, Ulrich. "Post-Ghazālian Theology: What were the Lessons to be Learned from al-Ghazālī?" In *Philosophical Theology in Islam: the Later Ashʿarī Tradition*, ed. Ayman Shihadeh and Jan Thiele. Leiden: Brill, forthcoming.

Ibn Rushd, Abū 'l-Walīd Muḥammad. *The Distinguished Jurist's Primer* [*Bidāyat al-mujtahid wa nihāyat al-muqtaṣid*], trans. Imran Ahsan Khan Nyazee, rev. Mohammad Abdul Rauf, 2 vols. Reading, UK: Garnet, 1994–1996.

Sabra, Adam. "Ibn Ḥazm's Literalism: a Critique of Islamic Legal Theory?" In *Ibn Ḥazm of Cordoba: the Life and Works of a Controversial Thinker*, ed. Camilla Adang et al., 97–160. Leiden: Brill, 2013.

Said, Yazeed. *Al-Ghazālī's Politics in Context*. London: Routledge, 2013.

Al-Sakkākī, Sīrāj al-Dīn. *Miftāḥ al-ʿulūm*, ed. ʿAbdul Ḥamīd Hindāwī. Beirut: Dār al-Kutub al-ʿIlmiyya, 2011.

Al-Samarqandī, Shams al-Dīn Muḥammad. *Kitāb ʿAyn al-naẓar fī ʿilm al-jadal*. MS London, British Library, Or. 3730.

Al-Samarqandī, Shams al-Dīn Muḥammad. *Kitāb ʿAyn al-naẓar fī ʿilm al-jadal*. MS London, British Library, Or. 3908.

Al-Samarqandī, Shams al-Dīn Muḥammad. *Sharḥ Fuṣūl al-nasafī*. MS Istanbul, Süleymaniye Kütüphanesi, Esad Efendi 3034, foll. 16a–19b.

Al-Samarqandī, Shams al-Dīn Muḥammad. *Sharḥ Fuṣūl al-nasafī*. MS London, British Library, Or. 11183, foll. 15b–19b.

Al-Samarqandī, Shams al-Dīn Muḥammad. *Ādāb al-ḥakīm Shams al-Dīn al-Samarqandī* [*al-Risāla fī Ādāb al-baḥth*]. In *Majmūʿa mushtamila ʿalā l-ātī bayānuhu: al-awwal* […], ed. Maḥmūd al-Imām al-Manṣūrī, 125–132. Cairo: Maṭbaʿat al-Saʿāda, 1353 [1934].

Al-Samarqandī, Shams al-Dīn Muḥammad. *Science of the Cosmos and the Soul* [*ʿIlm al-āfāq wa'l-anfus*], ed. Gholamreza Dadkhah. Costa Mesa, CA: Mazda Publishers, 2014.

Santayana, George. *Three Philosophical Poets: Lucretius, Dante, and Goethe*. Cambridge, Massachusetts: Harvard University Press, 1910.

Al-Sayyed Ahmad, ʿAzmī T. *Al-Ghazālī's Views on Logic*. University of Edinburgh: PhD Diss., 1981.

Schacht, Joseph. *The Origins of Muhammadan Jurisprudence*. Oxford: Clarendon, 1950.

Schneider, Egon and Friedrich E. Schnapp. *Logik für Juristen: die Grundlagen der Denklehre und der Rechtsanwendung*. München: Franz Vahlen, 2006.

Schöck, Cornelia. *Koranexegese, Grammatik und Logik: zum Verhältnis von arabischer und aristotelischer Urteils-, Konsequenz- und Schlusslehre*. Leiden: Brill, 2006.

Schöck, Cornelia. "Discussions on Conditional Sentences from the Year AH 17/AD 638 to Avicenna." In *Classical Arabic Philosophy: Sources and Reception*, ed. Peter Adamson, 55–73. London: the Warburg Institute, 2007.

Schmidtke, Sabine. "The doctrinal views of the Banu l-ʿAwd (Early 8th/14th Century): an Analysis of ms Arab. f. 64 (Bodleian Library, Oxford)." In *Le shiʿisme imamite quarante ans après. Hommage à Etan Kohlberg*, ed. M. A. Amir-Moezzi et al., 357–382. Turnhout: Brepols, 2009.
Al-Shāfiʿī. *Dīwān al-Shāfiʿī*, edited and redacted by Muḥammad Yakan. Beirut: Yakan and Mneimne Publishing Houses, 1400/1979.
Al-Shāfiʿī. *Dīwān al-Shāfiʿī*, ed. Iḥsān ʿAbbās. Beirut: Dār Ṣādir, 1996.
Al-Sharīf al-Murtaḍā, *Rasāʾil al-Sharīf al-Murtaḍā*. Qum: Khayyām, 1984.
Al-Shahrazūrī, Ibn al-Ṣalāḥ. *An Introduction to the Science of the Ḥadīth: Kitāb Maʿrifat anwāʿ ʿilm al-ḥadīth*, trans. Eerik Dickinson. Reading: Garnet Publishing, 2006.
El Shamsy, Ahmed. "The Wisdom of God's Law: Two Theories." In *Islamic Law in Theory: Studies on Jurisprudence in Honor of Bernard Weiss*, ed. A. Kevin Reinhart and Robert Gleave, 19–37. Leiden: Brill, 2014.
El Shamsy, Ahmed. "Al-Ghazālī's Teleology and the Galenic Tradition: Reading *The Wisdom in God's Creations* (*al-Ḥikma fī makhlūqāt Allāh*)." In *Islam and Rationality: the Impact of al-Ghazālī. Papers Collected on His 900th Anniversary*, ed. Frank Griffel, vol. 2, 90–112. Leiden: Brill, 2016.
El Shamsy, Ahmed. "Bridging the Gap: Two Early Texts of Islamic Legal Theory." *Journal of the American Oriental Society* 137.3 (2017): 505–536.
Al-Sharīf al-Murtaḍā, *al-Dharīʿa ilā uṣūl al-sharīʿa*. Tehran: University of Tehran Press, 1996.
Al-Sharīf al-Murtaḍā. *Al-Mulakhkhaṣ fī uṣūl al-dīn*. Tehran: Markaz-i Nashr-i Dānishgāhī, 2002.
Al-Shaykh al-Mufīd. *Awāʾil al-maqālāt*. Beirut: Dār al-Mufīd, 1993.
Shehaby, Nabil. "The Influence of Stoic Logic on al-Jaṣṣāṣ's Legal Theory." In *The Cultural Context of Medieval Learning*, ed. John Emery Murdoch and Edith Dudley Sylla, 61–85. Boston: D. Reidel Publ. Co., 1973.
Shehaby, Nabil. "*ʿIlla* and *Qiyās* in Early Islamic Legal Theory." *Journal of the American Oriental Society* 102 (1982): 23–46.
Sherif, Mohamed. *Ghazali's Theory of Virtue*. Albany: State University of New York Press, 1975.
Shihadeh, Ayman. *The Teleological Ethics of Fakhr al-Dīn al-Rāzī*. Leiden: Brill, 2006.
Shihadeh, Ayman. "The Argument from Ignorance and its Critics in Medieval Arabic Thought." *Arabic Sciences and Philosophy* 23.2 (2013): 171–220.
Shihadeh, Ayman. "Al-Ghazālī and *Kalām:* the Conundrum of his Body-Soul Dualism." In *Islam and Rationality:the Impact of al-Ghazālī. Papers collected on his 900th anniversary*, ed. Frank Griffel, vol. 2, 113–141. Leiden: Brill, 2016a.
Shihadeh, Ayman. "Theories of Ethical Value in *Kalām:* a New Interpretation." In *The Oxford Handbook of Islamic Theology*, ed. Sabine Schmidtke, 384–407. Oxford: Oxford University Press, 2016b.
Al-Shīrāzī, Abū Isḥāq Ibrāhīm. *Al-Maʿūna fī al-jadal*, ed. ʿAlī b. ʿAbd al-ʿAzīz al-ʿUmayrīnī. Al-Ṣafāh, Kuwait: Manshūrāt Markaz al-Makhṭūṭāt wa'l-Turāth, 1987.
Al-Shīrāzī, Abū Isḥāq Ibrāhīm. *Al-Lumaʿ fī uṣūl al-fiqh* [*with glosses by Muḥammad Jamāl al-Dīn al-Qāsimī*], ed. ʿAbd al-Qādir al-Khaṭīb al-Ḥasanī. Beirut: Dār al-Katānī, 2013.
Al-Shirwānī al-Rūmī, Kamāl al-Dīn Masʿūd. *Sharḥ Ādāb al-Samarqandī* [*al-Masʿūdī*], ed. Adem Güney. In "Kemâlüddîn Mesʿûd B. Hüseyin Eşşirvânî'nin (905/1500) Şerhu

Âdâbi'ssemerkandî Adli Eserinin Tahkik ve Değerlendirmesi." MA diss., Sakarya Üniversitesi, 2010.

Simon, Udo G. *Mittelalterliche arabische Sprachbetrachtung zwischen Grammatik und Rhetorik: ʿilm al-maʿānī bei as-Sakkākī.* Heidelberg: Heidelberger Orientverlag, 1993.

Sinnū, Ahyaf and Jirār Jihāmī. *Mawsūʿat muṣṭalaḥāt al-ʿulūm al-naḥwīya: Silsilat mawsūʿāt al-muṣṭalaḥāt al-ʿarabiyya wa'l-islāmiyya.* Beirut: Maktabat Lubnān Nāshirūn, 2010.

Steel, Carlos. "Avicenna and Thomas Aquinas on Evil." In *Avicenna and His Heritage: Acts of the International Colloquium, Leuven—Louvain-La-Neuve, September 8–September 11, 1999*, ed. Jules Janssens and Daniel De Smet, 171–196. Leuven: Leuven University Press, 2002.

Street, Tony. "Ṭūsī on Avicenna's Logical Connectives." *History and Philosophy of Logic* 16 (1995): 257–268.

Street, Tony. "Arabic Logic." In *Handbook of the History of Logic*, vol. 1: *Greek, Indian and Arabic Logic*, ed. D.M. Gabbay and J. Woods, 523–596. Amsterdam: Elsevier, 2004.

Strobino, Riccardo. "Per Se, Inseparability, Containment and Implication. Bridging the Gap between Avicenna's Theory of Demonstration and Logic of the Predicables." *Oriens* 44 (2016): 181–266.

Al-Subkī, Tāj al-Dīn and Taqī al-Dīn al-Subkī. *Ibhāj fī Sharḥ al-Minhāj*, ed. Shaʿbān Muḥammad Ismāʿīl. Cairo: Maktabat al-Kulliyyāt al-Azhariyya, 1401/1981.

Al-Subkī, Tāj al-Dīn. *Rafʿ al-ḥājib ʿan Mukhtaṣar Ibn al-Ḥājib*, ed. ʿAlī Muḥammad Muʿawwaḍ and ʿĀdil Aḥmad ʿAbd al-Mawjūd. Beirut: ʿĀlam al-Kutub, 1999.

Al-Suyūṭī, Jalāl al-Dīn. *Kitāb Bughyat al-wuʿāt*, ed. Muḥammad Amīn Ḥānjī and Aḥmad b. al-Amīn Shinqīṭī. Cairo: Maṭbaʿat al-Saʿāda, 1908.

Al-Taftazānī, Saʿd al-Dīn Masʿūd b. ʿUmar. *Sharḥ al-Imām al-Saʿd al-Taftazānī ʿalā al-Shamsiyya fī al-manṭiq li'l-imām al-Kātibī*, ed. Jād Allāh Bassām Ṣāliḥ. Amman: Dār Al-Nūr, 2011.

Tamer, Georges. *Zeit und Gott: hellenistische Zeitvorstellungen in der altarabischen Dichtung und im Koran.* Berlin, New York: Walter De Gruyter, 2008.

Tamer, Georges, ed. *Islam and Rationality: the Impact of al-Ghazālī. Papers collected on his 900th anniversary*, vol. 1. Leiden: Brill, 2015.

Toral-Niehoff, Isabel. *Al-Ḥīra: eine arabische Kulturmetropole im spätantiken Kontext.* Leiden: Brill, 2013.

Treiger, Alexander. "Al-Ghazālī's Classifications of the Sciences and Descriptions of the Highest Theoretical Science." *Dîvân: Disiplinlerarası Çalışmalar Dergisi* 30.1 (2011): 1–32.

Treiger, Alexander. *Inspired Knowledge in Islamic Thought: Al-Ghazālī's Theory of Mystical Cognition and its Avicennan Foundation.* London, New York: Routledge, 2012.

Al-Ṭūfī, Najm al-Dīn Sulaymān. *Sharḥ Mukhtaṣar al-rawḍa*, 3 vols, ed. ʿAbd Allāh b. ʿAbd al-Muḥsin al-Turkī. Beirut: Mu'assasat al-Risāla, 1987.

Al-Ṭūsī, Muḥammad b. Ḥasan. *Al-ʿUddat fī Uṣūl al-fiqh.* Qom: 1997.

Al-Ṭūsī, Muḥammad b. Ḥasan. *Al-Rasā'il.* Qom: Mu'assast al-Nashr al-Islāmī, n.d.

Al-Ṭūsī, Muḥammad b. Ḥasan. *Al-Nihāyah fī mujarrad al-fiqh wa al-fatāwā.* Beirut: 1980.

Al-Urmawī, Sirāj al-Dīn. *Al-Taḥṣīl min al-Maḥṣūl*, ed. ʿAbd al-Ḥamīd ʿAlī Abū Zunayd, 2 vols. Beirut: Mu'assasat al-Risāla, 1988.

Al-Urmawī, Tāj al-Dīn. *Al-Ḥāṣil min al-Maḥṣūl fī uṣūl al-fiqh*, ed. ʿAbd al-Salām Maḥmūd Abū Nājī. Banghāzī: Jāmiʿat Qāryūnis, 1994.

van Ess, Josef. *Die Erkenntnislehre des ʿAḍudaddīn al-Īcī. Übersetzung und Kommentar des ersten Buches seiner Mawāqif.* Wiesbaden: Harrassowitz, 1966.
van Ess, Josef. "The Logical Structure of Islamic Theology." In *Logic in Classical Islamic Culture*, ed. G.E. von Grunebaum, 21–50. Wiesbaden: Otto Harrassowitz, 1970.
von Wright, Georg H. "On the Logic of Norms and Actions." In *New Studies in Deontic Logic: Norms, Actions, and the Foundations of Ethics*, ed. Risto Hilpinen, 225–248. Dordrecht: D. Reidel Publ. Co., 1981.
Vasalou, Sophia. *Ibn Taymiyya's Theological Ethics.* Oxford: Oxford University Press, 2016.
Viney, Donald. "Process Theism." *Stanford Encyclopedia of Philosophy* (online), ed. Edward N. Zalta. 2014.
Vishanoff, David R. *The Formation of Islamic Hermeneutics: How Sunni Legal Theorists Imagined a Revealed Law.* New Haven: American Oriental Society, 2011.
Wagner, Ewald. *Grundzüge der klassischen arabischen Dichtung, Band I: Die altarabische Dichtung.* Darmstadt: Wissenschaftliche Buchgesellschaft, 1987.
Weber, Max. *Economy and Society*, ed. Guenther Roth and Claus Wittich. Berkeley: University of California Press, 1978.
Weiss, Bernard. "Knowledge of the Past: the Theory of *Tawātur* According to Ghazālī." *Studia Islamica* 61 (1985): 81–105.
Weiss, Bernard. *The Search for God's Law: Islamic Jurisprudence in the Writings of Sayf al-Dīn al-Āmidī.* Salt Lake City: University of Utah Press, 1992, second ed. 2010.
White, Peter A. "Ideas About Causation in Philosophy and Psychology." *Psychological Bulletin* 108.1 (1990): 3–18.
Wisnovsky, Robert. "Avicenna on Final Causality." PhD diss., Princeton University, 1994.
Wisnovsky, Robert. "Avicennism and Exegetical Practice in the Early Commentaries on the Ishārāt." *Oriens* 41.3–4 (2013): 349–378.
Wisnovsky, Robert. "Towards a Genealogy of Avicennism." *Oriens* 42.3–4 (2014): 323–363.
Al-Yazdī, ʿAbd Allāh b. al-Ḥusayn, and Saʿd al-Dīn al-Taftazānī. *Al-Ḥāshiya ʿalā Tahdhīb al-manṭiq li'l-Taftazānī.* Qum: Muʾassasat al-Nashr al-Islāmī, al-Tābiʿa li-Jamāʿat al-Mudarrisīn bi-Qum, 1405 [1984].
Young, Walter Edward. "*Mulāzama* in Action in the Early *Ādāb al-Baḥth.*" *Oriens* 44.3–4 (2016): 332–385.
Young, Walter Edward. *The Dialectical Forge: Juridical Disputation and the Evolution of Islamic Law.* Cham, Switzerland: Springer, 2017.
Young, Walter Edward. "Al-Samarqandī's Third *Masʾala:* Juridical Dialectic Governed by the *Ādāb al-Baḥth.*" *Oriens* 46.1–2 (2018): 62–128.
Young, Walter Edward. *The Kitāb ʿAyn al-Naẓar fī ʿIlm al-Jadal of Shams al-Dīn al-Samarqandī*, ed. and trans. Walter Edward Young; TEI Infrastructure by Frederik Elwert. [Digital critical edition collated from: MSS London, British Library, Or. 3730 and Or. 3908.] Online at pages.ceres.rub.de/ayn-al-nazar. Bochum: Ruhr-Universität Bochum, Centre for Religious Studies [CERES], 2019.
Young, Walter Edward. "Dialectic in the Religious Sciences." In *EI3*, forthcoming a.
Young, Walter Edward. *On the Protocol for Dialectical Inquiry* (*Ādāb al-Baḥth*)*: a Critical Edition and Parallel Translation of the Sharḥ al-Risāla al-Samarqandiyya by Quṭb al-Dīn al-Kīlānī (fl. ca. 830/1427), Prefaced by a Critical Edition and Parallel Translation of its Grundtext: the Risāla fī Ādāb al-baḥth by Shams al-Dīn al-Samarqandī* (*d. 722/1322*), forthcoming b.

Yunis Ali, Mohamed M. *Medieval Islamic Pragmatics: Sunni Legal Theorists' Models of Textual Communication*. Richmond, Surrey: Curzon Press, 2000.

Yücedoğru, Tevfik (et al.), eds. *Bildiriler: Uluslararası Molla Hüsrev Sempozyumu (18–20 Kasım 2011)/Proceedings: International Symposium on Mullā Khusraw (18–20 November 2011)*. Bursa: Bursa Büyükşehir Belediyesi, 2013.

Al-Zarkashī, Abū ʿAbd Allāh Badr al-Dīn Muḥammad. *Al-Baḥr al-muḥīṭ fī uṣūl al-fiqh*, ed. ʿAbd al-Qādir ʿAbd Allāh al-ʿĀnī et al., 6 vols. Kuwait: Wizārat al-Awqāf wa'l-Shuʾūn al-Islāmiyya, 1992.

Al-Ziriklī, Khayr al-Dīn. *Al-Aʿlām : Qāmūs tarājim li-ashhar al-rijāl wa'l-nisāʾ min al-ʿarab wa'l-mustaʿribīn wa'l-mustashriqīn*. Beirut: Dār al-ʿIlm li'l-Malāyīn, 2002.

Zghal, Hatem. "Métaphysique et science politique: les intelligibles volontaires dans le *Taḥṣīl al-saʿāda* d'al-Fārābī." *Arabic Sciences and Philosophy* 8.2 (1998): 169–194.

Al-Zuhaylī, Wahba. *Al-Uṣūl al-fiqh al-islāmī*. Damascus: Dār al-Fikr, 1986.

Zyzow, Aron. *The Economy of Certainty*. Harvard University: PhD diss., 1984.

Zyzow, Aron. *The Economy of Certainty: an Introduction to the Typology of Islamic Legal Theory*. Atlanta: Lockwood Press, 2013.

Index of Names

https://doi.org/10.1515/9783110552386-015

Index of Subjects

Bei Fragen zur Produktsicherheit wenden Sie sich bitte an:
If you have any questions regarding product safety,
please contact:

Walter de Gruyter GmbH
Genthiner Straße 13
10785 Berlin
productsafety@degruyterbrill.com